BEARING THE WITNESS OF THE SPIRIT

THE GOSPEL AND OUR CULTURE SERIES

A series to foster the missional encounter of the gospel
with North American culture

Craig Van Gelder
General Editor

• •

BEARING THE WITNESS OF THE SPIRIT

Lesslie Newbigin's Theology of Cultural Plurality

George R. Hunsberger

WILLIAM B. EERDMANS PUBLISHING COMPANY
GRAND RAPIDS, MICHIGAN / CAMBRIDGE, U.K.

© 1998 Wm. B. Eerdmans Publishing Co.
255 Jefferson Ave. S.E., Grand Rapids, Michigan 49503 /
P.O. Box 163, Cambridge CB3 9PU U.K.
All rights reserved

Printed in the United States of America

03 02 01 00 99 98   7 6 5 4 3 2 1

Library of Congress Cataloging-in-Publication Data

Hunsberger, George R.
Bearing the witness of the spirit : Lesslie Newbigin's theology
of cultural plurality / George R. Hunsberger.
p.   cm.
Includes bibliographical references and index.
ISBN 0-8028-4369-7 (pbk. : alk. paper)
1. Newbigin, Lesslie — Contributions in theology of
multiculturalism. 2. Multiculturalism — Religious
aspects — Christianity. I. Title.
BX7066.5.Z8N   1998
261'.092 — dc21   98-13661
                          CIP

Contents

Preface

This work is offered to God in the hope that it will encourage the praise of the nations to which God is due. My wife Gay and our children Lauren, Peter, and Anna Kate have begun that praise by their quiet and gentle patience as this work was done in several stages over the last twelve years. The community of God's people who have surrounded me with encouragement and support bear witness to the truth that I am here attempting to portray. This is especially true of two congregations, Christ's Community Presbyterian Church (Clinton, Mississippi) and Third Reformed Church (Holland, Michigan), three academic communities, Princeton Theological Seminary (Princeton, New Jersey), Belhaven College (Jackson, Mississippi), and Western Theological Seminary (Holland, Michigan), and two broader collegiality groups, the American Society of Missiology and the Gospel and Our Culture Network. These companions are in many ways the real architects of the thought and intent which this work represents. My own praise to God has been multiplied in the process of being borne along to express what the Spirit has made it important for me to say. Glory to God.

Special thanks is due to Bishop Lesslie Newbigin, whose kind helpfulness at many points in this study commended the doctrine he taught for so many years. Beyond the brief visits, his writings made him my mentor indeed. Upon his death in January 1998 he left to all of us in the world church a legacy of profound proportion. My hope is that I have represented him fairly and made his thought accessible to the church of Jesus Christ in a new and useful way. Appreciation must also be expressed to Princeton

Seminary mentors Sam Moffett, Charles West, and Charles Ryerson, who guided the initial research undergirding this book. The help of Judy Bos during the final stages of the preparation of the manuscript and the proof-reading of an earlier form of it by my former colleague Bill Durrett have been gifts of great importance.

Several notes will help the reader. Because this book interacts with major webs of discussion, there will be a large number of references to sources in Newbigin's writings as well as in the writings of others. References will be placed parenthetically in the text using the author-date system. The hope is that readers who do not need the details will be able to glide over them quickly, while those interested in more fully locating the discussion will be helped by the references in the text and by the endnotes. In the case of Newbigin's work, all occurrences of particular ideas will not be mentioned, only the ones most directly quoted. This should be sufficient to provide a map around his corpus for further research where that is desired.

While the normal author-date reference system is used for works by people other than Newbigin, for his writings each item is indicated by a code that tells the year of publication (the last two digits of the year) followed by up to four lower-case letters (drawn from the first letters of key words in the title). This will help the reader keep sorted out the sometimes numerous items published within a given year.

It is the intent of the author to use gender-inclusive language throughout but at the same time to preserve the integrity of quotations, many of which date to a time before care was exercised in this way. It should be noted that Newbigin in more recent writings has moved to this style, but his earlier work could not have anticipated later practice.

Biblical quotations are from the NRSV unless they are part of a larger quotation or otherwise noted.

GEORGE R. HUNSBERGER
Holland, Michigan

Abbreviations

BCC	British Council of Churches
CASA	Christian Agency for Social Action, NCCI
CISRS	Christian Institute for the Study of Religion and Society
CLS(I)	Christian Literature Society (for India)
CSI	Church of South India
CWME	Commission on World Mission and Evangelism, WCC
DWME	Division of World Mission and Evangelism, WCC
ET	English translation
IBMR	*International Bulletin of Missionary Research*
IMC	International Missionary Council
IRM	*International Review of Mission(s)*
ISPCK	Indian Society for Promoting Christian Knowledge
LCWE	Lausanne Committee for World Evangelization
LWF	Lutheran World Federation
NCCI	National Christian Council of India
NCCR	*National Christian Council Review*
NRSV	*New Revised Standard Version*
SCM	Student Christian Movement
SIUC	South India United Church (1908-1947)
SPCK	Society for Promoting Christian Knowledge
URC	United Reformed Church of England and Wales
WCC	World Council of Churches

Meetings and Assemblies

CHAPTER 1

Birthing a Missionary Theology
of Cultural Plurality

I first met Lesslie Newbigin on the occasion of his visit to Princeton Theological Seminary in 1984. He was presenting the B. B. Warfield Lectures that would later be published under the title *Foolishness to the Greeks*. As I listened to Bishop Newbigin's lectures I was struck by three things.

First, his vision of modern Western culture was clear and incisive. The analysis was not unique to him. He acknowledged his indebtedness to people such as Alasdair MacIntyre who had identified how important it was for an understanding of our culture to recognize its fundamental public-private dichotomy, a dichotomy which sorts things out according to whether they are "facts" appropriate to debate in the public ranges of life or "values" that are assigned to the protected private realm of "opinion." Newbigin captured the dichotomy clearly and showed its pervasive effects on a variety of facets of the social order; he then followed through with a sustained "missionary" encounter with those features of the Western world's ways of thinking and behaving. He held out both the dilemmas and the prospects for Christian belief and the church's vocation in such a world as the Western one. In the brief span of six lectures, he modeled for a coming generation what we must follow as a major agenda for a very long time into the future.

I was also struck by Newbigin's starting point in this missionary engagement with modern culture. Tucked away in the first ten pages of the

1

published version are the beginning principles that would guide him in the encounter, ten pages which too many readers skim past and miss. In those few brief comments he summarized the learnings from generations of cross-cultural missionary engagements and put them succinctly and almost matter-of-factly on the table as the rules which must of course govern any missionary encounter. His comments were pregnant with significance, as readings during the course of my doctoral program in ecumenics, missiology, and the history of religions had by that time shown me. He distilled out in a few basic affirmations a portrait of missionary approach that resonated with the best thinking in the field.

What was especially striking about his beginning point was that in what followed Newbigin worked in terms of the approach he had annunciated. Brevity about his method at the beginning did not mean for him a failure of memory when he employed the method. Successful or not in the project he was undertaking, he at least was sustaining an effort to be faithful to his beginning principles. This is what many critics miss. Without appreciating how thoroughly ingrained Newbigin is in the approach announced at the outset, it is impossible to judge him fairly — or to follow his lead genuinely!

The third thing that struck me during the course of Newbigin's lectures was something far more subtle, but ultimately more decisive for my own future path. At two distinct moments in the lectures, I heard what seemed to be a fundamental clue to Newbigin's theological rationale for Christian faith, life, and witness. He had given evidence throughout the lectures that there was something instinctively theological in the way he approached an understanding of culture, or of intercultural communication, or of the meaning and significance of the presence of the community called "church" among the world's peoples. At these two distinct moments, however, I was hearing what appeared to be the clue to the deepest foundational notions undergirding his theological perspective.

The clue I heard was this: twice, when it seemed that he had taken his line of argument clear to the bottom, to the most fundamental grounding point upon which his argument, his apologetic, his logic rested — his most basic axiom, as he might say — he said something like, "At this point we must resort to the biblical doctrine of election." (Hold on. It may not be what you think! Chapters two and three will amplify what Newbigin is getting at.) With that, he seemed to rest his case. It settled to the bottom with a gentle thud. Here was his deepest confidence, on which everything else depended.

The form in which I remember him saying it is not quite what the published text (nor even the audio tapes of the lectures) actually says, which still seems odd to me! I have scoured the text, and listened again and again to the tapes, and have found nowhere that it says exactly the words I remember so vividly. I can identify the places in the lectures where, I am certain, this point about election had gripped me. But my memory of what I heard him say had undoubtedly been colored by the fact that alongside the lectures I was reading other things Newbigin had written, most notably *The Open Secret* (78os) and "Christ and the World of Religions" (83cwr).[1] Both of these make the same point I was hearing in the lectures, with even more striking emphasis. This "clue" was not an oddity or a chance comment. As I would soon discover, he had been saying something like it for many years and in many ways.

The discovery of this fundamental clue to Newbigin's theology of mission and of cultures had a great impact on the direction of my own theological reflection. For years my interest had been focused on the relationship between gospel and cultures. I had entered doctoral studies with a desire to explore that more fully. I brought to that study an inclination to pose theological questions like "What does this mean?" and "What is God doing here?" Now Newbigin's theological grasp of these issues attracted my attention. I was particularly curious why he grounded his theology in what he would most characteristically call "the missionary significance" of the biblical doctrine of election. Tracking this initial clue would ultimately lead to the writing of a full dissertation on the way election functions in what I came to call Newbigin's "theology of cultural plurality," which I suggest is basic to his theology of mission in general (Hunsberger 1987). This present book offers to a wider audience the fruit of that dissertation's research.

Foundations for an Emerging Movement

Of course, it is not surprising that another effect of the lectures would be to draw me, together with a growing circle of companions, into the explicit missionary engagement with Western culture that Newbigin was challenging us to take up. In a sense, my life's experience before that had predisposed me for the challenge laid out in the lectures. It connected in deep ways with the missional instincts which had motivated me in the midst of university campus ministry in the late 1960s and early 1970s, as pastor for a fledgling congregation during much of the 1970s, in the course of a year's experience in Africa living and working alongside a community of political refugees, and in the role of teaching Christian faith and ministry in a liberal arts college program during the 1980s. Newbigin's challenge framed, in many ways, the calling toward which my life until then had been leading me. Moving later into seminary teaching only underscored that fact. I knew that the agenda Newbigin had set before us could not, and must not, be avoided.

As others in many places came to similar conclusions, initiatives of various sorts began to arise to fulfill this missionary vocation. In fact, it would not stretch the truth to say that Newbigin became something like a father to a movement. I refer to the "gospel and our culture" movement that has been spreading in a number of Western societies and touching numerous places in the postcolonialized world as well. The movement had its beginnings in Great Britain, where in the early 1980s Newbigin became involved in a British Council of Churches planning process to design some way to mark the notorious year "1984" when it arrived. His remarks about the kind of missionary encounter he envisioned for the churches of Britain led to the committee's invitation for him to spell out in more detail what he thought that would entail. The result was his first book to signal this agenda in an extended way, *The Other Side of 1984: Questions for the Churches* (83os84). From that beginning emerged the "Gospel and Our Culture Programme," originally a program of the British Council of Churches, later merged with the C. S. Lewis Society to form what came to be called "Gospel and Culture," and finally embraced by the British and Foreign Bible Society as part of "The Open Book" campaign.

These developments in Britain paralleled Newbigin's expanding in-fluence internationally. With the publication of *Foolishness to the Greeks* in 1986 and its sequel *The Gospel in a Pluralist Society* in 1989, widening circles of people in a variety of Western societies began to give attention to New-bigin's missionary challenge. The ferment of a new agenda for the churches began to appear in the nations of Europe, the U.S.A. and Canada, Australia, New Zealand, and South Africa. The scope of it is perhaps best illustrated by the Missiology of Western Culture project headed by Wilbert Shenk, which engaged the work of scholars from all parts of the Western world. In particular places, explicit movements have formed, somewhat on the order of the British initiative, to engage the agenda in a collaborative and local way. The most specific among them to date are the Gospel and Cultures Trust in New Zealand and the Gospel and Our Culture Network in North America (GOCN).

The latter network had its origins in a simple newsletter to exchange insights among a small circle of people inspired to "stay in touch" about this agenda and its relationship to North America. In November 1989 four of us gathered to ask the question, What more does this network need to be than people on a mailing list? Two things were obvious to us, and these guided the network in its formative stages. First, the Gospel and Our Culture agenda for us in North America must engage what is distinctly *our* culture in *this* part of the West. While we were indebted to Newbigin's more general analysis of Western culture, we knew that if we claimed to follow his agenda we must do our own hard work to engage our local, particular context. Second, while we recognized that many others were beginning to talk about the culture or about a theological response to it, we were convinced that such work needed to be done in ways deliberately missiological. These two, we believed, would be the special contributions that we as a growing collaborative network should make.

In the long run, a third assumed value has been evident as well: that the missionary engagement of the gospel with our culture implicates the church, including what it *is* as much as what it *does*. The North American GOCN has stressed, perhaps more than other expressions in the broader movement, the implications of this agenda for the life and witness of the church. The book of essays that shares the insights of the network during its formative years, *The Church Between Gospel and Culture* (Hunsberger and Van Gelder 1996), makes this clear. A book envisioning a missional ecclesiology for North America (*Missional Church*, Guder et al. 1998) carries the concern forward another step. At the present time in the GOCN's life, it is fair to say that the cutting edge of the movement is its focus on the formation of the missional character of the church (or perhaps its re-formation or trans-formation).

But the vitality of the forward edge in any movement depends on how well it is nourished at the roots. To form a missional mode of life and witness for churches depends on their capacity to recognize and engage the way the gospel addresses the culture in which they themselves are participants. That capacity, in turn, implies the presence of a theoretical framework about the nature of cultures, of the gospel, and of their mutual interaction, a framework with sufficient theological depth and texture to sustain Christian communities on their way to new patterns of life and witness.

It is that which this current study proposes to provide. This is not a book about the Gospel and Western Culture project, per se. It is a book about the theology of cultural plurality that lies beneath it and must continue to inform and guide it. It is a book about what is behind those first ten pages in Newbigin's *Foolishness to the Greeks*.

It is increasingly clear that the vocation of the Gospel and Our Culture movement cannot be fulfilled apart from solid moorings in a theological assessment of and appreciation for the inherent cultural plurality in the human social fabric. This is certainly true for the North American expression of the movement, and I am convinced it is true for other expressions of it as well. The Gospel and Our Culture project will flourish because it has deep theological roots in regard to cultural plurality, or it will languish because it lacks them.

As a cultural project, it demands intercultural theory. It requires that we know our *own* culture to be a particular human culture, and therefore a relativized and deabsolutized culture. It requires that we find companionship with churches among peoples of other cultures in order to discover together how each of our cultures is addressed by the gospel and how the gospel treats our cultures with dignity and yet calls them into question. As a gospel project, it demands hermeneutical theory. It requires that we learn how we are called to fundamental conversions of mind, practices, and identity. And as a project about the life and witness of the church, it demands missional and ecclesial theory. It requires an appreciation for the church's God-given vocation to embody and inculturate the gospel, and thus demonstrate and re-present it, in each particular society in which it finds itself.

At every point in the project, the fact of cultural plurality presses in. In North America, for example, the agenda cannot be engaged without accounting for the multiple ethnicities, the multiple cultures, which make up the larger cultural picture. It must engage the growing postmodern sense that all knowing is perspectival, that is, it involves knowing from some particular vantage point, from a particular perspective, and this gives shape and color to whatever is "known." The agenda also demands an honest look at issues of power and dominance in relations between peoples of diverse cultures, including the way Anglo culture dominates in North America or the way American culture dominates in the world. Unless these dimensions of cultural plurality are appreciated theologically, the whole project is vulnerable.

The absence of an adequate theology of cultural plurality is as problematic for the project's critics as for its proponents. To treat the project as simply a culture-negative one, as "culture-bashing," does not understand the larger picture within which the need of the moment is being assessed. Nor does it allow for the complexity of the culture-affirming and culture-critical aspects of the relationship between gospel and culture to unfold in a dynamic way. Just as easily, proponents of the agenda can distort the project by ignoring how fully the fact of cultural plurality qualifies all efforts to embody and articulate the gospel as limited and provisional ones. If it lacks the missionary eyes that Newbigin brings to the project, the movement can find itself missing the most fundamental challenges: discovering how the Bible reads *us* and critiques *us*, and hearing the call to a radical transformation regarding the contemporary modus operandi of the church.

An analogy with Newbigin's own biography illustrates what is needed. What Newbigin has done in regard to the Gospel and Western Culture agenda can rightly be considered the *sequel* — in his retirement! — to his long and full missionary career in India and in ecumenical dialogue. By analogy, this book represents the *prequel* to the Gospel and Our Culture agenda for those who come to it apart from such an extensive exposure to the issues of the missionary transmission of the gospel across cultural lines, for those who have not come by the route of self-conscious missionary theory or experience in cross-cultural encounters.

This book is an extended depiction of the theology of cultural plurality that is latent in Lesslie Newbigin's writings, offered with the conviction that such a theology is foundational for the project of engaging the gospel's encounter with any human culture, and in particular the culture which is any church's own culture. Its approach rests on two fundamental presuppositions: that issues of missionary approach regarding human cultures are and must be theological; and that issues of a theological approach to human cultures must account for and respond to the inherent plurality of those multiple cultures.

One contribution the book seeks to make is simply to lift out this facet of Newbigin's thought and help it become apparent. He does not always state it very explicitly and certainly never comprehensively. In fact Newbigin himself does not use the phrase "theology of cultural plurality" to describe his own work or intention. But because he has always been concerned to articulate the rationale for the mission of the church in a culturally plural world, it has inevitably meant that he would supply what the phrase indicates. Depicting the kind of theology of cultural plurality he provides will be successful if it renders his thought faithfully. If there is any contribution the present author makes in this, it will be by identifying the inner structure and framework of Newbigin's thought and organizing his theological reflections under this new rubric.

Another aim of the book is more ambitious. I propose that what Newbigin has done signals a field that needs to be more clearly focused and pursued. I wish no less than to be a kind of midwife to the birthing of such a field. I suggest it is crucial to frame this field because it is desperately needed for continuing work on a number of missiological fronts where a perspective regarding cultural plurality is at issue. The recent study process of the World Council of Churches on Gospel and Cultures, leading to the 1996 Conference on World Mission and Evangelism in Salvador which took up that theme, illustrates the heightened global importance of such conversations. Newbigin's way of offering a theology of cultural plurality, it will be argued, helps us sketch the contours of such a field and provides a considerable contribution to it.

The most ultimate aim of the book, however, has to do with its potential fruitfulness for pastors and other leaders of congregations, for denominational and parachurch staff who labor to encourage the faithful life and witness of the churches, and for theological educators charged with preparing leadership for those churches. The aim is to provide a theoretical undergirding for the church's missionary engagement, and for movements like the Gospel and Our Culture which seek to cultivate that. For people seriously asking how to live within the gospel's encounter with their own culture, the study hopes to help them find missionary ways of being and thinking and acting, missionary eyes for seeing their own and other cultures in light of the mission of the Spirit of God, and missionary instincts of compassion, humility, patience, and love for the journey.

Definition of a Nascent Field

At the outset it is important to define terms. Most simply put, "cultural plurality" is here taken to refer to the fact of the multiplicity of varied cultures which together cohabit the earth, seen in their similarities, differences, discrepancies, and interrelationships. So a "theology of cultural plurality" indicates a theological understanding of the significance of the plurality of diverse cultures present in and among the societies of the world.

Immediately, the smallest word of the phrase creates the most potential confusion. The ambiguous genitive ("of") in the expression opens the possibility for two different "theologies" about which we might be concerned. Mark Kline Taylor points out the dramatic difference which lies in these possibilities in his comments upon Paul Tillich's "theology of culture" project: "Is 'theology' the subject that addresses or deals with culture? Or is 'culture' the subject of the phrase, the possessor and generator of a theology?" (Taylor 1986:6). Taylor concludes that for Tillich the latter is the case, judging from the tasks he identifies as proper to the pursuit of what he calls a "theology of culture" (cf. Tillich 1959). But the project with which we are concerned has to do with the former. A "theology of cultural plurality" does not concern itself in this case with culture as that which "possesses a theology or a religious dimension" which invites theological reflection (Taylor 1986:6). Rather it attempts to respond theologically to the phenomenon of culture, cultures, and the plurality of cultures found in the world.

Whether these two can entirely be separated is an important question. If the genitive phrase is objective, that is, it speaks of a theology "about the fact of" cultural plurality, it is difficult to conceive of such a theology formulated in abstraction or isolation from theology "done from the context of" cultural plurality, that is, a theology which the plurality itself conceives and reflects. While it is the former which is the underlying theological project which this study intends to examine, a theology "about" cultural plurality which is born out of the experience of plurality adds an argument for the value of what it offers. A "theology of cultural plurality" in the objective genitive sense is best done by an ecumenical theologian, a missionary theologian, a theologian driven by the personal experience of plurality and the challenges it brings to the universality of the gospel of a missionary Christian church.

But the same dialectic is inevitable from the other side as well. A "theology from" plurality, in which case the plurality is the subject, makes a valuable contribution by virtue of the rich variegation which it offers as a wider basis for all theological reflection. The current blossoming of local "third world" theologies gives an example of the importance of this function. Such a project cannot help but contribute toward a universal theological perspective. But especially because of the nature of "plurality," if the theology is to be more than merely descriptive of the variety, it inevitably will ground itself upon some "theology about" the plurality, whether that is made explicit or not. Varied frames of reference are possible. Some commitment about which is the proper understanding of the meaning of the plurality will form the beginning point.

The project upon which Tissa Balasuriya embarks in *Planetary Theology* (1984) serves as a case in point. He argues from the multiplication of local theologies toward a "revolutionary global theology," which he asserts is lacking in Christianity. He urges that the "whole planet must be seen as a context for theology." He identifies the need for "a dialectical interchange between local theologies and a theology that tries to read the significance of global realities." Thus he proposes a theology for the planet as a whole (8, 14-15). But in that the aim is for a global theology spoken by the context (and thus many "contexts"), the approach cannot escape the necessity that there be some initial perspective "about" the nature and value of the plurality of "local" theologies. A "planetary theology" drawn from the "multiplication of local theologies" can only be normative by being cumulative or by the demonstration of a common perspective among the local theologies. But the assumption by which each alternative operates already implies a prior "theology about" the plurality. When the aim of a planetary "theology from" plurality is reached, it must depend on a "theology about" plurality for its evaluation and legitimation.

It is the vision of the nature and meaning of plurality that I am intending to examine in this study. To aim thus for a "theology about" plurality intends most particularly to serve the needs of a disciple church that looks for a faithful way to live in a pluralistic world in terms of its faith in a universal gospel. This form of the project is necessary for the church which is missionary by nature and which takes seriously the practical issues its mission faces. The construction of such a vision, informed as it must be by "theology from" the plurality itself, must necessarily remain limited by its provisional character and must acknowledge the perpetual testing which the "theology from" the plurality will give the vision. But that fact only amplifies the importance of reflection on the nature and meaning of the plurality itself.

The second area of the phrase which needs definition concerns what we have identified to be the object of the inquiry. To speak of "cultural plurality" moves deliberately beyond a theological approach that assumes for the term "culture" a monolithic and basically Western referent. This tendency is clearly evident in the classic work of H. Richard Niebuhr, *Christ and Culture* (1951). There he has provided a typology of Christian postures regarding "culture" that has determined the lines along which most subsequent discussion of the subject has taken place.[2] Yet it must be noted that his treatment, especially beyond the first few centuries of the Christian era, includes virtually no examples from outside Western civilization or from intercultural missionary encounters. This omission leads Donald A. McGavran to conclude about Niebuhr's view of culture that "while he recognizes its pluriform nature, the myriad cultures do not seem vivid to him" (1974:13). We may anticipate Newbigin's contribution in this field by observing his similar note that the lead given in "gospel and culture" discussions by theologians like Niebuhr and Tillich has unfortunately been done "by theologians who had not had the experience of the cultural frontier, of seeking to transmit the gospel from one culture to a radically different one" (86fg:1). In an article with a title which unambiguously revises Niebuhr's title ("Christ and the Cultures"), Newbigin moves beyond the basic paradigm of Niebuhr by showing that much of the difficulty of ecumenical fellowship lies in "the fact that at any one moment churches in different cultures will be in different relations to their cultures" (78ctc:14).

> A North American Christian, for example, highly critical of his own culture and very sympathetic to the relatively strange culture of India, is repelled when he meets a city congregation in India which is relatively unsympathetic to traditional Indian culture and very open to the West. Indian Christians coming to Britain are hurt to discover that Christians in Britain are much interested in Hinduism but much less interested in Indian Christianity. . . . The culture-critics (Niebuhr's first category) who belong to Church A and are in revolt against culture (a) will happily fall into the arms of the conservatives (Niebuhr's second category) who belong to Church B and seek to cherish and safeguard culture (b); but the mutual esteem is deceptive because it rests on a concealed contradiction. Both cherish culture (b) and both reject culture (a), but their reasons for doing so are mutually contradictory. (78ctc:14)

The specter of a plurality of cultures and divergent histories in their encounters with the Christian message produces a more complex set of issues than can be accounted for by a monolithic concept of "culture."

Taylor joins this critique when he says of Tillich's "theology of culture" approach that it contains an ambiguity (of which Tillich was not unaware) by virtue of "his stressing concretion while speaking frequently of singular culture." This, Taylor notes, has an anachronistic feel in an age of "pluralist sensibilities and consciousness of cultural specificity" (1986:4-5). Beyond the feelings of an age, the need to move beyond the singular is based upon the fact of the multiplicity of cultures which has had to be taken into account by that age. And for the missionary enterprise, only a lagging cultural imperialism can refuse the plural way in which the questions must be asked and the theological reflections focused.

The word "plurality" is purposely chosen to convey this plural sense of cultures. The phrase might have been cast otherwise. The term "pluralism" might have been chosen instead of "plurality," and in fact it is the more regular term in discussions concerning the plural religious setting. However, "pluralism" implies a certain form of commitment to the pluriformity. "Plurality" is to be preferred because it does not prejudice the case but speaks simply of the fact of it. "Theology of cultures" might serve the purpose just as well, except that it produces new ambiguities. As a phrase, it would suggest more the idea of a theology of the cultures themselves, taken either distributively or collectively. But here the focus is not on the cultures themselves but on the fact of their plurality. The fact that many diverse cultures exist and that in their pluriformity they must relate to each other in relative terms identifies the object of the kind of "theology" in view.

Third, it is important to add with more clarity the definition being employed for the word "culture." The approach followed here has companionship with that used by the evangelical anthropologist Paul G. Hiebert and the Roman Catholic theologian and missiologist Robert J. Schreiter. Hiebert identifies "most closely" with the development in recent years of "symbolic and cognitive anthropology" among anthropologists such as Clifford Geertz, Mary Douglas, and Victor Turner (1983:xix). He defines culture as "the more or less integrated systems of ideas, feelings, and values and their associated patterns of behavior and products shared by a group of people who organize and regulate what they think, feel, and do" (1985:30).[3] Schreiter places even more emphasis on the "semiotic" character of culture, which he sees as "a vast communication network, whereby both verbal and nonverbal messages are circulated along elaborate, interconnected pathways, which, together, create the systems of meaning" (Schreiter

1985:49). Such an approach has special value for the study of culture, he believes, for three reasons. First, the fact that it is interdisciplinary, drawing on such disciplines as "genetics, cybernetics and computer science, literary criticism, linguistics, sociology and social theory, psychoanalysis, philosophy, anthropology, and formal logic and mathematics," and has concern for "all dimensions of culture, both verbal and nonverbal, both empirical and nonempirical," gives the approach the needed "holism." Second, because it looks for the configuration of the "various sign systems in a culture," it permits "a closer look at how the identity of the culture and the identity of members of the culture are constituted." Third, it provides for seeing change as "more than deviance from identity" (51-52). Schreiter finds these potentials important for his investigation of the dynamics of "constructing local theologies."

Both Hiebert and Schreiter express their indebtedness to Clifford Geertz, and it is his definition of culture which most closely captures what will be the working model for the present study. Geertz defines culture as "an historically transmitted pattern of meanings embodied in symbols, a system of inherited conceptions expressed in symbolic forms by means of which men communicate, perpetuate, and develop their knowledge about and attitudes toward life" (1973:89).

Here we must anticipate Newbigin again in order to compare this "semiotic" definition of "culture" with his. Newbigin claims no sophistication for his own definition, which he draws from the Random House Dictionary.[4] That definition summarizes culture as "the sum total of ways of living built up by a group of human beings and transmitted from one generation to another" (as quoted in 78ctc:9 and with slight modification in 86fg:3). It is important to note, however, the comments he adds when he uses such a definition. These demonstrate where he places the accents. In the earlier essay which drew attention to this definition, he laid a fourfold stress upon matters he identified as important for theological reflection. First, culture is "a product of human initiative, not an unchangeable *datum*." Further, it is a "social" product, which the group creates, values, and transmits. Also, it is never something that exists other than "in transmission." Finally, it comprises the "vast variety of human ways of living," including "all of that which constitutes man's public life in society" (78ctc:9).

In a more recent comment, Newbigin emphasizes two fundamental dimensions of that "vast variety of human ways of living" which the concept of culture includes. Language, he says, is central to culture and "provides the means by which [people] express their way of perceiving things and of coping with them." Paired with that in importance is the fact that religion is a "part of culture." Religion he defines, in that respect, as "a set of beliefs, experiences, and practices that seek to grasp and express the ultimate nature of things, that which gives shape and meaning to life, that which claims final loyalty" (86fg:3).

Newbigin's definitions are not offered with the precision and rigor with which a professional anthropologist might give them. But they bear a sensitivity to the concerns of the field and his emphasis on the centrality of language generally corresponds with the "symbolic and cognitive" definitions indicated above.

Given the kind of definition we have given to the phrase "theology of cultural plurality," we may now begin to project the kind of issues which will enter into the picture when we pursue such a theology. We can expect that the project will involve some assessment of the origin and purpose of the plurality of the world's cultures. It will give attention to the meaning of the diversity that the plurality involves and the nature and importance of the interrelationship between the various cultures. Some response will be made concerning the purpose served by the mutability of cultures and the nature of the relationship of individual persons to their cultures. In addressing these and similar issues, a Christian and particularly a missiological theology of plurality cannot avoid touching upon such additional questions as those concerning God's creation of peoples who both "create" and are "created by" varying cultural webs of understanding and value, the relation of "religion" to "culture" and in turn the relation of "Christianity" to "religion," the meaning of "revelation" in the context of differentiated particular cultures, the nature of "conversion" in light of the cultural change it implies, and the possibilities for religious and ethical "norms" that transcend cultural particularities.

Gaps in Its Current Development

Attempts at a fully developed theological framework regarding cultural plurality are rare. A notable and welcome exception which by its presence highlights the gap is the contribution co-authored by Donald Senior, C.P., and Carroll Stuhlmueller, C.P., *The Biblical Foundations for Mission* (1983).

While their focus lies more on sociological perspectives than on cultural anthropological ones, their methodology makes strong use of both disciplines. Both their motivation for the study and the form of what emerges in it bear the marks of a clear agenda. They consciously write against the backdrop of "a new awareness of cultural and national identities" which have "swept through the globe like a brush fire." From the outset they affirm what guides their quest: "To be universal, capable of embracing and being expressed by all cultures and all peoples, is essential to the Gospel." Their intent is to plug the "somewhat surprising" gap in exegetical work on the question of Bible and mission, especially in light of "the crucial importance of the issue of universalism in the church today." It is noteworthy that their surprise arises from the fact that they find the gap "especially in the mainline churches" (1983:1-2).

The attempt of Senior and Stuhlmueller signals from the point of intersection between biblical scholarship and missiology the need for a more explicit and direct "theology of cultural plurality." The same signal arises where missiology meets religious studies. In *The Apostolic Imperative* (1985), Carl Braaten follows the lead of Paul Tillich and Wolfhart Pannenberg in calling for "a theology of the history of religions," a need he indicates is largely unmet, as evidenced by the emphases present (or, in this case, absent) in academic departments of religious studies. He is right to identify the subjective character of the genitive expression in Tillich's call ("a theology oriented around the history of religions"). More is certainly involved when one speaks of the history of religions as "the horizon within which Christian theology must make its case for the truth of the gospel and the scope of its mission." The tautology and ambiguity in the statement that "the future of Christianity itself depends on what happens when it brings the mission of the gospel into the midst of the struggles going on between the religions" does not obscure the fact that attention must be given to "what happens" in that meeting, and a theology of the history of religions is required for that, both in the subjective and objective genitive senses (1985:41-42). While Braaten's frame of reference here is the history of religions, the theology for which he calls cannot but involve a theology of cultural plurality at its base.

The failure to meet this need in discussions of missiological issues growing out of the fact of plurality can be illustrated from within two missiological orbits. In each case, it is in those very places where the theology of cultural plurality would appear to be most needed and where we might most expect to find it offered that we are disappointed. A close look at some of the "gospel and culture" discussions among evangelical missiologists and at some aspects of the ecumenical and Roman Catholic conversations regarding religious pluralism will show that in both arenas the development of mature theological reflection regarding cultural plurality remains a major need.

1. Among Protestants, it has been the so-called conservative evangelicals who until recently have done the most to engage directly the issue of cultural plurality. Their deep concern for a true communication of the gospel across cultural and linguistic frontiers, and their long and committed experience of working at that, have long since drawn them to a depth of cultural assessment and an engagement of the thorny problems of cross-cultural ministry that has been unparalleled among other Protestants.[5] The Lausanne Committee's Willowbank Consultation in 1978 gathered those who were leaders in that pursuit of a "gospel and culture" framework and provided in its report a serious step forward (Stott and Coote 1980). Yet it is at the very point of biblical theological foundations that the documents it produced are the weakest. In his essay on "Culture and the Old Testament" S. Ananda Kumar acknowledges, in limited fashion, the necessity to give attention to culture.

> Even though "culture" is not an explicit subject of the Old and New Testaments, biblical studies have made it clear that human cultures have played a far more significant role in biblical history than we may at first be prepared to recognize. . . . That culture forms an inseparable part of the content and context of the Holy Scriptures, yet at the same time stays below the surface, suggests both the value and the limitation of culture in the task of world evangelization. (1980:33)

But the purpose his essay pursues remains restricted: "The purpose of our study has been to see how and to what extent the Spirit of God used the cultural environment of the Old Testament writers as they contributed to the inspired record" (1980:47). Beyond the observable reluctance to investigate the significance of the culturally and historically conditioned character of human life, the tendency to focus theological reflection about cultures and the plurality of their forms on the narrowly circumscribed issue of the inspiration of written revelation mars the potential contribution an evangelical might make. The desire to guard that doctrinal conviction distracts the evangelical from asking deeper questions about the meaning of cultural plurality and searching the Scriptures for the clues to that meaning.

In the companion Willowbank essay on the New Testament, I. Howard Marshall treats only the relationship of the cultural context to the biblical text written within it, not what the teaching of the text might suggest about the meaning of those cultures which molded it. His purpose is "to consider the cultural environment in which the New Testament writings were created" (1980:20). His attitude that "the source material, in this case the New Testament, does not directly or explicitly deal with the concept of culture" (18) effectively sets aside the search for biblical help in understanding cultural plurality.[6] In fact, he so drives a wedge between religion and culture that he makes of the whole endeavor a moot point. To him, the relation of gospel and culture is "a difficult subject to probe since the New Testament is primarily a book about religion and not about the cultural life of Christians" (29).

At the critical point of asking about the connection between the Scriptures and the presence in the world of multiple cultures, the area in which one would expect evangelicals to make the strongest contribution, the Willowbank papers fail to address directly the most pressing dimension of the issue.[7] While Bruce Nicholls does approach more directly the needed foundation in his essay (1980), the theological groundwork he lays consists not in biblical theological reflection on the nature and meaning of plurality but in a reworking of the doctrine of special revelation with cultural diversity taken into account. "In his sovereignty God chose a Hebraic cultural form and transformed it over the centuries for his purpose, with the result that there is a supra-cultural character to his self-revelation" (53). His effort to preserve a sense of the normative character of the Bible as revelation is a commendable one, even if there are dangerous conclusions that come from it (to be taken up in the concluding chapter of this study). But while a theology of revelation must certainly be involved in a theology of cultural plurality, by allowing that to be such a dominating focus, Nicholls tends to leave aside a genuine search for what that very revelation has to tell us about the nature and purpose of the cultural diversities and particularities which we observe in the world.

This same tendency may be seen in the progression of thought in Morris Inch's contribution to the field, *Doing Theology Across Cultures*

(1982). Where we ought to find a biblical rationale for cultural multiplicity, we again find instead a defense of revelation as the "first issue," in terms of which we may view cultural diversity. The "tension between biblical authority and cultural integrity" is resolved for Inch if we hold a "high view" of both biblical authority and culture. But for him, following Donald McGavran, a "high" view of culture means that "the introduction of Christianity will have a direct effect on only a small minority of the cultural components — whether to encourage, change, or prohibit them" (22; cf. McGavran 1974:39). This view is "high" only regarding the neutrality and acceptability of all cultures. It is really a "low" view of culture regarding its importance or significance. In the end Inch is claiming that there is really no problem. Revelation is insulated from cultural relativity, so a search for the message of the Bible about cultural plurality is viewed as nonessential.

One of the Willowbank participants, Harvie Conn, has acknowledged his debt to that meeting as well as his sense of the continuing agenda it precipitated.

> Out of it came also a sense of frustration, which was felt by others there as well: It seemed that frequently the theologians and the anthropologists were using the same words but speaking very different languages. We needed to hear one another better, to work harder at learning one another's verbal symbols. (1984:5)

His book *Eternal Word and Changing Worlds: Theology, Anthropology and Mission in Trialogue* (1984) is an important attempt to further such a discussion. Even there, however, biblical theological foundations for understanding the plurality with which we wrestle are not forthcoming. He assesses the trends during the past century in each of the partners to the "trialogue" and suggests the way they must intersect on the road ahead. But he nowhere attempts to articulate a biblical perspective for viewing the nature and meaning of the plurality of cultures which has forced upon the partners a common agenda.

2. In an entirely separate arena, one which evangelicals have scarcely engaged but which for some Protestant and Roman Catholic theologians comprises the main agenda for a missiology faced with plurality, the concern is with religious pluralism. A plethora of literature has been generated on this subject discussing the ramifications of the experience of this plu-

ralism and the implications for mission that can be drawn from it. Even a quick glance at the character of that material demonstrates that practical words dominate the nature of the discussion. Most often, what is being discussed is the "encounter" between various religions. The "relationship" of one to another or the "attitude" which one holds toward another is most in view. Christian theologians and missiologists are concerned to develop "approaches" to the other religions, and "dialogue" is the most frequently discussed possibility. The attention of the discussions tends to focus on the "experience" of this plurality of religions known to our world.

Gavin D'Costa is right when he identifies the question of "attitude" toward other religions to be an essentially theological matter and one which lies at the heart of a host of practical considerations (1986:3). But his treatment of theological "attitudes" so restricts the field which the title of his book implies that he will address (*Theology and Religious Pluralism*) that the largest theological questions go not only unanswered but unasked. "The central theological question tackled in this book is whether salvation is possible outside Christianity" (4). But that focus leaves untouched the more basic question concerning the meaning of the fact of the very plurality which has made the question relevant. Still further, it does not address the fact of the plurality of cultures within which the religious dimension is one expression. Apart from addressing these questions more directly, the discussion of other theological questions will suffer.

When D'Costa comes to his concluding chapter he both shows the impulse that begs for a "Christian theology of religions" (as a part of what a theology of cultural plurality should involve, it should be added) and illustrates how easily it may be missed. Having argued throughout his book for what he calls the "inclusivist" attitude drawn from Karl Rahner, he proceeds to "tease out" some of the "implications of the inclusivist position, challenges which relate to issues such as dialogue, mission, truth criteria, Christology and ecclesiology" (1986:117). His book as a whole had dealt with "theology and religious pluralism." But when he turns the corner at last to suggest an attempt towards a theology "of" religions, it consists only in applying conclusions to practical matters or in drawing implications for other theological issues. It is a theology "for" pluralism without providing directly enough a theology "about" it.

A further observation must be made about the foundations D'Costa offers for the "theology for pluralism" which he does give. He argues that the "inclusivist" paradigm is superior to the "exclusivist" and "pluralist" para-

digms offered by others because "this inclusivist position intelligibly reconciles and holds together the axioms of the universal salvific will of God and
the axiom that salvation alone comes through God in Christ in his Church"
(1986:111). Regardless of the proof offered throughout the book that that is
the case, the argument suffers from a weakness at the outset. The question of
approach is set up on the "convenient" basis of the juxtaposition of "two
traditionally held Christian axioms": that salvation is "through Jesus Christ
alone" and that "God desires the salvation of all humankind," more commonly referred to by D'Costa as the "universal salvific will of God" (4). The
approach, he reasons, which best does justice to these two is the most
appropriate. The difficulty lies in the fact that he thus starts from a point
which requires much more assessment before it can be taken to be an
adequate beginning point. To affirm these two axioms begs the question as to
whether these are an adequate summary of the biblical materials. It leaves
aside the question of whether there might be in the biblical references
themselves a framework of understanding by which the "exclusivist" statements and the "universalist" ones may be seen as part of a whole and larger
picture of things. D'Costa too uncritically latches onto this pair of "axioms"
from Rahner (83; cf. Rahner 1969:391) without fully testing their validity as
the description of that which must be reconciled.[8]

 D'Costa is not alone in this insufficient care for the interpretation of
biblical materials bearing on questions of religious pluralism. Wesley Ariarajah provides in his book *The Bible and People of Other Faiths* (1985) a
second example of how easily this becomes a problem in discussions of
pluralism. Recognizing the ultimate importance of assumptions, especially
those concerning what the Scriptures say and teach, he attempts to even
out the ledger books. He argues that over against those Christians who hold
to "certain verses in the Bible which make exclusive claims for Christ," it is
possible to marshall another set of references which show "that there is in
the Bible another attitude to people of other faiths." Ariarajah declares his
intent simply: "All that I hope to do is to lift this up" (xi-xiv). But he
proceeds to conclude more than he argues for. Virtually leaving aside the
"exclusive" references from his final perspective, he claims for the "other
side" which he lifts up that it is "central to the spirit of the biblical message"
(58). That he has demonstrated a broader range of references than those
used by conservative "prooftexters" is obvious. That he has avoided the
same sort of "prooftexting" is not. He argues from the "theocentric" character of Jesus' life that Christians can, by imitation, "stand alongside people

of other faiths as children of the one God" without denying their witness to Christ.[9] But the basis on which he affirms that is the radical reinterpretation which says of Jesus that "he did not claim to be the full, final and decisive revelation of God, and it is difficult to see how such an exclusive position can be taken even on the basis of the Johannine verse, 'He who has seen me has seen the Father'" (65). But he must reckon with more than one verse on that other side, and the burden of proof rests on him to show how the verses from "his" side outweigh the verses of the "other" side as the "centre" of the biblical message. What he has failed to search for is the larger vision that could see a "centre" embracing all those "verses." Only that could handle the complexities of both the biblical text and the contemporary experience of pluralism. (One suspects that his inclusive position would be as unacceptable to a Muslim as the exclusivist position would be to a Hindu.)

The need, then, for a theology of cultural plurality goes beyond merely constructing sound cross-cultural strategies and methodologies by which the translation and communication of the Christian message take place. It also involves more than merely affirming pluralism, whether in religious terms or broader ones. When such theological foundations are not sought and directly discussed, the skewing of the discussions in matters related to plurality creates an accentuated divergence of posture.

For example, the focus of interest greatly affects the results. So Charles Kraft, whose interest as a Western missionary strategist falls on the problem of the communication of the gospel from his own to other cultures, approaches the subject of cultures with a different interest than does C. S. Song, who is searching for an indigenization of theology within his own Chinese cultural and historical heritage. Again, Balasuriya's interest as a citizen of the third world moves along socioeconomic "justice" lines. From each comes a different assessment of the meaning of cultures and cultural diversities. Disparate theological orientations only serve to complicate further the viewpoints.

This diffusion of opinion can be illustrated further from within evangelical discussions themselves by looking at the way "culture" is understood among evangelical missiologists and the way they see the intersection of ethics and culture. Robert Ramseyer identifies this as a basic problem in the anthropology of Charles Kraft. For Kraft culture has become a "value-free" or "neutral" language due to his bifurcation of form and meaning (Ramseyer 1983:114; cf. Kraft 1979:113). The same may be said of Donald McGavran, whom Morris Inch uses as a model. According to McGavran, "Christianity is wholly neutral to the vast majority of cultural components" (1974:39). Others, with Ramseyer, disagree. Bruce Nicholls challenges the usefulness of Kraft's principle of "dynamic equivalence" for contextualizing theology at just this point: "Culture is never neutral, it is always a strange complex of truth and error, beauty and ugliness, good and evil, seeking God and rebelling against him" (1980:56). Treating culture as "essentially a neutral language" leads to "a minimization of the importance of actual behavior" (Ramseyer 1983:114).

The problems which hurry into the picture whenever basic theological orientations are left unexpressed is immediately apparent. The lack of artic-ulation may represent a lack of self-understanding, in that arguments are based on assumptions of which one is unaware. Or it may involve a failure to disclose or clearly articulate and defend those theological assumptions of which one is fully aware. In either case, the result is the same. The thinking put forward in the debates can easily become fuzzy and inconsistent. Inade-quate theological footing for the discussions breeds either the impression that theological reflection is unnecessary for dealing with issues of cultural plural-ity or the equally problematic suggestion that there exists such a common theological understanding of plurality that there is no need to articulate it. In either case the gap has the potential to distort the discussion.

Specific attention to a theology of cultural plurality is necessary in order to bring to these diverging points of view the possibility of a mutual critique of preunderstandings. The development of such a theology would not in itself resolve the differences. But entry together into that field would provide the way to sort out the nature of the differences and bring to light what is too often unconsciously assumed. It is a field overdue for explicit reflection.

Prospects in Newbigin's Contribution

That we should expect to find a helpful and constructive theology of cul-tural plurality in the thought of Bishop Newbigin is suggested by four main factors. First, his missionary career has faced him with the challenges of a culturally plural world. Second, in the midst of his missionary engagements he has been involved in vigorous debate in three major arenas of discussion that are especially touched by the fact of cultural plurality. Third, the breadth of his experience and reflection have allowed him to bring into focused perspective a theological approach to plurality. And fourth, the mode in which he has tended to respond theologically has made a theology of cultural plurality its natural product. The display of these four factors will demonstrate that the prospects are good for finding in Newbigin a significant contribution.

Missionary Engagements with Cultural Plurality

Newbigin's missionary career began following his theological training at Westminster College, Cambridge. In 1936 he joined the company of the vast network of "missionaries" around the world whose daily struggle with "the issues involved in communicating the gospel to a people and a culture" had made of them "missiologists" (cf. 84bocm:10). Sent by the Church of Scotland, Newbigin eventually transferred his ministerial credentials entirely into the South India United Church, a 1908 union of Presbyterians and Congregationalists, and worked within that church until it became part of the 1947 union which resulted in the formation of the Church of South India (CSI) (cf. 85ua:70-72; 45ofmi). In that church he was elected to be one of the original bishops and served from 1947 until 1959 as bishop of the diocese of Madura and Ramnad (85ua:90ff.). The enlarged scope of pastoral oversight which this position gave him offered the challenge to pursue in practical terms the development of "a responsible church." The form of the church and its patterns of leadership became important issues to him as he watched the "spontaneous expansion" of the church of his area. His attempts to implement insights articulated by Roland Allen earlier in the century deepened the level of his struggle to understand and faithfully engage the movement of the gospel across cultural lines. In response to many local movements toward the Christian gospel among peoples who before had had no church in their midst, he stimulated and encouraged a program of early baptism, intensive training, and the cultivation of natural and Spirit-identified leadership (85ua:146-148; cf. Allen 1962).

The nature and location of Newbigin's work changed significantly in 1959, but it did not remove him from the necessity of engaging issues of the missionary relation to plurality. In some ways the change enlarged that experience. He took up the responsibilities of leadership in the International Missionary Council (IMC) during the two years leading up to its integration into the World Council of Churches (WCC) in 1961. His navigational work to help that integration occur and his leadership for the Division of World Mission and Evangelism (DWME) during its first years as a part of the structure of the WCC gave him an acquaintance with a wider spectrum of churches, cultures, and circumstances throughout the world. Living in the crossroad cities of London and Geneva brought him deeper into the missiological debates of the broader church. The vision for engaging cultures with the gospel, forged in the crucible of India, now was tested on the larger canvas of the world's multiplicity of cultures. The intensity with which the cross-cultural "missionary" vocation was being challenged during those years and in those circles forced a new clarity in Newbigin's thinking in defense of that calling.

In 1965 Newbigin returned from the cities of Europe to the South Indian metropolis of Madras. As Bishop of Madras in the CSI from 1965 until his retirement in 1974, Newbigin's sense of the cultural complexities of life in the modern world was further expanded. The city of Madras graphically illustrated what he saw to be true elsewhere. "A growing proportion of the human race lives in urban areas where each person is normally part of several cultural communities at the same time" (78os:162). The former patterns of social and cultural delineation could no longer be assumed for most people in the modern world. The increasing experience of "living with change" is exemplified in the urban condition which Newbigin observes, that "in the Madras of today the working community is probably of more significance as the context of discipleship than is the traditional kinship group" (163).

The fact that Newbigin's retirement to his home country in 1974 removed him from the place of his lifelong intercultural engagement in India does not mean that his encounter with cultural plurality was over. Three things ensured that it would not be. First, he retired to a position at Selly Oak Colleges in Birmingham, England, where it was his main work to "teach 'The Theology of Mission' and 'Ecumenical Studies' to those who were undergoing missionary training" (85ua:242). That provided a major period of reflection over the years of his missionary labors. During that time the essential lines of his thought in regard to cultural plurality coalesced and gained more direct expression. (His major work, The Open Secret [78os], was the fruit of that.) A second factor relates to another part of his teaching responsibility at Selly Oak. He gave instruction in Hinduism to help train teachers for their work in the field of religious education (85ua:243). The local Birmingham struggle over the form of its religious education syllabus at the same time stirred Newbigin's response. Cultural plurality, which had been his long experience in India, was now a pressing fact of life for England. Plurality was not left behind when Newbigin retired. Third, in the England to which he retired, Newbigin found a secular society that had become a pagan one (85ua:249). He discovered in the post-Christian West a formidable culture alongside all the other cultures of the world, which like the rest finds itself encountered by the gospel. His leading "questions to the churches" on the British scene (83os84) continued to the time of his death to be his personal agenda and are increasingly a point of discussion in places beyond the United Kingdom.

Missionary Dialogues About Cultural Plurality

It should already be obvious from this brief sketch of Newbigin's life work that he has been drawn into three major arenas of missiological discussion: the validity and character of cross-cultural mission, the necessity and forms of the church's unity, and the basis and mode of interreligious dialogue. What all three arenas have in common is the fact that they grow out of a heightened experience of "cultural plurality." And in each case, the participants in the discussion respond to the issues at hand out of some sense of the meaning of that plurality. In these three arenas or "orbits" of debate, the subject of a theology to undergird the reflection is infrequently and inadequately posed. But in each case there are theological assumptions operating beneath the surface issues in the discussion. Whether or not the discussion identifies its aim to be theological and whether or not a proposed course of action claims a theological basis, it must inevitably be there. Implicit in any Christian response to these issues is some foundational way of understanding cultural plurality.

A survey of Newbigin's involvement in each arena will show why we may expect that his theological approach to plurality gives promise for foundations that help to integrate the three.

1. *Cross-Cultural Mission.* The sense of the nature of "culture" gained within the social sciences has increasingly been brought to bear on the intricacies

of cross-cultural mission and communication. An appreciation of the integrity of human cultures and the acceptance of their relative character over against one another have become major factors in the definition of the gospel and formative influences on the understanding of its transmission and reception. Implications for both mission ideology and practical strategy have emerged from discussions such as these.

Culture confronted Newbigin from the very beginning of his missionary experience in India in the same way it confronts every missionary. He had come to live in a place "foreign" to him, among people whose basic orientation to living was sharply divergent from his own. The pastoral challenge of communicating a gospel which he assumed to be addressed to culturally "other" people as surely as to people of his own particular culture became and remained a deep commitment of his life. The development of his missiology, expressed ultimately and in its fullest form in *The Open Secret* (78os), traces his attempt to answer the question, How does a "gospel for all" meet and engage people in their particularities? His own entry into the wealth and riches of Tamil language and culture and his subsequent mastery of communication in that language became the constant medium through which he posed the question to himself. He maintained a pastoral approach, relating to people in the actual circumstances in which they daily lived. It has been his belief that the missionary movement of which he was a part represented a "penetration into the deepest recesses of human culture" (58obog:14).

In the earliest expressions of Newbigin's ecclesiology, the church's essential missionary character is emphasized (48rc, 53hg: chapter 6), especially its "duty and authority to preach the gospel" across cultural lines (48dacp). The need to labor to make that case grew in intensity when in the early 1960s he took on the responsibility of representing the "missions" concern in the heart of the ecumenical movement (cf. 62mdem). The theology for this was contained in the little booklet *One Body, One Gospel, One World* (58obog) and was given a more expanded treatment in *The Relevance of Trinitarian Doctrine for Today's Mission* (63rtdt) in an effort to affirm explicit cross-cultural missionary engagement. His concern is most pointedly illustrated by his insistence that the *International Review of Missions,* which he edited for the WCC, retain the "s" at the end of its title. At a time when "many of the most influential leaders in the mission boards wanted to eliminate the narrow category of missions and to speak only of the total mission of the church," he resisted in the interest of preserving "a specific concern for missions as enterprises explicitly intended to cross the frontier between faith and no-faith" (85ua:200). The same concern is evident in his essays on "Mission and Missions" (60mm) and "The Future of Missions and Missionaries" (77fmm).

The reflection of his "retirement" years has continued to explicate this essential dimension of the church's calling and engage the dynamics of intercultural communication and mission which it involves. This is evident in books such as *The Open Secret* (78os) and *Sign of the Kingdom* (80sk), and in articles and sermons such as "Christ and the Cultures" (78ctc), *Context and Conversion* (78cc), "The Church as Witness: A Meditation" (78caw), and "The Biblical Vision: Deed and Word Inseparable" (86bvdw). Increasingly his works have focused upon the gospel-culture encounter that occurs when the British (and broader Western) culture is the "foreign" one from the perspective of the gospel, as is the case in *The Other Side of 1984* (83os84), *Foolishness to the Greeks*, (86fg) and *The Gospel in a Pluralistic Society* (89gps), but also in lesser-known works such as "The Bible and Our Contemporary Mission" (84bocm), "Can the West Be Converted?" (85cwbc), "How I Arrived at the Other Side of 1984" (85hiao), "A British and European Perspective" (86bep), and "England as a Foreign Mission Field" (86eafm).

2. *Church Unity.* The fruit of the modern missionary enterprise has displayed itself in what William Temple called "the great new fact of our day," that is, the spread of the church into a vast number of societies around the globe. The relationship between the churches of many cultures has made itself one of the major agendas of contemporary missiology. Ecumenism, which began more as an intracultural discussion in the Western churches, has been removed from its concentration on the differences of tradition and denomination and made into an intercultural matter. More and more, the ecumenical debate has had to relate to the larger unity question of the whole of humankind and that trend occurs by analogy with the cultural dimension of the effort to achieve the visible unity of the church. The churches live within the cultures and carry the stamp of those particularities. The church's unity and the world's are alike in that they both wrestle with the alienating potential of divergent cultural identities. Building a "unity in diversity" continues to be an important concern for the church.

The challenge plurality presents to the unity of the church surfaced as a major agenda for Newbigin during his early years in South India. At a critical time when much of the leadership toward the union of the South India United Church (Congregational and Presbyterian), the Methodist Church, and the Anglican Church was passing from the scene in the early 1940s, his own leadership was drawn upon to help move forward the initiatives for a more comprehensive church unity in the region. All at once, the sense of ecumenism cultivated earlier in the Student Christian Movement (SCM) widened as he encountered the struggle for unity among churches whose spiritual traditions were rooted in diverse European cultures and histories and whose personal cultural roots matched that diversity within the Indian context. His efforts served as a major influence both toward the eventual union which produced the Church of South India in 1947 and toward the cultivation of ecumenical concern elsewhere around the world by means of the broad circulation given to his defense of the plan *The Reunion of the Church* (48rc; revised edition, 60rc). This involvement led Newbigin, at the suggestion of Alan Richardson, to continue to develop the ecclesiology implied in the defense, resulting in the publication of *The Household of God* (53hg). It also propelled him into the wider discussions regarding unity in the WCC.

Very early in the WCC's struggle to define unity, Newbigin urged that the neutral stance entertained in the 1950 Toronto Statement of the WCC Central Committee (i.e., that membership in the WCC did not commit member churches to any particular view regarding the nature of the unity they sought together) be clearly understood to be only a "provisional neutrality." He argued that it must be "the starting point, and not the way or the goal." It must not, he warned, be allowed to become a "permanent principle" (51cccw:253-254). His concern had been born on Indian soil. The calling of the churches made it a missionary necessity to resolve disunity. And to say that it is a missionary necessity is to say that unity most importantly comes to form locally as "all who confess Christ as Lord [are] recognizably one family in each place" (58obog:55). Newbigin urged as early as 1954 what the proper form of the church's unity must be:

> First, it must be such that all who are in Christ in any place are, in that place, visibly one fellowship. Second, it must be such that each local community is so ordered and so related to the whole that its fellowship with all Christ's people everywhere, and with all who have gone before and will come after, is made clear. (55qutr:31)

The further articulation of this vision in *One Body, One Gospel, One World* (58obog) was followed by a paper presented to the Working Committee of the Faith and Order Commission which became part of the report of the study committee on "The Future of Faith and Order" (59nuws). Newbigin's impact is clearly visible in the now famous New Delhi statement of 1961 and its dual focus on the local and particular Christian community ("all in each place") and the global and catholic church ("united with the whole Christian fellowship in all places and all ages"), the latter admittedly less forcefully articulated at New Delhi than it would be later at the Uppsala 1968 WCC Assembly (Handspicker 1970:148-149).

During the decade of the 1960s the unity of the church diminished as a focal topic in Newbigin's published works. (Although several publications early in the decade are worth noting: *The Mission and Unity of the Church* [60muc], *Is Christ Divided?* [61icd], and "The Church — Local and Universal" [62clu].) But following the Uppsala Assembly in 1968 the theme regained its earlier prominence. Again serving on the Faith and Order Commission, Newbigin made important contributions toward defining the emerging notions of "conciliar fellowship" and "unity in diversity." Throughout his life he continued to affirm the crucial nature of the unity of the church. His published works expressing that commitment include "The Call to Mission — A Call to Unity" (69cmcu), "Which Way for 'Faith and Order'?" (69wwfo), "The Form and Structure of the Visible Unity of the Church" (73fsvu), "All in One Place or All of One Sort: On Unity and Diversity in the Church" (76aopa), "What is a 'Local Church Truly United'?" (77wilc), "Common Witness and Unity" (80cwu), "The Basis and the Forms of Unity" (84bfu), "Faith and Faithfulness in the Ecumenical Movement" (84ffem), and "A Fellowship of Churches" (85fc).

In all of his involvement in this arena, Newbigin has struggled constantly to embrace both the universality of the church called into being by the gospel and the particularity of the forms the church must inevitably bear because of the nature of the gospel itself and the salvation it announces.

3. *Religious Pluralism.* The church's missiological discussions include the matter of interreligious relationship. With the political independence of the Third World and the resurgence of traditional values and religions came an enlarged call upon the church to form positive "nation-building" relations with people of other faiths and ideologies in pluralistic, secular societies. As "religious pluralism" has moved into the Western "neighborhood"

by the migrations of people of faiths other than Christianity, there has been a crescendo of concern to formulate appropriate Christian appreciations and responses in that setting as well. "Dialogue" has become the center of attention as a model for mission. The "uniqueness" of Christianity is pressed by a new challenge in the circle of "ultimate commitments."

Newbigin's missionary engagement with culture could not be conducted apart from the face-to-face meeting of religious commitments whose differences historically have been so often the occasions for the deepest division and strife. From the beginning, Newbigin entered with humility and boldness into the experience of this encounter. Religious pluralism is not for him a new phenomenon toward the end of the century, as it is to many in the West who have only recently encountered it in person and on their own turf. For him, it has meant the conversations of a lifetime with devotees of every gradation, much of that in the context of a society for which pluralism is an assumed pattern of human existence.

His early days in India found Newbigin in the regular company of Hindu scholars of the Ramakrishna Mission in Kanchipuram. Of the importance of those meetings he says,

> Along with the head of that community I shared in the leadership of a weekly study group in which we studied alternately the Svetasvara Upanishad and St. John's Gospel. We sat, Indian fashion, cross-legged on the floor and the leader in each case read the Scripture in the original language — Sanskrit or Greek — and expounded it, after which there would be an hour or more of questioning and discussion. These sessions were extremely rewarding to me. . . . I learned to see the profound rationality of the world-view of the Vedanta. (85ua:57)

Such personal experience as this laid the foundation for Newbigin's debate within the discussions about religious pluralism.

In his earlier writings, there is not a great deal that reflects directly on the question of religious pluralism. The encounter with Hinduism, and increasingly with the ideology of Marxism, forms in very large measure the backdrop for much of Newbigin's theology, even in that period. But religious pluralism emerges as a matter of direct reflection only minimally. It arises as a concern primarily in response to the "quest for unity through religion" (55qutr), a concern echoed again in his book entitled *A Faith for This One World?* (61ftow). The search for commonalities among the religions as a basis for common cause in the midst of the divisiveness of the world drew from Newbigin some preliminary thoughts regarding pluralism that would mature in his later writings. (This development will be traced more fully in chapter six.) With the publication of *The Finality of Christ* in 1969 his entry into the arena was clear (69fc).

His first years back in England upon retirement from India brought the issue to a place of central importance in his theological agenda. He entered into debate with the views of people such as John Hick, Wilfred Cantwell Smith, and Karl Rahner, and joined the reopened discussions continuing the "continuity-discontinuity" debate between Hendrik Kraemer and A. G. Hogg in the 1930s. Notable in this period were his essays on "The Basis, Purpose and Manner of Inter-Faith Dialogue" (77bpmi, revised to be chapter 10 of 78os), *Christian Witness in a Plural Society* (77cwps), "Teaching Religion in a Secular Plural Society" (77trsp), and "Christ and the World of Religions" (83cwr). His point of view regarding "dialogue" and the relation of the Christian gospel to people of other faiths has come to have such importance in the broader discussions that he figures prominently in the paradigms offered by many recent treatments of religious pluralism (e.g. Race 1982, Knitter 1985, and D'Costa 1986).

Bishop Newbigin has been deeply engaged in the discussions of all three arenas which we have identified as related to and in need of a theology of cultural plurality. It is important to note that through all of that engagement his most basic desire has been the pastoral-missionary task of communicating the gospel. He has attempted to understand the eternal gospel for the contemporary time and place and to bathe the present age in it. He has wished to apply the gospel and its implications to the ever-changing kaleidoscope of peoples, customs, and histories and to play his grasp of the meaning of the whole upon every new particular expression of life he encountered.

For him it has made perfect sense to do that ever since he came to see that the cross of Christ is "the one reality that can span the whole dimension, the height and the depth, the length and the breadth of human experience" (68coec:23). That vision came to him at a time of deep perplexity, when he "did not know which way to turn to find firm standing ground, in the midst of a time of personal humiliation and failure" (23). During that summer of his Cambridge undergraduate years when he worked among miners in the Rhondda Valley of South Wales, his sense of "total defeat" brought to focus a longtime struggle to gain the "will to believe" (the title of a book by William James which had challenged him). Of the experience he says,

> As I lay awake a vision came to my mind, perhaps arising from something I had read a few weeks before by William Temple. It was a vision of the cross, but it was the cross spanning the space between heaven and earth, between ideals and present realities, and with arms that embraced the whole world. I saw it as something which reached down to the most hopeless and sordid of human misery and yet promised life and victory. I was sure that night, in a way I had never been before, that this was the clue that I must follow if I were to make any kind of sense of the world. From that moment I would always know how to take bearings when I was lost. (85ua:11-12)

That vision of the cross which would always provide Newbigin with his bearings became more deeply embedded several years later when he wrestled toward his basic theological convictions. His Greek New Testament bears to this day the voluminous markings in the margins surrounding the text of Romans that attest to the study done during his theological training, again at Cambridge. For several months he poured over the text and commentaries on it. C. H. Dodd, he concluded, "made the Epistle palatable by removing its toughest parts." Demythologizing the "wrath" of God must also remove the "love" of God. Barth he read twice but found him "incomprehensible" (85ua:31). James Denney was the "decisive" voice for him. His study brought him to "a strong conviction about 'the finished work of Christ,' about the centrality and objectivity of the atonement accomplished on Calvary." This he marks as the "turning point" in his theological journey (85ua:30-31).

It can be added, as well, that Newbigin's vision of the cross as that which alone binds all things together has been the determinative starting point for all his subsequent thinking and ministry (68coec:23). The variety of particular cultural settings in which that ministry was carried out and the range of contacts with people from cultures beyond those settings provided more than an ample testing ground for this vision of a "universal" gospel. His ministry experience forced upon him the same issues with which the whole Christian community has had to wrestle in the modern age — a world of peoples come together bearing their vivid differences in thought, worldview, values, and customs.

Behind all of his interaction on issues growing from cultural plurality, and as a foundation from which he addresses them, lies this sense of the gospel. The "total fact of Christ" is central to his eschatology, his ecclesiology, and his missiology (cf. Reilly 1979:15-33).

Missionary Perspective Regarding Cultural Plurality

Lesslie Newbigin nowhere announces that it is his intention to supply a "theology of cultural plurality." But he is a theologian by habit and a lifelong missionary by trade. Wherever he has had occasion to address the issues any missionary encounters, issues that arise by virtue of the diversity of cultures, he has inevitably wrestled to give theological footing to the issue at hand. And his theological reflection over the course of a full lifetime has constantly found that it is precisely those issues of plurality which have posed the most urgent problems and challenges to the faith his theology sought to articulate. It is the central thesis of this study that the fabric of Newbigin's thought has been so inextricably bound up with the matter of culture and cultures that it provides an implicit "theology of cultural plurality."

That theology has not remained implicit only. His writings evidence movement toward an increasingly explicit theology of plurality. Especially since his "retirement" to Birmingham, his reflection upon years of work in India and in the ecumenical movement played upon the fact of cultures. In Birmingham he met yet another context in which plural cultures found themselves living side by side, struggling to understand what that meant. From the mid-1970s onward, Newbigin's writings exhibit an increasing clarity of focus on the issues of plurality. More and more they reflect a direct articulation of a theological foundation for understanding that plurality. A major statement was made in the pamphlet circulated by the British Council of Churches, entitled *Christian Witness in a Plural Society* (77cwps). Religious pluralism was directly addressed in articles such as "The Basis, Purpose and Manner of Inter-Faith Dialogue" (77bpmi) and "Christ and the World of Religions" (83cwr). Culture became an increasingly frequent topic in his writings: "Christ and the Cultures" (78ctc), "Church Growth, Conversion and Culture" (78os: chapter 9), "Context and Conversion" (78cc), and "Text and Context" (82tc). Drawing on the insights of several decades, these themes became the vehicles for making more explicit what had always been present in his work — a theology of cultural plurality.

In the introductions to two of his more recent books the presence of this explicit theology of plurality shows up dramatically as the overarching vision with which he approaches Western culture from the angle of "a foreign missionary." *Foolishness to the Greeks* asks "what would be involved in a genuinely missionary encounter between the gospel and the culture that is shared by the peoples of Europe and North America," asked against the backdrop of missionary reflection on "contextualization" (86fg:1-2). His critical understanding of the "gospel" shows how thinking in "contextualization" terms gives shape to the core of his theological perspective:

> In speaking of "the gospel," I am, of course, referring to the announcement that in the series of events that have their center in the life, ministry, death, and resurrection of Jesus Christ something has happened that alters the total human situation and must therefore call into question every human culture. (86fg:3-4)

He emphatically asserts that that very announcement is thoroughly conditioned culturally and it can never be otherwise. "The idea that one could at any time separate out by some process of distillation a pure gospel unadulterated by any cultural accretions is an illusion." But because the gospel is about the Word made flesh, that gospel, "which is from the beginning to the end embodied in culturally conditioned forms, calls into question all cultures, including the one in which it was originally embodied" (86fg:4).

Based on that perspective, Newbigin lays out the model it implies for any communication of the gospel across cultural frontiers, including the one between the gospel and the Western scientific worldview. The model is threefold:

> 1) The communication has to be in the language of the receptor culture. It has to be such that it accepts, at least provisionally, the way of understanding things that is embodied in that language. . . . 2) However, if it is truly the communication of the gospel, it will call radically into question that way of understanding embodied in the language it uses. If it is truly revelation, it will involve contradiction, and call for conversion, for a radical *metanoia*, a U-turn of the mind. 3) Finally, this radical conversion can never be the achievement of any human persuasion, however eloquent. It can only be the work of God. (86fg:5-6)

In other words, there lies a theology of cultural plurality at the very heart
of his project as a missionary to the United Kingdom and to the Western
world of which it is a part.

Newbigin's exposition of the "Fourth Gospel" (*The Light Has Come*,
82lhc), a Gospel much valued in India for its resonance with India's deep
spirituality, unleashes upon fellow Westerners the kind of impact his theology of cultural plurality implies the Bible should and must have on any
culture. He lays the groundwork by first questioning all our supposed
"objectivities." The critical study of any text, he says, "is never a value-free
enterprise." It always rests on some assumptions which for the moment
remain "uncriticized." Those prior commitments need to be exposed to
view. Newbigin's experience of living extensively in two very different cultures has taught him that it is only in the acknowledgment of those commitments, and the recognition that "there are very large gaps between the
cultural world in which the Gospel was written and both of these worlds,"
that a reader of the biblical text can be aware of the questions both worlds
pose to the text and, most importantly, "of the counterquestions which the
text puts to both" (viii-ix).

Newbigin moves to the task of hearing the Fourth Gospel only
through confidence in the Holy Spirit promised in it. The Spirit who bears
witness to Jesus, who guides disciples into truth, and who exposes the
"fundamental errors of the world" is given to the church as preparation
"for its missionary encounter with all the varied communities and cultures
of the world. These are real encounters by which both the world and the
Church are changed" (82lhc:ix). Here is Newbigin's theology of cultural
plurality coming to the fore.

Missionary Modes of Theological Reflection

Because the purpose of this study is to give full expression to this theology
by relating together both the later explicit forms it takes and the persistent,
if implicit, manner in which Newbigin has expressed it all along the way,
it is important to recognize from the outset several crucial characteristics
of Newbigin's "theologizing" which must inform any assessment of it. The
character of his theology, as much as his life experience undergirding it,
makes his thought especially promising in our pursuit of a theology of
cultural plurality. His theologizing is attached to his experience of cultural

plurality, and it is virtually unavoidable that his theology would provide foundations for wrestling with it, as the following observations show:

1. First of all, his has always been an ad hoc theology. Even though he arrived in India with a predisposition to seek the tangible unity of the church everywhere, owing especially to his SCM experience, it was the situation itself which drew him into that deep wrestling over the meaning of unity which became so important for the Church of South India and the whole ecumenical movement. His ecclesiology has deep roots in his India missionary experience.

Likewise, his longstanding concern with the issue of history and progress predisposed him to spell out a careful biblical eschatology. But it was as India's independence was being born and both the dreams for its development and the struggle between competing ideologies regarding its future were intensifying that his expression of that eschatology took form (cf. his Bangalore lectures on "The Kingdom of God and the Idea of Progress," 41kgip). Further articulations would follow in "The Nature of the Christian Hope" (52nch), "The Christian Hope" (53ch), and a chapter on eschatology in *The Household of God* (53hg:123-152).[10] During that period he also held an influential position on the committee that prepared the theme statement on "The Christian Hope" for the Evanston 1954 WCC Assembly.

Again, while he had experienced religious pluralism for many years in India, his writings on that subject showed up most profoundly upon his return to his native England. There he responded in the midst of England's new experience of such pluralism and its struggle for a way to ground that pluralism in the ideals and values inherited from its own past.

It has been characteristic of Newbigin that in every experience touching upon plurality he has wrestled at a penetrating depth with the meaning of the diversity and the result has always been the fruit of his own encounters with it. He has searched constantly for action based on a firm, undergirding theology. This forced over and over again the asking of ultimate questions of meaning and purpose, questions which for him grew from practical issues and must produce practical guidance. He has always articulated his theology "to the point" which immediately faced him and the Christian church he cared so deeply to pastor.

His theology has been produced "ad hoc" in another sense, as well. He did not set out to be a theologian, nor to write extensively his theological reflections. These occurred in the "heat of battle" as he was drawn toward the clear expression of his response to issues. Whether that was by participation in ecumenical meetings, because of invitations to lecture, preach, or write, or by reason of the inner conviction that a written or otherwise uttered response to the debate of the moment was required, it has generally been a particular occasion that has precipitated the expression of his theology. A survey of Newbigin's thought makes it obvious that at the most basic levels the major concerns to which he has tended to give theological attention and the major insights which lie at the heart of his reflections were to a remarkable degree formed during his early years, particularly those spent as an undergraduate at Cambridge, as a staff worker for the SCM in Scotland, and at Cambridge again as a theological student. But those seeds germinated in the soil of his missionary engagements and blossomed on the branches of the requirements for a missiology suited to the present moment and circumstance.

Even the volumes written by Newbigin showing the greatest scope of theological concern owe their origin to some lecture series. *The Household of God* was originally presented as the Kerr Lectures at Trinity College, Glasgow, in November 1952 (53hg:xi). *A Faith for This One World?* contains the William Belden Noble Lectures given in November 1958 at Harvard University (61ftow:7). The Firth Lectures, given at the University of Nottingham in November 1964, were published as *Honest Religion for Secular Man* (66hrsm:7). The Lyman Beecher Lectures at Yale University Divinity School, April 1966, were again given at Cambridge University as the James Reid Lectures and published as *The Finality of Christ* (69fc:7). Two sets of talks given in 1966 and 1971 at the Christian Medical College in Vellore, India, were later published under the titles *Christ Our Eternal Contemporary* (68coec: publisher's note) and *Journey into Joy* (72jij:v). More recently, his *Foolishness to the Greeks* contains the B. B. Warfield Lectures delivered at Princeton Theological Seminary in March 1984 (86fg:preface), and *The Gospel in a Pluralist Society* incorporates a series of lectures given at Glasgow University in 1988 (89gps). In all of these cases, the lectures addressed critical and pressingly personal issues that he was calling persons and churches to engage. They contained not abstract reflection around points of classical interest (although they demonstrate knowledge and perception regarding those issues) but rather attempted to articulate the meaning and implications of the biblical gospel for the current situation.

The exception (which serves to prove the rule) is *The Open Secret*

(780s). In this work, unlike any others, Newbigin used the circumstance of his teaching position at Selly Oak Colleges to draw together the essential lines along which his theology of mission had taken him. It serves as an important touchstone, therefore, for all of his other theological works, showing the basic foundations undergirding all his theological reflection. But more, it gives us a clear view of what he is attempting to do in those other works in that it describes his rationale for articulating the gospel to the variegated peoples of the world with a sense of its relevance and force in every historical experience.

The theology of cultural plurality to be detected in all of this bears marks that make it especially important. Newbigin, in dealing with such a wide range of practical missiological concerns which touch on cultural plurality, speaks from the inside of experiencing the dilemmas and ambiguities that make each of the issues troublesome, while he has witnessed within each set of problems the insights it can yield for a fuller understanding. Unlike some who deal only with a small field of issues touching plurality, he speaks to each issue with practical knowledge of the problems and potentials inherent in the others.

Further he speaks from both "sides" of the experience of modernity that as a global phenomenon makes an assessment of plurality so difficult. Newbigin saw secularization from both sides, both from the vantage point of an Eastern society receiving the brunt of its entrance upon long-accepted social and cultural structures of thought and action, and from the vantage point of the Western spawning ground of that secularization — first as that which was native to him and finally as the object of his missionary approach. Likewise, he wrestled with religious pluralism in both East and West. In both cases, this double vantage point contributed toward a unique bidirectional mode of thought about plurality. His thought is not merely Western reflection on it. Nor is it just Eastern. Rather, Newbigin bears sensitivities to both ways of approaching the issue and builds theologically upon the foundation of a bidirectional sense of the gospel's affirmation and critique of cultures. This guards him from the tendency — observable in many other voices regarding plurality — to discuss it only in monochromatic Western terms.

2. In the second place, Newbigin's theology is distinctly biblical. Such an assertion requires careful definition. To say that Newbigin's theology is "biblical" is first of all meant to distinguish it from dogmatics, or "system-

atic" theology, even when that may claim to represent faithfully the meaning of the biblical text. While his training in that discipline is observably rich, it has not been his direct attempt to take up certain logical categories as a schema for articulating "truth."[11] He works neither in the manner of a fundamentalist who develops from biblical prooftexts propositional statements that define God, man, salvation, and so on, nor in the manner of a contemporary theologian who employs the fruit of higher-critical methodologies in the attempt to give philosophical definition to the nature and meaning of life in terms suggested by modern thought.

First of all, his goal is different from that of a systematic approach. The questions and categories which draw his theological reflection are those which grow out of the life and missionary engagement of the church in reciprocal relation to those which grow out of the "book" of that community which has shaped its life and mission and critiques it still (86fg:56ff.). Thus the shape of theology must be both biblical, reflecting a sensitive reading of the text within its context, and contextual, fitting the multiple needs and requirements of the spectrum of cultural settings. The danger he sees for theology is that it would become captive to the culture which has crafted the categories and concerns it addresses. His experience of "seeking to communicate the Gospel for the first time to people whose entire framework of thought and imagination is shaped by other dogmas" teaches him that the theological task can never be complete (82tc:10-11).

> Until the end of time there will be a tension between the Gospel and every human culture and therefore every human language. And yet understanding is achieved. It is not (or ought not to be) that the missionary forces upon the hearers the culturally packaged version of the Gospel that he (necessarily) brings so that the converts become pale imitations of himself. Nor, on the other hand, is it that the missionary simply becomes an item absorbed into the receptor culture. There is — or by the grace of God there may be — a "fusion of horizons," a new perspective in which both understand each other and find that the Gospel is putting questions to both. Neither of the two cultures is treated as absolute. Both sides find themselves obliged to undertake self-criticism. The only absolute is Christ himself whom — through the Scriptures interpreted in the growing inter-cultural fellowship of the world-wide Church — both sides are seeking to know better. (82tc:11)

This "fusion of horizons" which Newbigin envisions as the ecumenical goal is what keeps him focused on the pursuit of a "biblical theology" for mission (and "of cultural plurality"). Further, its requirement that those in every culture must undertake self-criticism has implications for the methodologies by which it is pursued. He identifies a certain common ground shared by the higher-critical approach and the fundamentalist approach. Whether by laying claim to a supposed "neutrality" of objective historical investigation or by treating the Scriptures "as a 'scientific' account of the things recorded," each follows a "typically 'Enlightenment' approach: the autonomous reason dealing with 'objective' facts from the past" (83os84:43-48).

By thus relativizing the higher-critical method, Newbigin shares in common the critique of its role made in other quarters (e.g., Childs 1970; cf. the summary of Childs's view in Hasel 1975:49-55). He sees great promise in the discipline of "canonical criticism" and argues for "an examination of the way in which the text relates to the canon as a whole" (83os84:44). Such canonical interpretation moves beyond the efforts of past impulses in biblical theology. While Newbigin has in a couple of cases written works which give full exposition of specific New Testament texts (69sfbs, 82lhc) and in them shows sensitivity to the particular author's unique perspective and emphasis, his effort remains cast in the broader perspective of the texts as part of a larger "self-communication of the one whose purpose the story embodies" (cf. 79cjh:205). He is not so concerned with giving a biblical theological "description" of the "theology" of biblical authors or the "faith" of the people of God.[12] Neither is his chief concern to draw out in a comprehensive way the major themes that are woven like threads through the fabric of the Scriptures (although this comes closer to his intent and practice at certain points). He acknowledges the way he had been shaped by the biblical theology movement, which had provided "works on the biblical doctrine of work, of leisure, of marriage, of the state and of many other things," studies he identifies as "designed to show that the Bible could be trusted to guide us in the 20th century as well as in the past" (82tc:6-7). But with the possible exception of his volume on *The Holy Spirit and the Church* (72hsc) such thematic theology has not been his attempt.

Newbigin's concern has been to provide a missionary theological perspective consonant with and reflective of the unifying thrust of the Scriptures. The Bible, coming to us as it does in its "canonical shape," bears a "unity which depends upon certain discernible centres."[13] These centers are "the events, happenings in the contingent world of history, which are disclosures in a unique sense, of the presence and action of God" (83os84:49). He seeks to explicate the relevance of those "disclosures" because of his concern to interpret the meaning of history and his conviction that

> the meaning of the story [i.e., history] as a whole will have been grasped in the only way which is possible, not by induction from the generality of experience but by a revelation in the form of happenings which are grasped by faith as the self-communication of the one whose purpose the story embodies. (79cjh:205)

This understanding of the Bible as God's "self-communication," as revelation, lies at the heart of his approach. For Newbigin, the Bible is "the primal witness to what God has done" (84bocm:9) and thus it "renders accessible to us the character and actions and purposes of God" (86fg:59). As the "self-communication" of the God to whom the Christian community is committed, the Bible forms for that community "the determinative clue to the character and activity of the one whose purpose is the final meaning of history" (86fg:62). To read the Bible in this way — "as testimony of God's unique and decisive revelation of himself in Jesus Christ" — is for Newbigin "an integral part of the Christian commitment as a whole" (82tc:13).

Newbigin willingly faces the possibility of receiving the same charge as that laid at the door of Karl Barth, who was "accused of the sin of 'revelational positivism' because he insisted stubbornly on the fact that the theologian must begin by simply allowing himself to be informed by Holy Scripture that God has revealed himself in the way he has in fact done so in Jesus Christ" (82tc:11-12). The charge that this view cannot measure up to modern standards of rationality is met by Newbigin's insistence that "all rational inquiry starts with some axioms and models, and some procedures for reasoning." For the Christian community to proceed to think and live on the basis of a faith for which there is "no other way of substantiating it than simply to bear the witness" does not make it any more irrational than scientific discussions which depend upon "commitment to a 'scientific world view' which cannot be demonstrated as true from outside of its own commitments" (82tc:12).

The Bible, for Newbigin, bears the "character of witness" (83os84:50). This must be so for a book of historical self-disclosure by a living and acting

God. At the base, Newbigin approaches the Scriptures as revelation because in them he expects to encounter, and be encountered by, a living God. In his theological pursuits he seeks "personal knowledge" of that God.

> Thus when we speak of revelation and appeal to the bible for its form, we are not speaking of a series of propositions imposed by an alien power on the mind of man, invading and limiting the proper autonomy of his reason and conscience; we are speaking of the appeal of a personal love which seeks not to coerce submission but to evoke love. (84bocm:16)

As long ago as 1936, in a theology paper written as part of his theological training at Cambridge, Newbigin had already said what has remained his central conviction about the nature of the Bible.

> For we know a person only as he chooses to reveal himself, and only as our spirit is sensitive and trustful to respond to his revelation, and if the meaning of the world is personal then revelation is the only path by which it can be made known to us. (36r:2)

3. In all of his ad hoc biblical theology, Newbigin shows the capacity to maintain cogency and coherence. He works to establish a unified view of things, informed by the questions and clues that arise from all the particular places embraced by such a vision. The force of his argument inevitably pinpoints with precision the most basic assumptions and "axioms" on which any point of view is founded. Coming from long experience in intercultural and interlingual understanding, the knowledge of the function of culture and language as that which establishes the frame of thought and perception has enriched the capacity of an already incisive mind.

Newbigin's constant use of the criterion of "congruence," that our understanding of how God acts must be congruent with what we know about the persons God has made and with whom God relates, underscores the drive toward an inner coherence which Newbigin seeks to mold. In a comprehensive way, he touches on the all-encompassing issues of the meaning of world history, the purpose of human life, the plan of God, and the end toward which all things are moving. As he does so, cultural plurality is a reality of that world which is always near at hand. He always seems to be raising four basic questions, questions that correspond to what we might anticipate are needed for the purposes of a theology of cultural plurality:

What is the meaning of the plurality of cultures and how is that fact to be valued? What is the meaning of the fortunes of history by which these cultures are placed in relationship with one another? How is the Christian message to be understood in light of this plurality? What forms of Christian mission correspond to these understandings?

Displaying the impulses of the systematic theologian in his press for a cogent and coherent theological perspective, he yet remains distinctly biblical in his approach. His search is not for a master system defined in terms of the language and thought of a single cultural perspective but an understanding which grows from and within the tradition of the believing church present in the multiple societies and cultures of the earth.

Newbigin's theological work holds promise because in it we find a unique blend of the "normative" finality of the revelation of God in Jesus Christ and the thoroughgoing relativity of a theologian who sees the "conditioned-ness" of all human life, thought, and expression (cf. 86fg:6). It incorporates a vision of the unity and diversity present both in the Bible and in the church of any age (82tc:11; cf. 83os84:44). It arises as missiology: "the issues involved in communicating the gospel to a people and a culture" (84bocm:10). But because of that it becomes more. What originally has been formed as a "theology for" mission has become ultimately a "theology from" the missionary encounter. Such a theology provides at its heart a "theology of" cultural plurality.

Newbigin freely acknowledges that in regard to many of the issues he addresses he is not an accomplished specialist. Whether in the area of theology, of the history of religions, of cultural anthropology, of biblical studies, of the sociology of knowledge, or of the philosophy of history, his contributions do not claim a basis in a mastery of the field. He recognizes that he has always been more the generalist. That this is the case for an "ecumenical missionary pastor" should be no surprise. But his gained competence to speak responsibly in the varied fields with which he has been concerned, by means of an interactive dependence on specialists in each field, signals the nature of the contribution he makes. If he himself has become a specialist in any area, his experience and reflection have dictated that it would be in providing the inner structure of thought necessary for the missionary engagement of gospel and culture. It is this contribution which the present study intends to identify and examine.

In what follows I will display the lines along which Newbigin's theology of cultural plurality unfolds. One primary assertion I will argue is that Newbigin's theology of cultural plurality rests on the foundation of what he calls the "missionary significance of the biblical doctrine of election" (chapters two and three). In that notion lies the heart and "inner logic" of his theology. It will further be shown that his election-based theology of plurality works itself out most pointedly along three lines: the meaning of history (chapter four), the necessity of conversion (chapter five), and the limits of "religion" (chapter six).

In the concluding chapter (seven), the strategic model that emerges from Newbigin's theological foundations will be described. That will help to clarify the integrative potential of his theology of cultural plurality and to probe its implications for giving definition to the form the field should take and the agenda it must pursue. The important insights growing from Newbigin's theology will be identified and in some cases the potential for further development of the field will be explored in order to underscore the contribution his insights offer.

In all of this, the accent will be upon materials written prior to Newbigin's major works on the encounter with Western culture, showing the ground from which that encounter arises and the framework within which it is engaged.

CHAPTER 2

The Missionary Significance
of the Doctrine of Election:
Newbigin's Persistent Emphasis

When once asked about the origins of the particular missiological use to which he put the doctrine of election, Bishop Newbigin identified the period leading up to the publication of his major work on mission theology, *The Open Secret*. That is remarkable because the structure of thought by which he there construes the significance of election may easily be documented in published works spanning three decades prior to that time. This fact itself requires interpretation and in such interpretation will lie the demonstration that election has persistently provided Newbigin with the clue for understanding mission and that it is particularly in regard to issues surrounding plurality that it becomes a most important and essential theological foundation.

Before offering an account of the fortunes of the doctrine in Newbigin's hand, some definition is needed to show what he means by "election." In the early 1980s, Newbigin pressed the issue of election frequently as he engaged the modern renewal of the Hogg-Kraemer debate (83cwr). His critique of both sides in the debate for a similar omission shows the importance election holds in his view. "It is the weakness of Hogg and of his contemporary champions that they do not seem to have pondered the significance of the biblical doctrine of election." Kraemer, on this point, fares no better: "As far as I can see, however, Kraemer did not turn his attention in either of his two major works in this field to the missionary significance of the doctrine of election" (23-24).

The notion of election which Newbigin employs is distinctively biblical and missionary. It is biblical in that he refers not to a dogmatic formulation regarding the decrees of God and the status of the believer, but to the declarations in the biblical narrative which indicate the choosing action of God, particularly concerning his election of Israel to be his people and of the church to be his witnesses. It is missionary in significance because the narrative points beyond the reason for God's choice (which lies in God's own sovereign freedom and must therefore escape our full knowing) to the purpose for which it is made, which purpose is inherently missionary. Thus, with characteristic precision but uncharacteristic understatement, Newbigin says, "The Bible seems to teach consistently that God's gift of salvation (which is certainly intended for all) works by the principle of election, one being chosen to be the means of God's saving grace to others" (83cwr:23). Only when election is so understood in both biblical and missionary terms can the particularity and universality of the gospel be held together.

> This is where we have to invoke the biblical idea of election. If it is true that God fulfills his purpose of salvation not by making himself immediately accessible to every human soul considered as a separate entity but by means of events at particular times and places, this is only compatible with what we learn of God in Jesus if it is also true that these particular events are, in some sense, for the sake of all. This is what — as I understand it — the biblical teaching about election makes clear. As I have argued elsewhere, the doctrine of election is to be understood in connection with the biblical doctrine of man as a whole: that human beings are not to be understood as autonomous monads but always as mutually related; that salvation must therefore be in and through this relatedness; that therefore the saving deeds and words must always be mediated through one to another; . . . that those who have been chosen and called to be the witnesses of God's saving actions are so chosen and called in order to bring others into their saving power. (26)

This more recently labeled "missionary significance" of the doctrine of election has been deeply imbedded in his theological reflection from the earliest days in which that began to be shared in his writings. The form of its expression and its prevalence as a theme did not remain uniform in all the periods of his life. (This may begin to suggest the reason for Newbigin's impression that it was only in the 1970s that he gave attention to the doctrine.) But there has been a persistent tenacity to these ideas which even the periods in which they were lying somewhat dormant could not set aside. That the ideas so fully spelled out in *The Open Secret* can for the most part be found in detailed expression in writings as far back as the late 1940s and early 1950s should not be surprising to anyone who has read a large amount of Newbigin's work and recognized the consistency and repetition in it.

Three periods in Newbigin's life may be identified in regard to the way in which election figures as an important theme in his lectures and writings.[1] The first includes the late 1940s and most of the decade of the 1950s, the years during which he served the Church of South India as bishop of Madura and Ramnad. The period represents a continuation of his life and work as a pastor-missionary, now with an enlarged field for that work and with an increasing network of ties within the ecumenical movement. That shows itself in the very explicit, but almost casual and assumed, way he articulated the missionary significance of election during that period. The second period reflects the new concerns with which he had to deal as he moved back to the West in the late 1950s. The wave of optimism with which the growing sweep of secularization was being greeted drew him into a new set of concerns. In this period, including the 1960s and running into the 1970s, there was less direct reference to election, although its implicit presence in his thought gave a basis for his growing attempt to forge a sense of the meaning of history, especially the world history which the contemporary world increasingly shared as one history. The third period visible from a survey of his writings is that which emerges upon his "retirement" to England in the mid-1970s. There the issues of cultural and religious pluralism come to the fore, because he is now confronted with a newly plural England whose churches are entangled in a struggle to gain their balance. The reflections of a lifelong missionary, who now found himself facing his home culture and knowing it was in desperate need of an encounter with the gospel he had preached in India, drew him toward the issues of cultural diversity and the gospel-culture encounter. Election as a critical foundation for Christian faith and action emerged in vivid form once again, this time with more force and in a more pervasive way than ever. That it had now become the thread by which his missionary theology held together is evidenced by *The Open Secret* (78os), which depends upon it from beginning to end. The "Logic of Election" figures overtly as a fundamental rationale for Newbigin's engagement with Western culture in the 1980s and 1990s (89gps:chapter 7).

A survey of the discussions in which election appears in these three periods will serve both to describe the essential features of Newbigin's view of its missionary significance and to show the forces which nurtured and matured that view.

The Earlier Period

In the earliest period, the essential fabric of Newbigin's argument regarding election is already apparent. Substantial and extended discussions of its significance appear at critical points in some of the major writings of that period. Uniformly, Newbigin affirms the central importance of the doctrine for a biblical view of the church and its mission. "The Bible," he says, "is primarily the story of election, of the people whom God chose, and of the individuals whom he chose to play special parts in the story" (61ftow:77). This "choosing (election) of a people to be His own people, by whom He purposes to save the world" is the Bible's "central theme" (54wsot:75). Apart from it the fact of Jesus Christ cannot be interpreted (61ftow:77). That is because it represents an essential part of "the faith which Jesus accepted from Israel, in which his own deeds and words were rooted and without which they cannot be understood." The faith that God "is the Creator of all things," that humankind "is fallen from his true estate and involved in a common sin against the creator," and that God's action in Christ is "the culmination of a plan which begins with the choosing of a people" is the necessary context for understanding the fact of Christ (61ftow:61). These "fundamental doctrines" are presupposed by Christ and comprise, along with the redemption brought by Christ's action and the consummation promised on the horizon of the future, the heart of the gospel in Newbigin's earliest definitions of it (48dacp:23-24).

Newbigin is persistent and relentless in pressing how centrally necessary election is in the scheme of things: "God's purpose of love must be worked out through election" (48dacp:30). "God must deal with us according to the principle of election. One race is chosen in order that through it God's salvation may be mediated to others" (53hg:110-111). "God works by this method of election, of choosing one to be the means of bringing in the next" (54wsot:72-73). "God's purpose is fulfilled by a visible earthly fellowship of men and women — beginning with those whom he has first chosen, and spreading out to others" (56ss:45). Most emphatically, Newbigin presses this necessary principle as the foundation for our mission:

> the duty and authority of the Church to preach the gospel to all nations rests upon the fact that God has chosen it for this purpose, to be the witness, the first fruit and the instrument of his saving deeds. He might have chosen others. In the nature of the case, he must choose someone. In the mystery of his will, he has chosen us, the weak and foolish and insignificant. (61ftow:81)

There are four important dimensions to the construction of the doctrine of election given by Newbigin in this early period. These formed a foundational understanding essential to the treatments he gives in the later periods.

1. First, it is essential to observe the *core notion* which rivets Newbigin's attention. Election is "the choosing of one to be the channel of grace to his neighbor" (53hg:112). God chooses one to be the means of bringing in the next:

> Throughout the Bible we find it repeatedly stated that God has chosen certain individuals and groups, out of the general mass of their fellow-men, for some purpose of His. . . . God chose the Jews to be in a special sense His own people, to be the means of bringing salvation to men. (54wsot:72)

Herein lies the heart of Newbigin's early missiology, which was never isolated from his ecclesiology. "The preaching of the Gospel is indissolubly linked with the existence of a people called and set apart by God to be its bearers" (48dacp:29). It always spreads "according to the law that each one is chosen in order to be the means of bringing the message of salvation to the next" (53hg:161).

This understanding of election is tied in the most rudimentary way to Newbigin's sense of the purpose of God which lies in the reconciling of the human race to himself, not as individual monads who remain separate from each other but as persons whose reconciliation to each other is an essential facet of their reconciliation to God.

God deals with us through one another. One is chosen to be the bearer
of the message to another, one people to be God's witnesses to all people.
Each of us has to hear the gospel from the lips of another or we cannot
hear it at all. (61ftow:79)

His purpose is not to pick out an individual here and there for His
kingdom, but to re-create for Himself that one family which He purposed
in the first creation. (54wsot:73)

It is His purpose to create a new human race in which the divisions
caused by sin are overcome, in which men are at one with God, with one
another, and with themselves. . . . He desires to knit together into one
holy family the whole race of men broken by sin. Therefore He chooses
one man, one race, in order that through them others may be saved. Each
one who has been reconciled to God has to be the means by which others
are reconciled. (56ss:45)

This is the inner logic of salvation. By the very transmission of it from one
person to another, reconciliation between the partners in the communication takes place.

   This not only gives foundation for "the duty and authority of the
church to preach the gospel" (48dacp), but it is the basis upon which
Newbigin defends the very existence of the church as a concrete, visible
community bearing that gospel. Those chosen to mediate reconciliation to
others become by virtue of such a choice "the nucleus of a new redeemed
humanity" (53hg:111). The love of God, "mediated by the concern of man
for man," bears as its fruit the knitting of people "into a visible community"
and as its goal the knitting together of all "in one redeemed fellowship"
(53hg:113, 112). It is therefore "not chance but inner necessity" that the
gospel should reach us "in the form of an invitation to join a particular
human fellowship." Only in the church as "a particular, visible, historical
society" can we find the clue to the meaningfulness of human society and
God's dealings with it (48dacp:29-30). The principle of election makes plain
that "the centre of God's plan for salvation is an actual community of men
and women called by God for this purpose . . . , that through them God's
love may reach others, and all men be drawn together into one reconciled
fellowship" (56ss:46).

   In Newbigin's major work on ecclesiology, *The Household of God*, he takes up election at precisely the critical point in his overall argument. The debate between Protestant and Roman Catholic views of the church is inadequate, he suggests, in that those ecclesiologies equally tend to omit what he called the "Pentecostal angle" in the debate (53hg:102-104). In the chapter introducing that third "angle," treating the church as "the community of the Holy Spirit," lies Newbigin's major contribution for a wider ecclesiology. The chapter expresses climactically the complete and whole perspective for which the earlier part of the book argues and provides the foundation for the important later chapters on the often overlooked eschatological and missionary dimensions of the church. It is significant that in this critical chapter on the Holy Spirit Newbigin's major discussion of election takes place. The importance of the doctrine of election in the argument places it at the very heart of his ecclesiology. "It is clear," he says, "that no discussion of the nature of the Church can avoid dealing with the doctrine of election, and it is also clear that this must come in the context of our discussion of the Church as the community of the Holy Spirit" (53hg:112). The "clarity" of those connections which Newbigin asserts is nowhere better shown than in the concluding remarks of that section of the book in which he summarizes a theology of election — which could as well be called a summary of his theology of the church:

> The source of election is in the depths of God's gracious will "before the foundation of the world"; its context is "in Christ"; its instrument is the apostolic mission to the ends of the earth; its end is to sum up all things in Christ; and its means, seal, and token is the presence of God's Holy Spirit — opening men's hearts to believe the Gospel, knitting them in love into the fellowship of the body of Christ, giving them in foretaste the powers of the age to come, and sealing them as Christ's until His coming again. The life of the visible Church on earth is thus the reality within which alone the doctrine of election is to be understood. The Church on earth is no mere earthly shadow of an invisible and heavenly substance. It is both the first-fruits and the instrument of God's gracious election, for His purpose is precisely the re-creation of the human race in Christ. (53hg:113-114)

Newbigin, of course, could not develop such an ecclesiology without adding immediately the concern for the church's unity (53hg:114-122). This concern leaps from his discussion of election in other contexts as well.

Election functions in his thought as the foundation on which the call to unity is made. If God has chosen a people "for the sake of the world," it is a single people that he has chosen, "wherein men of all kinds and sorts are reconciled in one body through the cross." If this "people" is the witness and instrument for reconciling all men, how can those who are unreconciled with each other fulfill its purpose? Our disunities, Newbigin says, have "introduced a wholly wrong kind of particularity," unlike the particularity of God's choice which is for the purpose of being universal (61ftow:81-82). The "missionary character of the doctrine of election" (53hg:111) demands the pursuit of unity.

2. Secondly, Newbigin's treatment of the missionary character of election comes against the very *specific backdrop* of the offense taken at the particularity of the gospel, especially as that expresses itself on the lips of Indian culture. Were it not a gospel which claimed universal validity and authority, its "particular" rootedness in the history of Jesus, growing as that does from the history of the Jewish people, would pose no problem. But it is just such a gospel. And there is an "unbroken link" between that gospel which claims to be "the final and universally valid truth of human existence" and the community which announces it, "a particular human society, a particular strand chosen out of all the complex web of human history." The appearance that herein lies "an intolerable confusion between the particular and the universal" is offensive to those who wish to see history as "one whole" (48dacp:29).

The question arises in the modern missionary setting with a practical poignancy. As bishop, Newbigin knows the question that every believing Christian person must ask of the Bible from the standpoint of that person's own culture and the history which stands behind it. The hint of this question in Newbigin's pastoral piece offering a rationale for the study of the Old Testament as more than just for moral lessons and illustrations of eternal truths (54wsot:71-72) becomes even more vivid in the catechetical survey in *Sin and Salvation* (56ss:43ff.). The election of Israel to be God's people lies at the center of the story of God's "preparation" for salvation and cannot be dodged. "So we have to study the history of God's chosen people, the Jews." Newbigin's sensitive ear, by which he hears the pulse of the Indian spirit, perceives the question which shows why "this teaching is unwelcome" for many. "Why should I study the history of this obscure and unattractive tribe? Why should I not study what God has done for my own people and my own land? Can I not find Him in these things?" (56ss:44). Still more forcefully, Newbigin asks,

> [H]ow can it be that among all the tribes of the ancient world, *one* should be God's people? How can it be that the Christian Church, one particular strand of human history, should be the exclusive bearer of God's saving grace for mankind? (61ftow:78)

For Newbigin to raise these questions when he did was far from irrelevant. The attitude that a people's own cultural and religious heritage should serve as their "Old Testament," preparing them for Christ, had been forcefully advanced in India by people such as Pandipeddi Chenchiah. He had asked:

> Why in the name of reason and good sense should not God's dealings with my race be my Old Testament even as God's dealings with the Jew[s] was the Old Testament of Jewish Christian[s]? Why should there be only one path to Jesus and not two, one from Old Judaism and [the] other from O.H. (Old Hinduism)? (Thangasamy 1966:162)

His own answer was confident: "I can pick up material for an Old Testament in Hinduism, making selections in the light of what Jesus said and did" (Thangasamy 1966:162). But there was the rub. If, as Newbigin argues again and again, Jesus said what he said and did what he did based on assumptions which were distinctly Jewish, Old Testament ones (including the doctrine of election), then Jesus does not leave us with a vacuum which can be filled with whatever assumptions are at hand in a particular culture and its history. Herein surely lies the grave difference between Chenchiah's constant appeal to the "raw fact of Christ," which in Chenchiah's hand becomes nearly history-less and culture-less, and Newbigin's continual recourse to the fully historical and particular "total fact of Christ."

But it is the force of this sort of question, which Newbigin so frequently encountered and so keenly felt, which forged in large measure the way in which he framed his missiology and ecclesiology in terms of election. The more generalized form which the question takes when Newbigin addresses a wider audience than the Indian one does not blunt the fact that it is the question he has heard in the Indian context to which he is responding. Election, as the choice of one to bear salvation to another, is the way universality and particularity are held together. Just as the intent of salvation is universal, Newbigin insists, so we must maintain that "this element of particularity is integral to the Gospel message" as well (48dacp:29). The particularity of the "one chosen" and the universality of the purpose of that choice — to be a bearer of salvation to another — is what makes sense of our connectedness to the particular story of the Jewish people, because that story is the central thread of the world's history and the center point of the story is Jesus (54wsot:75-76). Thus Newbigin concludes that "precisely in its concreteness and particularity, [the Church] is the bearer of the universal salvation for the world" (61ftow:81).

3. That leads us to the third important aspect of Newbigin's thought in this early period. His most cogent and painstaking line of defense against the charge of "arbitrary favoritism" lies in his insistence that in election alone do we find a *divine method* which is congruent with the character of salvation. That there is a "must-ness" and an "inner necessity" attached to the doctrine of election in Newbigin's view has already been anticipated. God "must deal with us according to the principle of election" (53hg:110), "He must choose someone" (61ftow:81), his purpose of love "must be worked out through election" (48dacp:30). That must-ness derives from the fact that for Newbigin "the means by which the good news of salvation is propagated must be congruous with the nature of the salvation itself" (53hg:169). It is imperative for him that correspondence be maintained between content and method.

> The means which God employs for our salvation are congruous at every step both with the nature wherewith He endowed us, when he created us and the world of which we are a part, and with the end to which He leads us, which is that all things should be summed up in Christ. (53hg:110)

Newbigin approaches election with full knowledge that it is "unquestionably offensive to our human reason" (61ftow:78). One of the difficulties, he suggests, is an ethical one. "It is felt to be unworthy of a benevolent deity that he should show discrimination and pick out one race among others for his special favor" (61ftow:78). A clear understanding of the purpose for election would not only set aside the objection against it but argue for its necessity. The alternative, he asserts, could only be to look for "a relationship with God which is in principle accessible to everyone individually apart from any relationship with his neighbour" (61ftow:79). The unredeemed ego wants that in order to avoid being anyone's debtor and so asks, "Cannot God deal with me directly without bringing another person, another religion, another culture into the business?" It is precisely because it is God's purpose to "break open the shell of egotism" that, while he *could* do it otherwise, he *will* not. He chooses to give us a new nature that is "content to owe the debt of love to all men." Salvation as a "making whole" is inextricably bound up with God's choice of one to bear the message to another.

> God's plan for the salvation of the world is a consistent whole, the means congruent with the end. The end is the healing of all things in Christ, and the means therefore involve each of us from the very beginning inescapably in a relationship with our neighbour. . . . We cannot be saved except through and with one another. . . . The salvation of God is a consistent whole. From beginning to end it relates us to God only through a relationship with our neighbour. (61ftow:79)

Thus, "to demand that the knowledge of God's universal love be available to all men equally is to expect that I should know it without the actual experience of meeting my neighbour," which can never break the "circle of egotism" (48dacp:29).

Election, then, is "the only principle congruous with the nature of God's redemptive purpose" if we once understand that "salvation is corporate and cosmic" (53hg:110-111). Salvation is "not something for each individual separately but for the human race together" (56ss:45). Salvation which is born of God's love and gives birth to love for God and for others must take the tangible form of election. "Love only exists in actual concrete human relationships"; therefore an "actual community" is called to bear the love of God to others so that they too may be drawn into the "one reconciled fellowship" (56ss:45-46). God's purpose for the world

> necessarily requires that men's salvation should be not by an unmediated act of God directed to each individual human soul in isolation, but by the operation of a love which works on the plane of human history, mediated by the concern of man for man knitting men into a visible community. (53hg:112)

And this, Newbigin asserts, "can only be by the way of election" (53hg:112). It is not by chance, but by the "inner necessity of love's nature" that the "Gospel of God's love" reaches us by the election of one to bear the message to another (48dacp:29-30).

4. All of this, finally, rests on Newbigin's most *fundamental assumption,* the personhood of God. It holds an important position as the response he gives to another "difficulty" involved in the offensiveness of election. What he calls a "metaphysical" difficulty has to do with the feeling by many that it is "self-evident that particular events cannot demonstrate universal truths, that God is present always and everywhere, and that the idea that one particular series of events could be regarded as in any exclusive sense the acts of God, is impossible" (61ftow:78). Newbigin, in his response, gives a pointed if brief indication that herein lies "a great divide in human think-ing" (cf. 78ctc:16). The opinion he identifies stands opposite the belief in a personal God "at the heart of reality." But, he says, "If we believe in a personal God, we must believe that it is possible for him to act and therefore to choose the times and places of his actions" (61ftow:78). It is this personal character of God that he implies is wrested from the picture when there is a "demand that the doctrine of God's universal love be dissociated from the history of a particular people." That, he says, "is to expect it to conform to the pattern of general propositions or laws which are typical of human reasoning" (48dacp:29). God, he assumes, is not a composite of proposi-tions but a personal being with a will to choose and act.

We shall see this sense of the personhood of God recur again and again in Newbigin's thinking. In later periods, as we shall observe, it shows up in his emphasis upon "personal knowing," drawing on Michael Polanyi. But it is important to note at this stage, even though it lacks the explicit prominence which other features possess. Though it is directly mentioned much less frequently than those other features, it can be said to have a determinative bearing on the whole construction he gives to election. It is the theological root from which the strength of his affirmations about election have grown and from which those affirmations have continued to be nourished.

This point may best be illustrated by reference to a theology paper written by Newbigin during his course of training at Westminster College at Cambridge. In a senior paper on "Revelation" (36r), the foundational ideas upon which he builds his study bear a fascinating correspondence to all the ideas we have been noting. Both the corporate nature of salvation, with which he says election finds congruence, and the personhood of God, which means that election is certainly not ruled out but is rather most vividly implied, are inherent in the assumptions of Newbigin's formative years. Since the paper has never been published, the paragraphs containing these assumptions are included here in full:

> In a preliminary consideration of the subject we may fairly say that the central importance ascribed to revelation in Christianity depends upon two beliefs about the nature of the world and of man. Firstly the belief that the meaning of the world is personal. For if the final meaning of the world is less than personal, then it [is] best understood by those methods of scepticism and experiment which are the requisites of scientific enquiry, but which would be the complete destruction of any personal understanding. For we know a person only as he chooses to reveal himself, and only as our own spirit is sensitive and trustful to respond to his revelation, and if the meaning of the world is personal then revelation is the only path by which it can be made known to us.
>
> Secondly the belief that the meaning of man's life is in fellowship: if it were otherwise, we should not only expect that every man would be able to achieve for himself, apart from co-operation with his fellows, the necessities of physical existence and culture, and that pain and pleasure would always be distributed in mathematical accordance with sin and merit; but also that every man would be able to receive by direct revelation from God — apart from human telling — the knowledge necessary for blessedness. But if it be true that man was made for fellowship then we can understand not only the meaning of the co-operation which economic facts make necessary, and the strange incidence of pain and pleasure, so monstrously unjust by the standards of the law courts; but we can also understand the immensely significant fact that the revelation which is the key to our highest blessedness does not descend to us straight from heaven, but has to reach us passed from hand to hand of our fellow men along the chain of a historic community. (36r:1-2)

It is a remarkable clue that when reminded of these statements, which had lain unread in a stack of papers for probably the greater part of the fifty years since they were written, Newbigin expressed surprise that he had said that at such an early date. Equally telling was his verbal exclamation after hearing the paragraph arguing for the personal meaning of the world. It was emphatic: "There's John Oman!" The mentor whose influence had been so critical in his theological training (as he indicates in his autobiography, 85ua:28, 31) had left his mark in this important area. His insistence that there is not such a "thing" as grace, only a "gracious God" (cf. Oman 1917) had indelibly printed upon Newbigin's theology a similar insistence that only if there is a personal God is there meaning for the world and the people who inhabit it. On that basis, election was not only possible but true.[2]

It is interesting to note that nearly fifty years later a brief article would again bring together these two notions, wedded still to the doctrine of election, and in practically the same form and precision (83cwr:18, 23, 26). Whatever will be said presently about the movement and shifts in Newbigin's characterization and use of the doctrine of election, the continuity of the most basic notions connected with it gives proof that the heart of the idea has maintained itself throughout the years of his reflection. That it is a dominant and anchoring idea in his theology cannot be doubted.

The Middle Period

During the latter part of the decade of the 1950s, Newbigin's theological agenda began to shift in a somewhat dramatic fashion. It was not that his perspective had changed. Rather, he encountered a new challenge in his own study and reflection, in the ecumenical dialogues in which he was engaged, and in the growing spirit of secularism in the West (to which he was returning to live at about that time). Most simply put, the question which from 1948 to 1958 had absorbed his efforts was that of the authority for the church's mission. Now the question was becoming the authority for the church's faith. This change in questions reflects the change taking place at the time in missiological discussions. Focus on the church in mission was giving way to focus on the world as the locus of God's mission.

In Newbigin's rich interaction with these issues there develops an interesting, although potentially deceptive, lacuna. The substantial, direct discussion of the biblical doctrine of election so typical in his earlier writings does not appear. References to the doctrine are much more indirect and implicit. Only if we carefully observe the new lines along which his thought develops and their relationship to the way in which he had before articulated the "missionary character" of election will we avoid concluding that he had ceased to see its importance and realize that in the new implicit connections lies a wider application of the fundamental structure of thought.

Newbigin's book *A Faith for This One World?* (61ftow) signals the climax and culmination of his earlier focus on election. These lectures, given at Harvard in November 1958, were "an attempt to state the case for the missionary calling in the context of proposals for the unity of all religions" (85ua:165). While the uniqueness of that context sets the work apart from some other writings, the project remains the same as it had been on many occasions before. The two chapters containing the substance of his constructive position represent a matured version of the argument he had used in the article published in the preparatory volume for the Amsterdam 1948 Assembly of the WCC (61ftow:7; cf. 48dacp). The major question he addresses in both cases is the question of the authority of the church for its mission. The challenge he feels has maintained its force. He wants to help the church to "know with what authority it faces a world whose rules obstinately question its right to speak" (48dacp:23). "Christian missions," he recognizes, "have been constantly challenged to answer the question, 'By what authority do you do this?'" (61ftow:56).

But by the time those William Belden Noble Lectures had been given at Harvard on that continuing theme, new currents of thought had begun for Newbigin. A year earlier he had found himself traveling by plane to Bossey, Switzerland, for a meeting at which he was to present an address for which he was "unprepared." He spent the long night hours of the flight from Bombay to Rome "reading right through the New Testament and noting every reference to 'the world'" (85ua:152). That experience and the thought it triggered were to have deep consequences:

> The result of this was to set my mind moving in a new direction in which it was to travel for the next ten years. My thoughts for the past decade had been centred in the Church. This fresh exposure to the word of God set me thinking about the work of God in the world outside the Church. The result was a lecture in which I advanced the thesis that "what we are witnessing is the process by which more and more of the human race is being gathered up into that history whose centre is the cross, and whose end is the final judgement and mercy of God." . . . As far as I was concerned, this was the beginning of a shift in perspective which enabled me to understand the concern of people like [J. C.] Hoekendijk and Paul

Lehmann which I had failed to understand at Willingen [the 1952 meet-ing of the IMC]. It meant that I began the "secular decade" of the 1960s with some enthusiasm for the "secular interpretation of the Gospel," and was the more ready to see its weaknesses before that decade ended. (85ua:152-153)

The meeting at Bossey was a gathering of pastors and missionaries who aimed "to erase the boundary line which divides 'missions' from 'ecclesiology' and to ask the basic question, what it means to believe that the Church itself is a missionary body." But they thereby were dealing with another dividing line as well. "The boundary runs not between home and foreign, between 'Christian' and 'non-Christian' lands, but between Church and world, every-where." It was the assessment of Charles C. West, one of the editors of the published collection of the essays presented at the meeting, that it was this latter boundary which was the concern of the participants (West 1959:7-8). Surely that is the new concern evident in Newbigin's contribution (59guhc).

This led Newbigin in two directions. On the one hand, the major writings of the period give primary attention to the meaning of world history, especially the modern moment in which that history was appearing to converge into one unitary whole under the rubric of secularization. Already this theme emerges in *A Faith for This One World?* which begins on the note of the "rise of a world civilization," a "single world history" (61ftow:9-29).[3] That focus intensifies in *Honest Religion for Secular Man,* in which he critiques various Christian responses to the process of secular-ization, particularly that of Paul van Buren (66hrsm:54ff.; cf. van Buren 1963). It is Newbigin's major contention

> that the dynamism of the worldwide movement of secularization is rooted in the biblical faith which understands human history in terms of the mighty acts of God for the fulfillment of his purpose; and that, by the same token, to offer to men in the midst of a secularized world a version of the Christian faith denatured by the removal of the idea of the acts of God is to misunderstand completely both the Christian faith and the movement of secularization. (66hrsm:51)

In that, he accepts "frankly" the thesis of Arend van Leeuwen, whose inter-pretation of the process of secularization was in turn derived originally from the clue contained in Newbigin's "outline notes for a biblical approach to modern history," shared at Bossey (van Leeuwen 1964:16-17; cf. 66hrsm:69). "Secularization is the present form of the process by which the ontocratic form of society is broken up and men are required to make their own decisions about belief and conduct." It is "an extension of the prophetic attack . . . upon all structures of thought, patterns of society, idols whether mental or metal, which claim sacred authority over men" (66hrsm:76).

In this context, election does not play a significant role in Newbigin's thinking. The earlier hint (61ftow:80-81) that in the church's mission as "chosen for the sake of the world" is to be found "the clue to the meaning and end of world history" goes unmentioned. In his later discussion of *The Finality of Christ* (69fc) this concern with the interpretation of the contemporary moment in world history was to build toward the explication of the hint (cf. the chapters regarding "The Gospel as a Secular Announcement" and "The Clue to History"). But only in the much later reflection of *The Open Secret* (78os) would the full force of the insight be explicated, with its essential foundation in the biblical idea of election (cf. 78os:75).

Why does the election argument slip from view during the 1960s, especially in connection with the discussion of the meaning of history? Three things can be said. First, Newbigin's emphasis in that decade shifted from the "meaning of history" to the "meaning of the trend of the contemporary moment in history." Swept along with the tide of enthusiasm for the "secular interpretation of the Gospel," Newbigin moved along other lines than those with which he was concerned earlier and dealt with a different aspect of "world history" than that to which he would return later. That this does not mean a reversal regarding his view of the character and importance of election will be taken up in chapter four on "The Presence of the Kingdom: The Meaning of History," where this dimension of Newbigin's application of the doctrine of election will be treated.

Second, because Newbigin does not forfeit his view of the Church as the people of God in the world, election can never be far from the discussion. In the one place in which it does come to view in *Honest Religion for Secular Man*, the poignancy of his earlier discussions is felt. Personal humility, he emphasizes, should be the consequence of our election. In forgetfulness, the Church (as "old Israel" did also) tends to treat election

> as if it meant being chosen for special privilege in relation to God, instead of being chosen for special responsibility before God for other men. It has interpreted conversion as if it was simply a turning towards God for

purposes of one's own private inner religious life, instead of seeing conversion as it is in the Bible, a turning towards God for the doing of his
will in the secular world. (66hrsm:101)

This same implication of election, that we are chosen not so much for
privilege but for responsibility, is again emphasized in *The Finality of Christ:*
"The privileges to which conversion is the gateway are not exclusive claims
upon God's grace; they are the privileges of those who have been chosen for
special responsibility in the carrying out of God's design" (69fc:112-113).

This notion of humility becomes pronounced in the writings of this
middle period precisely in concert with the emphasis of the Newbigin-van
Leeuwen thesis: God's prophetic call to "secularize" every idolatrous pretension
warns the church not to misread its own election. While the overall interpretation of the then-current world scene offered in this thesis would disappear in
Newbigin's later writings under the corrective of the world's persistent pluralism and the virile resurgence of its religious traditions, the important insights
it precipitated remained. Newbigin discovered in the sixties how important it
is to view the gospel as a secular announcement, not just the faith of a Church
that "had become the religious department of European society rather than
the task force selected and appointed for a world mission" (66hrsm:103).

Third, the seeming lacuna is due to another important shift in agenda,
which grows alongside the one we have been surveying. The repercussions
from secularization in the sixties were most loudly felt within Western
society itself. There the fading Christendom was leaving in its wake the
most vivid and radical forms of secularized faith and the deepening crisis
of maintaining faith at all. If by the mid-fifties it had been characteristic to
conclude that *mission* had "become the problem," then by the mid-sixties
faith had become the problem. Parallel to Newbigin's attention to issues
concerning the world and its historical moment, a more decisive tendency
emerges in his writings. And within the framework of this shift election
begins to carry a new and determinative burden.

The writings of the period that includes the 1960s and early 1970s
address the question of authority in a new way. Whereas the earlier period
had responded to the challenge leveled at the church's authority to *preach,*
in this period we find Newbigin responding to a deeper challenge: by what
authority do we *believe?* The challenge of the church's authority for mission
has given way to the more serious challenge of the church's authority for
its very faith.

The shift is indicated by his motivation for writing the Firth Lectures (Nottingham University), given in 1964 and published under the title *Honest Religion for Secular Man* (66hrsm). The lectures responded directly to the influential book by Bishop John Robinson (1963). While written by a man he held in high regard, Newbigin "believed that his book was an attack on the very centre of the Christian faith." It was part of a "theological earthquake which was shaking the world of English-speaking Christians" and which was "a much more serious affair than the debate about missiology" (85ua:199).

In Newbigin's comment upon the effect which *Honest Religion for Secular Man* had we can see even more clearly the focus of his intention. It is his judgment that the book has been the most "successful" of all that he has written. He concludes about it:

> Very few experiences have given me more cause for thankfulness than the things that have been said to me in subsequent years by Christian ministers who were enabled by that small and halting effort of communication to recover their faith in God, and to continue their ministry in the Church. (85ua:199)

In the book he is responding to just that need: "Belief in God is no longer, for secularized modern man, a normal part of his mental furniture." He is attempting to reestablish the foundations for a biblical faith in "the revelation of God in Jesus Christ." He addresses the concern which has revised his agenda: "What does it mean to speak of knowing God?" (66hrsm:77).

Upon his return to India in 1965 to take up duties there as bishop of Madras, a similar concern can be observed in lectures given as an apologetic for the Christian faith. In both sets of lectures given at the Vellore Christian Medical College (in 1966 and 1971), the question of authority which he poses is the question of the basis for Christian faith. At its core, the question is epistemological. "'How do we know?' — I think that no presentation of the Christian faith can side-step that question — can side-step, in other words, the question of authority" (68coec:7). Upon his return to Vellore five years later the issue has only widened: "[W]e have to face the question, 'Why and how is the Bible an authority for me? Why must I accept what the Bible says?'" (72jij:4). "How and where, amid the irrationality and injustice with which the world is filled, do we find a clue to rationality?" (17).

Newbigin, who through his earlier writings had pastored a world church for whom there was a crisis of nerve regarding mission, now evangeled a world for whom the faith of the church had ceased to hold things together. Whether he was addressing the "problem of faith" of the one "who seeks to walk by faith" but is barraged with facts and perspectives that seriously question it (66hrsm:78), or approaching people outside of the faith who are hesitant about accepting from theologians their "most precise and detailed accounts of what God does or does not do" (68coec:7), a major part of Newbigin's agenda in this period was apologetics.[4] He sought to answer the question he put to himself: "How shall we speak of the knowledge of God in a way which is really honest?" (66hrsm:79).

It is in this connection that Newbigin began to employ the insights of Michael Polanyi (as he continued to do ever since in very crucial ways). Newbigin's apologetic asks, "What is the way by which we come to know anything?" (68coec:7). Drawing upon Polanyi's treatment of personal knowledge (1958), he first establishes that knowing is a learned skill and that it is an activity of persons in community (66hrsm:80-81; 68coec:7-9). Further, for a person to know means commitment and risk-taking, because all knowing "involves a committing of oneself to an understanding of reality which might be wrong" (68coec:9-10; 66hrsm:81-84). Given this understanding we are not left with the common view that "the highest role which can be assigned to faith is that it is an element in the achievement of knowledge, but can never be more than that" (66hrsm:85). Even for the scientist, there is a dimension of faith underlying the knowledge which is gained — "faith in the validity of the scientific method . . . , faith in the integrity of the community of scientists" (85). In fact, "objects of faith may have a higher degree of reality than the objects of our knowledge. . . . [I]t is difficult to deny there are realities which we know by faith" (86).

If this is so for all forms of knowing, it is more true for the mutual knowledge of persons. That knowledge "involves the recognition of another centre of decision which it is not in my power to control." It comes only "as the result of a mutual trust leading to a mutual self-revelation" (66hrsm:86). Such knowledge "is possible only through our sharing together in a common world of things and persons" (88). Therefore

> The mutual knowledge of persons is not something apart from our other knowledge. It is not an exception to the general rule which might be

allowed for but which could not govern our basic thinking. It is, on the contrary, the context and the precondition of all knowing. (87)

This, then, must be the context for any answer to the question, How can we know God? We know him only "through the shared world of nature and history" (88). Here Newbigin finds the great deficiency in Robinson's view. His book "left no room for a truly personal God" (85ua:199). Precisely this is the central affirmation of the biblical gospel, that "ultimate reality is personal" (66hrsm:89). The other major choice one could make in order to posit coherence for reality (the road traveled by ancient Greek and historic Indian thought) is that "personality, the distinction between me and you . . . , is seen as part of the world of unreality which ultimately is not significant" (68coec:18). The Bible presents an alternative, namely that

> the secret of unity and coherence lies, not in the power of your mind to unify and transcend experience, but in the existence of a Reality which is now present behind all the confusion of the visible world. The secret is in the mind of him who has created all things and who will bring order out of all this chaos. (19)

The Christian stands on the faith that this picture of reality is true, known in "the experience of a personal relationship of love and truth and faithfulness" (19).

It is easy to see in this construction the increasing way in which the impact of John Oman's "personalism" is making itself felt in Newbigin's thought. The connection between the personhood of God and revelation as the necessary means for "knowing" to occur between God and human persons can be seen from the earliest stages of Newbigin's thinking (cf. 36r:1-2). The link we have observed in the earlier period between this personal view of God and the missionary character of election shows up again here in this new connection in relation to Newbigin's concern to provide ultimate epistemological grounding for the Christian's faith. When finally pushed to the limits of the question "How do you know?" the Christian has only a simple and humble answer. For Newbigin, the answer "is not that he has decided to do this. The answer is that somehow or other Jesus has laid hold on him. 'You did not choose me, but I chose you,' said Jesus to his disciples, and that is the way it is" (68coec:21).

Election, then, plays a significant new role in Newbigin's theology as the personal, experiential basis for assurance that the Christian's commitment is worth staking one's life on (cf. 68coec:22). While this connection is not drawn out as fully as were the prior ones regarding the authority of the mission of the church, it comes at a critical juncture in the total apologetic argument (68coec:7-22, where the whole discussion about "authority" and "knowing" parallels closely the flow and detail of the similar argument in 66hrsm:77-99). This connection of election with the question of the authority for "faith" adds new depth to the continuing relevance it has for the identity and mission of the church. In this period as in the earlier one, while in many ways it is touched more lightly, election as the foundation for mission is affirmed, bathed now in the sense that it is foundational as well for the very faith of the church which testifies. The thread persists:

> In the middle of this world God has set His Church as his witness. (61icd:24)

> The Church simply is the body chosen and appointed by the Lord for this purpose . . . , the body chosen to bear the Name of Jesus in the world. It is only in this way that we can make sense of what the Bible teaches about election which is in a sense the fundamental doctrine of the Bible. (68wmc:3)

> We know three things: that all authority belongs to Jesus; that he will bring all things under his rule; and that he has chosen us as witnesses and agents of his purpose to do so. (68bima:28-29)

The Later Period

Among the mission theologies written in this century, Newbigin's *The Open Secret* (78os) stands unique in at least this one important respect: it alone weaves a comprehensive perspective around "election" as the central and dominant thread. In a more recent possible exception, Darrell L. Guder's *Be My Witnesses* (1985), the theme of election has a pervasive presence as well. However, election does not function as the essential integrating notion of Guder's theology, as it does for Newbigin. It can also be demonstrated that Guder's use of election is dependent upon what he has learned from Newbigin (Guder 1985:xiii).

Again, H. H. Rowley's biblical theological work on election (1950) and its important role in Johannes Blauw's watershed "survey of the biblical theology of mission" (1962) does not negate the assertion. In neither work does election become the governing notion which provides the basis for mission. In fact, it appears as potentially poised against mission. In many other mission theologies election receives only passing notice (usually in regard to Genesis 12), if any at all. In none does it appear as the rationale for mission and the fabric of the forms which mission must take. For Newbigin, it is both.

That election is so consciously and completely played out by Newbigin as the integrating theme in *The Open Secret* is remarkable in two respects. In the first place, the book is consciously intended to develop the argument contained in seed form in Newbigin's earlier study paper published in 1963, *The Relevance of Trinitarian Doctrine for Today's Mission* (78os:vii-viii). That paper, in turn, was itself an attempt to move beyond the inadequacies of the earlier *One Body, One Gospel, One World*, which Newbigin thought was "too exclusively church-centred in its understanding of mission" (85ua:198-199). In neither of those earlier works, however, does election appear as part of the argument. But in the more complete development of Newbigin's trinitarian missiology during the 1970s, as he taught and lectured during the early years of his "retirement," election holds a determinative position in the case for mission. That is true not only for *The Open Secret* as a whole but for the chapters in which he focuses attention on the three persons of the Godhead (chapters 4 through 6) in particular. The "trinitarian basis for mission" that Newbigin had long espoused has now become virtually "an exposition of election."

There had been hints in that direction in a dictionary article he wrote regarding "trinitarianism":

> Its importance for missions may be suggested in the following points. (1) Jesus Christ cannot be introduced to those of another religion simply as "God." He can only be introduced as the Son of the Father. (2) The sovereign freedom of the Holy Spirit over as well as within the church is the starting point of missionary renewal. (3) The church's mission is the clue to world history, but is subject to the Father who over-rules all things according to his will. (71t:607)

But now Newbigin is no longer just hinting. What accounts for this new clarity?

The other intriguing feature in this turn of events is the fact that in Newbigin's own sense of the situation he marks the mid-1970s as the time when election became for him a key notion in his mission theology. In personal conversation on one occasion he expressed surprise at the fact that his use of the election argument had spanned the whole length of his ministry. In fact, the ways in which he uses the doctrine of election as a foundation for mission in *The Open Secret* are not at all new in Newbigin's thought at that time. While he wrote that book with a new consciousness that election formed the center for his mission theology, the structure of thought surrounding it and the various facets of "inner logic" it provides had shown up in his writings in the earlier periods we have surveyed.

While at a couple of points the election argument is expanded and more fully elaborated, none of the details in his use of the doctrine of election in *The Open Secret* are new. For example, Newbigin makes more of the election of Jesus. The progressive narrowing down of the focus in the Old Testament finally results in the narrowing to one man "who bears the whole purpose of cosmic salvation in his own person." From there it broadens again, "a few are called to be bearers of the secret" (78os:37-38). But this expanded treatment is not substantially different from earlier expressions of the same idea (cf. 53hg:113; 56ss:44; 61ftow:77-78, 80). The stronger emphasis at this time is most probably to be attributed to Newbigin's reading of Karl Barth's *Church Dogmatics* upon his return to England in 1974 (85ua:241; cf. Barth 1957b).

Another example concerns the lengthy treatment given to the implications of Romans 9–11. If even God's elect people, the Israelites, finally end up in the position of having to receive salvation from the hand of others, the Gentiles, then the principle that "salvation can only be in mutual dependence and relatedness" is affirmed. Even the elect "can receive the gift of salvation only through those who are not the elect" (78os:84-86). Newbigin credits the insights derived from this passage as those which "most focussed" for him the determinative character of the election perspective. But here again, the idea is not new in his writings at this later time but had been noted at several points before (cf. 53hg:150; 61ftow:79; 66c:315-316).

This unusual consciousness of Newbigin's that the election foundation for his missiology was only forming in the mid-1970s adds importance to the question with which we were left when we observed the way that the trinitarian basis has in the end become embraced by the notion of election. Why? How may these things be explained? Essentially, it will be argued here that the explanation lies in the lacuna of the former period (the 1960s). That explains why election has appeared to Newbigin to be a new insight in the 1970s and why election now dominates the trinitarian basis. This can best be demonstrated from within *The Open Secret* by showing (1) that the essential features of Newbigin's use of election in the early period have returned in full bloom due to the new circumstances of the pluralism agenda of the 1970s; and (2) that the use of election has been substantively enriched by the focus in the middle period on world history and the personal basis for faith and knowing.

The problem which reemerged with new force for Newbigin in the seventies was the problem of particularity, which uniquely challenges all those who hold faith in a gospel which claims universality. Somewhat muted in the decade of the "secular" with all its euphoric hope that the world was coming into one single history and that the unity of humankind was coming within reach, the problem gained renewed momentum as the diversities and particularities found new ways to manifest themselves. Newbigin began a period of reflection over his forty years of missionary service at a time in which the England to which he retired found itself in the first throes of reckoning with the empire come home to roost. Religious pluralism, especially, had become a topic not just for missionaries in remote parts of the world. The challenge now was not to find "a faith for this one world" but to make room for all faiths. Against such a backdrop, the apparent lacuna of the prior period came to an end, and Newbigin's thought returned to election as he faced this new challenge of pluralism.

It is significant that the chapters most saturated with the notion of election are those most determinative in the development of the plan of the book. As a foundation for the articulation of a trinitarian understanding of mission (which follows in his chapters 3 through 6), Newbigin raises the persistent question of a lifetime, the question of authority (chapter 2). Mission faces first of all the question concerning the right to preach, the right "to call men and women out of their traditional allegiances, and to invite them to accept — with all the cost involved — the yoke of obedience to Christ" (78os:13-14). At the most basic level, Newbigin's response shows the lines along which he has for years been accustomed to answer. His authority lies in the authority of Jesus, which is "the authority of God himself present in the life of men" (16). Ultimately, he says,

> I make this confession [that Jesus is Lord of all] only because I have been laid hold of by Another and commissioned to do so. It is not primarily or essentially my decision. By ways which are mysterious to me, which I can only faintly trace, I have been laid hold of by one greater than I and led into a place where I must make this confession and where I find no way of making sense of my own life or of the life of the world except through being an obedient disciple of Jesus. (19)

Thus Newbigin places into the picture the rationale for believing which became important in his writings of the middle period. But immediately alongside that answer comes the other, which had been for so long his rationale for preaching:

> God chooses men and women for the service of his mission. To be a Christian is to be part of a chosen company — chosen, not for privilege, but for responsibility. The doctrine of election, so central to the whole of the Bible, is necessarily central for a true understanding of missions. It has been misconstrued. . . . But no doctrine of the Christian mission can be true which does not recognize that it is God's sending, and that he sends whom he will. (19)

Thus the fruit of his thought in response to both questions of authority — the authority to preach and the authority to believe — comes together at the outset of his most complete mission theology. And election forms his answer to both questions.

Newbigin returns to this question of authority in chapter 7, and again it comes in response to the central problem, particularity. Following the development of his basic trinitarian framework, Newbigin shifts to a discussion of "some of the theoretical and practical problems that the church must meet in pursuing its missionary calling" and begins that series of discussions by addressing the "scandal of particularity." In this chapter on "The Gospel and World History," which serves as prelude to his later discussions regarding justice, conversion, and interreligious relationships (chapters 8 through 10), he most thoroughly demonstrates the relevance of the doctrine of election for contemporary missiology. The scandal of particularity which he sees to be "at the center of the question of missions" finds its answer "in the doctrine which permeates and controls the whole Bible — the doctrine of election" (72-75).

Three critical observations should be made regarding the importance of the argument Newbigin develops in chapter 7. First, a comparison of the way in which he poses here the question of the scandalous character of particularity and the way he before asked the question of authority (chapter 2) demonstrates that Newbigin is sensitive both to the question of the Hindu (and others whose commitments differ from Christianity) and to the question as raised in the post-Christian West. In chapter 7, Newbigin describes the scandal as he has heard it from the lips of the Hindu peoples among whom he had lived much of his life:

> Is it really credible that the Supreme Being whom I and my forefathers have loved and worshiped for forty centuries, is incapable of meeting my soul's need, and that I must await the coming of an agent of another tradition from Europe or North America if I am to receive his salvation? What kind of a god are you asking me to believe in? Is he not simply the projection of your culture-bound prejudices? Come! Let us be reasonable! Let us open our treasures and put them side by side, and we shall see that your symbols and mine are but the differing forms of one reality shaped according to our different histories and cultures. If God is truly God — God of all peoples and all the earth — then surely God can and will save me where I am with the means he has provided for me in the long experience of my own people. (73-74)

But he also hears with equal potency the question which is asked "with a confidence and vehemence unusual fifty years ago," even "within the Christian church" (13-14).

> Why not join with the sincere adherents of all religions in seeking the fullness of the truth to which they all aspire?
>
> Why not join with all people of goodwill in tackling the real human problems of hunger, oppression, sickness, and alienation, instead of seeking more adherents for your religious group?
>
> Is your [missionary] enterprise not an offense against the unity of mankind? Is not the just unity of all peoples a matter of such urgency that to propagate something so divisive as religion is almost a crime against humanity? (14)

The two settings in which he hears the question create a double backdrop against which he writes, and in a sense this presents Newbigin with a continually double agenda. Both the reaction of the adherents of other faiths and the sentiments of the members of the Western churches provide the impulse for his theological work.

Second, it should be noted that in chapter 7 election lies at the heart of an interpretation of the historical character of human existence which had become such a vivid matter for Newbigin during the 1960s. Hints are visible even in his earlier writings regarding his sense that election, along with the church's mission which is based upon it, provides the clue for the meaning of world history. While those hints were not fully developed in the middle period, his engagement with the issue of world history in that period has enriched those hints as they are now picked up again in this chapter of *The Open Secret*.

In the chapter, Newbigin first shows how election speaks to the central question of missions, namely "the problem of relating God's universality to his particular deeds and words." It may readily be noticed, Newbigin claims, that in the New Testament "these two themes are interwoven without any apparent sense of incompatibility." In fact, "universality and particularity do not contradict one another but require one another. How can this be so?" (74-75). It is to this question, "How?", that Newbigin applies the answer which he finds in the doctrine of election.

The Bible presents "the story of a universal purpose carried out through a continuous series of particular choices." This means that God "does not accomplish his purpose of blessing for all peoples by means of a revelation simultaneously and equally available to all" but chooses one for the sake of the many. Our understanding of this pattern must of course refuse to treat God's choice as "limited privilege." But the pattern must be of this sort if we are to guard the integrity of what it means to be human. "The human in the Bible exists only in relationship with other persons and only as part of the created world." This is true because God himself is not "an isolated spiritual monad." Therefore "there can be no salvation for man except in relatedness. No one can be made whole except by being restored to the wholeness of that being-in-relatedness for which God made man and the world." From this "fundamental insight concerning the nature of man" arises "the biblical insistence that God's universal purpose of salvation is accomplished through the choosing of particular people" (75-78). Newbigin concludes:

God's way of universal salvation, if it is to be addressed to man as he really is and not to the unreal abstraction of a detached "soul," must be accomplished by the way of election — of choosing, calling, and sending one to be the bearer of blessing for all. The biblical doctrine of election is fundamental to any doctrine of mission which is addressed to men and women as they are in the fullness of their shared life in history and in nature. (79)

Thus the mission of the church which has in its hand a gospel to be transmitted to others is inseparably linked with the fact and nature of creation, tied at the same time with the ultimate, universal destiny of the world and its people as planned by the one who created it all. The fundamental connection of God's electing choice to this overall plan is seen by Newbigin in the assertions of Paul in the early verses of Ephesians.

> The whole action has its origin in the eternal being of the triune God before the creation; it has its goal in the final unity of the whole creation in Christ; and meanwhile the secret of this cosmic plan, the foretaste of its completion, have been entrusted to these little communities of marginal people scattered through the towns and cities of Asia Minor. (79)

However, to find thus the solution to the dilemma of universality and particularity in the "essentially narrative" story told in the Bible only drives the problem one step deeper. When we hold to "the biblical picture of world history as centered in a series of 'acts of God,' among which his act of choosing, calling, and sending a people to be bearers of his universal purpose of blessing has a central place" (87), we must face the question, "By what right do we talk in this way, and how does this talk relate to the history of the world (and of the Mediterranean area) which we read in the writings of secular historians?" (91).

First of all, this problem is not to be resolved by reducing the importance of their "happenedness" and resorting to "truths which are eternal and universal" and which lie behind the Christian stories (91). These "so-called eternal truths are the attempts we make at particular moments in the story to grasp and state how things are in terms of our experience at that point." But,

> the Bible does not tell stories which illustrate something true apart from the story. The Bible tells a story which is *the* story, the story of which our

human life is a part. . . . It is not that there are stories which illustrate "how things are"; it is that we do not begin to understand how things are unless we understand how they were and how they will be. (92)

As Newbigin tackles this problem of positing a decisive significance for the history of the whole world in the story of "one of the minor ethnic communities of the Near East," he makes several observations about "modern scientific historiography." It is first of all to be understood as something which itself is not universal but "a product of a particular culture." Second, historiography involves the handling of its tools and the arranging of historical information "by a human being whose work is also shaped by the interests and influences of his time and place and culture." Ultimately, then, one cannot answer the question, "What events are significant for human history as a whole?" apart from "some idea, if only a provisional one, about the shape of the human story as a whole." The point of any story is "normally . . . clear only at the end. Our difficulty is that we are still in the middle of the story: we can investigate the past, but the future is hidden and we do not know the end" (93-95).

This necessary limitation inherent in the nature of history brings "revelation" into the picture. For the significance of any event to be understood "in a way which is valid for all" it is necessary that "the point of the story has been revealed even before the story has come to its end." No amount of research can do what revelation must at this point. The Bible is understood within Christian tradition to be precisely that, a disclosure of the end of the story, and hence its shape, in the events it narrates. From this source has come "into our culture" the very "idea of a universal history" (95-96).

How then does the biblical story "of God's dealing with man by the way of election" relate to the story of humankind as seen in "a modern history of the world" (97-98)? The answer, according to Newbigin, must begin with the affirmation that "the biblical story is not a separate story. It is not a special history ('salvation history') apart from human history as a whole. The whole story of mankind is one single fabric of interconnected events, and the story the Bible tells is part of it." As such it is subject to the "critical probing of the historian" (98). But the Christian believer approaches the interpretation of the significance of history with a presupposition no less valid than those of the Hindu, Marxist, or Western academic —

the presupposition that the point of the whole human story has been revealed here; that in Jesus the whole meaning of the story is disclosed; that everything else, including all the axioms and presuppositions and models developed in all the cultures of mankind are relativized by and must be judged in the light of this presupposition. And the presupposition is the one which has shaped and has been borne by the believing community which is the church, from the first disciples to this day. (99)

It is of the very essence of the Christian faith that it thus presents "a way of understanding world history which challenges and relativizes all other models by which the meaning of history is interpreted" (99).

This election-based interpretation of history leads to a third critical observation to make in regard to chapter 7, namely, its integral connection to the relationship drawn in the prior chapters between election and the trinitarian basis for mission. In both the chapter on the Father (chapter 4) and the one on the Son (chapter 5), specific reference is made to an election rationale whose "inner logic" will be spelled out in chapter 7 (78os:37), where also will be more fully explored the implications of treating the kingdom of God as something which "must be such that it binds each of us to *all* as part of its very character" (implying a view of human history as "one interlocking reality") rather than something which "must be equally available to all and to each in his time and place" (implying a view of the human soul as "a distinct monad having an eternally unsharable destiny") (56-57). In fact, in both of these chapters the essential earlier fabric of the missionary character of election together with its implications for an understanding of world history play a central role.

It is the leading assertion in Newbigin's exposition of mission from the perspective of "Proclaiming the Kingdom of the Father" that

> we are talking about the origin, meaning, and end of the universe and of all man's history within the history of the universe. We are not dealing with a local and temporary disturbance in the current of cosmic happenings, but with the source and goal of the cosmos. (32)

Careful to preserve the distinction between election to the status of "beneficiary" and election to the position of "bearer" of the blessings of God, Newbigin emphasizes the narrowing way of election central to the Bible's "universal history" (33-37). God's "universal purpose of blessing is not to be effected by means of a universal revelation to all humanity" but by a process of selection, a few being chosen for the sake of all. Narrowed finally upon one man, Jesus, the heart of God's universal purpose comes to light in "the way of the cross": "He bears witness to the presence of the reign of God, not by overpowering the forces of evil, but by taking their full weight upon himself." The "secret" of that purpose was revealed to disciples, who then were granted to be made "witnesses," "chosen by God," of the resurrection which was not a "reversal of a defeat" but "the manifestation of a victory." The Lamb that was slain (cf. Revelation 5:1-10) "and he alone, can and does reveal [history's] meaning to those whom he chooses. As they follow the Lamb on the way he went, they bear witness to the true meaning of what is happening in the history of the world." It is Newbigin's conclusion that such apocalyptic passages of the New Testament as this one "sketch for us the public history of the world in a form which is shaped by the cross and resurrection of Jesus" (37-41).

As he moves on to mission as "Sharing the Life of the Son," Newbigin affirms that the kingdom of God is in the New Testament not only proclaimed but actually present (44). Its presence in Jesus implies its presence from that time forward in the church.

> The church is a movement launched into the life of the world to bear in its own life God's gift of peace for the life of the world. It is sent, therefore, not only to proclaim the kingdom, but to bear in its own life the presence of the kingdom. (54)

But this precipitates an important question: "With what right can we dare to speak of the presence of the kingdom in the life of the church?" (54). The history of the church, Newbigin acknowledges, gives reason for serious pause regarding the legitimacy of the claim.

The ultimate answer he gives rests on the election structure of thought. "The particular happening of the living, dying, and rising of Jesus, the 'fact of Christ' as a happening at one time and place, must, so to say, enter into the stream of historical happenings and become part of its course." If "God's reign concerns history in its unity and totality, we . . . must share in its power . . . by participating in the life of that society which springs from it and is continuous with it." The company of people chosen to be the bearers of God's gift on behalf of all is the necessary form in which "the new reality which [Jesus] introduced into history was to be continued through history." By this means it is possible for the "single happening" of Christ, located as it was "at a particular point of place and time in the whole vast fabric of human affairs," to be "of decisive significance to all" (57-58).

The wedding of former elements in Newbigin's complex of thought regarding election which we have thus far observed in *The Open Secret* is applied specifically, in later chapters, to critical contemporary concerns. While the chapter on "Mission as Action for God's Justice" (chapter 8) does not mention election as such, it is not hard to understand its dependence on the framework offered in the first seven chapters. The final two chapters deal with cultural plurality and religious plurality respectively. These chapters were refinements of materials which had already been published, in which in an ad hoc fashion he had begun to engage the issues of pluralism into which he had become immersed in the 1970s. (Chapter 9 was based in part on "Christ and the Cultures" [78ctc] and chapter 10 was based on "The Basis, Purpose and Manner of Inter-Faith Dialogue" [77bpmi].) In each case, election is the key to his approach.

Newbigin's discussion regarding conversion and culture (chapter 9) rests upon a triangular model of the relationship between the gospel and cultures in which "the three points are the local culture, the ecumenical fellowship representing the witness of Christians from other cultures, and the Scriptures as embodying the given revelation with its center and focus in the person of Jesus Christ" (172). It is at the point at which the Scriptures are included as possessing special authority that there arises, particularly from those within the modern scientific world, a challenge which at the very deepest level affects "the integrity and authority of the Christian mission" (173). One dimension of that challenge especially touches the nerve of the particularity inherent in salvation which works by God's election. The Bible

> arises out of the experience of a people, or a group of peoples, among all the peoples of mankind. It is indelibly marked by their cultural peculiarities and it is embodied in their languages. How, then, can it be absolutized, given an authority over the products of other cultures? (173)

That the Bible is located in "one particular part of the whole fabric of human culture" is inextricably tied to its own story that "God chose the clan of Eber from among all the seventy nations that made up the human family" and to Christianity's "central" dogma that "God has chosen one people among all the people to be the unique bearer of his saving purpose for all nations" (174).

It is precisely this which "contemporary Western culture" finds impossible to believe and wherein lies the offensive nature of the view that the Scriptures ought to have authority over other particular cultures.

The response Newbigin gives to this reaction lies at the most elemental level of reasonable reflection upon the issue. He contends that

> here two different dogmatic systems confront one another, and I know of no set of axioms more fundamental than either of them, on the basis of which it would be possible to demonstrate the truth of one of these dogmas and the falsity of the other. According to one dogma, world history is in some sense a coherent whole, and it is therefore possible to affirm that certain events have a unique significance for the entire story. According to the other dogma, there are no events which have such unique significance and therefore no universally valid affirmation can be made about the meaning of history as a whole. (174)

Here, then, is a "clash of ultimate faith-commitment" between the Christian's affirmation which is "part of the total faith-commitment to Jesus as Lord" and that which rests upon "the dominant 'myth' of contemporary Western culture" (174).

When Newbigin takes up the matter of interreligious relationships in the final chapter (chapter 10), election as the clue to the meaning of history again figures prominently in the discussion. For Newbigin, the personal starting point for meeting the neighbor of another religion is the humble position of "a witness, one who has been laid hold of by Another," from which position one can "only point to Jesus as the one who can make sense of the whole human situation." It is a necessary corollary to the belief that Jesus is the "light" that we both acknowledge light wherever and whenever it is to be found in the midst of human activity (religious and otherwise) and point to it as that which makes the path "clear" and that which stands in opposition to "deeper darkness." But the "terrible thing about human nature is our capacity to take the good gifts of God and make them into an instrument to cut ourselves off from God, to establish our independence from God." This tragic dynamic of human life is exposed and remedied in the cross of Jesus, a "unique historic deed, which we confess as the true turning point of universal history." The "unique incarnate Lord" there "confronts the claim of every religion with a radical negation" (197-200). So, in the end, the revelation of God's saving love and power in Jesus entitles and requires me to believe that God purposes the salvation of all men, but it does not entitle me to believe that this purpose is to be accomplished in any way which ignores or bypasses the historic event by which it was in fact revealed and effected. (200-201)

This leads to Newbigin's respectful anticipation that through dialogue there is much for the Christian to learn. If salvation, which works by the way of election, is

a real consummation of universal history and not simply the separate consummation of individual personal lives conceived as abstracted from the public life of which they are a part, it follows that an essential part of the history of salvation is the history of the bringing into obedience to Christ of the rich multiplicity of ethical, cultural, and spiritual treasures which God has lavished upon mankind. (202)

In other writings of this period on themes related to the nature and mission of the church and the pluralism in which that mission must take place, a similar dependence upon the "inner logic" of election is easily observed. Newbigin's ecclesiology (cf. 80pfnd:7), his view of conversion (78cc:5), his understanding of religions (83cwr:23-24, 26), and his approach to witness in a plural society (77cwps: 8, 17, 25) all make recourse to the "missionary significance of the biblical doctrine of election" at critical points in the argument.

But during this period, another major agenda was emerging in Newbigin's lectures and writings alongside these facets of the missiological one. England, which he and others "had been accustomed, especially in the 1960s," to speak of as "a secular society," he now came to recognize was "a pagan society." He saw himself as the "easy victim of an illusion" which his reading of the Gospels should have corrected. "No room remains empty for long. If God is driven out, the gods come trooping in" (85ua:249). Therefore, Newbigin gave himself to what he called "the greatest intellectual and practical task facing the Church," namely, "the development of a truly missionary encounter with this very tough form of paganism" characteristic of Western society (249). The primary expressions of his challenge to the churches in that regard (83os84 and 86fg), while they do not in major and extended ways make explicit use of the structure of thought surrounding his missiological use of the doctrine of election, do nevertheless show that his case rests on that structure of thought.

In *Foolishness to the Greeks,* the most complete basic treatment of this theme, it is at three critical junctures in the argument that election appears. Most critically, election is important to the rationale Newbigin gives for biblical authority (86fg:50-64). Authority can only be understood on the basis of a proper appreciation of conversion as a "paradigm shift," a change of "plausibility structure." The Christian for whom authority is located in Jesus and therefore in the Bible where he is portrayed, bases that confidence neither on an irrationality, as the Western worldview would assess it, nor on a rationality based only on the presuppositions of the worldview of the Western scientific culture. Rather, the basis lays claim to "a wider and more inclusive rationality" found in the biblical account of "the character and actions and purposes of God." The root of this conversion lies not in the ability "to make a sort of gigantic hermeneutical leap" but in the fact that Christian believers have been "chosen and called — not of their own will — to be witnesses of Jesus to the world" (53, 59).

Herein lies the most important feature of the hermeneutical circle, for Newbigin. "The Bible comes into our hands as the book of a community, and neither the book nor the community are properly understood except in their reciprocal relationship with each other." Thus, the "hermeneutical circle operating *within the believing community*" is precisely "the clue to understanding the nature of the Bible itself" (55-56).

> The Bible functions as authority only within a community that is committed to faith and obedience and is embodying that commitment in an active discipleship that embraces the whole of life, public and private. This is the plausibility structure within which the faith is nourished. (58)

That the church is this company of those who have been "laid hold of by Another" in order to live in such a relationship to the biblical account and thus are chosen to be in public the bearers of this "secular announcement" is Newbigin's critical beginning point for the "missionary encounter between the gospel and modern Western culture." In the encounter, "the first party will be represented by a community for which the Bible is the determinative clue to the character and activity of the one whose purpose is the final meaning of history" (62).

The importance of the public character of this community is underscored by Newbigin in a later reference to its "chosen-ness" (98-100). That the Old Testament people of God were chosen had in view the coming day when God's reign would break upon the full world scene. The ironic form in which that reign came in Jesus, that "the king reigns from the tree," masks the announcement from the world. By the resurrection that way of reigning is proclaimed as victory, but only "to those chosen as witnesses," who are "sent forth to proclaim and to embody in their common life the victory of Jesus, the reality of the reign of God." Because the community brought into being by those witnesses is drawn from all the nations, the church can never be a "private religious cult" but is "the public assembly to which God is calling all men everywhere without distinction."

The third reference to election also has to do with the resurrection. Because the resurrection has revealed to chosen witnesses that in the cross there is victory, the church "can never identify any political order with the reign of God" (125-127). All political agendas are tested by this stratagem of God: "the cross of Jesus as the central event of history" as attested by witnesses chosen to bear the message from one to another.

Thus, while the nature of the subject with which Newbigin deals in *Foolishness to the Greeks* does not call for the thoroughgoing display of the "inner logic" of election that is seen in *The Open Secret*, it is obvious that his thought rests on the foundation it provides. As is highlighted in his expansion of these themes in *The Gospel in a Pluralist Society* (89gps:chapter 7), he has confidence to undertake such an ambitious encounter as the one between the gospel and Western culture precisely because his sense of mission is the one found in *The Open Secret*. His authority for believing the gospel and preaching it unashamedly comes from the experience of being laid hold of by Another, gripped from his earliest days by the vision of That One's cross as that which alone gives meaning and purpose to the whole breadth of life and history. And the nature of the human condition and God's provision for salvation within it makes the passing of the word about the cross from one to another by the way of election the natural and required method.

CHAPTER 3

The Missionary Significance
of the Doctrine of Election:
Newbigin's Unique Perspective

Many of the lines along which Bishop Newbigin expresses his notion of the "missionary significance of the biblical doctrine of election" bear a marked affinity with other treatments of election. In several very important respects, he moves in concert with impulses shared by others who have attempted to forge a biblical missiology for the latter half of the twentieth century. The contributions of Old Testament biblical theology have drawn the attention of virtually all mission theologians to the basic "act of God" found in the choice of Abraham to father a people who would be uniquely "God's." At the same time, the sensibilities of an age that watched the decolonization of the world have led to the constant probing of missionary thought for personal models that breed more humble approaches toward the "other." The recultivation of the Western missionary's servant attitude has of necessity become a high priority. The "election" of God portrayed in the Bible has had to be contended with as a potential culprit restricting this better attitude unless it could be understood in fresh ways. Newbigin has not been the only one to address these concerns and offer important reflection on the missionary dimension of election.

But for all the similarity, Newbigin's interpretation of the significance of election stands apart. Rarely, if ever, has anyone else given it the prominence which it has in his mission theology, and for no one else does it hold so foundational a place in the rationale for mission.[1] In the particular nuances by which he interprets election and in the uses to which he puts that interpretation there are facets of missionary significance which are unique to him. What for others are unexpounded hints or unobserved applications receive wide-ranging treatment in Newbigin's effort to see coherence in the "character and actions and purposes" of the One who is both a choosing God and a missionary God.

It is the purpose of this chapter to identify these strikingly unique nuances in Newbigin's use of election and to show that those are there precisely because his mission theology is responsive to the issues raised by cultural plurality. These unique features will be shown as they emerge from a comparison of Newbigin's thought with other assessments of the meaning and significance of election, particularly within the missiological discussions that seek biblical foundations for contemporary mission. At the outset, two preliminary comments must be made to place Newbigin's treatment within this context of discussion.

1. Newbigin is a fellow-traveler with those who see the character of election in the Bible as predominantly corporate. As the mission of God emerges into view in the Old Testament, it does so in terms of the election of Israel to be God's people. The bridge to the New Testament Church maintains that essential perspective. Newbigin's discussion of election takes place within the recognition that this corporate aspect is central. It thereby unfolds in sympathy with approaches such as that of James Daane (1973). Daane's observation that the "first case" of election in the Bible is that of the nation, Israel, leads to his focused critique of past tendencies in the theology of election:

> This light from the Old Testament has largely been ignored by all those ecclesiastical traditions which have formed a doctrine of individual election, for all of them try to define the election of individuals by a direct reference to an eternal divine decision. Such a direct reference to eternity tends to produce a highly individualistic, ahistorical conception of election. (99)

While Newbigin does not as directly challenge that historic development, his thought agrees with the critique by its emphasis on the corporate.

The perception that the biblical emphasis lies upon the election of the nation and then the church is more generally received than it is pointedly applied. Paul Jewett, for example, admits that "in the Bible the elect are generally spoken of as a class, not as individuals per se" (1985:47). Yet he proceeds to devote ninety-three pages to his discussion of "Election and the individual," while spending only seventeen pages on the corporate aspect of election. Similarly, G. C. Berkouwer shows sensitivity to the corporate character of election: "We are repeatedly struck by the lack of tension between the election of the individual and the election of the Church. The emphasis of Scripture is definitely not on the individual" but on the individual as "incorporated into the great community of the Church" (1960:309). His treatment nonetheless places the stress on issues dealing with the election of the individuals who are to be included in the church, rather than the election of the church itself as a corporate whole.

Newbigin follows the biblical clue with more consistency than that by carefully couching the matter of individual election within the larger issue of the election of a people. The question is not "Why has God chosen this or that person?" but "Why has God chosen a particular community of persons among all the peoples of the world?" This corporate question is what makes election missiological for Newbigin. But he recognizes also that this must be played out fully in such a way as to bring those missiological implications to bear on the persons who have been chosen into the community. His assumption is that a community is composed of individual persons whose individuality is affirmed, not denied, by their being incorporated into a chosen community. Newbigin does not exclude the individual dimension of election, nor is individual election for him an "abstraction" (as it is for Wolfhart Pannenberg, cf. 1977:47); rather it forms a critical facet of the social fabric of the chosen group.

This individuality which Newbigin sees as inherent in corporate election comes as a necessary implication of the shift which takes place in the New Testament regarding the basis for inclusion. Participation in the Israel of the Old Testament was essentially by way of race, of biological ties. But in the New Testament, it is by faith that incorporation is secured. The gospel that calls women and men into the community calls for their very personal and individual response as the affirmation of their inclusion. Thus the faith principle, while it does not undo the emphasis on the corporate, attaches individuality to it.

2. In Newbigin's usage, the term "election" refers to the "chosenness" of those who comprise God's "people." The passive position this implies for the people who are the object of Another's choice forms the beginning

assumption from which Newbigin works. To read in the Bible that Israel was the elect nation or that the Church is the new "chosen race" means for him that at the outset we must understand that a choice has been made regarding the people thus designated as the "elect." The maker of that choice has thereby determined that certain things are now true of them. A theology of election has the task of ascertaining what those things are, based on an understanding of the character and purpose of the One who has initiated the choice.

While there are, as we shall see, large areas of correspondence between Newbigin's thought and that of Karl Barth, it is important to note at this point the significant difference in their uses of the term "election." Newbigin uses this word for the "electedness" of human persons, while Barth prefers to use it for the "electing" choice of God, his primal decision to be "for man" in and through Jesus Christ. By "election," Barth refers to the over-arching "intention" of God to "choose" in favor of humanity (1957b). In contrast to that, Newbigin refers to those particular actions by which God's overall purpose is brought about. For the one, it refers to the origins of the mission of God in the deepest recesses of his "willing." For the other, it speaks of the method by which the ultimate purposes of God are being carried forward. Generally, it may be said that Barth's term "election" corresponds to Newbigin's sense of the "purpose of God" and that Barth's term "calling" would more nearly correspond to Newbigin's use of the term "election" (cf. Barth 1962:577-592). Thus Barth can speak of "the election of grace" as "the sum of the Gospel" (1957b:13-14), while Newbigin would never see in election the content of the gospel, always its method. This difference is made vivid by the absence in Newbigin's writings of the definite article of Barth's characteristic phrase, "the election"!

The semantic divergence here is not without deeper significance. It reflects a difference in the two structures of thought. Barth challenges the notion that dominated the thinking of the Reformers. They related the biblical doctrine of election to the eternal decree of God made "independent of Jesus Christ and only executed by Him." To the contrary, Barth asserts, "election" refers to the "divine decision made in Jesus Christ" (1957b:60-76). Newbigin affirms, of course, that the "total fact of Christ" is a particular event which has significance for the whole of the world and its history. And he stresses that it is by incorporation into Christ, "the chosen One," that anyone else's election is established (cf. 53hg:112-113). But by the term "election" he means something other than God's "deciding" for the world. In Newbigin's usage, the term does not designate God's eternal decree which fixes human destiny; nor does it refer essentially to the "electing act" of God in the cross. Rather, it designates God's acting personally and particularly in history, selecting a people to be uniquely his own. Therefore, the focus of attention for Newbigin is not the "decree" of the Father (as for the Reformers), nor the "decision" in the Son (as for Barth), but the "selection" established by the historical converting action of the Spirit. This involves a movement of thought different from Barth's. Barth begins from the generality of "the election" in Christ and then incorporates within that perspective the particularity of the chosen community and the election of the individual (1957b: paragraphs 33-35). Newbigin, on the other hand, begins from the particularism of "election" as the selecting actions of God in history and shows that the clue for understanding the generality of God's purpose for the world is to be found in that pattern of "selection." This explains why Newbigin invariably takes Abraham as his point of departure, while Barth begins emphatically from the election of Jesus.

A further contrast may be drawn by observing how Barth moves from the general "election" to the particular "elect." In his effort to avoid any semblance of a doctrine of "double predestination," Barth maintains that God's election cannot be "identical with the determination of these private relationships as already made," neither the determination that one is "elected" nor "rejected." In election "the will of God is determined concerning all men." But the particular determination of each one is a different matter. "It is only in that one man [Jesus] that a human determination corresponds to the divine determining. In the strict sense only He can be understood and described as 'elected' (and 'rejected')" (1957b:43). Even Barth finds it unavoidable, however, to speak of those who are made distinct by their "calling" (which enables them to be "assured of their election by faith") as the "elect" (410-417). One gets the feeling that Barth does so only grudgingly. He is willing to admit to the problem of the historical distinction between the "elect" and the "rejected." But by construing election as the "primal decision" (50) and by affirming its "altogether Yes" character (13) he creates a structure of thought more designed to set aside the "problem of the antithesis," the problem of the "un-chosen," the "nonelect" (cf. Berkouwer 1960:322ff.; Senior and Stuhlmueller 1983:83).

This problem Newbigin does not seek to avoid. By refusing to separate

God's determining (Barth's "election") from God's determination (Barth's "calling") Newbigin preserves a brute historicality that affirms and faces the dilemma Barth too neatly dispatches. That is not done by returning to the idea of a "determination of those private relationships as already made." Rather, it envisions a determination of private relationships as *historically* made. As we shall see, it is precisely in such a concrete historical pattern of "election" that Newbigin finds the resolution for the very dilemma of "antithesis" it poses.[2]

Not the Reason but the Purpose

Newbigin stands among those who search for the purpose of election. It is to him a betrayal of trust for believers when their minds "are concerned more to probe backwards from their election into the reasons for it in the secret counsel of God than to press forward from their election to the purpose for it, which is that they should be Christ's ambassadors and witnesses to the ends of the earth" (53hg:111). The chief importance of the doctrine of election is that by it the church is made to be the people "by whom [God] purposes to save the world" (54wsot:75). God's people are the visible community which expresses "His purpose to create a new human race" (56ss:45). The "cosmic range of God's purpose," which is "nothing less than the uniting of the whole cosmos," is in the Scriptures linked firmly "to God's action in choosing and calling a particular people" (78os:79). All of this makes clear the duty of the church, for "if we fail to preach the Gospel to others we flout the purpose with which He chose us to be the unworthy bearers of it" (48dacp:30).

This represents a different approach from traditional Calvinism. The focus shifts away from analyzing what can be known (or, what cannot!) about the decrees of God concerning the eternal destiny of each individual soul (which reduces the notion of salvation to a question of soul-destiny). Instead it gives attention to the historical intention God has for the choice of some, namely that they should now live uniquely on behalf of the others who are not yet the "chosen." Newbigin's approach revises the traditional question: "God could have chosen others, but he has chosen us. We cannot say why. But we know the wherefore: he has chosen us to be the bearers of his promise of blessing of all mankind" (77cwps:25). Thus his treatment of election carries the same force as James Daane's critique of what he calls "decretalism." But while Daane focuses his critique on the important point that in decretal theology "God's decree is not identified with his freedom, but with his essence, and thus with God himself" (Daane 1973:31), Newbigin's critique of historic Calvinism charges that it has distorted the gospel in that the truth of election has been "taken in isolation out of its proper relation to the truth of the incarnation." Although it is an "undoubted truth that God can choose and regenerate by the secret working of His Spirit whomsoever He will," if our starting point is not rather "the fact of Christ," then "the missionary task will be no longer integral to the very being of the Church." The answer to young William Carey will stand, because we will be led to the unmissionary view that "the Spirit is directly given to every man and His witness requires no confirmation from any other source." What is missing in the traditional approach is the insight that our election is to be seen in concert with that of Jesus, "the elect of God, His beloved, His chosen One. Our election is only by our incorporation in Him. We are not elect as isolated individuals, but as members of His body." Only by viewing election from this vantage point will we be able to preserve a proper ecclesiology that sees at the center not an "invisible number of the elect known only to God" but an "actual visible society" (53hg:112-113).

By his emphasis on the purpose of election, Newbigin is in league with many in this century who have similarly emphasized the responsibility side of the matter. The dictum of H. H. Rowley that we are chosen "for service" provides the slogan for the dominant trend of missiological reflection on election during the latter half of this century (1950; cf. Blauw 1962). Much of the trend has matured under the impact of Barth's powerful case for revising our sense of "the goal of vocation" and the purpose toward which that vocation is directed (1962:520-576). Barth's "correction of Calvin" (as Newbigin calls it) moves us away from focusing on the "possession, use and enjoyment of the salvation of God," which makes of the church merely an "institute of salvation," a "*medium salutis*" (561, 567).[3] Rather, the heart of our vocation must be construed biblically, and "it is common to all the biblical accounts of calling that to be called means being given a task" (573). The essence of this task, the vocation of Christians, "is that God makes them His witnesses . . . of His being in His past, present and future action in the world and in history, of His being in His acts among and upon men" (575).

Fundamental to Newbigin's perspective, then, is this conviction that election is about the purpose God intends by the choice, not the reason God has for making the choice. Many corollaries come alongside this notion to fill out his sense of the logic of election. The remainder of this chapter will identify those by noting four recurring and characteristic phrases in Newbigin's treatment of election which respond to the fundamental questions that concern him: 1. What is the importance of emphasizing purpose? It is so that we are reminded that election is "not special privilege but special responsibility." 2. How must the purpose of election be defined? Its purpose is that by it we are made "bearers of the blessing," "bearers of the witness of the Spirit." 3. Is purpose alone sufficient for understanding election? No, it is "the end as well as the means." 4. How does the purpose of election resolve the issue of the universal and the particular? It works by the principle of "one event with significance for the whole." The way Newbigin responds regarding each of these issues will show the affinity his view has with other views while vividly demonstrating the unique contribution it makes.

It will be primarily in relation to those who share the general concern for the purpose of election and who see its focus to be on responsibility that I will compare Newbigin's view of election with that of others. There may be truth, in regard to some approaches, in Paul Jewett's claim that the "so-called 'teleological' approach to election, an approach that emphasizes that those who are elect are elect and chosen for a task, is not meant to explain election in a logical fashion" (1985:31, n. 1). However, this survey of Newbigin's view has already shown that this is not the case for him. The comparison of his view with other constructions will further demonstrate how fully he intends to show an inner logic to election as the clue for understanding the action of God in the world and the mission of the church which God has called into being.

Before proceeding, it is important to note that in Newbigin's writings he does not engage in any polemical way the specific views others hold, except for classical Calvinist approaches, as observed above. He points out instances in which others have failed to take proper notice of the doctrine and indicates where such failures may lead. But he does not directly compare his construction of the missionary character of election with the way other missiologists speak about it. Therefore the comparison that follows offers this writer's assessment of the ways Newbigin's perspective is both unique and uniquely able to serve the requirements of a theology of cultural plurality.

1. Not Special Privilege but Special Responsibility

It is still true that for some people the biblical doctrine of election contains only the notion of "exclusive privilege." That causes some missiologists to reject the whole idea as an unuseful throwback to another age. Given the context of contemporary religious pluralism, for example, Wesley Ariarajah prefers to emphasize a biblical strand of thought poised over against that of Israel's "self-understanding" as the chosen nation. His assumption that election is primarily a "status" matter and that it breeds only an "exclusive" approach to the peoples of other nations leads him to search elsewhere in the Old Testament to establish a basis for "God's universal relationship with all nations." This he says he finds in the "parallel tradition" regarding God as creator and hence as universal lord and provider. He concludes that "it is in this context that we must look at the doctrine of election," because the self-understanding of a group that it is chosen "is valid only insofar as it does not violate the doctrine of God as creator" (1985:5-11).

C. S. Song likewise appears to see only an exclusivity in election. He sees it at the heart of what he calls Israel's "political theology of the covenant" by which they built a "racial and religious community that was closed to outsiders." The prophets challenged such a view. He claims for them that they "must have realized that covenant understood as election was doing Israel a disservice" and therefore "could no longer identify with" it (1982:32-34). He, like Ariarajah, looks to other "self-disclosures" of God parallel to that in the midst of the chosen people, emphasizing the priority of creation over redemption (40; cf. Song 1975:19-50).

Many others take a less radical view in response to the observable tendency for the idea of election to breed a sense of special privilege. Rather than dismissing the doctrine or juxtaposing it over against the doctrine of creation, they seek to transform the way in which election has been understood historically by including the dimension of its purpose. "Chosenness" means to be assigned a function (cf. Pannenberg 1977:49).

The emphasis on "election for service" has received its wide currency most probably due to the major missiological contributions of H. H. Rowley and Johannes Blauw. Rowley, in his classic biblical-theological work on *The Biblical Doctrine of Election* (1950), was expanding on a hint contained in his earlier survey of *The Missionary Message of the Old Testament* (1945). He maintains that "the purpose of the election [of Israel] is service, and when the service is withheld the election loses its meaning, and therefore fails" (1950:52). The concern which drives his "teleological approach" is his interest to find in the doctrine that which leads to humility rather than pride (17-18). Chosenness means for Israel seeing itself "not so much as destined to receive honour from men as called to fulfill the purpose of her election in the service of men" (19). Privilege, while redefined by Rowley as the privilege of serving God, inevitably remains in the picture (45). But the weight now falls on the responsibility of the elect (166ff.).

Th. C. Vriezen adds concerning this shift that the Old Testament has as its primary concern regarding election not "the foundations of a certainty of salvation" but a proper attitude on Israel's part as the chosen people of God: "privilege has not been extended to Israel that she might become infatuated by it, but that she might recognize it as a commission" (1953:32, quoted in English translation in Blauw 1962:22-23). Drawing on these and similar sources, Blauw concludes that "Israel is not so much the *object* of divine election as *subject* in the service asked for by God on the ground of election. . . . Therefore election is not primarily a privilege but a responsibility" (23).[4]

The same trend that Blauw in a sense "codified" in the early 1960s in his watershed work gathering the fruit of thirty years of biblical studies is carried forward in the work done by Donald Senior, C.P., and Carroll Stuhlmueller, C.P. They provide a service for mission theology in regard to biblical scholarship similar to that of Blauw by gathering up the reflections of the two decades subsequent to his publication (Senior and Stuhlmueller 1983). Stuhlmueller, in his intriguing sociological approach in the Old Testament section, includes a chapter on election, which he says is "not a peripheral idea" but is "at the center" and is "intertwined" in Israel's history and culture (83). Using the scholarship of Horst Seebass, he also sees the teleological dimension of election. Seebass's study of the Hebrew term *bachar* indicates that the two essential features of its Old Testament usage are that (a) it "means a careful choice," and (b) it "implies a *special purpose or mission*" (94; cf. Seebass 1977:74, 82-83). Given the purpose element,

> Israel's election is to be considered under these terms: a choice by a personal God, in favor of a helpless people, with promises and gifts to be held as loaned and borrowed, never as possessed and owned, as signs of love rather than indicators of power, as goods to be shared instead of riches to be hoarded and defended. (87)

The dominant perspective here is one which struggles against the risk that those who know themselves to be "elect" will slip into a "false and vain self-glory," a "highmindedness," a "self-exaltation" and "pretentiousness," tempted to it by what G. C. Berkouwer calls the "Great Misconception" which severs election to salvation from election for service (1960:322-330). The concerted effort in mission-sensitive theology has been to set aside an egoistic particularism which cuts the nerve of mission. Darrell Guder, as has been noted, shows how pervasively this notion must be incorporated in any contemporary mission theology by doing so in his own (1985).

With this movement and motivation Newbigin is compatible. As we have seen in the prior chapter, his search is for a conception of the logic of election which will not violate the tone and tenor of the gospel of God's gracious dealings with humanity but will set aside every egoistic impulse. It shows what lies at the heart of his motivation to notice that he finds in his own election the most humble basis for his meeting with someone of another faith. What makes possible the otherwise inconceivable entrance into "simple, honest, open, and friendly communication" with the other person is not to arrive at the conviction that "he also is saved" within the terms of his religion. Such a claim to "have access to the secret of his ultimate destiny" does not resolve the dilemma of the antithesis (78os:196-197). Rather it is in the understanding that election is for a purpose and the purpose is witness:

> I meet him simply as a witness, as one who has been laid hold of by Another and placed in a position where I can only point to Jesus as the one who can make sense of the whole human situation which my partner and I share as fellow human beings. This is the basis of our meeting. (78os:197)

This hunger for missionary humility and the rejection of everything which perpetuates human egoism leads to Newbigin's persistent assertion that election is not for "special privilege" but for "special responsibility" (53hg:149).[5] The Jews were chosen "not for themselves but for the sake of the world." Punishment followed when they "behaved as though they were God's favourites" (54wsot:72). God's people "are not called because they are better than others; nor are they called because God wants to save them only. They are called in order that through them God's love may reach others" (56ss:46). The object of election is not to bring a person to the "acceptance of his own personal destiny; it is for the fulfillment of his role in God's plan for the salvation of mankind. It is a calling to responsible participation in the events which are the key to world history" (66hrsm:44). Too often the church has acted as though "God had arbitrarily chosen certain people for eternal blessedness and equally arbitrarily left out other people from the blessed purpose." But it is not to "the privilege of eternal blessedness" that we are primarily elected. The central question is never one concerned with "what is going to happen to my little soul" but the bigger question about "the hallowing of God's Name, the doing of His will, and the coming of His Kingdom." In that context the church must be seen as "the task-force appointed by God," those called to "a particular responsibility . . . in order to bring eternal blessedness to all, in order to fulfill His purpose in creation" (68wmc:3). Over and over again, Newbigin directs the attention of his listeners and readers to the plain reminder of election's purpose in the words of Jesus: "You did not choose me but I chose you. And I appointed you to go and bear fruit" (John 15:16).

In *The Open Secret*, his major articulation of an election missiology, Newbigin continues to draw attention to the difference between focusing on the privilege implied in being chosen and focusing on the responsibility (78os:19, 35, 75, 82). But in one of those contexts another phraseology is employed which shows how Newbigin's concern for the proper attitude has deepened. As before, he uses his characteristic word "bearers" to affirm that "those who are chosen to be bearers of a blessing are chosen for the sake of *all*" (34). Here, he contrasts that role as "bearers" against the attitude which is the constant temptation: "exclusive beneficiaries." This he does as well in his proposal for the manner of *Christian Witness in a Plural Society:*

> The Church is the bearer of the work of Christ through history, but not the exclusive beneficiary. God purposes the salvation of all. For this purpose he has chosen a people. Because that people have over and over again fallen into the sin of supposing that they have a claim upon God which other men do not have, they have over and over again been punished and humiliated and have had to hear the word of God spoken to them from others. . . . Whenever the Church has imagined that it had a claim upon God which others did not have, it has already fallen away from grace. The Church is servant and not master. It is appointed to a stewardship on behalf of all, not to a privilege from which others are excluded. (77cwps:17)

In all that has been mentioned thus far, Newbigin is not unique. He perhaps raises these concerns with greater frequency and tenacity than others do. But in terms of his teleological approach, his concern for promoting humility among those who are "elect," and his emphasis on special responsibility over against special privilege, the lines of his thought are similar to those observable in much contemporary missiology. However, a closer scrutiny of the source observation which drives his emphasis on purpose and responsibility will show an element of uniqueness, the importance of which will increase as we view other aspects of his understanding of the doctrine and compare them with the views of others.

It has already been observed that Newbigin frames his notion of election in response to the basic question that he has heard from the mind, if not the lips, of the Hindu person with whom he has been associated for most of his adult life: "Is my ancient religion not good enough? Why must I receive this message of salvation from you? How is it that God has chosen one particular strand of human history to be his people? Does he not love all people equally?" This frame of reference is important to note because it alters the point of approach to the doctrine of election. For others, the reference point is the person who, having heard the gospel, believes. This is true for "decretal theology," which seeks in the decree of God an understanding of the rationale for God's choice of those who are his people. It is also true for the theology of Barth, who seeks to understand the "determination" of the elect as those whose calling it is to be Christians, receiving by faith the "divine election of grace" revealed in the life, death and resurrection of Jesus. Both seek to give to the "chosen" ones an understanding of what that "chosenness" means. They answer the basic questions, What does it mean for me to be "elect"? and, How does that relate to other people who do not now share my faith?

Newbigin, on the other hand, while answering similar questions, answers in a different order and from a different perspective. He begins with the question asked by one outside the Christian faith looking in. It is the question about the chosenness of the "other" who comes to them as a witness, the one who asks them to believe. "How is it," they ask, "that 'that one' is chosen, out of all the streams of humankind? How does that chosenness of the other relate to me?" He is posing the question — for which election is both the problem and the solution — from the position of those hearing from the supposedly "elect" their message of universally applicable salvation rather than from the position of those who possess the status of "elect" by virtue of which they present a "universal" message. He will answer that latter question, but only in terms of the requirements laid down by the former. This patently missionary and cross-cultural reformulation of the question is what makes Newbigin's invocation of the doctrine of election so persistently pointed and at the most elementary level makes his construction a unique innovation.[6]

There are at least three important consequences of this. The first is that it revises the way a Christian is invited to respond to the teleological dimension of election. It is not a matter of looking within myself and transposing my inner thoughts and self-understanding as one of God's chosen people so that I set aside my egoistic concentration on the privileges and benefits which that affirms for me. It leads not first to such introspection but to the position and question of the one my gospel addresses. I am invited to consider election by looking from without, stepping into the shoes of the one who sees me as claiming to be one "chosen of God," looking back from the place where we have all had to stand once ourselves and asking the question which we all should have asked at one point or another. The responsibility to be simply a witness, a servant, then comes neither by a mystical experience nor by legalistic requirement but as a practical matter of discipleship in the realm of living social relationships.

In the second place, when the question is thus transposed from an inner, personal, theological-psychological one into an interpersonal, socioanthropological one, it changes the nature of the issue. The question now does not so much concern the genuineness of the universal offer of salvation by those who are "elect" as it does the validity of the universal claim which the offered salvation makes. This leads Newbigin to the root of the apologetic questions and the connection between the authority to believe and the authority to preach. It also means that his description of the "inner logic" of election applies itself more thoroughly than do the perspectives of others to issues raised by cultural plurality.

Third, the locus of the essential clue to the teleological dimension of election is not to be found in the decree of God, nor even in the cross of Christ, although it cannot be detached from either. Rather its locus is to be found in the action of the Holy Spirit, the one who chooses and calls witnesses together to be the church. If there is a second "key verse" of the Scriptures that pervades Newbigin's articulation of an election logic, alongside the already mentioned John 15:16, it is Acts 10:40-41: "But God raised him on the third day and allowed him to appear, not to all the people but to us who were chosen by God as witnesses, and who ate and drank with him after he rose from the dead" (cf. Acts 1:8). This is so implicit in Newbigin's mind that the chapter in *The Open Secret* which finishes the trinitarian section by reference to the Spirit does not include any direct reference to "election" or his "election rationale" for mission. But the chapter is saturated and bathed in that perspective. The very title of the chapter embraces the whole of his conception: "Bearing the Witness of the Spirit." It is "by an action of the sovereign Spirit of God that the church is launched on its mission. It remains the mission of the Spirit" (78os:65). The sending of the Holy Spirit, who is "the" witness and who makes the disciples of Jesus to be witnesses also, is for Newbigin the essential corollary of the doctrine of election.

2. Bearers of the Blessing

The idea that election, understood biblically, means being chosen for a "purpose," that is, "for service," has been enlisted on the one hand to make the case for a "theology of church growth" (Charles Van Engen 1981:121-160) and on the other hand to make a case for a "theology of liberation" (Juan Luis Segundo 1978:138-139 and David Lowes Watson 1984). This illustrates that the large agreement regarding the fact that election includes purpose finds no corresponding agreement concerning just what that purpose is. To affirm that chosenness means to have been assigned a task does not yet define the task (cf. Pannenberg 1977:49). The slogan, "elect for service," which has come to be used so generally, is assumed to settle the issue of the purpose for God's choice. But it only begs the question. What sort of service? And to what end?

It is notable, therefore, that Newbigin does not use the general phrase, "elect for service." That gives evidence that he is concerned to establish more precisely the nature of the "divine vocation" which God's election gives and what it means for God's people to be the "instrument of the divine purpose."[7] Newbigin's careful development of the inner logic of election brings him to a pointed definition of its purpose, unlike many who define it in such generic terms that it fails to answer the basic questions which election raises, or others who assign definitions too quickly without sufficient consideration of the implications involved. According to Newbigin, the purpose of election is that those chosen will be the bearers of the blessings of salvation, which is transmitted from persons of one "people" to persons of other "peoples." The purpose therefore is to "bear the witness of the Spirit." By this very means of transmission of the news of Jesus Christ, the salvation it announces takes place in the reconciliation of persons as they are becoming reconciled to God, thus establishing "wholeness."

Newbigin differs from the view that God elects his people to be a mere *instrumental mechanism* for his salvation activity. To say that Israel was chosen by God in order to be the "recipient and guardian of God's special revelation to the world" and to be the "channel for the Redeemer to enter human history" (Kane 1976:23) makes of the nation's function such a pragmatic instrumentality that it voids the notion of election of its living dynamism.

The tendency in this direction might be expected in a dispensational missiology such as that of George Peters, who sees God's choice of Israel as a way to mediate between himself and the world of nations (1972:23). In his view, the call of Abraham "is the beginning of a divine counterculture designed both to arrest evil and unfold the gracious plan, salvation and purpose of God" (90). Israel's function to be "the priesthood of God among the nations to mediate God's revelation, salvation and purpose" has been "transferred temporarily to the church of Jesus Christ which has become the witness, the priesthood, the servant, the light, the salt. Thus in the present dispensation the church is God's mediating agency not of salvation but of the message of God's salvation in Christ Jesus" (23). For Peters, Israel bears a form of agency which the church does not (mediating salvation itself) and that agency is not now dropped but only delayed until in the future Israel is taken up again in God's hand as a historical instrument (23-25).

But this is the tendency, also, in other missiologies which employ a "redemptive-history" hermeneutic for interpreting the Bible. Harry Boer, for example, traces with meticulous care the "redemptive line" which by God's determination proceeds to Abraham, "who becomes the father of the nation from which shall arise the universal Messiah, the Son of Man" (1961:137). Boer's understanding of the purpose of election is dominated by that fact: "To [Abraham] and to his descendants was given the special function of preserving in its integrity the messianic line culminating in the coming of Christ and in the second universal diffusion of the grace of redemption," that is, Pentecost (68). To this he adds that "the dispersion of mankind at Babel and the separation of Israel to a peculiar service among the nations were but steps on the way to a larger purpose" (138). These two historical facts, "the calling of Abraham and the separate existence of Israel," must therefore be seen as "integral and essential parts of the divine plan to redeem the world" (138). Such an approach as Boer's assigns to Israel more a function as the machinery of history than a dynamic and living vocation as its ordained purpose. His sense that Israel has "the mandate to be the mediator of God's salvation to the gentiles" is clearly subordinated to and to be interpreted by his contention that Israel was elected "to be the bearer of the redemptive process" (140).

In his classic work establishing the hermeneutic on which Boer depends, Oscar Cullmann slips into the same difficulty (1964). His concern is less that of the preservation of a biological redemptive line (as is the concern of Boer) and more to display the "continuous time process" of God's redemptive activity, the historical line of events which are determined and fulfilled in their mid-point, the death and resurrection of Jesus Christ (32-33). The election of Israel, then, as a part of the redemptive process, "takes place with reference to Christ and reaches its fulfillment in the work of the Incarnate One" (108, cf. 136). The election of Israel is a "preparation," which only in its "connection with the unique mid-point" is able to "preserve its actual redemptive value" (136-137). "The divinely willed concentration upon this one small line" serves this representative function: that "the history of *one* people becomes determinative for the salvation of *all* men. . . . God chose one community, the people of Israel, for the salvation of the world" (116).

The difficulty with Cullmann's view becomes most visible in the context of his description of the compressing and reducing process of Old Testament history by which the many become the few, and finally the one. The "progressive reduction" takes place, he says, because "the people of Israel as a whole do not fulfill the mission assigned to them" (116). What exactly this mission was does not anywhere become clear in Cullmann's treatment. That is because Cullmann's view of election is tied not to a missional purpose but to a historical instrumentality as a part of the redemptive process. Therefore it lacks a sense of the living relevance for Israel of her election, as is illustrated by Cullmann's struggle at the conclusion of his work to link faith and election as a way to establish the individual person's relationship to redemptive history (217ff.).

In all these approaches, a loss of the people-ness of the chosen takes place. Salvation becomes a cosmic engine, the parts of which God freely conscripts from the sceneiy of history. The question this fails to answer is, How are the people who are chosen themselves involved in the unfolding of it all? And why should God do it this way? Is there any rationale for making salvation a process and making the choice of a particular people a part of that process? In these approaches, no reason is offered.

Newbigin differs as well from the view that God elects his people primarily to be an *illustrative showcase*, a tangible facet of God's self-revelation. Here Newbigin's view is closer, but nonetheless distinct in that he casts a wider portrait of the purpose of election.

At the most basic level, this approach emphasizes, as does I. Van Dijk, that in God's choice of Israel we find an "election to service in the life of revelation, in the Kingdom of God" (1917:232, quoted in English translation in Berkouwer 1960:319). In similar fashion, Th. C. Vriezen believes that election "places a whole nation in the world as a place of the revelation of His Kingdom" (1953:34, quoted in English translation in Berkouwer 1960:320). Johannes Verkuyl notes that "countless recent studies" — by people such as G. von Rad, Walter Eichrodt, Bachli, and G. E. Wright — emphasize something similar: "God chose Israel in preparation for the complete unwrapping and disclosure of his universal intentions" (1978:92).

Jakob Jocz plays out the thought. "Israel and revelation are correlatives," he says. Israel's function is the transmission of divine truth. Therefore her history is *"special history* — an object lesson of God's dealing with mankind." The history of the church, as that of the Jewish people, has "revelational" value as the "community in which God reveals himself" (1958:1-5). While he later adds that "Israel has been chosen to hear and to repeat the burning, searing words, 'I am the Lord,' to the nations of the world," which has a more directly missional slant, that verbal implication is intended to support the major assertion that the very existence of Israel and the church has as its purpose a revelation by God in historical form (168). That remains the emphasis.

For Jocz to introduce the notion of "object lesson" makes more specific how the election to service is conceived to be an election to the service of revelation. Hendrikus Berkhof gives an expanded portrait of the meaning of Israel that adds vivid color to the idea. He suggests that the "vicarious service" to which Israel was called and chosen — and of which she was "probably only at times aware" — may be described by the term "experimental garden." The term "conveys fairly accurately to modern readers the ultimate purpose of Israel's way; in an experimental garden the soil and what can be done with it are tried out, so that other fields, to which these experiments are applicable, may benefit from it." In this facet of Israel's life Berkhof sees her "election to service for the good of the whole world." The "abiding relevance" of that election is that "Israel has shown once and for all how unfruitful we humans are in our faithfulness to God and our neighbor; and then, too, how unimaginably faithful God remains to mankind which ever and again seeks life apart from him" (1979:244-246).[8]

The basic image here can be turned any number of directions, as Charles Van Engen in fact does. Under the umbrella notion of "witness to the world" he teases out this "display" sense of the purpose of election. He sees Israel's "mediatorial role" best illustrated in its "priestly function." Israel was chosen "to protect, care for, illustrate, and call attention to the presence of YHWH." Israel was "a special people entrusted with the exhibition to the entire world of the presence of YHWH in the world . . . , a sort of 'model' to all the nations, both in her sufferings as well as in her successes." God's election of a particular community has in view "their being a sort of showcase, a prototype, of what He intends for all mankind. . . . In their communal, practical everyday life they must really BE that exhibition model which they are intended to be" (1981:134, 144-145).

In other words, in this view the purpose of election can be summarized to consist in the "presence" of the chosen community. So argues Robert Martin-Achard when he says, "The evangelization of the world is not primarily a matter of words and deeds; it is a matter of presence — the presence of the People of God in the midst of mankind and the presence of God in the midst of His People" (1962:31). He affirms that "the *raison d'etre* of the chosen people is to exist; its presence gives testimony to the divinity of Yahweh, its life proclaims all that God is for it and for the world" (1959:30, quoted in English translation in Blauw 1962:32). This is Israel's "mission," its mediatorial "function," its offered "light." With this view Wolfhart Pannenberg concurs. As is the case for Israel, so it is for the church: "the primary relationship of the church to mankind at large is a symbolic witness borne by the church in its very existence" (1977:37).

Newbigin would surely agree that Israel's and the church's calling includes these "showcase" dimensions. God does choose Israel in order to "reveal and effect God's will for all mankind" (48dacp:29). The church in its very being, by its "presence" in the world, fulfills the foundation of its mission (58obog:20). The church is the "sign" of the Kingdom of God (80sk), as it is also sent "to bear in its own life the presence of the Kingdom"

(78os:54).[9] Newbigin stresses as much as any of these representative voices the importance of the very existence of the church and its revelational significance.

But the primary difficulty with the "showcase" views just surveyed (a difficulty which the "mechanism" views share to an even greater degree) is that they have a tendency to define the purpose of election in a way that is "abstracted" from the actual life of the elect community in intimate daily relationship with people among and around whom it lives. On some level in God's cosmic scheme of things, an illustrative function is being performed. In some corporate sense, its presence in the world reveals something. But these views fail to show the engaging personal and corporate dynamic by which God goes about bringing this illustrative revelation to the people beyond the elect community or the ways in which the persons in the elect community are themselves agents in that process.[10]

For Newbigin, it is true on the one hand that "it is the community which has begun to taste (even only in foretaste) the reality of the Kingdom which can alone provide the hermeneutic of the message" (80sk:19; cf. 89gps:222-233). But it is equally true that "the church is its proper self, and is a sign of the Kingdom, only insofar as it continually points men and women beyond itself to Jesus and invites them to personal conversion and commitment to him" (80sk:68). There is in Newbigin's assessment of the purpose of election a more deliberately missional approach that stretches wider the sense of the church's mission and the nature of its witness. He will characteristically speak of the church's calling to be the "sign, foretaste and instrument" of the Kingdom of God, and it is the latter term that enlarges the picture. (The word "agent" might capture it in more personal terms!) God chooses Israel to be "bearers of the blessing" and the church to "bear the witness of the Spirit," and these imply as much a calling to active representation as to tangible demonstration. Election engages the people of God in an active process in which salvation is revealed by the witness of person to person and community to community, a witness that includes the communal portrait it presents to the world but is not exhausted by that. Apart from this wider view, the concern that the elect should not be focused on themselves and their privileges by virtue of election would be thwarted. Instead they are led only to a view that in essence invites them to see in their own life as a community the whole substance of the purpose of their election, and thus the purpose and goal of God, creating a new form of introversion. But with the wider missional view, the "witness" purpose of election constantly forces the elect people to recognize in their election a vocation "for others."

Newbigin also defines the purpose of election in terms that more completely develop its "innermost" logic, which responds to the greater difficulty with the approaches emphasizing the illustrative, revelational, or "showcase" dimensions of purpose. They do not adequately address the most pertinent set of questions: Why did God choose to reveal himself and his universally gracious salvation in such a particularist way? Why did God choose to give an "object lesson" by means of such concentrated dealings with one particular people? What inner logic shows why God should choose one nation to "symbolize" his relationship to the whole world? Why did God not choose multiple "symbols," a pluralism of "experimental gardens," or some method of universally individuated revelation that would meet each person in her or his own place directly?

This is tellingly obvious when many state or imply, without giving a reason that it is so, that election was the "necessary" thing for God to do, particularly after the "fiasco" of Babel.[11] Perhaps none says it so emphatically as John Piet. Babel, he says, "is the picture of disintegration and disorder, the reason why God must choose, a choice which begins decisively with Abram" (1970:40). But the statement that Babel means that God "must" choose is entirely undefended. He goes on:

> But while the necessity for God to choose is plain, the way in which Israel should rectify the situation remains obscure. In other words, Israel's theology is not as clear when she looks to the future as when she looks to the past. In order to have meaning, however, election must have a forward as well as a backward look. It must result in purpose, and this purpose must encompass a circle wider than the elected one. (40)

Again, the "musts" are given no justification. To each the question "Why?" must be asked. Exactly why should (or "must") God work by means of particular election? Is there a necessity for it? And if so, what is it? Newbigin, unlike others, gives careful attention to just this question because he understands that the offense is not just the critique that God by his election is "arbitrary," as is assumed by Blauw (1962:129) and De Ridder (1971:18). That much can be cared for by the assertion that in God's particular choice is found his "mission of service to the nations" (Vicedom 1965:48). But the question goes beyond that to the offense of particularity itself. It is this question which leads Newbigin to his sense of the "must"-ness of the divine method of election.

Newbigin explains that the necessity lies in three areas. First, election is required by *the nature and destiny of humanity*. Human life is by nature historical and social, each person intimately connected to each "other." It is by reference to the future end and purpose of life that meaning in the present social and historical context is to be found. The revelation of that goal and meaning can come only within the social and historical life of humanity. This God does by choosing some to be those in and by whom the end is now present and made known. By this method it is shown that one particular event can have significance for the whole.

Second, its necessity is due to *the personal character of God*, which is therefore also the character of the creatures divinely made to be "like" God. "Personal knowing" comes by the free choice to entrust such knowledge of oneself to another.[12] It occurs by an act of "willing" and is received and known by an act of commitment. As a person, it is not only possible but essential for positing meaning for the whole of existence for God to choose the time and place for self-disclosure. To proceed by particular acts of revelation in a historically particular fashion is merely consistent with "personal" character.

Third, its necessity is found in *the nature of salvation* as God has willed to achieve it for the world. Salvation means "wholeness," which must include the restoration of social justice and interpersonal relationships. The method of election means that I cannot be made whole apart from my neighbor, on whom I have depended for the message of God's reign. By virtue of the reconciliation between the witness and the receiver of the witness inherent in the method of election, it is congruent with the end envisioned in salvation. The humility required to receive the message from another corresponds to the humility by which the grace of God must be received as a free gift.

This care to describe the inner logic and necessity of the method of election in response to the question of particularity is what guides Newbigin to his most central definition of the purpose of election: to bear the witness of the Spirit. In that respect, his approach is distinct even from those who like him define that purpose as "witness" or "proclamation" or whose sense of Israel's calling to be a revelation by "presence" includes that.[13] His unique sense of the nature of the scandal of particularity, viewed as it is from the position of the one for whom the elect is the "other," leads him to a more penetrating display of the necessity of election and its fitting correspondence with a vocation of "witness."

3. The End as Well as the Means

I have noted that Newbigin recognizes that it is not only essential to acknowledge the purpose dimension of election but to emphasize it. And by his dynamic and missional depiction of that purpose, his emphasis is enhanced in that it more thoroughly responds to the pressing question "Why must it be so?" Precisely because there is an answer to that question, Newbigin does not allow an emphasis on the purpose of election to negate the fact that it nonetheless has something to do with the possession of the benefits of salvation.

We can see this in the way his language shifts — and with observable precision — regarding the necessary point that election must not mean "special privilege." When the contrast is between "privilege" and "responsibility," there is a clear-cut distinction: we are chosen "not for privilege, but for responsibility" (as in 78os:19). But when the terms of the comparison are shifted, those chosen are considered to be "bearers — not exclusive beneficiaries" (34). In the first case the two terms refer to attitudes, and one is clearly God's objective whereas the other is as clearly not. In the latter case the terms mark identity. In the distinction he makes, the appearance of the qualifier is significant because Newbigin's contrast is not between being a "beneficiary" of salvation and being its "bearer" but between seeing oneself only as beneficiary and seeing oneself as both beneficiary and bearer. Only in the yoking of the two identities are we enabled to recognize that we are not "exclusively" the ones for whom the benefits are intended, but neither are we excluded from them. To fail to embrace both is to short-circuit the essential connection between salvation and service, a connection which works both ways: salvation for service, and service for the real salvation of those who hear and believe the message and thus also become its servants.

For some, the modern emphasis on election "for service" forecloses any sense at all in which it continues to "dispense" salvation upon those chosen. In reaction to an attitude of exclusivity as "beneficiaries" they distance themselves from saying anything that might seem to give it a place to flourish. But in many cases, a reverse "exclusivity" results. Such can be demonstrated in the dominating approach of Rowley. Because he sees the basic distinction to be made as that between being "destined to receive honour from men" and being "called to fulfill the purpose of . . . election in the service of men" (1950:19), Rowley affirms that God's choice "is ever election for some purpose" (39). "Whom God chooses, He chooses for service. . . . The divine election concerns exclusively the divine service" (42). Even in regard to individuals, "they are always chosen for service . . . , for the specific task that is assigned them and for the service God requires of them" (95). For both the corporate and individual dimensions, Rowley excludes the notion that election has any bearing on the issue of salvation and prefers to see in it the choice of Israel to the national function of service and revelation to the world. Robert Cushman may be technically correct that Rowley does not exclude a sense of privilege accompanying this election "for service" (1981:199). But that obscures the fact that Rowley limits the conception of "privilege." For him, there is privilege in election only because "in the service of God is man's supreme privilege and honour" (1950:45). This means for Rowley that there is not a fundamental difference between the election of Israel for its role as the bearer of the revelation of God and the "election" of other nations "for a service that often carried no measure of privilege" (121-122). The Old Testament, he says,

> is concerned with the election of Israel, and with the election of others in so far as its purpose touches Israel. It neither affirms nor denies that God chose Greece to achieve cultural heights far beyond Israel's. For it is not interested in culture, but in religion. It claims that in the realm of the spirit Israel is the unique Chosen People, and that to her and through her in an unparalleled degree God designed to reveal Himself and His will. (1950:138)

Others join Newbigin in opposing the conclusion that to emphasize the purpose of election must lead to a "service only" view of it.[14] Typical of his argument is Newbigin's response to the implications of Johannes Hoekendijk's world-centered missiology articulated in the early 1950s in reaction to the then-dominant church-centered approach. He protests against Hoekendijk's view that the nature of the church is "sufficiently defined by its function" by pointing out that "it is precisely because she is not *merely* instrumental that she can be instrumental." Possessing in its life the Holy Spirit who is the earnest of the inheritance, the church is already a foretaste of that coming salvation. The church "can only witness to that inheritance because her life is a *real* foretaste of it, a real participation in the life of God Himself" (53hg:168-169). He is here sensitive to the question which must be put to Rowley as well: If election is solely unto service, and that service is "to reveal [God's] character and His will" (Rowley 1950:39), to what end does that lead? Is there a real purpose to God's purpose? Does he choose some to serve in order to achieve a more ultimate purpose of salvation or simply in order to do it? Newbigin drives hard at this point: "If we answer the question, 'Why should I become a Christian?' simply by saying 'In order to make others Christians,' we are involved in an infinite regress. The question 'To what end?,' cannot be simply postponed to the *eschaton*" (53hg:169). For Newbigin, the fruit and benefit of salvation must be part of the experience of the chosen witness if that witness is to have any force as it meets the neighbor.

Further, Newbigin argues again from the ground of congruence. But in this case it is not the congruence of election as method with the nature of human life and the personal character of God that is most pointed. Rather it is the congruence of election with the nature of salvation, the healing and making whole of all things. The church can only fulfill its task of reconciling people to God in Christ "insofar as she is herself living in Christ, a reconciled fellowship in him, bound together in the love of the Father. This life in Christ is not merely the instrument of the apostolic mission, it is also its end and purpose" (53hg:169). It is the beneficiaries of salvation who can credibly attest to its truth and in whose lives are embodied the very thing for which they are the means. The reconciliation which is an inherent part of the offered gospel is also the direct fruit which comes from a salvation which works by way of election, of one bearing the message to another in the cross-cultural encounter.

To insist that the elect church is at the same time "the means and the end" maintains a comprehensive sense of the scope of salvation. The alternatives do not. If the church is seen as merely those who enjoy the benefits of Christ, then salvation is shortened from including a sense of personal and social reconciliation and mission becomes a strategy for gathering those who are being "snatched out" of the world (68wmc:3). If the church is only for the function of service, salvation is likewise reduced from including an offer of a salvation that brings reconciliation now, and salvation is left as only a future prospect. The eschatological tension of present and future salvation, of socio-historical wholeness and ultimate destiny is preserved only in terms of a union of salvation and service, beneficiary and bearer, means and end. By arguing for such a union, Newbigin affirms the essential historicality of God's plan of salvation, thus providing a foundation for understanding the meaning of the world's history as a whole and the meaning of all particularities within that whole.

Thus, Newbigin refuses to deny the personal benefit dimension of salvation, although he bathes it in cautions against presumption, pride, and self-centeredness. By plumbing the depths of what service and salvation mean and how they are intimately related in the "bearing of the witness of the Spirit," he places on a more firm and humble footing the conviction that the benefits of salvation are only received as grace. To know that the benefit is carried for the sake of another is a reminder that God could have chosen another to bear the blessing, that God in fact chooses the unworthy, and that the blessing itself has come through the encounter with a neighbor who had been chosen to bear it.

4. One Event with Significance for the Whole

The Bible presents us with "the story of a universal purpose carried out through a continuous series of particular choices" (78os:75). That thesis, which suggests a harmony for which "God's way of election" is the key, presents what is perhaps the most dramatic and important difference between the approach of Newbigin and that taken by others who emphasize the purpose of election. The doctrine of election, which most take to be exactly the "problem for doing mission" in terms of Old Testament thinking (Sundkler 1965:14ff.), Newbigin takes to be the solution.

The problem of the universal and particular is perennial. In the traditional, individualistic approach to election in which it was treated primarily in terms of "predestination," the tendency was to particularize God's manner of dealing with humanity in such a way that no connection was maintained with the cosmic, universal dimension (except in a unity posited to exist in God's mind and decree). On the other hand, a modern trend to emphasize the universal and cosmic sense of the salvation of the whole *oikoumene* has run the opposite risk of universalizing God's relation to humanity in such a way that no connection is maintained with the particular and historical (except in the affirmation that the salvation of the whole distributively includes each one in it).

There have been some who have suggested that because "election" has been demonstrated convincingly to "have no connection with favouritism" there is "therefore no ground for the reproach still often heard within the younger Churches of Asia (an echo of the reproach from the neo-Hindu side?): 'We do not like a God who has favourite peoples and favourite persons'" (Blauw 1962:23-24). But the issue has not gone away and those like Newbigin who have heard the continuing "offense" keep us sensitive to that. Only by facing such a challenge as the question to which he responds can we move beyond simply observing that in the calling of Abraham in Genesis 12 there is a universal element which "coincides" with the particular calling in order to provide an Old Testament basis for mission.

Further, to simply assert that "this universal meaning of the election of Israel" is established by the purpose relationship — "particularism" as "the instrument for the universal ends of God with the world" (Blauw 1962:22, 24) — does not yet address the issue fully enough. What remains is to explain *how* the particular serves a universal purpose. What is the inner connection of logic and practicality that keeps the suggested relationship from being an attractive but ultimately impotent response to the "scandal" which it is mission theology's place to answer?

It is generally assumed that universality and election stand poised against each other in at least "apparent contradiction" as an "ancient," a "primordial paradox" (Cushman 1981:204ff.).[15] For Israel's election to be "placed within a more comprehensive context" by its association with Abraham means that the "tension between a particularistic and a more universalistic interpretation of God's election of Israel has been effective from this point on through Jewish history" (Pannenberg 1977:49). The sense Israel had of its election by a divine "act of gratuitous love" paradoxically "provided an opening to universalism." Such love would "strain at the narrow boundaries of Israel and reach out to the *goyim*" (Senior and Stuhlmueller 1983:317-318).

Some find these "great contradictory themes" resolved by the link between the principles of election and substitution (Sundkler 1965:12-14). Boer, for example, argues that God's particularistic narrowing ("severe limitation") of "the scope of His soteric dealings with men" was effected because of the "manifestation of universal intransigence" at Babel. The election of Abraham, and with him Israel, forms part of the redemptive movement "from universalism to universalism through a process of contraction and expansion." That the call to Abraham had a "universal reference" points toward the fact that in the narrowing, "God never wholly relinquished His hold on the nations" but "preserved them for an eventual confrontation with the redeeming Spirit" (1961:67-68). Pentecost, therefore, becomes important as the return to a kind of suspended universalism.

Cullmann, upon whom Boer depends in large measure, finds in "the principle of representation" the most suitable framework for the consideration of election. "The history of *one* people becomes determinative for the salvation of all men" only in terms of the understanding that "the election of the people of Israel takes place with reference to Christ and reaches its fulfillment" in his work (1964:116, 108). Once accomplished, this "progressive reduction" from people to remnant to Christ reverses itself to become a "progressive advance from the one to the many" (116-117). Election is thus tied to redemptive history. Universalism is left behind until finally it may be rejoined.

Blauw, meanwhile, attempts to find a foundation for mission within the particularism of the election of Israel (1962:34-40). In his search for resolution between a particular election and a universal mission, he rejects the earlier suggestions of Rowley and others as inadequate. Their notion that election gave way to monotheism, then universalism, and finally mission, was an attempt to show the teleological dimension of election to be that which resolved its relationship to universalism (Rowley 1950:59ff.). Blauw, however, finds that progression "impossible to glean" from the Old Testament (Blauw 1962:30). He prefers another route. From a "universalistic" point of departure, the Old Testament portrays the election of Israel as a covenant by which God "steps actively into history" (30, 35). The covenant produces "expectation for the future," an expectation which is essentially Messianic (44ff.). That Messianic expectation "bears the character of universalism wellnigh continually" (45). Such a "universal-eschatological-Messianic salvation" expectation forms what Blauw concludes to be a "missionary mentality," upon which foundation a more explicitly centrifugal sense of mission emerges in the New Testament (52-54).

The more recent work of Stuhlmueller makes a similar effort to "trace the dramatic breakthrough from election to world mission" in order to tackle what constitutes "a major stumbling block" for any development of "a mission statement for the 'un-chosen'" (1983:89, 83). The breakthrough reaches its "full and clear expression" of the purpose of election in Second Isaiah, who "involved the larger secular world intimately in Israel's salvation," by which declaration he "expanded the doctrine of Israel's election to include universal salvation" (107, 106, 98).

What all of these approaches have in common is the assumption that election poses a problem to mission, and that occurs precisely because it is poised as an opposing idea to universality. They all attempt to find a universalism which is not undone by the particularity of it all. There is common agreement that the Old Testament story tracing the "elect" people begins on a note of universalism. Election enters the picture and disturbs that universalism and with it the potential for a conception of mission. The tension between the particularizing choice and the universal intent of God, it is believed, must find some resolution in favor of the universality if mission is to take place. If this cannot be found in the Old Testament, then it must be sought in the New. But in either event, election is viewed as a problem for universality and mission.

For Newbigin, election is the essential clue for resolving the "problem" posed by the "scandal" of particularity and thus the foundation for a universal mission. The universalism which forms the beginning point of the Old Testament story is preserved in and by election as the means by which God provides that each will receive from another the blessings of salvation. This Newbigin sees as the inner logic by which universality contains in it the necessity of an inherently missionary particularism. Such a particularism is at the same time permanently established as universal in its design, function, and intent. Election has built into it an inherent logic of universality which does not need a shift or correction. It needs only for its inner logic to be perceived and preserved.

While Newbigin's thought shares much in common with Cullmann's observation that the story of election in the Old Testament shows a "repeated narrowing of the focus to a smaller and smaller remnant" until election finally narrows down "to the one who bears the whole purpose of cosmic salvation in his own person" (78os:37), it operates according to a different logic. The narrowing election of a people is not construed as a departure, temporary or otherwise, from God's universal dealings with humankind, but as the necessary way for his provision of salvation to be universal. To choose one to bear the message to another corresponds to the salvation of which the message speaks and the nature of the persons to whom it is addressed. Thus he does not make the election of the people of God essentially different from the election of Jesus, as the redemptive history approach tends to do. The saving action of Jesus stands as one particular event which bears significance for all in the same way that the witnessing action of the elect is a particular event with significance for the whole.[16]

In the end, Newbigin concurs with Carl Braaten's assessment that "biblical universalism . . . is an historical project. It requires a mission in history to give the universal promise a matching content" (1977:53). David Bosch picks up Newbigin's instinctive clue regarding election and relates it to the "embarrassment" many feel because of the Old Testament's "apparently exclusive concentration on Israel." The embarrassment is due, he says, to "an inability to understand the Old Testament revelation as historical." The "concentration on Israel" and its position as chosen is not "unmissionary" but "precisely the opposite." In the history of the elect nation is to be found the "continuation of God's dealings with the nations." To be "truly missionary" a religion must be historical (1978:38-39). Election is not an embarrassment but the requirement of a universal meaning that embraces particular historical moments and places.

Whereas many observers conclude that in the Old Testament "the idea of mission either occurs only sporadically or is missing altogether" (Blauw 1962:30; cf. Hahn 1965:20), Newbigin, like Bosch, recasts the question by his formulation of the missionary character of election. The issue is not whether or not there is a "commission." The issue is God's intent in calling a people and the inner logic of that calling in relation to his purpose for the whole world. Election to bear the blessings of salvation to another made the chosen people witnesses to the presence and person of God. This they articulated in their affirmations of that faith in the very documents of the Old Testament, even if they did not do so by direct "outgoing" mission to the Gentiles. By their presence among the nations in the flow of public events and their voice of praise to the God who called them, the people of Israel bore ahead of time the witness to the reign of God coming.

It should also be noted that the effect of Newbigin's construction is to reverse the dictum of Rowley that Israel's "world mission" is the corollary of its election (1950:59-67). From the perspective of the consciousness of Israel and the development of its people's faith that may be said to be true.[17] But Newbigin turns that around by looking not at Israel's sense of its election but at God's design for it. If an answer is to be given to the scandal of particularity, it must be given in terms that demonstrate the universal intention and dimension of the particular choices God makes. For Newbigin, then, election is the corollary to the mission on which God has come.

It is the implication of the nature of his intent to bring wholeness to a world that includes persons who have an essential social relationship to each other. It is the method of reconciling such persons to each other and himself that is implied by his own personal nature. Newbigin treats mission as the starting point in terms of which election displays its inner rationale. Election is the central clue, but it is the mission of God about which it provides the clue. Election is the corollary of mission founded upon a trinitarian basis.[18]

Conclusion

Two things may be said in conclusion. First, the accumulation of the various ways in which Newbigin's treatment of election is distinct is to be attributed to the Indian setting in which much of his theological formulation has been fashioned. His view is most distinctive in that (1) it purposes to respond to the probing question of the Hindu observer who asks "why?" and "how?"; (2) it describes the congruent "fit" of election as a divine method with the personal nature of God and the social character of both human life and the divine salvation which brings wholeness, all of which stand counter-poised against dominant notes of Hindu thought; and (3) it claims for election that it is the solution to the relationship of the particular and the universal, attaching it to the assumption that one event can and does have significance for the meaning of the whole of history, as over against the axiom of Hindu faith that it does not.

Second, the testing of the adequacy of Newbigin's distinct view of the "missionary significance of the biblical doctrine of election," especially as that touches the issue of universality and particularity, will be accomplished best by showing how he builds on that view and applies its insights to the meaning of history in eschatological perspective (chapter four), the boundaries of the church and the necessity of conversion (chapter five), and the intercultural encounter of religions (chapter six). Newbigin's notion of election becomes pointedly expressed in each of these three areas, which lie at the center of the concern about cultural plurality. By tracing his line of thought in regard to each, the ability of his notion of election to provide a foundation for a theology of cultural plurality will be tested and on that basis an articulation of the contours of that theology can be made (chapter seven).

CHAPTER 4

The Presence of the Kingdom: The Meaning of History

The rich diversity of the world's peoples and the wide range of their visions of the meaning of things tend to mute all suggestions about a common meaning to their shared life and history on the planet. Yet it has always been characteristic of the Christian faith to make the claim that it possesses and offers just such a sense of the meaning of the whole. Bishop Newbigin is not alone when he repeatedly asserts that in Christ, and in the gospel which announces him, is to be found the clue to the meaning of history (63rtdt:24). Any talk of the "finality" of Christ must certainly mean this (69fc:62-65). To preach the gospel is to make "the tremendously bold claim that God really has a purpose for the world and for all men, and that we have the secret of that purpose, and that all men should join with us in obeying and fulfilling that purpose" (54wsot:75). "Christian faith," Newbigin asserts, "is itself an interpretation of history" (69fc:55). The acts of God in history "are the clue to its meaning and direction" (66hrsm:49).

But Newbigin makes this assertion in an even bolder fashion. It is the church, the chosen community of God's people, that "one particular strand in world history," which is the clue to its meaning (61ftow:80; 48dacp:30). In particular, it is the church's world mission which is "the central clue to world history" (61ftow:105, 81).[1] The Christian mission is not the clue

> in the sense that it is the "winning side" in the battle with the other forces of history, but in the sense that it is the point at which the meaning of

113

history is understood and at which men are required to make the final decisions about that meaning. (63rtdt:37)

To make the assertion in this way inexorably draws election into the picture. An unelaborated suggestion to that effect may be found in an early statement Newbigin makes: "God's purpose of love must be worked out through election . . . ; if we resent it, we make the history of the human society on earth ultimately meaningless" (48dacp:30). More pointed is the acknowledgment lying at the crux of his argument in *The Open Secret*, where he has taken "the doctrine of election as the clue to the understanding of the role of mission in world history" (78os:91). This argument so often developed before to show the way the gospel gives meaning to world history is now placed at the climactic center of Newbigin's mission theology.[2] While it was not always articulated in such a direct manner, his mission theology has come to be founded explicitly on "election" as both the "inner logic" of a trinitarian basis for mission and the "answer" to the scandal of particularity (cf. 78os:73-75). With that "election missiology" established, Newbigin proceeds to develop on that basis the theme which forms a bridge to the questions of Christian action in a culturally plural world: "The Gospel and World History" (78os: chapter 7). Growing in the soil of election, his theory regarding the meaning of history yields the fruit of a foundation for a theology of cultural plurality.

Newbigin's concept of the "missionary significance" of election is an integral part of the fabric of his perspective on meaningful history. It is the intent of this chapter to show that essential relationship by first tracing the lines along which Newbigin has consistently argued that the history of the world as a whole has meaning. Then we shall look at the applications he makes of that meaning regarding the basis for Christian action in the secular life of the world and a proper interpretation of contemporary world history. Finally we shall identify the implications for a theology of cultural plurality which grow out of his view of history.

The Clue to the Meaning of History

Newbigin spent the greater part of his life in the thought-world of the Indian subcontinent, sometimes absorbing its deep spirituality and humility, sometimes questioning its deepest convictions, and always attempting to frame a statement of his gospel in terms that showed most vividly its alternate vision of the gracious God who disclosed his purpose for the world through Jesus Christ. Of major concern to him has been the "great divide" between the visions of history held in Christianity and in Hinduism.[3] His theological agenda has in many ways been set by the simple acknowledgment that "it is characteristic of Hindu thought that it regards the question of historicity as unimportant" (69fc:50). The quest for a clear and convincing apologetic for his own faith in an essentially historical revelation of salvation has always been a deeply personal one. He shows how pointed the matter is:

> I have never forgotten the astonishment with which a devout and learned teacher of the Ramakrishnan [sic] Mission regarded me when he discovered that I was prepared to rest my whole faith as a Christian upon the substantial historical truth of the record concerning Jesus in the New Testament. To him it seemed axiomatic that such vital matters of religious truth could not be allowed to depend upon the accidents of history. (50)

These two visions represent varying ways to seek "unity and coherence behind and beyond all the multiplicity and incoherence which human experience presents to us." The one finds unity in a "reality behind the multiplicity" and the other in "an end yet to be obtained." The first is the cyclical vision of the "wheel" and the second the linear vision of the "road." The "endless movement and change" on the circumference of the wheel "means nothing" because reality lies in the "timeless, motionless center." In contrast, "coherence and harmony" in terms of the road are to be found only "at the end," when the journey is complete (69fc:65-66).

The two explanations of coherence found in advaitic Hinduism and in historic Christian orthodoxy involve fundamentally different notions of the "eternal" or the "supreme being." They follow what Newbigin calls the "two main lines" by which the human mind has interpreted the eternal. It may be taken to be "a motionless centre equidistant from every point on the moving circumference" or it may be interpreted as "personal will which moves towards the fulfillment where all that is now opposed to it will be wholly subdued to it" (66hrsm:50). For the former, multiplicity and change are regarded as "a mere veil which has to be torn away in order that we may have access to ultimate reality"; for the latter, they are regarded as "the place where we are to meet with and know and serve the divine purpose."

The former looks for salvation by "absorption into the Supreme Being," while the latter seeks it in "reconciliation to the Supreme Being" (61ftow:39).

This, according to Newbigin, lies at the root of the difference in the doctrines of humankind contained in the respective Scriptures of each perspective. In the Upanishads, "the ultimate truth about man is sought in his interiority, in the deepest recesses of his being where all relations with the sensible world and with other human beings have been left behind." The contrasting view of the Old Testament is that "the truth about man is seen in his relatedness to his neighbor and in his responsibility to God for both his neighbor and for the world in which God has placed him" (79cjh:202). At stake is the question whether "man is to be understood ultimately in terms of his inward, private spiritual life alone" or "in terms which include both this and also the public life which he shares with the whole of the rest of mankind and with the world of nature" (203).

Newbigin's discussion of the meaning of history unfolds against this backdrop. Painted against the scenery of a different religious climate, other issues might have come to the fore instead. But Newbigin's Indian setting brought vividly to his attention the fundamental importance of this watershed divergence of elemental axioms regarding history.

The importance of the observation did not stop there, however. For within Western thought as well, a viewpoint similar in effect to the Hindu view of history has shown itself. Not only in the "popular Hellenistic thought" which characterized the Roman world into which the early church ventured, but in modern attitudes formed by the scientific worldview characteristic of Enlightenment culture there is to be found a negative assessment of the possibility of maintaining the importance for the whole of any of the "accidental happenings of history" (78os:26-27; 86fg:96-97). "Our culture," Newbigin says, "is offended by the idea that the Absolute should be made known in contingent happenings of history." He quotes the affirmation of Lessing which he says has almost become "an axiom" for modern Western culture: "the accidental truths of history can never become the proof of necessary truths of reason." What the culture supposes to be the "autonomy of reason" is threatened by any "claim of revelation in particular happenings" (83os84:51-52).

This tendency to look elsewhere than to the historical for meaning Newbigin finds present in the attempt to address the gospel to the secular age in existentialist terms. In that approach "the whole attention is centred not upon the public history of mankind . . . but rather upon the personal spiritual history of each believer." Rudolph Bultmann's assessment, for example, is that "eschatology is not at all concerned with the meaning and goal of secular history. . . . It is concerned rather with the meaning and goal of the history of the individual and of the eschatological community" (66hrsm:44-45; cf. Bultmann 1962:116).

As further examples of the "divide" over history, Newbigin mentions the views of William E. Hocking and A. G. Hogg. In Hocking's view of faith, Newbigin finds a "radically different" conception than that of the Bible. For Hocking, "it is axiomatic that faith is an individual experience of timeless reality." The history in which he is interested is that of the individual's "apprehension of the eternal as love." Newbigin contrasts this view with the Bible's picture in which "the eternal emphatically *has a history,*" a fact which corresponds to the "fundamentally social character of religion" (61ftow:48).

Newbigin critiques Hogg for failing to see the essential "happened-ness" of the events reported in the gospel, a failure evidenced by his in-sistence over against Hendrik Kraemer that the significance of the biblical account lies in the "content" of the events, not in their "occurrence" (69fc:50-52). It is this which leads Hogg to insist that "a loving Father must necessarily have made his saving revelation available to everyone, apart from particular events in history" (83cwr:20, 26). Thus Hogg, Hocking, and others suggest that the path to true knowledge of God comes by way of induction from "general religious experience," a path which lies over against the perspective that we grasp the meaning of the story as a whole "by a revelation in the form of happenings which are grasped by faith as the self-communication of the one whose purpose the story embodies" (79cjh:205, 69fc:62-63). Between these two opinions, according to New-bigin, there is a "radical incommensurability."

At the very base of the issue, Newbigin finds the question to be that of a rudimentary choice between divergent axioms:

> Here two different dogmatic systems confront one another, and I know of no set of axioms more fundamental than either of them, on the basis of which it would be possible to demonstrate the truth of one of these dogmas and the falsity of the other. According to one dogma, world history is in some sense a coherent whole, and it is therefore possible to affirm that certain events have a unique significance for the entire story.

According to the other dogma there are no events which have such unique significance and therefore no universally valid affirmation can be made about the meaning of history as a whole. (78ctc:16; cf. 78os:174)

This is the critical beginning point from which Newbigin constructs his view of the meaning of the common history of humankind. For him, it is a "conflict between two ultimate beliefs" (79cjh:205). When one chooses one or the other as a starting point, the choice is a "decision of faith" (61ftow:39). Each is, in that sense, fully a "starting point." "You cannot," Newbigin says, "demonstrate in advance that either of these is the right starting-point. . . . It is validated — if at all — only as the outcome of this process of exploration" (69fc:63). The issue then in the discussion about the meaning of history is not the "tools" that one uses (such as the critical skills of the modern scholar) but the "presuppositions, axioms, models, analogies, and paradigms" which one must inevitably bring to the task and by which an interpretation will be made. It is the same for the Hindu, the Marxist, and the Western academic, no less than for the Christian believer (78os:98-99).

It is God's pattern of working by way of election which provides Newbigin the clue for establishing this beginning point.[4] Election affirms, as was shown in the last chapter, that "one event bears significance for another" in that one person is chosen to bear salvation to another. The choice of Abraham as one who was to bear the blessing for all, the choice of the nation to bear among all the nations the salvation purposed for the world, the choice of Jesus to bear the sins of the world, and the choice of witnesses to his resurrection, are all particular choices within the actual history of humankind. It is an ultimate faith commitment that meaning and relationship to the divine purpose should come in such a way that "one among all the cultures should have this unique position" (78ctc:16). To accept this clue is to choose one of the fundamental dogmas regarding the possibility of historical meaning. To choose the other alternative and in any way to suggest that it represents the biblical posture is to miss the biblical teaching about election, in Newbigin's assessment. It is the inner logic of election which clarifies the appropriateness of accepting it as the starting clue.

If it is true that God fulfills his purpose of salvation not by making himself immediately accessible to every human soul considered as a separate entity but by means of events at particular times and places, this is only compatible with what we learn of God in Jesus if it is also true that these particular events are, in some sense, for the sake of all. This is what — as I understand it — the biblical teaching about election makes clear. (83cwr:26)

Within this election perspective, history is seen not as a succession of mere "illustrations" of "how things are" in an ultimate reality beyond the multiplicity and change but as events which have "actually happened" and which have bearing on the meaning of other things which actually happen (cf. 78os:91-92).

While it is true that Newbigin at the most elemental level claims for election, and the church's mission which is established by it, that it is the beginning and essential "clue" for the meaning of world history, a starting point which is a decision of faith which cannot be demonstrated by any prior principle, there are in fact two prior principles which function for him as the means by which the adequacy of any beginning model must be tested. These are the bases upon which he affirms that election must be the beginning clue and by which he finds alternate clues and opinions deficient. Two assumptions must find full expression for Newbigin in any "right" approach to the Christian faith and the meaning of history. First, God is personal. Election gives adequate explanation because it describes God's actions as those of one who is personal. "If we believe in a personal God, we must believe that it is possible for him to act and therefore to choose the times and places of his actions" (61ftow:78). Second, human nature is social. God's purpose "has in view, not 'the soul' conceived as an independent monad detached from other souls and from the created world, but the human person knit together with other persons in a shared participation in and responsibility for God's created world" (78os:86). Therefore, "the saving deeds and words must always be mediated through one to another" (83cwr:26). A clue to the meaning of history, to be adequate, must measure up to these two standards. Herein lies Newbigin's most basic faith commitment.[5]

If election provides the clue that one event can indeed have meaning for all events and therefore history can be viewed as a coherent whole, then it must be asked what criteria are to be used to determine which events bear that significance and what significance they convey. The beginning point for determining the answer to that question must be the acknowledgment that "historical inquiry is never an ideologically neutral enterprise" (78ctc:19). Newbigin argues that the historian's attempt to understand the past must begin by seeking to grasp it in terms of the thought-world which he inhabits and to which he is committed. His effort is shaped by his culture. He can only understand the past by means of analogies in his present experience. (78ctc:20)

We cannot "make sense of a mass of information" apart from "the language we use, the models and analogies" furnished by our culture (78os:94). Therefore, the decision about what events are significant — the necessary process of selection in which every historian engages — must be "based upon the provisional judgment of the historian, which again depends upon his own understanding of and commitment to the course of events in his own time" (69fc:70). Newbigin's stance is unqualified on this point: "All understanding of history rests upon some provisional belief about the meaning of the whole" (79cjh:200).[6]

But if "there is no standpoint which is above all particular standpoints," then "can there be such a thing as universal history?" (69fc:71). Newbigin affirms that there can be, but it can not come by the generally received route of induction from the data. "Such concepts as 'research,' 'study,' and 'observation' are irrelevant" because of the particular difficulty inherent in the very nature of what is involved in a universal history. The story can only be told when the teller of it "has seen the meaning of it" and has a sense of "the point" of the story (78os:94-95). Newbigin embraces the idea which seems to him to be plain, if to others it might appear naive, that "if history has no end, it has no meaning" (61ftow:95-96).

> Normally the point [of any story] is clear only at the end. Our difficulty is that we are still in the middle of the story: we can investigate the past, but the future is hidden and we do not know the end. Our different ways of writing history, our different pictures of the story, are our ways of expressing our different beliefs about its end. (78os:94-95)

Therefore, there can be a genuinely universal history "only if, by some means, the teller has become convinced about the end of the story while he is still in the midst of it" (69fc:71). This requires that in some way or other "the point of the story has been revealed even before the story has come to its end" (78os:95).

Revelation thus enters the picture as an "unavoidable" element. It enters in such a way that it gives greater substance to Newbigin's argument than might otherwise be judged, due to the fact that he states in a qualified way what he believes more strongly (using the word "normally," 78os:94, 69fc:71). Even his vivid analogy of a building site strewn with the materials for a construction whose shape is unknown to the observer until the architect's drawings reveal it has more potential force than he teases out. There is a potential flaw in the analogy: an experienced observer *could* judge a great deal from the site itself! The illustration as he poses it does not seem to require the strong conclusion he draws that "the concept of revelation is not an alien intrusion into the process of responsible human knowing. There is no other possibility" (78os:95; cf. 68coec:19).

But the analogy's potential flaw turns out to be its strength, for within the illustration lies something deeper. As much as an experienced observer *could* detect from the materials at the site, the ultimate shape of the project would still be knowable only at the end or by viewing the architect's blueprints. Likewise, as much as other clues may exist among the data of history, the essentially important clue must be the purpose in the mind of the one to whose plans it will conform (68coec:19). Knowing the "meaning" of history implies to Newbigin discerning the "purpose" to which it is directed. The idea of purpose, in turn, is tied to his most basic assumption: "to speak of purpose is to speak of a personal will known by words and acts which express and foreshadow something which is not yet visible but which is real now and will be visible at the end. It is to speak, in other words, of revelation" (66hrsm:51; cf. 61ftow:95-96). The personal character of God requires the pattern of "selected" historical actions that as "disclosures in a unique sense, of the presence and action of God" (83os84:49) are "the self-communication of the one whose purpose the story embodies" (79cjh:205).[7]

In particular, it is in Jesus that this decisive revelation has taken place, in "those events in which God has disclosed ('revealed') the shape of the story as a whole, because in Jesus the beginning and the end of the story, the Alpha and the Omega, are revealed, made known, disclosed" (78os:95-96, 99). The Christian claims finality for Christ by endorsing "the judgment of the apostles that in his life, death and resurrection God himself was uniquely present and that therefore the meaning and origin and end of all things was disclosed" (69fc:76). The "fact of Christ," as Newbigin enjoys calling it (following his mentor Dr. Carnegie Simpson), is "the decisive point, the turning-point . . . in God's long and patient wrestling with the human race" (69fc:75-76). It fits with the personal character of God, the social nature of humanity, and the cosmic scope of God's purpose of redemption that the center of that redemption should be a "deed wrought out at an actual point in history and at a particular place" (53hg:109-110). By virtue of the "incarnation of the eternal Word of God" (83cwr:28),

> the public history of mankind will be seen as a coherent reality which has a real centre and a real end. The centre (in the Christian understanding) is the life and death and resurrection of Jesus. . . . The end is the new creation of which the resurrection of Jesus is the first-fruit. (79cjh:204-205)

It is important to note that Newbigin's emphasis on the personal history of Jesus as the center should not be misunderstood to mean that the revelation of history's meaning is entirely contained in that "center-point." This is what Maurice Wiles appears to have missed in his reading of Newbigin. While agreeing with much that Newbigin says in the article critiquing Wiles's thought, Wiles finds occasion to counter that he does not see

> that he has made out his case that there would have to be *one* event of a different order of decisiveness, or that that one event would have to take the form of a divine self-communication as distinctive and direct as he postulates. (Wiles 1979:212, emphasis his)

Perhaps in the article Wiles had in hand such an impression is left. But Newbigin is clear in the spectrum of his writings that Jesus is the "center" but not the whole of the revealing. His emphasis lies in the fact made so vivid by the biblical doctrine of election, that "the central thread of the history [of the world] is the story of God's people. And the centre point of the story is the birth, life, death, resurrection and ascension of Jesus and the coming of His Spirit to His disciples" (54wsot:76). He is concerned to show the bearing which this "one particular series of events" has on the meaning of world history (83os84:51). He reports with approval the judgment of Kraemer that Jesus' personal history forms "the heart of the 'connected series of divine acts'" (83cwr:18). But the crucial significance of "the fact of Christ" for world history lies in the fact that it is of the same piece of cloth. It is not an essentially different "revealed clue" than the rest of the story of God's dealings with humankind, particularized especially in the history of his people. The exodus from Egypt, the "central" act in the Old

Testament, and the resurrection of Jesus, the "central" act in the New, are only the "climactic acts in a story in which God's mighty power is seen at work throughout the whole history of the chosen people" (66hrsm:47). Thus there is no real disjuncture when the line of Israel is narrowed to just One, as "the whole purpose of God for the world is concentrated in the single thread of events enacted on a hill outside Jerusalem," but only a focusing of the longer and larger thread (61ftow:80). Immediately Newbigin notes the broadening out again as the chosen witnesses are sent into their mission!

This is not to say that Newbigin does not count the events of Jesus' life, death, and resurrection as unique. "The revelation of God which is concentrated in the Cross of Jesus Christ is the revelation of a holiness which *is* and which is in agony until what ought to be is" (69fc:68-69). That unrepeatable act has its own particular and unique bearing on the meaning of history, a bearing not shared or diffused. But what we are saying is that the events of Christ's history are not of a different order than all others in which God has been present in particular, self-disclosing acts within history. It is Newbigin's sense of the principle of election which guards this sense of the continuity of God's revelation. Christ's election and that of the people of God before and after him are of the same sort, equally yielding a disclosure of the meaning and end of history, equally sharing the character of "one event which bears significance for the whole."

Implications for Christian Responsibility

Newbigin's discussions regarding the meaning of history have always had the purpose of validating and formulating Christian political involvement. (This he indicated in personal conversation in October 1986.) His concern for this is so strong that the capacity of any philosophy of history to sustain deliberate action toward the creation of a better human society is one of Newbigin's assumed criteria of judgment. It joins together with the personhood of God and the social character of humanity as an essential requirement for a valid theology of universal historical meaning. It is on that basis that he criticizes the idealist view that in "common mystical experience" we find "a harmony beneath all the multiplicity and movement of this world" — "it would destroy in the long run the will to create an ordered world" (61ftow:53). On the other hand, he argues that the belief — implied to be that which we all harbor — that "it really matters whether my insights are translated into action on the stage of public events" requires that we see more than "truths, values, experiences" in past events and acknowledge that their "happenedness" is important. Otherwise we invite a future generation to adopt a way of understanding our present which voids it of significant historicality (79cjh:203). To deny the "happenedness" of past events cuts off the significance of actual actions in the present. Essential to faith is the "happenedness" of the events which "form the clue" to history. That faith "will be expressed in a life of discipleship in the shared life of humanity, seen not just as illustrations of the faith or as exercises in personal spiritual growth, but as participation in the story whose centre has been discerned in the events" (79cjh:205; cf. 66hrsm:44).

Newbigin sees such a commitment to act as necessarily involved in any belief about the meaning and end of history. He yokes the belief and the commitment in his assessment that any historian must understand things "in terms of the thought-world which he inhabits and to which he is committed" (78ctc:20). The conviction which a "teller" of the story has about the end of the story yet to come will "necessarily be at the same time a commitment to act in a certain way in the history which is being written today and tomorrow" (69fc:70-71). Every stance from which the meaning of history is construed is a "decision of faith" on the basis of some provisional clue and every such decision is at the same time a commitment to actions consistent with that chosen starting point. When that starting point is the Christian one he outlines, just as is the case with any other, it must issue in committed participation by which "we shall find that not only God's ordering of our personal lives, but also God's ordering of the course of secular history has a shape, a pattern which is discernibly related to his purpose to sum up all things in Christ" (63jsmc:2-3).

Newbigin's interest is not only apologetic. His apologetic is made in the interest of his pastoral-missiological concern for Christian involvement. The interpretation of the meaning of history which the gospel renders requires of the Christian believer action in two forms:

> this must mean a provisional interpretation of the meaning of contemporary secular events (discerning the signs of the times) and concrete action in the various sectors of secular life directed towards the true end for which God has created humanity and the world (Christian obedience in the common life). (78os:100)

The question of meaning for history can only be "answered in action," and the Christian confession about that meaning can only "make good its claim to truth . . . through actions in which this confession is embodied in deed" (78os:100-101). Just how it is that the gospel's clue to the meaning of history forms the foundation for concrete Christian action is a task to which Newbigin constantly applies himself, and in the next section we will observe the rationale he offers. Newbigin's attempts at various stages in his life to interpret the "current" scene will then be assessed in terms of the overall scheme of action implied by his assertion that the gospel of Christ and the world mission of the church are the clue to history.

The Basis for Political Action

In Newbigin's estimation, the basic problem facing a theoretical foundation for public action is the relationship between the meaning of world history as a whole and meaning for the individual person within it.

> On the one hand, how can one secure determined and effective action to achieve a new order of society within history without invoking the power of an ideology which dehumanizes man and treats him as a means rather than an end? On the other hand, how can you treat seriously the personal destiny of every human being without robbing human history as a whole of any intelligible meaning? How can you have meaning for history as a whole except by surrendering the meaning of each human life, or how can you have meaning for each human life except at the cost of meaninglessness for human history? (66hrsm:55)

Put in theological terms, the problem concerns "the difficulty of seeing the right relation between God's purpose for the individual soul, and God's purpose in history as a whole" (41kgip 4:5).

This problem was hinted at in the earliest period of Newbigin's life as one posed by the assumptions undergirding the Christian notion of revelation: to hold that "the meaning of the world is personal" without seeing that "the meaning of man's life is in fellowship" leads to "an individualistic mysticism very remote from the genius of Christianity," while a sense of the "fellowship" meaning of human life apart from "a personal interpretation of the world" is all too compatible with "tyranny" (36r:1-3). That certainly lies in the background throughout Newbigin's career. But he has given the clue much greater force through his vision of the reason for the "dilemma" the problem involves. That was expounded as early as 1941, when it formed one of the central themes of the very important but never published Bangalore lectures on "The Kingdom of God and the Idea of Progress" (41kgip: lectures 2 and 4). Here it becomes very clear that in Newbigin's thought

> the difficulty arises from the fact of death. For death removes every individual abruptly out of history, before history has reached its goal of perfect fellowship, which is also the proper goal of the individual['s] growth. Death thus creates for each man the dilemma which was our starting-point. It makes it impossible that his participation in the task of creating a perfect fellowship should lead him personally to his own perfection. Therefore the hope of finding his own perfection in an other-worldly heaven, becomes a rival in his mind to the desire to labour for that perfect fellowship on earth which he knows he cannot see. . . . There-fore man and striving cannot and does not lead in a straight line to the full realisation of the Kingdom. Death, failure, corruption, bar the way. And hence arises that tragic dilemma when a man seems forced to choose between seeking the perfect goal of history which he will never see, and seeking perfection for himself in an individual survival of death. (41kgip 4:6-7)

That has been a persistent theme in Newbigin's writings ever since.[8] The dilemma with which death "mocks any hope for a total liberation of man in history" poses two ways to find meaning, either in the "future of the common human life" or in the "future destiny" of the individual (78os:115-116). The former dehumanizes the individual, according to Newbigin, making the person the tool to an end that cannot be shared, and the latter sets aside responsible participation in the common life of humanity in order to pursue egoistic ends.

Newbigin finds examples of each of these choices not only in the general ways in which human cultures have sought to resolve the dilemma but also in expressions of the Christian hope and secularized versions of it. He suggests that the alternatives may be seen most graphically in the Berlin Wall, with a "grim totalitarianism" on one side and a "screaming futilitarianism" on the other. Such stark images create for Newbigin the urgency of demonstrating that neither is satisfying and both lack an integral view of the personal and corporate nature of humanity.

The choice for individual meaning over against meaning for history as a whole can of course be seen in the tendency within Christian experience to focus hope on the "state of being beyond death," believing that "the aim of the Christian life is to be found in another world which [one] enters by the act of dying" (41kgip 2:2, 8; 68coec:41). But the Bible's image of the end is not that of a "disembodied survival for the individual" (79cjh:205). God's purpose is not "a collection of individual spirits abstracted one by one from their involvement in the world of matter and in the human community." Therefore, "the Christian hope is no selfish quest of private salvation" (53ch:109-111). Such a view would negate the view of history as "a real drama with a coherent meaning" and reduce it to "a non-stop revue, an endless series of solo items," a show which as a whole "has no plot and no conclusion" (59scmt:183).

The effect is the same for the existentialist attempt to restate the gospel, in which attention is focused on "the personal spiritual history of each believer" rather than "the public history of mankind" (66hrsm:45). For the existentialist, "the only meaning of events is the meaning which the individual gives to them." The dichotomy this view preserves is that "between a purely personal, inward and spiritual world . . . and the outward world of historical events," a dichotomy similar to the "Hindu distinction between the real world of the self and the realm of Maya." These modern parallels of the "popular Hellenistic thought" of the first century are likewise critiqued by the gospel which announces events "determinative" for nature and history as well as the human soul (69fc:54-55; 68coec:41).

The issue in all these cases is "whether 'salvation' refers to the destiny of a soul conceived as an entity apart from the total human person, or to the destiny of the human person considered realistically as part of history and nature" (79cjh:205). But the death-produced dilemma suggests an alternate possibility. One might choose to seek meaning not in the individual person but in "the vision of a future age of freedom and justice for all" (78os:117). Various beliefs in "social progress," especially those nurtured by Western Enlightenment culture, follow this route (86fg:134; 41kgip 1).

One of the most emphatic examples is Marxism, and in this feature of Marxism lies Newbigin's primary critique of it. The tone of that critique is important to note, because Newbigin finds much of value in Marxism precisely in regard to this issue of history. In the only work in which he attempts a direct and in any sense complete statement regarding Marxism, the line of critique which we shall note presently does not in fact appear (74cfm). When the article does touch on Marxism's view of history, it does so with affirmation and approval. Crediting the Jewish upbringing of Karl Marx, Newbigin notes ways in which Marxism "reflects the biblical faith." As over against Hinduism, Marxism believes that "human history moves towards a goal." The Marxist also believes that "truth is known in action," a "profoundly biblical insight." Both the Bible and Marxist thought envision "a messianic people which is the bearer of God's purpose through history" (74cfm:23). In this latter "apocalyptic twist to the Enlightenment scenario" of progress, Marxists are "more biblical . . . than the liberal Protestants," who used language of the Kingdom of God to "domesticate" Christianity within the culture's dominant notions of social advance (86fg:134). Marxism presents a "secularized version of the biblical hope," which "as an interpretation of history rests ultimately on the Old Testament vision of a meaningful future for the public life of humanity" (78os:116-117). Newbigin finds Marxism to provide much "more useful" concepts for restating the gospel to a secularized world than those of existentialism, especially for the peoples not living in the Western world who are filling with hope as "development" looms on the horizon (66hrsm:45-46).

But Marxism, along with other visions of social progress and utopian dream, has not been able to avoid the negation of the meaning of personal histories in the quest for meaning for world history. Here, Newbigin says,

> it is no use mincing words: if our final hope rests upon a state of society which is to exist on earth at a later date, then those are right who are willing to liquidate living human beings today for the sake of the goal which in any case they will never see. On this view, the men and women living today can only be means to an end, and there is no final judgment upon any human action except the judgment of what is expedient from the point of view of the social process. (53ch:111)

Such views "marginalize the human being" in that they maintain a logic by which "the individual human person has no final significance" (86fg:135; 68coec:40). The drive for a "perfected human social order" (53ch:111), which properly invites human action in the interest of the public life, does so at the expense of the meaning of the life of the actor who constructs such an order. The actor is cut off before the perfect has come and cannot participate in that which has been worked for. That is the effect of that "formidable road block," death (cf. 61ftow:96). Marxism itself has had to face this, claims Newbigin. He quotes a Marxist philosopher as saying that "from the point of view of the progression of nature, death is entirely sensible, but from the point of view of a given individual, death is senseless and places in doubt everything that he does" (68coec:41). The fact of death underscores the need for "an understanding of the human situation which gives meaning to the whole drama of human history without in the end evacuating each man's personal history of meaning" (63jsmc:3).

It is Newbigin's conviction that the gospel answers with

> a faith regarding the final consummation of God's purpose in the power of which it is possible to find meaning for world history which does not make personal history meaningless, and meaning for personal history which does not make world history meaningless. (66hrsm:46)

If the historicality axiom — that certain events can have significance for the whole of history — is the one which alone gives a basis for public action, then it is only the biblically eschatological version of it which gives such a basis in a way that both individual and cosmic dimensions of meaning are preserved. The Christian gospel transcends the dilemma which death creates because it addresses both the root cause of death (sin, by way of atonement) and the tragic wedge death drives between the individual and the whole social order.[9] The death and resurrection of Jesus lie at the heart of New Testament eschatology, which alone can give a meaning to world history that preserves the integrity of the personal and social character of the life of humankind. The human situation, which requires some "reliable report" from beyond death about the end to which the world proceeds, hears testimony to that in the gospel of a risen Christ who defeated sin and death.

The Christian, then, has a basis for acting "with confidence and with a sense of direction" because "his faith rests upon the resurrection of Jesus from the dead" and because of the knowledge that "the end of all things is his reign" (61ftow:101). There is a real resurrection in the Christian's personal future and that personal future is in a real human society brought to completion under the just and peaceful reign of God, "a city which is at the same time the gift of God and the true goal of the story of civilization"

(79cjh:205). To look for that city and live life in terms of its character and certainty is to maintain the hope of "a consummation which embraces both the public and the private life of men and women" (83os84:35).

The potential that the private and public meanings of life might be divorced, which has long fueled Newbigin's attempt to clarify how the announcement of the reign of God unites meaning in both respects, has provided for him a lens through which to observe how thoroughly Western culture has come to adopt just such a fracturing. The thrust of two of his major efforts to address the missionary encounter of the gospel with Western culture (*The Other Side of 1984* and *Foolishness to the Greeks*) has been to display this feature: "As we have seen over and over again in this study, this dichotomy between the private and the public worlds is the central clue to the ideology that governs our culture" (86fg:132; cf. 83os84 and an earlier anticipation in 63rtdt:55). Newbigin calls for the church to refuse to withdraw to the private realm and to see its discipleship as a requirement to be "signs and agents of God's justice in all human affairs" (86fg:133). In this the contemporary church is to emulate the earliest church, which, in Newbigin's judgment, "declined to accept the status of *cultus privatus*" which it had open to it in the Roman Empire (79cjh:200-205). Instead that church "called itself the *ecclesia tou theou*, the public assembly to which God is calling all men everywhere without distinction" (86fg:99-100; cf. 83os84:33).

This "split between the public and the private" is "healed" only by a true eschatology, one which sees that "death and resurrection are the connective terms between this present life and the re-created life of the new age" (86fg:136). While that eschatology validates and requires Christian action in the public realm, it also qualifies all our pretensions that the perfect society can be "the direct result of our efforts" (41kgip 4:1). Here we meet in Newbigin the most essential element of his eschatological vision as it critiques all utopian or triumphalistic missiological aims. A humble and servant church travels the way of the cross, which leads down into the chasm of death and judgment. It is only in the church's risen Lord that it has real connection to the other side of the chasm, where there arises the holy city where God's purposes are consummated and brought to completion. This vision has been shared from the earliest of Newbigin's lectures and writings up to the latest.[10] It may best be represented by a full reference to one of his more recent and succinct tellings of the vision:

We do not see the future of either our own personal selves or the world we share with all people. The curtain of death shuts off our view. But Jesus has gone before us through the curtain. The road disappears from view down "into a dark valley, into whose depth we cannot peer. Jesus has gone down there before us and has appeared victorious on the other side. He is himself the path, the way that goes through death to life (John 13:36–14:7). As we follow that way, we have before us, beyond the chasm of death, the vision of the holy city into which all the glory of the nations will be brought and from which everything unclean is excluded. (86fg:136)

The vision which promotes our action gives us pause about it as well. The chasm, death, is a reminder that "all the patterns we are weaving are flawed, that all our achievements are ambiguous, and that none of them leads directly to the perfection we seek" (78os:118). "There can be no straight road," in other words, "from this life to the goal that alone gives it meaning" (86fg:136). Newbigin invites us to lose ourselves in the service of God's cause and make the confession that "though I cannot create the city, God can raise up both me and my works, purged in the fire of judgment, to take a place in the life of the city." Knowing that "because Christ is risen, my labor in the Lord is not futile," we are moved to "work tirelessly for the best possible among the actually available political alternatives" (78os:118-119; 86fg:137). All ideological programs are critiqued and qualified by the fact of death, and all quietistic escapes are challenged and corrected by the fact of the risen Lord of the world (cf. 83os84:37).

It is this line of thought with which M. M. Thomas takes issue in his review of Newbigin's *The Other Side of 1984* (Thomas 1984). He believes that Newbigin's discussion is "so overweighted on the eschatological side that the framework is close to" what Thomas would call "a social pietism in which political struggles cannot be taken seriously." To show this, he quotes a lengthy passage, the center of which is the sober realization that "both our selves and all our works must disappear and be buried under the rubble of history" (321; cf. 83os84:37). He says that Newbigin is right to "move away from absolutizing the realm of politics" but believes he has ended up by "making politics too fragmentary." According to Thomas, Newbigin's view does not give sufficient place to the need to grapple with actual ideologies "in order to relate the eschatological hope to the historical hopes based on a realistic appraisal of the natural and social forces operating in the historical situation for good and evil" (321).

The assessment of this critique must take into account the long and kindly relationship and interaction these two men have had. Thomas indicates his debt to Newbigin's early lectures given in 1941 at Bangalore on "The Kingdom of God and the Idea of Progress" (Thomas 1969; cf. 41kgip). Thomas found help in Newbigin's presentation of "the eschatological character of the gospel of the kingdom as contrasted with the Utopian." While he expresses some regret that following that time Newbigin's "theological pursuits became too oriented to Church Unity rather than to the church's witness in relation to Indian religions and society," the regret was balanced with the acknowledgment that "he never lost touch with the fields of religion and society, as it was inherent in his concern for mission. And he was always prepared to enter these fields with zest" (Thomas 1969; cf. 85ua:214ff.). But Thomas has continued to feel that Newbigin "of course has the theologian's fear of translating the eschatological and evangelistic insights into the historical meaning of the concrete political and social revolutions of our time for the humanity of men" (Thomas 1969). That fear — which it would be more accurate to call a "pastor's fear" — Thomas senses is still at work and causes Newbigin to shy away from asserting with any real force a continuity between our "eschatological hope" and our "historical hopes."

This same issue was raised by Thomas in the context of the partially published debate in which the two were involved in the late 1960s and early 1970s. (See pp. 280-282 in this volume for a survey of the exchange of comments referred to here as the "Thomas-Newbigin debate.") In the end, the debate revolved around "koinonia" (which theme will be taken up in the next chapter), but its original focus was on "salvation and humanization." Thomas's concern in that debate was to stress a continuity between the present and the future: "the Kingdom of resurrection-life, whether for individual or community, does not start only after death; it begins and is partially realised here and now, within the dimension of a history facing death and disintegration" (1971:9). This he says in response to a discussion of Newbigin's in which he had asserted that a true eschatology must take into account death and judgment and find ultimate meaning in terms which make sense of them. Thus, "the human community cannot be understood in fully personal terms from a point of view which has no perspective beyond the death of the individual human person" (69wwfo:119).[11]

Thomas's objection is a telling criticism in that it asks whether action can be sustained towards the achievement of our "historical hopes" if we adopt Newbigin's perspective. Thomas's intuition on this point senses how taut is the tension Newbigin draws between the meaningfulness of present labor for movements of peace and justice and the realism that all the fruit of such labor will become the "rubble" of history. The discontinuity between present labor and future realization would certainly appear to be necessarily the more ultimate and therefore dominant conviction. That in turn would appear to discourage the sort of serious political action Thomas seeks to support. More must be said about this dimension of the criticism presently. But two points must first be made in relation to the way Thomas argues for an alternate vision.

First, Thomas too quickly identifies "eschatology" with the "future." This appears to be his sense of the phrase "eschatology and history" by which he seems to make reference to the future and the now (1984:321). (What he appears to mean about Newbigin is that his position is over-weighted on the "future" side.) But for Newbigin, eschatology is the revelation of the last things, made and begun in Jesus Christ. The reign of God is "now" already, even while it is "yet" to come. His understanding of eschatology molds his view of the meaning of history; it does not stand poised over against history as some sort of alternate to it. History is eschatological. Thomas, by casting eschatology as a "future-oriented" idea ("eschatological hope" versus "historical hopes"), loses this present sense of eschatology and thus fails to view history in terms of the future brought into it already, witnessed by the sign community which is both instrument and foretaste of the presence of the reign of God (cf. 78os: chapters 3-6). His restrained view of the importance of an actual Christian community as the witness to that reign (to be noted more fully in the next chapter) contributes to this difference in eschatological perspective.

Ironically, it is because Thomas does not emphasize "the future brought into the present" that he gives insufficient attention to the future dimensions of the biblical eschatological vision of the "city," the restored human community, the new creation in the form of a new heaven and a new earth. That future dimension is required by the New Testament witness to judgment (cf. 53ch:111-112). Thomas misses the argument of Newbigin which rests on the fact that the New Testament announces a coming "day" on which all of history will be halted by a radical "making new" in the return of Christ. This is what supplies Newbigin with his vision of "chasm."

The chasm of ultimate and final judgment on all the deeds of human persons and societies must be as squarely faced as the chasm of death, which breaks the connection of an individual's history from the progression of world history. Were this more directly addressed by Thomas, he would recognize the "dilemma" of personal and world meaningfulness created by death and judgment that lies at the heart of Newbigin's attempt to articulate the meaning of history.

Second, Thomas expresses his critique from a point of view formed on the basis of a very different starting point from that of Newbigin. His concern to relate eschatological hope to "historical hopes" begins to hint that his fundamental clue to the meaning of history and therefore the meaning of mission (in that order, and not the other way around as is the case for Newbigin) lies in "a real appraisal of the natural and social forces operating in the historical situation" (1984:321). The deliberate choice he is making here is the one between a theological and an anthropological starting point.

> One may start with the ultimate, the Divinum, and come to man's historical destiny. But there is no reason why the historical destiny of the human being, i.e. anthropology, could not be the point of entry for the understanding of man's ultimate destiny in the purpose of God, i.e. his eternal salvation. And there is every reason to believe that in general this latter is the best point of entry today. (1971:9)

In a more recent article on religious pluralism, Thomas underscores even more emphatically that which is most foundational for him: "in our present day pluralistic situation, anthropology understood in its broadest sense is the right point of entry into historically relevant and challenging interfaith theological discourse" (1986:106). It is under the rubric of anthropology that Christology makes its contribution. "The anthropological debates underlying our common search for the historical future of humanity in our technologically united world" present Christianity with the challenge "to restate and reformulate its Christology in the context of Christian participation in the common search for new forms of community" (1986:106).

This difference in starting points Newbigin misses when he expresses his agreement with Thomas's reply to Peter Beyerhaus that "Christian missionary thinking cannot be either theology or anthropology except as either of them is related to Christology" (1971:7). Newbigin's reading of that, which interprets it to mean that "the true starting point of a doctrine of the Christian mission is not theology nor anthropology but Christology" (71rsh:71), misses both the more explicit statement in which Thomas indicates his choice between theology and anthropology and the importance of the conception which he has of Christology, drawn from the tradition of Indian theologians "from Keshub Chunder Sen through Chenchiah and Chakkarai to Paul Devanandan." Jesus is seen as "the Divine Man, or the New Adam, the bearer of the New Humanity, the New Creation" (Thomas 1971:18). The "misunderstanding" which Newbigin had earlier anticipated could arise from Thomas's view — namely, the idea that "it is from the events of the secular world that one learns what God's will for man is" — has its grounding in this anthropological approach (69cmcu:259).[12] Newbigin's own position stands in critique of Thomas's choice. There *is* a reason why "the historical destiny of the human being" cannot be the point of entry. It cannot possibly be known by phenomenological observation and induction because it is future, not past. History cannot itself supply the model for understanding the end and therefore the meaning of history. The end, for Newbigin, can only be known by a revelation from the One "whose purpose it is" to bring it to that end. The gulf is wide between the starting points of Thomas and Newbigin as well as between the paths by which they hope to know meaning and destiny. The path of induction means that eschatology serves a mission fashioned by the aspiration for humanization. The path of revelation means that mission serves an eschatology established by the death and resurrection of Jesus.

We may now return to consider in what ways the force of Thomas's critique of Newbigin must be assessed. It may first be said that it would be unfair to require of Newbigin that he be an "activist" or even possess the "spirit of an activist." His thought must be judged on the merits of the arguments, not on the basis of his "theologian's fear" or any similar thing. The intent of his discussions is to clear away the mental hindrances which would deter Christians from involvement, to enable them to be "free both from the fear of rapid social change and from the idolatry of it" and to work "for the healing of the divorce between the life of faith and the secular world and for the discovery of patterns of holiness relevant to the world in which modern technology has placed us" (62rsce:5). He wishes to give for the mind safeguards against false eschatologies, false paths, and false Christs (cf. 63rtdt:38-51).

In addition, it is important to observe that in Newbigin's own experience he gives evidence of the pastoral power of his vision. The recognition that the "chasm" of death and judgment means that even our best works must ultimately go down into the rubble of history gives a security of hope and confidence which enables work to continue at the very moment of disappointments, failures, and tragedies. I myself pastored a congregation for five years that subsequently experienced a sad and destructive division and finally was dissolved altogether, and for me the realism which promises that my works will become rubble also affirms that for them to join that rubble now cannot negate their value and meaning. Their value lies in their connection to the living Jesus who has himself already descended into the chasm of death and come out on the other side in his resurrection. Far from discouraging action, this is a perspective that encourages it and enables it to flourish in hope, because hope lies in the living Christ rather than in any tangible permanence of our accomplishments. This vision invites us to live in accordance with the words of the apostle Paul: "Be steadfast, immovable, always excelling in the work of the Lord, because you know that *in the Lord* your labor is not in vain" (1 Corinthians 15:58, emphasis added).

This was Newbigin's own experience too. In a sentence which must in its writing have been filled with pathos (as we can detect by reading it against the backdrop of his view of the chasm), he speaks of relinquishing to the rubble of history five years of work fashioning a creative response to the need for identifying and training leaders for the village churches in the Diocese of Madurai: "My successor did not approve of these ideas and the programme was not continued" (85ua:148). He has been able to learn from the rubble of history in a place like Cappadocia, "once the nursery of Christian theology," but now a place where he and his wife had to worship by themselves because "there was no other Christian to be found" (85ua:241). What he has learned from the rubble sets priorities for the vibrant life of the present. On seeing the simple and joyous faith of a newly formed village congregation of which he was not aware until he was taken unexpectedly to it, he reflected,

> I suppose that much of our more impressive work could be easily swept away. These handsome buildings of ours, these magnificent colleges and schools and hospitals which rightly win the praise of the world — they could well be swept away by the hurricanes that are blowing in Asia and the world. But I do not think what I saw this morning could be blown away: it is too close to the ground. (51sid:83)

This personal power of the teaching notwithstanding, the problem remains to be faced. The question of continuity between our action now and our hope in the future plagues every affirmation that acknowledges the reality of the chasm of death and judgment. In the Bangalore lectures in 1941 Newbigin began to approach the problem, recognizing the possible objection that his view would "not satisfy our longing to have a part in a great purpose which really and visibly leads to a goal" (41kgip 4:11). But to dismiss the objection as Newbigin does because such a longing is "egotistical" evades the real problem. If we are personal creatures of a personal God who wills and works to achieve certain purposes, is it not of our nature to wish for fulfillment for the work of our hands? Inherent within Newbigin's thought are better answers, sometimes touched upon. If no "straight road" from our works to the consummation of God's purpose can exist, then help must be supplied by giving more complete definition to the "eschatological continuity" which, Newbigin affirms, does exist.

Newbigin approaches what is needed in *The Open Secret* when he comments that he and his works will be "raised up" and will "take a place in the life of the city" (78os:118). But the grim reminder that "neither I nor my achievements are of themselves fit for the kingdom of God" tends to more than cancel out that prospect (118). In none of the published versions of his vision of the chasm is there as helpful a discussion of this point as there was in the last of the four Bangalore lectures. Parallel to the resurrection experience of Jesus, we will be raised up in such a way that

> all the faithful labour of God's servants which time seems to bury in the dust of failure, will be raised up, will be found to be there, transfigured, in the new kingdom. Every faithful act of service, every honest labour to make the world a better place, which seemed to have been forever lost and forgotten in the rubble of history, will be seen on that day to have contributed to the perfect fellowship of God's Kingdom. (41kgip 4:2-3)

> That perfect society, the fully accepted and accomplished rule of God in men's hearts[,] therefore, is the object of a Christian's hope and longing. And he knows that even though he himself must go out into the blackness of death, and that even tho[ugh] all his efforts for the creation of a better society on earth must in the end be buried and forgotten, yet none of this is lost. In that day it will all be found to be there raised up, transfigured. (41kgip 4:8)

A restoration of features such as these would strengthen Newbigin's case immeasurably. They would serve to give more lively substance to the exhortation he borrows from Albert Schweitzer and sprinkles liberally throughout his reflections, to see in our participation in the world "acted prayers for the coming of the kingdom."[13]

The Interpretation of Contemporary History

"Acted prayers" grow from the soil of a commitment to an interpretation of the meaning of history as a whole. But that interpretation must always apply itself to the current moment in history and become a practical discernment "of what is going on, of what are the issues, of what are the forces at work" if it is to provide any basis for "taking part in the public life." For the Christian, it is not a responsible action to "simply leave a vacuum" in regard to "the effort to interpret current history." Unless history is a "meaningless jumble" and God is not, after all, working out a purpose, "it is necessary to interpret — even if only in very modest, tentative and provisional terms — what he is doing" (69fc:81-82).[14] While "the processes of history" must never be confused with "the revelation of the Kingdom of God," Newbigin counts it as "our business as Christians to understand what God is doing with the world" (60whsl:21).

Newbigin has continuously put his hand to this particular plow. He has counted it a part of the requirement of the gospel that it be "proclaimed afresh and each new day re-interpreted as it must always be in the language of each new generation and each new culture" (72sad:71). But the relationship is reciprocal. Casting the gospel "in the language" must also mean interpreting and challenging the day, the generation, and the culture at hand.

Newbigin's effort to interpret the times through which he was living stands out most vividly in two periods. The first was during the late 1950s and the first half of the "Development Decade" of the 1960s, when the interpretation of the emerging "unitary history" of the world under the impact of the process of secularization became an absorbing part of his theological agenda. During this time he wrote on such themes as "The Gathering Up of History into Christ" (59guhc), A Faith for This One World? (61ftow), and Honest Religion for Secular Man (66hrsm). In these and other writings, Newbigin joined a chorus of optimism in the spirit of that time.[15]

For the ten to fifteen years following that there was a transition phase during which he increasingly critiqued the reflections of that earlier period. In part that was due to the emergence of a more revolutionary mood replacing the "development" hopes of the 1960s and the inwardness of "spirituality" replacing the outward-oriented "secularity" (85ua:252). These new circumstances, as indicated in a published address on "Living with Change" (74lwc) and in his contribution on "Mission and Missions" to the "Recent Thinking on Christian Beliefs" series in *The Expository Times* (77mm), opened the way to the more critical appraisal of secularity evident in writings such as *The Finality of Christ* (69fc) and "The Secular-Apostolic Dilemma" (72sad).

By this time, Newbigin was also experiencing the impact of pluralism upon Western culture. This altered the lines of his interpretation and opened up the second major effort he has made to interpret the contemporary world in light of the gospel. In works such as *Christian Witness in a Plural Society* (77cwps) and "Teaching Religion in a Secular Plural Society" (77trsp) are to be found the seeds of Newbigin's focused attempt in the 1980s and 1990s to foster a missionary encounter of the gospel with Western culture, a project involving a fresh reading of the times.

The movement which this trek represents must, of course, have some relationship to the kaleidoscopic shifts in world events as well as in the moods of the times during which Newbigin's interpretations of contemporary history were made. But in all the range of his thinking, at no other point is there as obvious a vulnerability to being swept along with a current of thought as has occurred in relation to "interpreting the times." Particularly, his "shift in perspective" toward an "enthusiasm for the 'secular interpretation of the Gospel'" in the 1950s and 1960s and his subsequent disillusionment with the conclusions to which that was leading illustrates how risky such interpretation is. Newbigin's assessment that he had become the "easy victim of an illusion" when he failed to see that a "secular" England must become a "pagan" England apart from a seriously biblical foundation shows that he himself is most aware of the dangers inherent in making an interpretation of things "as they are" (85ua:249; cf. 86fg:131-132). This has brought an increasing carefulness to claim for such interpretations no more than is certain.[16]

However, the later realization that he "was partly carried along" by the very currents which in other ways he "fought against" (85ua:252) does not make null and void any or all further attempts to interpret the contemporary history of the world of cultures. To the contrary, the very fact that on this issue Newbigin is again and again willing to be self-critical — more so on this feature of his thought than on any other — and learn from times of mistaken judgment strengthens the possibility that his ability to distinguish the works of God from those which oppose God is a growing one.[17]

It must also be said that Newbigin's efforts to interpret the times are an application of his essential theology of history, not an argument for it. The force of his argument as we have outlined it above does not depend on the validity of his interpretation of a particular current in contemporary history. If his view requires that interpretation be made, it equally requires that it be qualified as but a part of all our public action, which must become the "rubble" of history. His provisional attempts in this regard do play a supportive role in the substantiation of the theory for which he argues. In the sweep of history and the interpretation of the moment to which it has come, there will be "signs which confirm the understanding which is given . . . in the Bible" (69fc:86). But the understanding does not stand or fall on that basis.[18]

The elements of continuity which underlie the changing face of Newbigin's assessment of the meaning and significance of the contemporary scene may best be observed by tracing the various factors which contributed to the rise of his "enthusiasm" for the appreciation of the secular character of the modern world and the factors which moved him on from that perspective to the analysis of the roots of Western culture that later occupied him. By noting the similar impulses at work in these two "shifts" in his perspective, the governing vision beneath the changing applications will come to light.

Enthusiasm Regarding Secularization

The spark that ignited for Newbigin the shift from a decade of focus on ecclesiology to a decade of "thinking about the work of God in the world outside the Church" was occasioned by a 1957 conference of pastors and missionaries at Bossey in Switzerland (85ua:152-153). On the way there by plane, in preparation for his own contribution at the meeting, he read through the New Testament, noting every mention of the "world." The fruit of the study was an essay which argued "that what we are witnessing is the process by which more and more of the human race is being gathered up into that history whose centre is the Cross and whose end is the final judgment and mercy of God" (59guhc:82). While it had the effect of bringing him rather suddenly on board in regard to a growing trend of thought, there were antecedent trends within his own range of reflection that prepared the ground for his entry as a major actor in the discussions which would follow.

The immediate spawning ground for his thinking was his (by then) twenty-year missionary experience in the Indian church. He was full of the unblushing optimism of a decade of life in a united church in a newly independent and postcolonial India. The hope for the future embodied in a succession of "Five-Year Plans" signaled to Newbigin dramatic changes.

> I believe that this great new upreach of vital power which is expressing itself in the whole life of the country — in rural development, in industry and technology, in politics and social change — is in the last analysis the fruit of the meeting of the Gospel with the soul of India. I do not mean only the Gospel as the missionaries have brought it, but the Gospel reflected and refracted in a thousand ways — yes, and distorted too — in the civilization of the West within its literature, its service, its jurisprudence, its political ideas and in many other ways. India is responding to that contact now for the first time with her whole strength. (57tfd)

Never far from Newbigin's mind was the defense of Alexander Duff in answer to those who criticized him for teaching young boys English literature, language, and philosophy: "I am laying a mine which, when it explodes, will blow up Hinduism." The fact that Hinduism had seemed to respond to the blast as an essentially unchanged sandbank became less and less the whole story for Newbigin (61ftow:10-11). The gospel was having a more dramatic effect than had been imagined.

Particularly, it was the element of "progress toward a goal" — symbolized by the Five-Year Plans and embracing as it did a linear notion of time and history — that meant a radical new dynamic was forming in a society whose understanding until now had been dominated by a cyclical view. Before his very eyes he was watching the "dawning of history." This he had observed faintly as he moved from village to village in his early years as a bishop. "One can say that these villages belong to prehistory rather than to history. Or perhaps one should say that they are just emerging into history" (51sid:44). The ancient social fabric remained strong.

> But we are still at the dawn of history here in these villages. A tremendous ferment is at work and it is impossible to predict the future. . . . The Gospel is here present and operative at what looks like a vital growing point in human history. (51sid:48-49)

More and more it would occur to him that the "dawning" was widening in its effect and indicated a momentous change for Indian society. He refers a number of times in his writings of this period to the impression that had been made on him years ago (before he was a Christian) by the book of J. L. Myres which bore the title that provided the necessary image: *The Dawn of History* (59guhc:83; 66hrsm:13). Its first chapter, "The Peoples Which Have No History," focused what was now happening. "Today, these peoples who have no history are being drawn irreversibly into the current of a single world history" (61ftow:26).

So it was that he spoke during this period with an approach inevitably "shaped by the situation as it is in India," giving him "an angle of vision which can enable some things to be seen more clearly than from a purely Western point of view" (59guhc:81; 66hrsm:7-8). From that angle, he saw a special significance to the emerging "single history" which all peoples were understood to be coming to share (cf. 63jsmc:3). If "the people of East Asia," for example, "are being drawn out of their separate pools of existence into the current of a single history," it means not only the technologically facilitated gathering of their "separate experiences into a single history" but also their common experience at the present time of coming into having "history" at all. For them, "a cyclical understanding of human experience is being replaced by an understanding in linear terms," one which sees life "in terms of progressive development, in terms of planning which looks forward to permanent and irreversible changes in the human situation" (60whsl:21). The world's peoples are being drawn into a unitary history based not on any religious faith or ideology but on "a shared secular terror and a shared secular hope," the latter of which was represented by the term "development" (66hrsm:13).

The dynamism which was forging such a unitary history was the process of secularization. Newbigin defined the process as having two aspects:

> Negatively, it is the withdrawal of areas of life and activity from the control of organized religious bodies, and the withdrawal of areas of

thought from the control of what are believed to be revealed religious truths. Positively it may be seen as the increasing assertion of the competence of human science and technics to handle human problems of every kind. (66hrsm:8)

From the Western "Christendom" point of view, the negative side was the most keenly felt. But Newbigin called attention to the difference it makes when the process is experienced from the Indian angle. There the process

> is accomplishing the kind of changes in patterns of human living for which Christian missionaries fought with such stubborn perseverance a century and a half ago — the abolition of untouchability, of the dowry system, of temple prostitution, the spread of education and medical service, and so on. (66hrsm:17)

That is the consequence precisely because "secularization is a process in which men are set free from total envelopment in sacral forms of society" (66hrsm:68). "The effect of this is to destroy beyond the possibility of repair the ancient sacral types of society" (63jsmc:3).

Growing out of the original spark, Newbigin developed the suggestion that "we must interpret" this gathering up of history under the effects of secularization

> in terms of the apocalyptic teaching of the New Testament, in terms of the fact that world history is in the grip of Christ, is being propelled by him towards its ultimate issues, propelled through tribulation and conflict to a final consummation in which the judgment and the mercy of God which are set forth in the Cross are finally and conclusively worked out. (59guhc:83)

Drawing on that insight, he went on to assert that the very idea of a secular order, "a system of thought and practice which lies, so to say, outside of the direct responsibility of religion, but in which the will of God is to be done, is a Christian idea" (61ftow:21). The dynamism within the global process of secularization is "rooted in the biblical faith which understands human history in terms of the mighty acts of God for the fulfilment of his purpose" (66hrsm:51). Therefore, we inherit a new situation in which we have neither a Constantinian "Christian sacral society" nor a pre-Constantinian "pagan sacral society" but a society "which has been secularized irreversibly by the operation of forces originating in the Gospel itself." Whether we may speak of the "vast revolution of expectations" or the "quest for humanization" or the very "conception of a single human destiny," these marks of the present impact of secularization have their roots in the Bible and in the preaching of its Gospel (63jsmc:4-6; 69cmcu:262). While "the force which is drawing all nations into a single history is immediately a secularized Christian eschatology," it is "ultimately the revelation in history of the origin and end of history — namely Jesus Christ" — which forged in the "so-called Christian west" the notions of history and progress which are now having their impact everywhere (60whsl:22-23).

This suggestion, first made in embryonic form at the Bossey conference in 1957, was the germ idea which helped fashion the influential thesis of Arend van Leeuwen's *Christianity in World History* (1964, cf. 16-17). Newbigin picks up that thesis and affirms that he "frankly accepts" it in its "main outlines" (66hrsm:69, 38). Simply put, Newbigin summarizes van Leeuwen's thesis: "the worldwide extension of the process of secularization, which has proceeded with such immensely accelerated speed in the past twenty-five years, is a form of the impact upon the non-western world of biblical history" (50).[19] Specifically, for van Leeuwen secularization is the present form of "the struggle of the prophetic faith in the living God to overcome . . . the ontocratic pattern of society," that pattern which "rests upon a total identification of the orders of society with the order of the cosmos" (28). Thus Newbigin considers secularization to be "an extension of the prophetic attack" on the ontocratic pattern and a "continuation of God's age-long education of man" (76). The Christian then must be able to interpret "the source and character of this dynamic society which is becoming the common society of mankind" and as well be able to show "how it must disrupt the ancient cyclical understanding of human life and raise new questions concerning the nature and destiny of man, questions which ultimately lead to the question of Jesus Christ himself" (63rtdt:45).

Newbigin is always the evangelist. For him, the controlling factor in the advancing of such a thesis as the one he endorses along with van Leeuwen is the measure of its correspondence to the continuing saving purpose of God in the world. The feature of the process of secularization which he especially emphasizes is the effect it has on raising the ultimate question of faith in Jesus Christ. His vision of the soul of India meeting the gospel "reflected and refracted in a thousand ways" moved compellingly to the conclusion of the matter, that is, that "India must surely go on to faith in Christ as the sole Redeemer, or into godless scepticism" (57tfd).

As a process, secularization sets people free. Personal choice and responsibility come into the picture immediately when there is a breakdown of the "ontocratic" pattern by which the religious norms govern the actions. Secularization "requires of the individual man a capacity to take decisions which, in traditional sacral societies, he would not have to take." Therefore secularization is a "summons to greater personal freedom, and to the responsibility which freedom entails" (66hrsm:68-69). The choices made may align themselves to the biblical sources of the ideas and values mediated through the process of secularization or they may "lead to a radical cleavage or even to open enmity," as van Leeuwen points out (1964:333).

These two possibilities provide evidence of the critical fruit of global secularization, in Newbigin's assessment: "the 'de-sacralizing' of great areas of human life is all part of the journey by which God leads the world to the ultimate issue of faith or unbelief in Jesus Christ" (63rtdt:62). This is the current form of "the coming into history of the light by which all men are finally and personally exposed and judged" (66hrsm:69). The results of Christ's coming into the world are being worked out in this process which "places all men in a critical situation, a situation charged with the possibilities both of ultimate salvation and ultimate loss" (61ftow:22); people are led "right to the ultimate issue of absolute surrender or final rejection." So in the present unitary history "the central issues are being determined by the whole complex of ideas which derive ultimately from the revelation in Christ" (59guhc:86-87). Within the biblical picture of the nations drawn into the "one decisive act of judgment and mercy in Christ we are to understand most inclusively the events of our time" (61ftow:24). This does not merely provide the background for mission but is "one aspect of the fact, which the Bible teaches us to acknowledge, that the world mission is the central clue for the understanding of world history as a whole" (59scmt:185).

It is this forcing of the "ultimate issues" to which Newbigin makes reference when he interprets contemporary history "in terms of the apocalyptic teaching of the New Testament" (59guhc:82). Here we find a striking difference between the biblical emphases in the respective approaches of van Leeuwen and Newbigin. Van Leeuwen is right, according to Newbigin, to see in the "prophetic attack upon the ontocratic pattern of society the element in the Bible which makes biblical faith a secularizing agent"

(66hrsm:37). But Newbigin's own choice of the apocalyptic teaching of the New Testament as the primary clue presents a contrast which points to several fundamental elements which Newbigin is attempting to retain.

First, it maintains an important connection to the basically eschatological foundation for the meaning of world history as a whole, based on the revelation of the end of the story in Jesus who is the beginning of that end. Only from the sense of the meaning and end of the whole which is revealed in Christ is Newbigin's specific interpretation of current trends derived.

Second, it ensures that the prophetic attack does not lose connection with its source. He questions (in a way that appears to be directed to van Leeuwen) whether a "truly secular spirit can be sustained if it loses contact with that which gave the prophet his authority to speak," namely a "God who is for man against all the 'powers'" (37). To ground his analysis in New Testament apocalyptic firmly roots it in the revelation of coming judgment and mercy. A solely "prophetic attack" easily becomes a moralism, or worse, a new "law."[20] The breaking loose of the hold on life of ontocratic societies is intended not as an end in itself but as an opening to discover the grace of God in the Jesus Christ who comes again.

Third, the emphasis on New Testament apocalyptic introduces the necessary caution inherent in the warning about "Antichrists."[21]

> Thus . . . history converges towards a single final issue: Christ or Antichrist, the true Saviour of the world, or the bogus saviours who purport to offer mankind final security and well-being in terms which belong to this world, that is to say, which belong to this side of death. (59scmt:185)

The apocalyptic vision points ahead to a "city" which is the gift of God, not a human product. It is in the city, which in the 1960s became a grand symbol of the secular hope, that we find "the place where man's calling to mutual relatedness and man's commission to subdue the earth have their sharpest focus." But the reminder of Antichrist tells us to expect that while "the city is the symbol of man's supreme achievements in 'subduing the earth,'" it is "also the scene of his most horrible perversions of that divine commission" (78os:77).

By 1974 Newbigin would be found observing that "one finds today much less optimism than ten years ago about the process of secularization." It had been assumed that "in due course" the secularization would overtake "the social and religious and cultural patterns of Asia and Africa," but by the mid-1970s that was not so certain (74lwc:19). Several important lines of thought can be traced that show why Newbigin was now doubting the earlier bold assertion that "the relation of every man to Christ is becoming more and more inescapable, more and more inevitable, more and more central" (59guhc:86).

The enthusiasm for the process which secularized and desacralized the world was based on the "illusion" that failed to see that "men cannot live for long in an ideological vacuum" (75rim:27; cf. 85ua:249). It was this weakness which he had begun to critique in his major work having to do with secularization, *Honest Religion for Secular Man* (66hrsm). Newbigin believed that Rudolph Bultmann, Paul van Buren, and John A. T. Robinson all in one way or another had divested the Christian faith of historical or personal substance. Their reinterpretations to account for and speak to a secular age had missed the requirements which that process makes for a meaning-producing faith. Van Buren, by understanding any talk of "God" as expressing a noncognitive "blik" ("view") by which we orient our way of acting, offered a reinterpretation which would "destroy the possibility of a creative Christian participation in the process of secularization" (54-76; cf. van Buren 1963). Bultmann offered personal meaning but without a basis for positing meaning for the whole of history "by the removal of the idea of the acts of God" (44-51; cf. Bultmann 1962). Robinson's assertion that "reality at its very deepest level is personal" alongside the rejection of "the effort to persuade oneself of the existence of a super-Being beyond this world endowed with personal qualities" has the effect of removing "the whole pungency, the whole reality from the Christian experience of God" (88-93; cf. Robinson 1963). It had come to disturb Newbigin that the enthusiasm for secularity was leading in these directions. It gave beginning evidence that to desacralize also tends toward the stripping away of the substance of the very biblical faith which furnished its dynamism. The corollary that as a consequence this destroyed meaningful history and thwarted — ironically — meaningful participation in the process of secularization made this development unacceptable.

In each of the cases just mentioned, Newbigin is noting the loosening of the ties between the "prophetic attack" on all ontocratic patterns and the foundation of authority upon which that prophetic attack was first made, the reality of a personal God. This contained grave dangers which began to point out the illusion of thinking that an "ideological vacuum" is possible.

Specifically I suggest that if the mastery which is given to man through the process of secularization is not held within the context of man's responsibility to God, the result will be a new slavery; that if the dynamism of "development," the drive to a new kind of human society, is not informed by the biblical faith concerning the nature of the Kingdom of God it will end in totalitarianism; and that if the secular critique of all established orders is not informed and directed by the knowledge of God it will end in a self-destructive nihilism. (66hrsm:38-39)

If it is true that "the worldwide spread of the secular world-view which Christianity has brought to the birth is not a religiously neutral event" (61ftow:22), then neither are the responses of the societies which absorb its impact. With increasing precision, Newbigin responded in terms of the most essential answers to the question, "How are we to interpret God's action in history and so learn to commit ourselves to obedient partnership?" (69fc:83).

(a) That which is disclosed in Jesus Christ is the very character and will from which all that is proceeds. (69fc:83)

(b) This disclosure of the character and will of God in the midst of human history is met not by success but by rejection. (69fc:84)

(c) But this is not the last word. . . . Because of his resurrection faith, the Christian will expect and will find that defeat is turned into victory. (69fc:85)

Encounter with Western Culture

In light of that growing critique of the earlier enthusiasm over the fruits of secularization, and upon his return to a "pagan" England in the mid-1970s, Newbigin directly addresses the need for an encounter of the gospel with Western culture, the great purveyor of the secularization spawned by biblical faith which now had lost its own grasp on that faith. That encounter is marked by a clarity about the fact that no area of public life, not even the state itself, "can be completely secular in the sense that those who exercise power have no beliefs about what is true and no commitments to what they believe is right" (86fg:132). All claims to "religious neutrality" notwithstanding, the educational system of even a "secular" state "is not and cannot be religiously neutral" (140). There is not any possibility that a process of desacralizing will create a neutral society, for if nothing else the process brings its own structure of belief. In the case of the West, the strength of its scientific worldview has meant that other "faiths" are relegated to the private realm and allowed no significance for public life.

There are three areas of thought in Newbigin's earlier discussions that show signs of a certain ambivalence, containing unresolved hints which in this later period will gain clarity and give greater focus to the critique of Western culture. The first of these has to do with the specter of cultural domination. On the one hand it is affirmed that "the cultural and political and economic expansion of the white races" has been "halted and reversed" (61ftow:9, 14). On the other, it is said that a "world civilization" has come into being which is "a product of the West" but supposedly a "detachable and potentially independent" product (14). It is acknowledged that the "modern scientific world-view" is really a Western one but it is at the same time construed to be a culture shared somewhat evenly by all societies. To cut loose the process of secularization from its culture of origin blurs the element of continuing cultural domination which happens even in the period following decolonization. The admission that "from one point of view, development might almost be described as the substitution for the traditional cultural values of a set of values derived from western Europe and North America" vividly shows the problem (63jsmc:3). Newbigin more clearly distinguishes the issues involved when he later warns against uncritically adopting "the current pattern of development aid" by showing the similarity between the missionary imposition of a "colonial image" and the current "substitution by the peoples of Asia and Africa of a new hierarchy of values" (65fe:418). The fragility of the very notion of "development" shows the cultural assumptions which lie inherent within it, defined by and in the favor of the "developed" nations of the world (cf. 69wwfo:128-129). While many might have wished to believe otherwise, the "development" of the 1960s followed the basic pattern of the colonial era. "The prevalent values were those of the Western nations" (78os:104). As this perception grew for Newbigin, his language shifted from speaking of the "modern scientific world-view" to a more culturally specific reference to the "Western scientific world-view." The outcome is his "missionary encounter" with that Western culture.

The second area of ambivalence in the early period has to do with the enigma represented by Asia's eager acceptance of Western science and technology while rejecting its underlying philosophy of history. Asia's religions respond with renaissance and its forms of national organization reflect secular humanist ideals, but it seems insulated from infection with the roots of those ideas in Western culture.[22] Newbigin's (and van Leeuwen's) thesis had asserted that secularization moves Eastern peoples from a dominant cyclical view of history to a linear, progress-oriented one. And yet, he notes time and again, Asians eagerly embrace the modern scientific technical apparatus and worldview while maintaining their traditional cyclical view and do it "without even suffering from mild indigestion" (59guhc:81).[23] Even more generally he observes, "Non-western peoples are eager to master every element in the science and techniques of the western world, but almost totally uninterested in enquiring into the roots of the tree on which these fruits have grown" (66hrsm:25).[24] This "paradoxical situation" tends to undercut the major thesis which at that time was being defended. At the very least, it begs for explanation concerning why the Hindu frame of reference so easily detaches the science from the roots of it and accepts the former into its own thinking. Why is monism "more hospitable to the modern scientific world view than is the thought world of the Bible" which gave rise to it?

The answer to this question emerges in Newbigin's more recent reflection on the essential distinctives of Enlightenment culture. He sees as its most crucial element the "abandonment of teleology," the elimination of the idea of purpose (86fg:34-35). The scientific structure fabricated without recourse to purpose is exactly compatible with the Eastern religions which "do not understand the world in terms of purpose" (39). Newbigin's earlier concentration on the Hindu image of the wheel gives way at this point to the image of the dance, "an interpretation of movement and change without invoking the idea of purpose" (39). Here is the clue to the earlier enigma.

If Western scientific culture can be embraced by Asia and leave monism intact, then it is not unexpected that the Western Enlightenment culture should be inclined to gravitate toward a similar monism. This becomes increasingly obvious to Newbigin as he wrestles with the third area of ambivalence to be found in the earlier period. It might be called "the ghost of Christopher Dawson." There is a haunting quality to the scattered references to Dawson's work in Newbigin's writings. In particular, it is Dawson's suggestion that "western civilization, if it lost its living relationship with the biblical faith, could be re-absorbed into the monistic spirituality of Asia" which fascinates Newbigin (66hrsm:50).[25] At first, he indicates that Dawson's prediction "seems much less likely now than it did when Dawson wrote." But shortly after that comment, he turns to support Dawson's contention by reference to the aforementioned enigma of Indians highly trained in science but retaining "the cyclical, non-historical pattern of advaitist Hinduism" (50). He continues in a similar vein when he goes on to say that "it is not fanciful to suggest" as did Dawson that Western civilization could "sink back again into the timeless monism of the ancient pagan religions of Asia" (56).[26]

Newbigin's later reflection more and more sides with the view that Dawson was right. In his 1974 article on "Living with Change" his assessment is that at the time Dawson wrote his suggestion, "it seemed unlikely"; but "to-day it seems an obvious possibility" (74lwc:22). Still later, Newbigin identifies the recent trend toward viewing the Christian story "from the perspective of the general religious experience of mankind" as very much like the choice made in Indian religion. Now Newbigin refers to Dawson's comment as a "prophecy" when he notes, "Contemporary English Christianity, sharing the general loss of faith in a significant future which has followed our loss of a sense of a national role in world affairs, is strongly tempted to go this way" (79cjh:209-210). As the potential for the fulfillment of Dawson's suggestion comes more and more to view, Newbigin becomes clearer about the companionship of Western Enlightenment culture and Eastern monistic culture. This, once again, shows up with force in his observation that both are alike in that they abandon the notion of purpose in their understanding of the world of change.

Implications for a Theology of Cultural Plurality

Newbigin's view of the meaning of history builds on his sense of the missionary significance of the doctrine of election. It adds to the foundation "election" provides for a theology of cultural plurality. The most direct and poignant implication to be gained from his treatment of history emerges in his strong reaction to any suggestion of a "salvation history" *(Heilsgeschichte)* of another character than or in any way isolated from the natural, secular history of the world. He at times can use a phrase such as "salvation history" in fairly neutral terms (e.g., in 77mm:261). And his view that the clue to the meaning of the world's history lies in the series of "acts of God" recorded in the Bible, whose center is the life, death, and resurrection of Jesus, certainly puts him in the stream of those who speak in these terms about the strand of history in which these acts of God took place. But he is continuously sensitive to the implications of viewing that history as of a special character over against (above?) the unfolding of the rest of the history of humankind.

By the "acts of God," Newbigin is careful to note, he does "not mean, certainly, a series of events which are separable from the whole fabric of human history, a *Heilsgeschichte* which is separate from the history of the world. No such separation can be made, for the whole fabric is woven from one piece" (66hrsm:51). He is quick to "safeguard" his identification of God's "saving acts" with the "one particular strand in world history" involving God's people by pointing out that in doing so he is

> not implying that that is something which exists or can be understood in any kind of disjunction from world history. It is part of world history, that part from which we understand the whole. It is the clue to world history. . . . [T]he special story with which [the Bible] is concerned is in no kind of isolation from the rest of the world's history but is bound up with it. (61ftow:80)

Secular history is not "mere background for the story of the Church," nor "mere scenery for the drama of salvation" (63rtdt:24). What election makes clear is that the history of God's acts and God's people bears universal salvation for the world "precisely in its concreteness and particularity," that is, its occurrence as part of secular history (61ftow:81).

For Newbigin, only such a substantial identification of the history of salvation with the history of the world for which it is intended can provide the clue for understanding the multiplicity of the world as a coherent whole (69fc:65ff.). It can only be "an illusion" to speak of "two kinds of history — sacred and profane, salvation history and secular history" (86fg:61). That illusion fuels the withdrawal of theology into the private sector of the modern public-private dichotomy (69). This withdrawal is complete if salvation history is "portrayed as something quite distinct from the ordinary history depicted by secular historians and immune from their critical investigations" (48).[27]

Newbigin preserves a determined historicality regarding the personal disclosure of God in the particular acts by which his saving purpose for the world becomes known by the way of election, one chosen to bear it to another. Such a thoroughgoing historicality is the only way to unite into one the meaning of the whole history and at the same time protect the integrity of each particularity. Newbigin finds in the notion of a separate "salvation history" an emphasis on its universal "otherness" which removes from particularities their relevance and meaning. He feels the same tension that C. S. Song mentions when he asks of Oscar Cullmann how "the nar-rower redemptive history and the universal process come into interplay? How are they related? Are there mutual interactions between them?" (1982:24). Song has difficulty with Cullmann's "principle of election and representation," because Cullmann leaves it unarticulated in missiological terms and thus fails to show that one strand of history is chosen to bear salvation to others. Therefore he rejects as a "caricature" Cullmann's image of a "straight-line God" (which is Song's caricature of Cullmann's view! 1982:25) and prefers to speak of a "historical pluralism" of histories and meanings of history (1975:30ff.). This essentially follows the same path that Chenchiah took in India when he suggested that Hinduism be the Indian Christian's Old Testament. But this approach breaks the total sense of meaning in another direction. It maintains the significance of particularities but strips from them all the possibility of bearing significance for the meaning of history as a whole. Some other source than the events of history must be found, then, if any such universal meaning is to be had. That can only lead back to idealism.

Newbigin stands between the classical biblical theological approach and the Asian theological approach and offers a view which holds radically to both the integrity of particularity (and with it the meaning of individual persons) and the potential for universal meaning. By doing this, he roots the Christian mission neither in a "symbolic" representation of a universal principle of salvation (as does, e.g., Pannenberg, 1977:36-41) nor in a diffused presence of God's creating power (as is the case for Song, 1975) but in the public, secular announcement of the end and meaning of the story of which all of us are a real and meaningful part (cf. Newbigin 69fc:46ff.). The basic authority for the Christian mission, and by virtue of that an essential element in Newbigin's theology of cultural plurality, is to be found in the form of a personal "commitment to a belief about the meaning of the whole of human experience in its entirety," which makes "a claim regarding the entire public life of mankind and the whole created world," and which is shared in a community which is "a movement launched into the public life of mankind" (78os:17-18).[28]

To this set of observations must be added several further implications for a theology of cultural plurality which are indicated by Newbigin's approach to historical meaning.

1. In the essay in which Newbigin has most directly and fully attempted to outline his theological approach to "Christ and the Cultures," Newbigin includes as the centerpiece his clarification of the two fundamental assumptions regarding historical meaning which represent the "great divide" (78ctc:16). He knows that the attitude taken toward them must play a determinative role for the assessment of cultural plurality and the framing of a theological and missiological approach to it. His choice in favor of the possibility that "certain events" may "have a unique significance for the entire story" opens the way for a theology that both offers a universal gospel and respects the uniqueness of cultures.

2. Newbigin's descriptive presentation of death as the final threat to meaning — the meaning of the world or the meaning of the person — provides the foundation for qualifying and relativizing all cultures. The judgment coming, which shows itself already in the fact that all our achievements must go into the chasm of death and join the rubble of history, testifies that "culture is not an ethically neutral entity" (cf. 78os:161). Culture itself is not an evil. But because it is a human product it bears the marks of the human propensity to resist and undercut the rule of the creator of the world. The correction of culture comes as present and future historical meaning are bound together in "communion with the Person" (74lwc:27-28) who has gone before us across the chasm and meets us from the other side in his resurrection life. A "commitment to the Purpose" he bears means we will value cultures as treasures which belong to him and in sober realism refuse to allow them to become idols. We will work instead for their transformation on the pattern shown us in the secret entrusted to us for the world. Thus we can "live in commitment to ceaseless change and yet remain truly human" (74lwc:28).

3. The importance Newbigin places on a determined historicality must have an impact on how we do theology and how we appreciate its conclusions. History, and God's self-disclosure in it, are the foundation for coming to know "how things are."

We do not begin to understand how things are unless we understand how they were and how they will be. Our so-called eternal truths are the attempts we make at particular moments in the story to grasp and state how things are in terms of our experience at that point. They are all provisional and relative to time and place. (78os:92)

This is the only way open to us if the source to which we look for universal meaning is "certain events which have significance for the whole" rather than to a "general religious experience" by which we intuit and/or induce "eternal principles" that are the meaning of the world of change and multiplicity. It is also the nature of knowledge which is personal, given by revelation in time and location by one whose personal character and will has formed the meaning and end of history. Theology is then of the nature of "testimony" (83os84:50).

4. This understanding of the theological task sets certain conditions for a Christology constructed in view of cultural plurality. First, the church "must be continually in earnest about re-examining its own tradition, seeking to grasp it afresh in terms of its new and expanding cultural experience." In that regard, the specter of "syncretism" must always be faced, especially in the West at the present time. Second, the church in every place "must do its Christology in fellowship with other churches, giving and receiving correction and illumination." Third, such "ecumenism" must maintain a widened range: the church "must do its Christology in dialogue with those who inhabit cultural worlds outside of the Church," which is implied by the affirmation that the secular announcement in our hand belongs to the Lord of history and it interprets its bearers as well as the ones to whom it is born (78ctc:21).

CHAPTER 5

Conversion and Community: The Boundaries of the Church

Conversion as Boundaries

It was never within Bishop Newbigin's normal pattern of expression to speak in terms of the "boundaries" of the church. In fact, he was always eager to undo the tendency of the church toward a "corporate egotism" which sees mission solely in terms of its own "preservation and extension" as coterminous with God's work in the world. He is careful to remind the church that "God's saving work is always spilling over far beyond the bounds of the Church" (72sad:71). The church's mission is such that by its calling to exist for the rest of humankind it must always be the "beyond bounds" people, offering its gospel to those outside. Therefore, "there will be no fixed boundaries because God's saving purpose in Jesus Christ is not limited by our membership rolls" (73snhc:10). He prefers to define the church by its "centre" rather than by its boundaries, first because "to say exactly where the boundaries of the church lie" is "difficult" — even "impossible," and second because to attempt to define them exactly "always ends in an unevangelical legalism" (80sk:68).

But Newbigin is far from the attitude that the issue of boundaries is unimportant or that the call to personal conversion — the crossing of the boundary — is inappropriate to the mission of the church. In the vivid image he frequently uses to illustrate conversion, Alice, of "Through the Looking-Glass" fame, is found gazing at the mirror which bounds her own world from the one on the other side. "The resurrection," Newbigin suggests,

> is rather like that mirror. It is the boundary line between two worlds: in one of them everything leads up to death and death is the end; in the other everything starts from death and death is the beginning — and there is an infinite vista of new possibilities which we can only guess at. (68bima:17)

Likewise, in full view of the challenge of Hindu reaction to it, he affirms the concreteness of the Christian community as a people who make "extraordinary claims" (67srd:10), and that the visible, historical character of the church necessarily brings into the picture the issue of boundaries.

This issue has found its way to center stage in several important discussions in which Newbigin has been involved. In the ecumenical arena of the mid-1960s, he and others wrestled with the relation of conversion to the "rapid social changes" of the day and the requirements of Christian discipleship and mission in regard to them. Particularly important in that debate are his article on "Conversion" (66c) and his books on *Christ Our Eternal Contemporary* (68coec), *The Finality of Christ* (69fc), and *Honest Religion for Secular Man* (66hrsm), much of it written in response to the views of Paul Löffler (1965, 1967a, and 1967b), Kaj Baago (1966), and Emilio Castro (1966). The debate stimulated a bit later by M. M. Thomas's *Salvation and Humanisation* and carried in part on the pages of *Religion and Society* moved more and more toward the issue of "koinonia" and the relationship of conversion to the visible form of the church (see pp. 280-282 in this volume). During the 1970s, Newbigin's attention shifted toward the issues of culture and plurality and in that context he again addressed the issue of conversion, particularly in "Context and Conversion" (78cc), *The Open Secret* (78os), "The Centrality of Jesus for History" (79cjh), *Sign of the Kingdom* (80sk), and "A British and European Perspective" (86bep). Most clearly in this later period, conversion came to be seen in its important connection to the issues raised by the "missionary encounter of the gospel with Western culture" into which Newbigin had thrown himself (83os84; 86fg).

It is in the context of the latter discussion that Newbigin most boldly puts the question to which all of these discussions speak. In his most complete statement of the "encounter" *(Foolishness to the Greeks)*, he arrives at the most critical point in the case he makes and there lays bare the way in which the boundary issue emerges:

> The argument hitherto leads to this preliminary conclusion. In the missionary encounter between the gospel and our culture, the first party will be represented by a community for which the Bible is the determinative clue to the character and activity of the one whose purpose is the final meaning of history. The boundary between this community and the society for which the Bible is not determinative is marked by the paradigm shift that is traditionally called conversion. (86fg:61-62)

This "paradigm shift" is a movement to a new "plausibility structure" that is viewed as granting a "wider rationality" than that provided in the regnant plausibility structure of the culture — the scientific worldview that leaves out of the picture the matter of "purpose." Therefore, those who by conversion "belong to this community inhabit a different plausibility structure from that of their contemporaries" (62), a fact which marks the boundary. Necessarily involved in "the missionary encounter of the gospel with the modern world" is a call to this sort of "radical conversion."

> This will be not only a conversion of the will and the feelings but a conversion of the mind — a "paradigm shift" that leads to a new vision of how things are and, not at once but gradually, to the development of a new plausibility structure in which the most real of all realities is the living God whose character is "rendered" for us in the pages of Scripture. (64)

It is obvious from these comments that Newbigin's view places the issue of "boundaries marked by conversion" in a crucial relationship with his core understanding of the nature and life of the church. A visible communality, therefore, forms an essential feature of his ecclesiology. As well, the relationship of the Christian community to the societies it lives in and among must rest on such an understanding of its "conversion" origin. Mission, therefore, depends on an appreciation of the significance of the boundaries of the church. Further, the numerous and intricate cultural and intercultural "encounters" in which Christians and their gospel are involved on a daily basis hinge on the perspective taken about boundaries. It is the purpose of this chapter to show the ways in which Newbigin's view of conversion has a formative impact on these issues. It will not be difficult to observe in the process how his view rests on his understanding of the "missionary character of election" and the meaning of history which derives from it.

In Tension with the Local Culture

Whether in the face of "the dogma that all religions are the same, and that therefore conversion is either meaningless or wrong" — a notion so resilient within Hindu thought (68coec:84) — or in response to "conversion as an ecumenical problem" (Löffler 1967a:252ff.), Newbigin has steadily maintained that "the calling of men and women to be converted, to follow Jesus, and to be part of his community is and must always be at the center of mission" (78os:136). His starting point for such an assertion is the teaching of Jesus as that is paradigmatically represented in the first chapter of the Gospel of Mark. The "announcement of the coming Kingdom" and the immediate appeal to "repent, and believe the good news" provides definition for the "radical decision" pressed by the presence of Jesus (65fe:148-149).[1]

Newbigin takes the Greek word *metanoein* to specify in the New Testament what we mean by conversion (in this he follows Paul Löffler, 1965:95-96). Drawing and amplifying upon the Old Testament notion of "turning" *(shuv)*, in which terms the prophets (including John the Baptist) called on God's covenant people to "re-turn" to their loyalties and obedience, the New Testament issues a call to make a "U-turn of the mind" (80sk:70; 86fg:58). Given its context in the framework of the announcement that the reign of God is present in Jesus, "conversion, then, means being turned round in order to recognize and participate in the dawning reality of God's reign" (69fc:96), "the true future of the whole creation" (65fe:149).

While, because of its Old Testament connections, the biblical concept of "turning" must be seen as having "primarily a collective connotation" (Löffler 1965:97), Newbigin's understanding has always incorporated the essentially personal character of conversion. The fact that the prophetic call to "return" is "addressed to the people as a whole does not exclude but leads on to the idea of its applicability to the individual," as the Old Testament idea of a believing remnant makes clear (66c:310). This personal quality is made vivid in the introduction Newbigin gives to the last of his 1966 addresses to the Christian Medical College at Vellore. The issue of conversion arises as the topic of that lecture, he says, because "there comes a point at which a decision has to be made, a commitment has to be made" (68coec:81). He concludes the series with a personal appeal to his listeners: "To be converted means for you, I think, to let Jesus have the last word in regard to your life, to let him have the full surrender of your life, to let him have the key that unlocks the inner chamber of your house" (93). For Newbigin, conversion always involves as one of its "intrinsic elements" an "inward turning of heart and mind," an "inward relationship of faith" (69fc:98; 66c:312).

Newbigin sees this inward, personal dimension predominantly in cognitive form. In his later writings, he introduces the use of Thomas Kuhn's notion of "paradigm shift" as "an analogy — and no more" for describing the personal adoption of "the new way of understanding the total human situation in which the Cross is seen to be the power of God and the wisdom of God" (78cc:4; cf. Kuhn 1962). This, Newbigin says, "is the result of a radical shift of perspective which is called conversion" (78cc:4). Such language makes obvious what has been true all along, that Newbigin sees as the fundamental character of conversion that it consists in a mental revision of the ways things are perceived "to be." So in *Foolishness to the Greeks* he is careful to point out that conversion is one of the mind and not just of the will and the feelings (86fg:64). Thus, at the most basic level, conversion has to do with the most assumed aspects of a person's cultural "givens," the frames of reference by which the world is seen to "make sense."

This inner marking of boundaries is complemented by a still wider and tangibly external range of cultural change implied in Newbigin's notion of conversion. Along with "personal commitment," conversion involves both "a pattern of conduct, and a visible fellowship" (68coec:92). Tangible actions from within an actual community lie inherent within the "Follow me" which comes on the heels of "Repent and believe." The implications of the last part of the triad — "a visible fellowship" — will especially concern us in the next section of the present chapter. But it is essential at this stage to underscore the importance to Newbigin's view of the second dimension of the content of conversion, which in many ways forms the connecting link between the inward and communal dimensions. "Biblically understood," he insists, conversion means being so turned round that one's face is towards that "summing up of all things in Christ" which is promised, and of which the resurrection of Jesus is the sign and first-fruit. It means being caught up into the activity of God which is directed to that end. (65fe:149)

Here is the second half of the turning to "recognize and participate" in the dawning reality of the reign of God. "Conversion in the Bible is the turning of a man to Christ so that he may become a partner in Christ's work and a witness to God's Kingdom" (65fe:421). The converted one is "turned" towards being a "participant in and an agent of God's reign" (69fc:112). "Truly understood, preaching is the announcement of God's kingdom, and conversion is conversion to its service" (65fe:421).

Mingled together in those affirmations are both ethical and missional facets, both participation and agency in the reign of God. In regard to each, Newbigin is concerned to stress that true conversion is never only an inward and personal, mental and religious, "U-turn." It always has real sociocultural consequences. Tangible patterns change. The repatterning of lived life must occur, and this unavoidably has a boundary-marking effect. Such is the intent of his assertions about the necessarily ethical character of conversion. To "participate" in God's reign means making "a total break with both personal and 'structural' injustice" (80sk:31). The call to conversion is "a call . . . to behave differently here and now in all sorts of private and public responsibilities" (66c:311).

> There cannot be a separation between conversion and obedience. To be converted in any sense which is true to the Bible is something which involves the whole person. It is a total change of direction which includes both the inner reorientation of the heart and mind and the outward reorientation of conduct in all areas of life. (78os:150-151)

That the call of the gospel is "a call to concrete obedience here and now" means that the response to it must take concrete, culture-fashioned form.

By holding to the essential ethical nature of biblical "conversion" Newbigin wishes to avoid the possible assumption that conversion is only an inner, religious phenomenon and, therefore, has no necessary outer form. Such an idea would seem on the surface to guard against any imperialistic imposition of culture-specific norms on the variety of the world's Christians. It would seem to foster freedom and mutual acceptance. But it leads instead to a greater vulnerability to the more deadly force of the status quo. If a relationship to Christ is "purely mental and spiritual, unembodied in any of the structures of human relationship," then it is "liable to be influenced by all the accidental — and potentially sinful — facts of human cultural and political life" (69fc:106-107). The older error of thinking that conversion is "a purely inward religious experience which does not intrinsically and of itself involve certain decisions about conduct" finds no real "correction" in the suggestion that there are "two conversions," the second of which follows as "a later diaconical decision based on other supplementary theological principles." Both ideas have in common that they fail to see in the one conversion of which the Bible speaks the power to produce change precisely in the social context where unity and reconciliation are needed (69fc:93).[2]

The strength of Newbigin's concern to see conversion as a religio-ethical unity and avoid the conception that it is "a purely religious phenomenon separated from its social context" is most obvious when he critiques Emilio Castro for maintaining a "remnant of the wrong idea" even while giving a refutation of the "two conversions" suggestion (69fc:94-95; cf. Castro 1966).[3] Newbigin points to Castro's argument that "the liberation of the children of Israel from Egypt" is what "makes conversion possible" for them. This, according to Newbigin, preserves the view that conversion is inward and religious, unconnected to the social nexus. His own correction of the picture — construing the earlier belief of the Israelites while still in Egypt (Exodus 4:30-31) as their point of conversion — fails to offer anything different since Israel was simply called at that earlier time to receive God's act of deliverance on their behalf, not to rise up and throw off their oppression. Castro's point does not suggest a bifurcation between religious conversion and social responsibility but conversion as a response to God's redeeming initiative.

What, then, accounts for the severity of Newbigin's critique, which functions here with such a fine-toothed comb? It can only be attributed to the strength of his concern to maintain the unity of a conversion large enough to respond to the challenges made by those looking elsewhere than to Christian conversion for the resources to enable the transformation and humanization hungered for in the modern world. For this, the church must be recalled from the tendency by which it has "interpreted conversion as if it was simply a turning towards God for purposes of one's own private inner religious life, instead of seeing conversion as it is in the Bible, a turning towards God for the doing of his will in the secular world" (66hrsm:101).

But immediately, another potential problem surfaces. The affirmation of conversion's ethical quality may yield a tendency to become legalistic by imposing requirements which strip conversion of its character as grace. This may happen in the case of a view such as that of Paul van Buren, who, Newbigin says, sees conversion only in ethical terms. The idea that the essence of conversion is entirely captured by the phrase "I intend to behave in the following way" fails to explain sacrificial and costly "intentions" and "behaviors," and it gives no place for the most distinctive of all Christian behaviors, "forgiveness of one's opponents." The denial of a real foundation for action in the inward commitment to a living Person can lead only toward a purely ethical and therefore legalistic path. "All conversion has an ethical content, but conversion is an event which is more than its ethical implications. To deny this is to leave the order of grace and freedom and to go over into the world of legalism and bondage" (66hrsm:70-74; cf. van Buren 1963:126-134).

The problem looms larger than just in relation to the denial of the reality of the inward and spiritual character of conversion, however. The strength of Newbigin's affirmation of the ethical dimension of conversion and the concretion of a new pattern of sociocultural behavior requires that he respond again and again to the many ways in which this emphasis tends toward legalism in one or the other of its many forms. Missionaries themselves can fall into this trap when they have "in effect identified conversion for practical purposes with the abandonment of whatever appeared to the evangelist to be the moral evil in the situation" (e.g., polygamy, 69fc:73; cf. 78os:15lff.). Likewise, we become "victims of the law instead of bearers of the gospel" whenever we allow a separation between a commitment to the cause indicated by the ethical patterns of conversion and the commitment to the person who is the foundation of the ethical pattern (80sk:68-69). This, in fact, is the reason Newbigin uses the expression "patterns of conduct." He wants to ensure that conversion is seen as a new pattern "and not a law." The New Testament, he says, "doesn't impose a whole new complicated legislation, but it does give patterns, pointers, suggestions of what it means to be converted" (68coec:89).[4]

The concrete action which conversion implies includes also a missional facet. The one who "participates" in God's reign is also its "agent." Conversion is "the turning of a man to Christ so that he may become a partner in Christ's work and a witness to God's Kingdom. It is the enlisting of men in God's service for the fulfillment of His purpose for the world"

(65fe:421). This becomes obvious in the case of the earliest disciples. From the Gospel accounts of their callings we can learn "first of all, that the call is addressed to all; secondly, that those whom God actually converts are few; and thirdly, that those whom He converts are converted not for their own sake but for the sake of all." His pledge to make them "fishers of men" meant that they were going to "sound the same call to conversion" which they had heard (68coec:87). They issue that call not in the confidence that it will prevail by a weight of argument but knowing its credibility to be "as much a matter of faithful endeavor and costly obedience as of clarity and coherence of argument" (86fg:64), an understanding which links the missional and ethical facets of the "new pattern."

The tendency of the church to understand its calling and election as privilege instead of responsibility precipitates for Newbigin the concern that here also there not be a misapprehension of the force and intent of conversion. He wishes to avoid the self-centered approaches to conversion that relate it only to personal salvation or to self-aggrandizing extension of one's own church rather than to a commitment to God's mission. Of conversion he says,

> It is not, *in the first place,* either saving one's own soul or joining a society. It is these things only secondarily, because the new reality is one in which every soul is precious, and because there is a society which is the first-fruit and sign of the new reality. (65fe:149)[5]

This fact must have a bearing on what we think about so-called church extension. Mission cannot be defined as a mere "reproduction of the church from which the missionary came" (65fe:147). Conversion is not "the turning of a man to Christ . . . simply to increase the size and power of the Church" (421).

In Tension with the Missionary Church

It is this mission facet which surfaces the most critical issue for a theology of conversion that attempts to seriously account for our culturally plural context. If conversion means an essential paradigmatic shift and active revision of ethical living patterns — that is, it involves the altering of culture-fashioned aspects of the way persons perceive and act — and the already converted possess a mission role to call all humankind into such "conversion," then how is that mission not an audacious, arrogant, and proud enterprise? As Newbigin recognizes, "To claim finality for Christ in this sense is to imply a summons to men to forsake other claims to ultimate loyalty and to be converted to him. This is the point at which the claim seems actual and threatening" (69fc:87). How can this fail to alienate by an ethnocentric imposition of the culture of the converted upon the cultural heritage of the not yet converted? In other words, if we do not land in an ethical legalism — whether in the form of a pietistic moralism or an ideological idealism of the right or the left, then do we land in an ecclesial imperialism, an extension of the church as a form oriented toward the preservation of the benefits and privileges of the already converted? In both cases, the problem is a cultural domination of one person or group by another which absolutizes what is itself relative and subject to the judgment of God. How can this be avoided while maintaining such a notion of conversion as Newbigin describes?

This way of putting the question identifies the concern that lies at the foundation of Newbigin's "conversion" discussions. It is not surprising that the path by which he chooses to resolve the dilemma is tightly interwoven with his sense of the missionary character of election and the implications of that "biblical doctrine."

The first way in which Newbigin responds to the challenge of cultural imperialisms is to underscore what has already been anticipated. Mission, for Newbigin, grows out of the knowledge that "one is chosen to be the bearer of the message [in this case, the call to conversion] to another." In the context of the conversion discussions, Newbigin refers to this principle by using "the phrase we have all become accustomed to using," *pars pro toto*, the part for the whole (66c:313; cf. Löffler 1965:98 and 1967a:260; Weber 1963). Following Löffler, Newbigin grounds this principle in Jesus' deliberate choice of a representative "twelve." "Jesus didn't just issue a general invitation and the number of acceptances happened to add up to twelve" (68coec:87). The twelve, it must be acknowledged, "in some sense represent Israel" (69fc:97). Both Löffler and Newbigin apply that sense of representation to the relation between the church and the world.

But on this point Newbigin moves beyond Löffler in that he asks with more incisive precision just what is meant by that "representation." In what sense may we say that the twelve — and thus the Christian community of which they are the embryo — stand as *pars pro toto* in regard to the world? It is critical in this connection what the word *pro* is taken to imply. "Does this little preposition mean 'with a view to,' or 'instead of'?" Newbigin decidedly favors the first, "the sense that [the Church] is sent in order that the rest of the world may be converted" (69fc:97). To him, the meaning seems "quite clear" in the text of the Scriptures: "the words 'You did not choose me, but I chose you' are immediately followed with 'that you may go and bear fruit'" (66c:313). Thus he quotes with favor Löffler's comment on the eschatological tension contained in the phrase, which works against "the sense that the rest of the world is adequately represented by the Church and needs no conversion" (69fc:97): "The temptation with 'conversion' has often been to short-circuit this very eschatological tension, either by reserving it for the few who are saved, or by letting it be submerged in a universalism which does not recognize any form of definite commitment" (Löffler 1965:99). Newbigin refuses the kind of universalism that Löffler thus describes.[6]

Yet, Newbigin finds some evidence in the Bible that "the other meaning is not altogether excluded" because "God's plan of salvation is not limited to the visible fellowship" (69fc:97).[7] This dimension of the way the Church must be seen as a "part for the whole" is taken up in a later discussion regarding "The Form and Structure of the Visible Unity of the Church" (73fsvu). He offers there a "working definition" of the church as "the provisional incorporation of mankind into Jesus Christ." With this definition Newbigin emphasizes that the church, as "the 'first-fruits' of the harvest which is intended to include all men," gathers to worship "as the representatives of all mankind." This he takes to be the reason why the church cannot — and must not — see itself as a "private or sectional organization." That the church is representative in this sense means for Newbigin that it must refuse to withdraw into "the status of a *cultus privatus*," to which modern Western culture tends to relegate religion. It must choose to live as a *cultus publicus,* an *ecclesia theou,* as did the early church within the Roman Empire (126-128).[8]

Newbigin is also emphasizing that the church which is "first-fruits" can only be the "provisional" incorporation of humankind into Christ. This is true in that its membership is "only a small part of mankind" which it represents. Because of that, the church cannot as yet "reflect in its forms the full richness and variety of mankind" which it is destined to do (73fsvu:128).

While he acknowledges that this more universalist meaning of representation is not altogether excluded, he does insist that the church's functional and instrumental character of representative service for the whole of mankind does not negate its own incorporation into Christ as a real "communion with God." It shares now in the "end" which it representatively signifies as God's plan for the whole of creation. Only because it is genuinely "first-fruits" can it also be representatively a "sign and instrument" (73fsvu:129).[9]

The definition Newbigin explicates here — "the provisional incorporation of mankind into Christ" — remains very ambiguous in his discussion of it, and it is even more so in light of things he says in other places. It has on the surface of it the feel of a statement which might be made by a proponent of the view that since the church represents humankind in this way, conversion is not then needed by all but is sufficiently supplied "instead of" them. It would seem to imply that, representatively, all humankind is, in some sense other than "potentially," actually "incorporated into Christ." But this contradicts his meaning elsewhere. Conversion and incorporation remain inseparable for Newbigin. Incorporation into Christ is by means of conversion, which is always "conversion to Christ" (cf. 78os:156). This is required if the church is to maintain the sense that it is the "sign . . . of God's new creation" and "not the whole of it" (69wwfo:119), while at the same time knowing that it is a "sign of the Kingdom only insofar as it continually points men and women beyond itself to Jesus and invites them to personal conversion and commitment to him" (80sk:68).

Newbigin's definition here must be interpreted in light of the full range of his common and pervasive language about the church. That which describes the resurrection of Jesus ("sign and first-fruit") describes also the converted person as well as the church collectively (65fe:149; 66c:322). Newbigin constantly calls the church the "earnest (arrabon), first-fruits, foretaste, sign, servant, witness and instrument" of "God's purpose, plan and mission regarding the whole world."[10] That "purpose" he frequently specifies: The church is the sign and instrument of "God's Kingdom, his new creation, his new humanity, his purpose to unite all things in Christ, his total plan of salvation for the world."[11] Both the focus, which lies on the church as the sign of the "purpose" of God, and the care with which he clarifies that the church cannot be equated with the product of that purpose, the "Kingdom, new humanity, new creation," show a manner of thinking which does not lead to seeing the part as "in place of the whole" but rather "in order that the whole may be converted" (66c:313).[12]

The church's proper view of its missional identity is the beginning of an answer to the challenge of cultural imperialism. The part is placed in service to the whole. Newbigin adds a second — and ultimately more determinative — response to our question. It also bears the impress of the election frame of reference. Whether in the Old Testament *(shuv)* or in the New Testament *(metanoein)*, "conversion is the work of God. It is He who turns the heart again" (68coec:85). Jesus comes in the spirit of Old Testament prophecy and "converts." "He actually went out and as it were laid hold of people and turned them round so that they faced His way. . . . In this sense of the word their conversion was His work" (66c:313). "A visible community takes shape by his deliberate, individual and concrete acts of calling" (69fc:96-97). That perspective Newbigin has found to be confirmed in his own experience and the experience more generally of the church. He affirms the soundness of Roland Allen's "central thesis" that "it is the [Holy] Spirit who brings about conversion" and equips and guides the church thus brought into being (78os:146). Every conversion "is a fresh act of the Holy Spirit" (69fc:104), a "free and supernatural work of the Holy Spirit" (78cc:6). The Spirit works sovereignly (78os:146, 154; 62clu:26).

Nowhere does Newbigin press this issue as forcefully and relentlessly as he does in the text of the 1978 Church Missionary Society Annual Sermon (78cc). In that address he begins by calling for the proper starting point for the cross-cultural expression of the gospel, which can never begin with the "context" unless we wish to end in the realm of law instead of grace. We must start with conversion, the "radical shift of perspective" which brings the church into being. And that shift "is strictly speaking not a human accomplishment at all but a supernatural work of God." This new perspective "you don't choose; you are chosen" for it. Those thus chosen are distinguished only in that they are made "the *locus,* the place from which the total human situation is seen in a new perspective," one which "so radically questions the accepted perspective of the surrounding culture" (4-5).

From this he draws out essential implications. The church, by its calling, is made the "*locus* of that miracle by which the paradigm shift which we call conversion happens" (78cc:6). But it is neither the author nor agent of conversion, which remains a miracle of the Holy Spirit. The body owes its life to the Spirit, but the Spirit is not "domesticated" within it. This is the point Newbigin makes in critique of Ralph Winter's explication of what he sees to be the two structures of God's mission, "modalities" — the church, composed of those nominal Christians who make a first-level church-membership choice — and "sodalities" — the mission, composed of those who have made a second-level commitment to be engaged in God's mission (6ff.; cf. Winter 1974). The most important line of critique Newbigin wishes to make (and in the presence of the very mission society which Winter takes to be one of the prime examples of his "sodality" structure!) is that the key to mission is not, as Winter's view would imply, the level of commitment and the ensuing strategy of highly efficient mission structures or programs of "contextualization" (13). Rather it is the action of the Spirit. A survey of conversion experiences shows that the variety among them is great: "there is no one road by which men come to Christ." Our words and deeds are given a place, but "conversion is truly a work of God." From the evidence he has seen, Newbigin can only conclude that "there is no direct proportion between the organised efforts of missionary agencies and the actual event of conversion" (7). The *locus* — but not the cause — of such conversion is the church

> where through the faithful following of Jesus by ordinary men and women along the way of the Cross the situations are created where the Holy Spirit can do his own sovereign work of bearing witness to Christ and bringing men and women to conversion. (12)

This theme has important consequences for the question we have raised about imperialisms. First of all, it makes it "crystal clear that mission is not simply church extension, but that it involves something more radical, more paradoxical, more costly — a kind of *kenosis* which is an echo of that from which all Christian mission begins." Newbigin draws insight on this matter from his personal reading of the "original documents" of the controversy surrounding Robert di Nobili, an early Jesuit missionary to India. Di Nobili's approach illustrates the way the church in mission must refuse to see itself as the cultural embodiment of the form which every newly converted Christian community must bear. In contrast to those who were extending "the Portuguese Church" by gathering out individuals from the Indian world "to remove them to the Christian world" represented by the mission station, di Nobili chose to be "present within Hindu India, present with all his powers," to form there a new community to be "the first-fruit for Christ of Hindu India in all the fullness of its culture and spirituality" (65fe:147, 150). Out of such an emptying into a culture, Newbigin is convinced,

> God is able to raise up something which is not a reproduction of the
> church from which the missionary came, but a new creation — the first-
> fruit of a whole new community remade in Christ, a fresh adumbration
> of the new life in Christ in the idiom of this people. (147)

The gospel, in this understanding, must be *given into* another culture
with the trust that the Holy Spirit will fashion the form which both conversion and the church must take (cf. 78os:146-147). "The given structures
of society in any historical situation," therefore, "will be those which shape
the structures of the Church." Provisional though the acceptance of those
structures may be, to accept them is "entirely congruous" with the church's
"proper character as the provisional incorporation of all mankind into
Christ." It must not be forgotten that two principles operate together in
this regard. Discerning the proper structures for the church in any place
must be done both "in relation to the actual structures of human society
as they are today" and "from within the given reality of the Church," a
reality "rooted in a certain history" (73fsvu:129-133). Newbigin's stress on
the first of these two is prompted by the frequent and easy identification
of the present form of the church as that which must be assumed in every
new setting in which the church takes root. That route can lead only to
legalism and imperialism.

Only from the perspective which looks for this "fresh adumbration"
of the gospel in each new culture into which it is given can the danger of
"domesticating" the gospel within one's own culture be avoided.

> It is of the essence of the specifically missionary task that it involves
> crossing over into another human situation, in which the Gospel has to
> be articulated in the terms of that situation. . . . Without this, the Gospel
> becomes too easily denatured by a process of domestication. (63rtdt:43)

The temptation is an old one, to rely on "the pressure of the law to mold
new churches into conformity to Christ" (78os:147). The earliest church
was confronted with such an issue in the matter of the Gentile converts
(Acts 11 and 15). Rather than being made into "mere extensions of
Judaism," they were fully received in terms of their own uncircumcision
(69fc:104-105). "The churches in Corinth and Ephesus and Rome were not
to be mere extensions of Judean Christianity. The gentile converts were not
to be Jewish *Assimilados*" (103). This was decided because of the prior

decision of the Holy Spirit evidenced by the conversion of Cornelius. In the face of that, "the church has to keep silence. It is not in control of the mission. There is another who is in control, and his fresh works will repeatedly surprise the church" (78os:67).

What has been said here about the form of the church as it arises in new cultural settings must be said also about individual conversions in every setting. Newbigin claims for every "fresh work of the Holy Spirit" in conversion, especially as that occurs for one who hears the gospel communicated across cultural lines, a necessary and "radical discontinuity" with all former expressions of Christian discipleship.[13] He maintains "the possibility of a certain radical independence of the newly converted over against the old" if conversion is to be true and not merely "an act of my religious imperialism" (66c:320). Just as there is "no one road" leading to conversion, so "the precise character" of the paradigm shift we call conversion "will vary with circumstances" (79cjh:209). Newbigin applies this, for example, to the special case of the industrial worker, the content of whose conversion "will be determined by what we believe to be God's purpose for industrial life" (65fe:149). Given the potency of the practical circumstance, he asks whether it is not so that converts in any given social situation

> can develop into a living Christian community with their own leadership conforming to the language, style and culture of their community, or whether they have to emigrate from their culture, attach themselves to one of the middle-class congregations in the neighborhood, and depend permanently for leadership upon men trained in the style of a typical English college or seminary. (80sk:66)

This discontinuity could not, of course, be absolute without creating a virtual *apartheid* separation of churches, as Newbigin admits occurred in the case of di Nobili (69fc:105). "There is a visible historic chain all the way." Jesus "trains and sends out apostles. They go to the nations, make converts, ordain elders. But it is never *merely* a visible human chain. The Spirit is sovereign" (62clu:26). Therefore a tension must always emerge. "Every conversion is a particular event shaped by the experience of the convert and by the life of the Church as it is at that place and time" (69fc:91). The question which must always remain open for debate is "What elements of continuity are necessarily involved between the old community and the new convert?" (105). That is because

There will always be, and there should be, a tension between that element
of discontinuity which is created by the fact of true conversion and the
element of continuity without which there is no Christian Church. . . .
It is useless to try to remove the tension involved by trying to deny either
side of it. The Church grows and justifies its claim to have the clue to
history only by living with this tension. (108-109)

This tension is especially pressing when it comes to the ethical content
of conversion. The critical question becomes "Who has the right to decide
the ethical content of conversion at any time or place — the evangelist or
the convert?" (78os:152). If the church bearing the gospel has that right or
the evangelist preaching it "presumes . . . that he knows in advance and can
tell the potential convert what the ethical content of conversion will be,"
then the "virus of legalism" has a place to enter and the mission "has become
simply church extension." In such a case the missionary has become the
"lord over the gospel instead of being its servant." Newbigin illustrates this
point with the example of the early converts in Uganda, where the missionaries were certain that "the abandonment of polygamy was an indispensable
element in conversion." But the converts saw in their conversion more a
call "for humility and for willingness to share the work and the hardship
of the poor" and a break with the system of slavery (cf. John V. Taylor
1958:45-49). This and similar examples lead Newbigin to assert, about
polygamy or any other matter: "I deny an absolute identification of conversion with a particular ethical decision." Anything other would introduce
law in place of grace and enforce a cultural imperialism (66hrsm:73-74;
78os:152-155).

The compelling insight which Newbigin maintains by this approach is
that there must always be a reciprocal relationship between the prior Christian community and the new convert in such matters. While admittedly the
church "very much" determines the content of conversion for the new convert, "every true conversion is a new creative event which — in principle —
may call in question the existing life of the community" (69fc:109). Therefore,
"conversion does not mean *simply* being incorporated into the given community." It may "carry as one of its consequences profound changes in the
structure of the community," as, for example, the conversion of the Gentiles
did regarding the early Christian community (104).

As would be evident to anyone acquainted with the writings of Roland
Allen, Newbigin depends very heavily on his thought. He strongly concurs

with the thrust of what he calls Allen's "passionate, sometimes irritating but usually inescapable argument" on this issue of continuity and discontinuity, which he identifies as the "central issue" to which Allen devoted himself (69fc:107ff.; 66c:320ff.). Newbigin draws upon Allen's quest for what makes up the essential *"tradendum."* Newbigin states cautiously that he might not accept Allen's "clear cut lines" and would not say as Allen does that all but "the Scriptures, the Sacraments of baptism and the Lord's Supper and the Ministry" are to be "excluded" (66c:320-321). But he finds the issues well drawn. And he declares that in his own experience of evangelism he has seen

> how the gospel can spread and living churches can be multiplied and grow if one is willing to refrain from imposing Western patterns of ministry and training, and to allow those whom the Spirit touches within the life of village communities to develop styles of leadership congruous with the native culture. (78os:146)

That is enough to convince him that "Allen's central thesis is true."

Here we have an enlargement on what Newbigin means when he says that it is impossible to fix the exact "boundaries" which do and must lie at the point of conversion. The boundaries, such as take form, are not fixed ones. They are provisional, as is the church itself. Newbigin invites us to live at the intersection of two tensions. The first one arises when we understand that conversion is a boundary because there is a radical discontinuity between the former way of seeing and acting and the new pattern in Christ. But it is not an absolute discontinuity, for conversion is always a lived, concrete reality which can never be divorced from some culture, some way of living. Therefore, the old pattern and the new are in tension. The second tension has to do with the fact that to be in Christ means that from the outset there is a radical discontinuity between the new convert born of the Spirit and the Christian community which presented to that convert the witness of the Spirit. This discontinuity is not absolute either. That is because the witnessing community, at least in part, fashions the new conversion, as does also the culture from which the convert comes. Both forces are at work in the form which the conversion takes. Neither does so absolutely, or else there will be a denial of the Spirit and of the integrity of the new relationship to Christ, either by syncretism on the one hand or legalism on the other.

It is within this framework that Newbigin formulates his fundamental explanation of the intricate relationship between gospel and culture as

> a continually developing relationship within a triangular field of which the three points are the local culture, the ecumenical fellowship repre-senting the witness of Christians from other cultures, and the Scriptures as embodying the given revelation with its center and focus in the person of Jesus Christ. (78os:172)

Within this field the two types of tension I have mentioned intersect. Within it, also, conversion may be affirmed as "boundaries," construed with sensi-tivity to the cultural plurality of human existence and thus able to expel the arrogance of legalism and imperialism and at the same time maintain the testimony of the Spirit to the biblical call to a U-turn of the mind and life.

Boundaries as Community

The continuity of the new convert with the prior Christian community is at issue in two of the missiological points of view with which Newbigin interacts most deeply. Represented by M. M. Thomas and Donald McGav-ran, the two perspectives are in many ways widely divergent, as Newbigin recognizes (78os:149-150). But regarding the points on which Newbigin most forcefully debates their views, there is a remarkable similarity. Both, in essence, are attempting to carve out a place for the cultural freedom of the convert (and the community of converts which forms in a given cultural setting) vis-à-vis the prior existing Christian community.

A certain companionship exists between Newbigin's orientation toward the sovereign freedom of the Spirit and independence of the convert, which is drawn so vividly from di Nobili and Allen, and the approaches of both Thomas and McGavran. Thomas's call for a "Christ-centred secular fellowship outside the church" (1971:13) is an attempt to find the "form" of the church most contextually appropriate within the heart of a society experiencing the humanizing renascence of its ancient religious traditions under the impact of secularization. With the amendment that di Nobili "separated sociological realities entirely from renewal in Christ" by not reckoning with the seriousness of caste divisions — an amendment not far distant from Newbigin's concern about di Nobili's virtual *apartheid* approach — Thomas associates himself with di Nobili's "experiment of forming the Church within the Hindu community" (1972:73-74). On the other hand, McGavran, by the use of his "homogenous unit principle," encourages the gathering of new converts into the church in such a way that their freedom to "form" that church in terms of their own cultural traditions is allowed and maximized. A primary part of his rationale for facilitating such freedom and independence in the fostering of "people movements" is the articulation of Paul's missionary methods by Roland Allen (McGavran 1981:135-137).[14] Newbigin affirms the similarity between McGavran and Allen in their common conviction that "missions have been wrong in their insistence that it is their business to impose on younger churches ethical standards laid down by the sending churches as an essential part of their work" (78os:146; cf. 144-157). So in both cases, for both Thomas and McGavran, the critical principle of freedom from cultural imperialism and from the legalism attached to it is of primary concern. What Newbigin calls for, with his view that conversion is a sovereign work of the Spirit, these two are attempting to fashion. Each in his own way is simply carrying Newbigin's basic principles to practical conclusions.

It is also not unimportant to observe that both of these men share Newbigin's background in India, one as an indigenous and ecumenical lay theologian and the other as an expatriate evangelical missionary. But their different experiences there have caused them to deal with very different facets of the Indian social setting, and their differing approaches lead to models of mission that tend toward mutual antagonism and even "condemnation" (cf. 78os:147, 149). In fact, the internationally known institutions with which each has been associated (the World Council of Churches and the Fuller Theological Seminary School of World Mission) represent to many people the polar opposites in mission. They have come to be paradigmatic figures for the widest sort of diversity on the current missiological landscape.

This difference between the two makes all the more important Newbigin's interaction with their views. These two viewpoints move in sharply divergent directions from a commonly endorsed beginning principle. They represent twin examples of the effort to make radical application of Newbigin's own thesis. His interaction with each, therefore, provides a unique illustration of the intricacy which Newbigin identifies as an unavoidable feature of the relationship between conversion and culture (cf. 78os:155, 165, 166).

These discussions become illuminating especially because they show Newbigin in response to movements on the extreme provocative edges of what he himself has enunciated as the proper approach. They show how he believes Thomas parts company with di Nobili as well as how McGavran and Allen "lead out into sharply diverging lines of action" (78os:147). As a consequence, the range and scope of his principles are clarified and we are shown their necessary limitations. Here we can expect a kind of refinement that is either not possible or not evident in abstraction.

As we take up each of these "debates" — for which Newbigin promised "there will always be room" (69fc:105) — we will especially note the course taken in regard to the continuity of new convert and prior Christian community and the view of culture and the church on which it is founded. In the process, we will observe several important features of Newbigin's ecclesiology which emerge from his view of conversion. The Thomas debate will highlight his view of the necessity of the church and, therefore, the priority of the church for mission in word and deed. The McGavran discussion will emphasize his view of the unity and, therefore, the ecumenical form of the one church in a culturally plural world.

Continuity with the Past

The so-called Thomas-Newbigin debate grew out of long years of appreciative association with each other (cf. 85ua:73; Thomas 1969). Newbigin's assisting role in the inauguration of the Christian Institute for the Study of Religion and Society with which Thomas was associated from its inception in 1955 (85ua:145), the deep involvement each has had in various facets of the work of the WCC, and their common efforts to stimulate the theological and missiological reflection of the Indian church have made them frequent companions. Their mutual respect has given them freedom for critical and creative interaction on the most pressing of issues.

In the late 1960s and early 1970s they drew each other into dialogue on the issues with which this chapter is concerned, conversion and community.[15] The debate emerged from discussions which each had begun to have independently. At the Mexico City 1963 meeting of the Commission on World Mission and Evangelism (CWME), Thomas had begun an exchange with Hendrikus Berkhof on the subject of "the form and content of the salvation which Christ offers men in the secular world" (Löffler

1968:10; cf. p. 13, n. 2). Paul Löffler urged that the dialogue be carried forward in print, and it was under his editorial guidance that that was done (Löffler 1968). Newbigin's contribution to the *Festschrift* for Bengt Sundkler (69cmcu) offered an assessment of that dialogue.

On the other side, Newbigin had given an address at the Nasrapur Consultation of the National Christian Council of India (NCCI) in March 1966. His contribution on the subject of "conversion" stood over against the position of Kaj Baago, whose article published that summer (Baago 1966) drew out the lines along which Newbigin would engage the issue further (66c; cf. 69fc, chapter 5). Thomas entered that discussion while carrying forward the matter of salvation in the secular world with the publication of his book *Salvation and Humanisation* (1971). Because he took issue with Newbigin at several points in the book, Newbigin gave it an extensive review in *Religion and Society* (71rsh) and the debate was on. A published exchange of letters (72bck) and other material which never made it to publication produced a vivid display of the pregnant issues touching "conversion and community" (see pp. 280-282 in this volume for notes regarding unpublished materials in the debate). While the debate proper soon dissipated, the issues raised have continued to receive the attention of each (cf., e.g., Thomas 1986).

The major theme of the debate, the nature of *koinonia* and the forms of the church (Newbigin 69fc:102, 105ff.; Thomas 1971:38), may best be approached by beginning with Newbigin's response to the challenge of Baago concerning whether "membership in the visible fellowship" is integral to conversion. Newbigin here faces a question that brings to the fore and challenges the third element he says is involved in conversion, "a visible companionship" (69fc:96; 66c:312). If the purpose of God cannot be identified with the "aggrandisement of the community," as his case against a "church extension" model has shown, "in what sense, then, is 'membership in the visible fellowship' integral to conversion?" (69fc:102). Is baptism, incorporation into a Christian organization, the acceptance of the label "Christian," and the adoption of the traditions and customs of the "Christian community" required for one to "belong to Christ"? (102, 105f.; cf. Baago 1966:331). Or, as Newbigin has summarized Baago's question, "Does a Hindu have to become a Christian in order to belong to Christ?" (66c:316). Newbigin finds it easy to set aside Baago's tendency to load the question by assuming a lot of "colonial baggage" in the word "Christian" (69fc:106). But the question itself raises more fundamental issues. They are essentially of the same character as the challenge faced by the whole perspective based

on the biblical notion of election, a challenge issued in its most direct form
against the claims made by the Christian church in its mission: "Can you
really think that you, of all people, are entitled to invite the whole world
into your fellowship?" (61icd:21; cf. p. 12).

Newbigin's basic affirmation in this regard carries the same weight
that he placed on the personal and ethical dimensions of conversion. "This
inward turning immediately and intrinsically . . . involves membership in
a community" (69fc:96). "The New Testament knows nothing of a relationship with Christ which is purely mental and spiritual, unembodied in any
of the structures of human relationship" (106). The essential confession of
every new convert embraces belief not only "in the finality of the revelation
of God in Jesus Christ, but also in the necessity of this community as part
of the response to that revelation" (91). If the biblical description of "conversion" as Jesus introduced it early in his ministry is to be followed, it must
be so. For it is a "visible community" which takes shape because of the
deliberate, concrete and sovereign call of Jesus which converted the first
disciples, and every disciple thus converted is placed in it (96).

Turned another way, the question asks about mission strategy: "Does
fidelity to Christ require us also to try to draw men into the fellowship of
the visible church?" (69fc:100). All that Newbigin says about refusing to
adopt a church extension model would seem to lead to a negative answer
and give preference to unselfish service to those outside the church. But to
say that conversion must not be a mere extension of the church does not
mean that it does not include incorporation into a visible community.

> True conversion involves *both* a new creation from above, which is not
> merely the act of extension of the existing community, and *also* a rela-
> tionship with the existing community of believers. The real question is:
> What is the relation between these two? (107)

This was the issue in the important case of Acts 15. The outcome did not
only affirm that the model of extension was being refused and the Spirit's
freedom beyond the existing church was being acknowledged. The Gentiles
were baptized and fully embraced. "While there was no question of making
the gentile converts mere extensions of Judaism, they were certainly incorporated into a visible and definite community" (104).

It is in respect to Newbigin's affirmation of the necessity, in true
conversion to Christ, of participation in a visible Christian fellowship and

Baago's apparent denials that "the Church is essential" that Thomas enters the debate. His concern is to raise the question which lies between these positions, the question concerning "what form the Church should take." He criticizes both Baago and Newbigin for "confusing and mixing" the two questions (1972:70). Because of that, Newbigin, he believes, "misses narrowly" the most crucial issue, that of "the transcendence of the Church over religious communities, which makes possible the Church's taking form in all religious communities" (1971:38). The debate which ensues is a real one precisely because Newbigin's treatment of Baago's challenge had included his strong caution against the "domestication" of the form and structure of the church and his affirmation of the "radical independence" of the new convert, and there can only be mutual rejoinder between he and Thomas because they both wrestle with the limits ("boundaries") of the independence of the newly converted. They jointly pose two questions: What lies within the legitimate range of choices regarding the form of the church in any cultural "place"? And, what necessary continuity must that form bear with former choices made in other parts of the Christian community? The result is a struggle to define more closely what is the *tradendum*. How is it identified with or differentiated from that which Allen enunciated? Is there more or is there less which must comprise the essential "givens" of genuine "belonging to Christ"?

The answers offered to these questions hinge on the way each responds to the three interlocking issues which emerge as the crucial ones in the debate, especially in the interests of a theology of cultural plurality. The points on which they struggle have to do with (1) the relation between the "new humanity" and the "church"; (2) the relation between "freedom" and "transcendence"; and (3) the relation between "religion" and "culture." A survey of their interaction on each issue will bring to light their tendencies on the question of the *tradendum* and illustrate the implications for a theology of cultural plurality in Newbigin's thought.

1. Thomas is right when he says that the relation of the church to the new humanity is "the crucial issue of difference between us in our understanding of the Church" (1972:72). He insists that Newbigin does not take seriously enough his admission that the church cannot be identified with the new humanity and that the new humanity is the wider reality (1972:72; cf. Newbigin 71rsh:72-73). Newbigin, to him, "seems to think that Church is the 'substitute' for the New Humanity" (1972:72). Newbigin responds to Thomas's challenge to show where he sees "the new humanity in Christ

outside the Church" (Thomas 1972:71) by pointing to a passage in *The Finality of Christ* (69fc:83-84), which he implies Thomas has missed in his "scan" of Newbigin's writings (72bck:75-76). More importantly, he suggests the place where the greatest depth of divergence lies with a telling, if unpursued, observation: "I think that much of the difficulty of our debate arises from the fact that this phrase is being used in a number of different ways" (76).

In the debate as a whole, the extent of the difference of meaning the two attach to the phrase "new humanity" is never clarified. But it lurks in the background and obscures the discussion on many other points. It seems to be this which Löffler picks up and asks them to address. He argues that different New Testament Christologies are attached to different New Testament approaches to mission. He sees especially two: a *basileia* orientation and a salvation orientation. He links to the first Thomas's reference to a "Christ-centred secular fellowship outside the Church" and to the second Newbigin's formulation of a company of people "at the centre of this saving purpose" (Löffler 1973:1-2). But this distinction of ecclesiologies — a kingdom "team of messengers who spread the news of the beginning kingdom" as over against a salvation-oriented "clearly recognizable community of the church" — neither clarifies nor resolves. On the one hand, it would seem more appropriate to relate Thomas's "secular fellowship" to the salvation motif with its concern for making whole the land, its social structures, its justice and peace — in other words its humanizing dimension. On the other hand, the kingdom motif stresses yielding loyalty to God over all other rivals, which would tend in the direction of an explicit community and the breaking of solidarities. Newbigin himself denies the link Löffler suggests between his view and the salvation theme by showing that his view of the church grows in direct relationship with the kingdom orientation. The presence of the kingdom is attached to the call to follow Jesus. Therefore, "the creation of concrete human community bound to Jesus is the *immediate* implicate of the announcement of the kingdom" (73ck:1). He quotes Pandipeddi Chenchiah, an earlier Indian theologian, to illustrate "the ultimate absurdity of attempting to drive a wedge between Church and Kingdom." Chenchiah asserts that the day of Pentecost was "a fatal day to the Kingdom, and a glorious day for the Church" (quoted by Newbigin from Christopher Duraisingh 1972:17). But "if this is so," says Newbigin, we would obviously "have to push the fatal day farther back and say that it was a disaster for the Kingdom when Jesus called men from their work and said 'Follow me'" (73ck:3).[16]

If Löffler's paradigm is inadequate, at least his probing underscores the lack of sufficient common definition of underlying differences. The real difference lies in the phrase "new humanity," which was never clarified in the debate nor made central to it. It was too easily assumed that it meant essentially the same thing to both parties. But that was not so. For Newbigin, the new humanity is that to which God is moving the world of his creation as the consummation of his reconciling and saving purpose. It focuses upon the ultimate destiny of humankind in the final restoration and summing up of all things in Christ. But for Thomas, the phrase appears rather to focus upon the maturing (evolving?) nature of what it means to be human in the current process of historical development. It is not a destiny of which we have the first fruits now so much as the reality which is now in operation and maturing toward its ultimate expression. A fundamental difference in eschatology is again at the foundation of the disagreement (cf. the previous discussion in chapter four). Each shares some elements of the eschatology of the other, but the picture with which each functions is very different. Hence Thomas sees much more presently realized "new humanity" than does Newbigin. Newbigin sees a much more tangible future dimension of the realization of it than does Thomas.

The most problematic dimension of this ambiguity lies in Thomas's insistence that "koinonia," biblically speaking, "does not refer primarily to the Church or the quality of life within the Church, but that it is the manifestation of the new reality of the Kingdom at work in the world of men in world history" (1971:19). Newbigin's exegetical challenge on that point is echoed by Alfred Krass, who joined the latter stages of the debate (71rsh:76; 72bck:75; Krass 1971:1; Krass 1972b:1). Thomas's protests (on the claimed authority of John A. T. Robinson and Christopher Duraisingh) can do little more than add a precarious "common sense" reading of Colossians 3:10 (1972:87-88). But that hinges on an undefended identification of New Testament language regarding re-creation and renewal in the image of God with the process of humanization Thomas observes in contemporary India. Herein lies the crux of the matter. Thomas makes a convincing case that in India,

> when the idea of religious fellowship in Christ, of the Christian congregation, led to the idea of a secular fellowship in the total village or the total college community, humanisation was already at work. It soon had its impact on the larger Indian society. (1971:12)

But he equivocates without arguing the connection by equating an observable manifestation of a process of humanization with the "new humanity" which is God's goal and the "final destiny of man" (cf. 1971:18). Why the current manifestation is to be taken as the "goal" and not merely a fruit of the outworking of the goal through the identifiable Christian community is not clarified or defended. For Thomas to conclude, "Salvation itself could be defined as humanisation in a total and eschatological sense" sets his notion apart from Newbigin's. This has a confusing impact on the debate in that the difference is never sufficiently clarified.

2. The second major issue in the debate is the relation between "freedom" and "transcendence." The latter is Thomas's word (used variously and, therefore, confusingly at times in the debate). He argues for "the transcendence of the Church over religious communities" (1971:38). His first principle upon which he founds that idea is that the New Humanity, that is, "the humanity which responds in faith and receives the liberation of Jesus Christ as Lord and Saviour" is transcendent over the church (1972:71).

> Once we acknowledge that the Christ-centred fellowship of faith and ethics transcends the Christian religious community, are we not virtually saying that the Church can take form as a Christ-centred fellowship of faith and ethics in the Hindu religious community? (1971:40)

For Newbigin, to ask the question does not answer it, as it appears to do for Thomas. He answers from the perspective we have noted, that the form of the church is a matter which has continual freedom and must of necessity be subject to the full range of cultural dynamics in a particular setting, including prior religious ones. It must be open to the surprises the Spirit brings. But that "radical independence" is possessed by the "Church," and that must be properly understood. The freedom itself is rooted in the nature of the church as a radically social, historical, visible, actual community. Therefore, it is unclear to Newbigin what could be meant by the transcendence of the Church "over religious communities."

> There seems to be a kind of spiritualisation of the Church here which I cannot accept. I think that the Church cannot escape from the fact that it is an institution which shares many of the characteristics of other human institutions (including the tendency to be more concerned about

its own self-aggrandisement than about the purpose for which it exists).
I do believe that the Christian faith is, in a sense, transcendent over other
faiths. . . . But I also believe that this Christian faith has to be embodied
in an institution which is a human institution among other institutions
and cannot claim a kind of "transcendence" which sets it free from the
limitations and temptations which beset all institutions. (71rsh:75)

Well into the debate Newbigin confesses, "I still feel that you are really
docetic in your thinking about the Church. You seem to envisage a form
of Christian corporate entity which never has existed and which never could
exist" (72bck:78).

Newbigin's ecclesiology persistently drives against any approach
which does not give full place to the essential historicality of the church.
The charge of docetism which he makes against Thomas's view is echoed
in his critique of John Macquarrie's book, *Christian Unity and Christian
Diversity* (76aopa; cf. Macquarrie 1975).

There is a curious docetism about the argument of this book, the suggestion that, because unity has an aspect that is inward and spiritual, it
follows that the visible and historical forms which unity must take can
be dismissed from consideration. (76aopa:297)

But "we are not discarnate spirits," he says. Biblically described, those who
are in Christ are "incorporated in a visible and recognizable company of
people who break bread together and in this act are made participants in
his life" (297, 296). Similarly, in the earlier and most complete exposition
of his ecclesiology, he raised the same caution regarding the tendency of
Protestant theology since the Reformation. While he does not there use the
word "docetic," that is clearly the implication of his remarks:

The Reformers have given us an intensely dynamic conception of the
Church. . . . The obvious defect in this conception . . . is that it gives
no real place to the continuing life of the Church as one fellowship
binding the generations together in Christ. It makes of the Church
practically a series of totally disconnected events in which, at each
moment and place at which the word and sacraments of the Gospel are
set forth, the Church is there and then called into being by God's creative
power. (53hg:48)

He illustrates the problem by reference to the paper by Karl Barth in the pre-Amsterdam 1948 volume on the church. Barth, he says, takes this dynamic doctrine "to almost this extreme point" in which Newbigin's self-acknowledged "exaggeration" has stated it. Barth's oft-repeated phrase "The congregation *(ecclesia)* is an event *(Ereignis)*" leads Newbigin to conclude that "the eschatological has completely pushed out the historical." In Barth's view "there seems to be no place in the picture for a continuing historical institution, nor for any organic relation between congregations in different places and times" (53hg:48-49; cf. Barth 1948).

Newbigin, then, refuses any sense of "transcendence" for the church which would remove it from the necessities of actual historical life, and this cannot but mean that it will be an actual, recognizable fellowship. What becomes clarified during the debate is that Thomas's sharp reaction, which appears to work against that notion, is due to the particular character of "religious community" in the Indian context. Thomas agrees with Newbigin that this ghettoizing communalism which Christianity has inherited in India "was forced upon it by the religious communalism of Hinduism" (1972:88; cf. Newbigin 72bck:78). But he insists that an approach is needed which will not reinforce but "break the traditional communal pattern of religious life" (1972:88; Krass affirms that idea, 1972b:1).

Thomas's suggestion that Newbigin is not as keen on achieving this does not mean that Thomas himself is immune from the problem. The rationale for his "secular fellowship within the Hindu religious community" argues from the acknowledgment that the Hindu as well as the Christian religious community is a "socio-political-religious" whole, and he seeks a fellowship which can remain within that "solidarity" (1972:73). Newbigin points out that the nature of such a proposal makes it obvious that Thomas also supports the sustaining of a communally knit "unity of religious, cultural and social bonds" (72bck:77-78).

3. This is the point at which the third major issue in the debate becomes relevant. Newbigin would not object to Thomas's desire to break down the communalist pattern which segments off ("privatizes"?) the Christian community. His difficulty is more with the strategy by which that is proposed and Thomas's failure to account in a clear way for the relation between "religion" and "culture." Thomas believes that the transcendence of the Church over religious communities makes possible "the Church's taking form in all religious communities" (1971:38). The critical question which Newbigin asks is about the meaning he attaches to the word "reli-

gion." One of the two concrete examples Thomas gives concerning what he is proposing, the "Christ-centred Secular Fellowship" of those involved in "the struggles of societies for a secular human fellowship," fails to convince Newbigin because merely being "open to transcendent forgiveness" does not demonstrate "Christ-centredness." The people concerned would certainly deny such a designation (72bck:76; cf. Thomas 1972:70, 72). The second example speaks of "adherents of other religions . . . who have gone beyond the recognition of Christ as the Ideal to the faith-response, however partial, to Him as Person as 'decisive for their existence'" (Thomas 1972:72). This "Christ-centred Fellowship of Faith in Hinduism" cannot avoid, however, the implications of such a "faith-response," whatever the degree. This case is "totally different" from the first, according to Newbigin. It is a fellowship which is "religiously separating itself decisively from Hinduism" (72bck:77).[17]

Newbigin challenges Thomas on the point of claiming that the "Christ-centred fellowship" he envisions within Hinduism is "within" it religiously as well as otherwise. He questions whether this is "sociologically realistic." A form of the church which breaks no solidarities is impossible if there is genuinely an explicit link of faith in Jesus. If someone is religiously, culturally, and socially a Hindu and

> at the same time, his allegiance to Christ is accepted as *decisive*, as — therefore — over-riding his obligations as a Hindu, this allegiance must take visible — that is social — forms. He must have *some* way of expressing the fact that he shares this ultimate allegiance with others — and these ways will have to have religious, social and cultural elements. (72bck:78)

Thomas's own distinction between "religion" and "faith" includes the recognition that faith "always expresses itself in Religion. . . . Religion always changes its form to express the central Faith" (1972:70; cf. 1971:40). If that is so, he should concur that a "Christ-centred faith" within Hinduism will express itself in that religion of which it is a part and the result will be disruption in some form (cf. Newbigin 72bck:79). Newbigin makes that case by pressing Thomas on the example of di Nobili. He employed the principle which has been typical in Christian movement across cultural and religious lines, namely that the "specifically religious elements in the total socio-cultural-religious complex" were distinguished from the rest. In di

Nobili's arguments with the Franciscans, he "distinguished between practices which were religiously neutral and those which implied a religious
belief incompatible with the Christian faith" (72bck:80).

This would lead to an unspoken criticism of Thomas's view as very
quietistic. It becomes conservative, in the long run, to imagine or support
a form of the Church within Hinduism which would not be disruptive on
this point. Newbigin warns of this when he guesses at the sectarianism
which a proliferation of such movements, disconnected with one another
or other expressions of the church, might produce. In a hundred years,
might there be "a litter of small Indian sects embodying in a fossilized form
the particular ideas about secularisation, dialogue etc. which happen to be
fashionable just at the moment?" (72bck:81).

The critical problem lying behind these issues is the definition given
to the "slippery" word "religion." Thomas follows Paul Devanandan in his
definition, which emphasizes the cultic practices and communalist expressions which faith makes (1972:70; cf. Devanandan 1983:10-13). In that
sense a new faith might conceivably not alter those external forms. Under
that definition, culture as well is less than holistically conceived but speaks
of the veneer of behavior which expresses the religion formed by the faith.
In Newbigin's definition, however, a holism regarding culture as "the total
way of life of a people" informs his understanding of religion as well. It
involves elements of the culture which lie at its very heart. It connotes "those
beliefs and practices which are concerned with what we believe to be ultimate and decisive" (72bck:80). His definition reflects more a cultural anthropology than a theological or philosophical one. The former is essential
for laying foundations for a theology of cultural plurality. Thomas, on the
other hand, has allowed his theological distinction between faith and religion to lead him to an understanding of culture and religion which is
problematic.

When all of this has been said, it is that part of Newbigin's review of
Thomas's book with which Thomas did not take issue (regarding the nature
of evangelism, Thomas 1972:74) and which, therefore, was little discussed
in the debate which followed, which contains one of Newbigin's most
important critiques of Thomas's suggestions. His two points, which we have
seen are integral to his understanding of conversion, are "(a) The Gospel
is greater than our grasp of it; (b) The human situation is more varied and
complex than any generalisation of ours can cover" (71rsh:78-79).
Thomas's proposal is in danger of missing these points by making of

"humanisation," a generalization of the need of our time, an absolutizing of the gospel. It may not represent the particular need of thousands in this time, and it may not represent what in another time must be stressed. In other words, to make it the gospel is to overparticularize and domesticate what can never be so much in our control. It may do in a new form what Thomas critiques the communalized Indian church for doing in the past.

In the course of this debate, the issue of the essential *tradendum* of the Christian faith remains the deepest one. Newbigin challenges the lack of clarity in Thomas's definitions. In one of Thomas's phrases, "the humanity which responds in faith and receives the liberation of Jesus Christ as Lord and Saviour" (Thomas 1972:71; cf. Newbigin 72bck:76), Newbigin finds what is virtually a definition of the church, and in Thomas's use of the phrase "Christ-centred fellowship of faith" Newbigin can only see what would make one example not Christ-centered and the other a Christian religious fellowship (72bck:77). The sense that Thomas is uncomfortable with that because he wishes the net he throws to gather a wider circle grows as the debate continues. From an earlier and fairly clear statement that "'Christ-centredness' in the sense of acknowledgement of the centrality of the Person of Jesus Christ is the essence of Faith" (Thomas 1972:70), he moves on to speak of "partial but real acknowledgement" (72). He addresses the question of the essential and minimal requirement of faith and asks, "What is that minimum except faith-acknowledgement of the centrality of the Person of Jesus Christ for the individual and social life of mankind?" (74). The minimum appears to get even more frayed at the edges when he speaks about those who "are acknowledging Jesus as the reality of the transcendent criterion and resource for humanisation, but who cannot acknowledge Him in the traditional religious terms as 'Lord and Saviour'" and calls for "a new definition of the 'substance' of what it is to acknowledge Christ Jesus as Lord and Saviour" (90). He clearly wishes for some acknowledgment of faith as being present in many who cannot or do not acknowledge Jesus in the ways by which the church has historically acknowledged him. Newbigin's firmness on such points, assuming an "acceptance of Jesus Christ, as we know him through the Bible, as the absolute Lord of all things," indicates the faith that he believes must be part of the *tradendum*.

The dominant concern on Newbigin's part throughout the debate with Thomas is the affirmation that the church is and must be a visible and recognizable fellowship. "The acceptance of Jesus Christ as central and decisive creates *some* kind of solidarity among those who have this accep-

tance in common." There is no determinative and universal answer —
beyond "meeting together to celebrate with words, songs and formal actions" — to the question how far that must extend. But it appears to him
"almost inevitable that some common cultural forms and some common
social bonds will develop among those who are united by a strong faith in
Jesus" (72bck:78). There *will* be forms of the church, whatever those forms
may look like.

It comes as no surprise, therefore, that in Newbigin's missiology this
fundamental necessity of the church's historical form plays a large role. He
frequently asserts the priority of the life of the community of God's people
as the basis for the other aspects of its mission.

> The Church, living in the power of the Spirit, is the privileged place where
> the Spirit bears witness and draws men and women to Christ. The words
> and deeds that flow from this presence of the Spirit are — equally —
> occasions by which the Spirit acts. (86bvdw:2; cf. 58obog:20)

Words and deeds are "held together in the life of a fellowship" (75rim:27;
82ccee:148). Here he finds the way to resolve the dilemma of choosing a
priority between words and deeds, proclamation and service, witness and
justice (cf. 61ftow:87-92).

> The true relation between the word and the deed is that both must be
> visibly rooted in the same reality; namely in that new community which
> is created and indwelt by the Holy Spirit. . . . [T]he word illuminates the
> deed, and the deed authenticates the word, and the Spirit takes them
> both to bear His own witness to the Resurrection. (65fe:422)

In this sense are we to understand the central role Newbigin assigns
to the church in his more recent apologetic formulations. Addressing the
question of authority, and especially what authority the Bible has in the
encounter of the gospel with modern Western culture, he affirms that "the
Bible functions as authority only within a community that is committed
to faith and obedience." The hermeneutical circle operating within the
community means that "tradition and Scripture are in a constantly developing reciprocal relationship." Therefore, "it is not the Bible by itself but the
church confessing the mystery of faith that is spoken of as the pillar and
bulwark of the truth (1 Tim 3:15-16)" (86fg:58).

But there is no hermeneutical circle between this community and that which lives outside of this faith. That boundary must be defined by other models, "such as are suggested by the biblical image of death and birth" (86fg:58). Conversion as a boundary marker, and the community as that which the boundary marks, are intimately tied to the witness that the Spirit continues to give to the gospel.

Continuity with the Future

The questions posed by Baago, Thomas, and others from the Indian context tend to emphasize the side of the continuity question that has to do with the past. How must a new convert be related to the traditions of the prior church? What are the essential requirements of "visible community" inherent in true conversion? What are the legitimate forms which that may take in the case of new converts, and what does that imply for the renewal of older forms? In the midst of such issues the question of continuity with the historical church lies at the center. An eager openness to the future easily tends to close off the past.

Newbigin's interaction with the views of Donald McGavran shows that the church growth movement pushes in the same way for the freedom of forms and the adoption of local indigenous cultural patterns. But the emphasis is not quite the same. The tendency to emphasize the past-associated present cultural setting has an inherent vulnerability toward closing off the future. This future side of the continuity question is what Newbigin in essence raises by challenging the idea that cultures are basically "closed" to change and influence. He identifies the danger that such insular "forms" of the church tend to close off the future of mutual life, accountability, and reconciliation among the churches formed in the various cultural settings of the world, thwarting the proper witness of a "universal" church. How will these churches in each segment of humanity have continuity with all others which share the future with them or follow after them?

As was the case with Thomas, Newbigin addresses McGavran's views because there is a certain commonality. It is by a process of affirmation and critique that Newbigin uses McGavran as both a spokesman and a foil for the articulation of his theology of conversion in the context of his major work on mission theology (78os, chapter 9). The affirmation goes beyond a shared concern for the times and places where the church shows little sign of growth and for the multitudes of people beyond the church who have not heard, or have heard and rejected, the gospel. Again, it is more than a common appreciation for the legitimacy of a distinctive "missionary" role in the life of the church. Most importantly, Newbigin finds in McGavran a critique of the "mission station" approach very compatible with his own critique of "church extension." In the mission station ("the perfect contradiction in terms"!), "converts are detached from the natural communities to which they belong, attached to the foreign mission and its institutions, and required to conform to ethical and cultural standards which belong to the Christianity of the foreign missionary." Being himself concerned to maintain the freedom of the new convert and the sovereignty of the Spirit, Newbigin affirms the truth in McGavran's charge that missions have "fallen into the old legalist trap" by "adopting practices which put in the center, not the liberating gospel, but a series of demands for conformity to ethical and cultural standards set by the missionary" (136-143).

In these respects, Newbigin finds McGavran's views very similar to those of Roland Allen. Both have in common a conviction "that missions have been wrong in their insistence that it is their business to impose on younger churches ethical standards laid down by the sending churches." Newbigin associates the language McGavran uses to describe how missions "have confused 'discipling' with 'perfecting'" with Allen's way of describing their reliance on "the pressure of the law to mold new churches into conformity to Christ, when they should have trusted the power of the Holy Spirit working through the Word and sacraments of the gospel in the life of the community." They both view as essential to conversion a commitment "to Jesus Christ in the fellowship of his people" (78os:146-147). Newbigin affirms the place in which these two stand together against all impositions of law which set aside the freedom and sovereignty of the Spirit in conversion.

If McGavran's position is so like that of Allen and Newbigin, how then is it that his proposals would not provide the proper corrective? Can they be embraced? Or do they in some way fail to follow the insight to fitting conclusions? Setting aside an initial critique of McGavran's emphasis on numerical growth as too easily leading to a "conquistador" approach that becomes again "self-aggrandizement" (78os:141-142), Newbigin proceeds to challenge the vision McGavran suggests for church growth at two basic points: its ethical implications and its ecumenical implications.

1. *Ethical Implications.* While McGavran's distinction between the missionary task of "discipling" and the pastoral task of "perfecting" preserves the "radical independence" of the converted, it strains the tension between the personal and ethical dimensions of conversion to the breaking point.[18] Given that the two functions may be seen as separate ones, can the implications of the two be separated in the event of conversion? This is the question Newbigin poses. He is convinced they cannot. The gospel by which people are "discipled" is always, even when the evangelist takes care not to reimpose law, a call to repentance and to a "following" after Jesus which involves doing the will of God. Newbigin acknowledges that in this path lies a very hard road to travel. But the tension must be faced and the attempt constantly made to escape from legalism "without becoming ethically irresponsible." While making sure that it guards itself against identifying conversion with a "particular set of ethical decisions," the church "must speak to the best of its ability about what obedience to Christ will involve." The separation of discipling and perfecting does not adequately understand that "discipling" is essentially the Spirit's work, and the witness of the church which the Spirit uses is "the witness given when proclamation is linked to the full ministry of the suffering Servant of the Lord who discerns, encounters, and bears in his body the sin by which the world rejects God's rule," that is, "the church's struggle towards 'perfecting'" (78os:151-157).

McGavran's concern for the multiplication of churches in each piece of the "vast mosaic of different cultures" parallels that of Newbigin to preserve the freedom in every cultural setting for the Spirit to form the church there which comes about by way of conversion. Both move away from the habit of domesticating the gospel in such a way that the church is "extended" in an alien form into other cultures (78os:157; cf. 138). But McGavran's fuller view on the matter presents another question to Newbigin. If the resident culture is that in terms of which are to be defined the forms of conversion and the community it produces, then how will the church be a sign and instrument of the rule of God which judges and seeks to restore all things? Are we left with the church as a mere "holding pen" for a future rescue? How does a more dynamic view of salvation as "wholeness" enter the picture?

Newbigin critiques McGavran on two points at which these issues arise. First, he challenges McGavran's understanding of cultures as each "psychologically closed to the rest of the world." Such a static picture is not true to the realities of the world. "Every human community is changing."

None is free from mutual influence and interaction with others. In most modern situations, people live in an interwebbed network of cultural communities. All cultures "are involved in the tension between the new and the old." The struggle between "conservatives" and "reformers" means that static neutrality on matters of cultural tension or change is impossible. The basic anthropology McGavran uses is faulty and therefore "misleading" (78os:160-163).

More critically, that gives rise to a second difficulty with his view. To call for the "adaptation of Christianity to the culture of each piece of the mosaic" with the understanding that "God accepts world cultures" has the tendency to "absolutize" cultures "over against the gospel." Newbigin asserts that "culture is not an ethically neutral entity, and cultural change cannot be a matter of ethical indifference" (78os:160-163, 137). This stands in contrast to McGavran's bold statement that "Christianity is wholly neutral to the vast majority of cultural components" (1974:39).[19] Here Newbigin's identification of cultural dynamics with the biblical language about the "powers" becomes crucial. "The powers of state, religion, law, and custom," though created by and for Christ, "conspired and combined to crucify" him. By his death they are disarmed and "their claim to absolute authority has been disallowed" (78os:159; cf. H. Berkhof 1962). Because of this realist perspective on the grandeur as well as the travesty which human cultures represent, Newbigin affirms that, as "sign, instrument, and foretaste of God's purpose for all human culture," the church must "so live, act, and speak within each culture that its words and its deeds and its life communicate in a way which can be understood the judgment of God upon that culture and his promise for it" (78os:163). To embrace culture "as it is" is not the implication of the radical independence for which he argues; that lies in seeking and following the will of the free Spirit who in conversion both affirms and judges all cultures.

2. *Ecumenical Implications.* In the remainder of the chapter in which this assessment of McGavran's thought is made (78os:164ff.), Newbigin leaves off his direct critique of the church growth perspective. But it is worth noting that in the more general discussion which follows, his attempt to form a full perspective on culture moves him ultimately toward the necessity for the unity of the church. This he had anticipated in his direct comments on McGavran's views. In a side comment made while entertaining the hypothetical possibility of following the homogenous unit principle in a city like Madras, he says he is leaving aside the fact that "most Christians

in Madras would reject this on ethical grounds, believing that it is an essential part of Christian witness to affirm the unity of all in Christ" (162-163). The shades of "apartheid" always hang over the "independence" of the convert. But here is exactly where his concern for unity enters. The force behind the argument against a sending church or a mission effort "domesticating" the gospel in terms of its own culture applies equally to the receiving culture. When all in each culture acknowledge "that the gospel cannot be completely domesticated within any culture," there will be a mutual and continuing critique harmonious with the purpose of God "to unite all of every culture to himself in a unity which transcends without negating the diversities of culture" (168). McGavran's plan produces cells too isolated for the effecting of such a unity.

This unity provides the essential balance for "independence" in Newbigin's theology of conversion in the midst of plurality. His understanding of unity as an implicate of conversion lies behind his oft-repeated claim that "only a universal fellowship can be the adequate bearer of a universal Gospel" (61icd:12).[20] That such strivings for unity in visible, actual historical terms do, in fact, produce such a multiplex unity "without negating the diversities of culture" is demonstrated in his own experience by the life of the Church of South India of which he was so intimate a part. Returning to Madras once after an absence of eighteen years, he recounts,

> I did not find that they had become uniform: on the contrary I found a rich variety of styles in worship and practice. What I found [were] congregations less concerned about their own affairs and more ready to think in terms of God's will for the life of the city as a whole, less like competing clubs each trying to enlarge itself and a little more recognizable as sign and foretaste of God's kingdom. (76aopa:299)

The quest for such unity in diversity is the common future of churches in every culturally particular place.

CHAPTER 6

The Gospel as Secular Announcement:
The Limits of Religion

Part of the surrender by which the Western churches have withdrawn into the "private sector" has been the abandonment of the claim to hold, in the gospel, the clue to "the understanding of the whole public life of mankind." A failed attempt to define a "salvation history" separate from the public history has left as the burning issue "the question of the relation of Christianity to the other religions," the church generally accepting in the process a position as "one of the forms of private *gnosis*" (79cjh:200-201).

This has come about, according to Bishop Newbigin, over against the example of the early church's refusal to do that in its own pluralistic setting and over against the gospel to which it gave expression as a "secular announcement" about the meaning and end of the public life of all humankind. This way of characterizing the universality of the gospel and the uniqueness of Jesus Christ sharpened steadily in Newbigin's focus from the 1960s onward. The seed is found in the notion that "the idea of a secular order" (i.e., "a system of thought and practice which lies, so to say, outside of the direct responsibility of religion, but in which the will of God is to be done") is "a Christian idea" (61ftow:21). That notion combined with Newbigin's sense of conversion as a "secular act," a perspective shared with Paul Löffler in the discussions of the mid-1960s and most emphatically expressed in *The Finality of Christ* (69fc; cf. Löffler 1965:97).[1] His discussions of the gospel as "The Clue to History" (chapter 4) and "Conversion" as the point at which the finality of Christ comes to its sharpest focus (chapter 5) are grounded in a firm conviction about "The Gospel as a Secular Announcement" (chapter 3).

> It is not the teaching of a new way of personal salvation after the manner of the Buddha. Nor is it the announcement of a theocratic kingdom in the manner of Islam. . . . It is neither simply the announcement of a new religious doctrine, nor the launching of a new secular programme. . . . It is the announcement of the decisive encounter of God with men. . . . It concerns the consummation of all things. Its character as "final" lies in this fact. (69fc:48-49)

The gospel, therefore, is a revelation not in the sense of a "disclosure of eternal truths" but as "the launching of an action which looks to the consummation of all things; its relation to ordinary secular history is of its essence" (69fc:50). The gospel is first and foremost, for Newbigin, the "concrete events of history — secular events, if you like to put it so" in which "God shows himself as Saviour," a description he applies equally to Old and New Testament events (72amtj:5). Here, at the heart of the gospel, is the pattern made clear by the missionary character of election. It concerns the actions of a God who works by means of particular events which bear significance for the whole — by way of election. And preeminent among all these "events" is that one which appeared in the person of Jesus in the presence of chosen witnesses, the new "fact" that "the kingdom of God is at hand."

This means that it is certainly true of the gospel that "in its original form it is a news-bulletin." Therefore, it "does not mean 'There is a God,' or 'You ought to be good.' It is not about 'religion.'" Rather, it is simply an announcement of a fact. "And the *news* is that this fact is now present in a way that has to be faced and demands decision. It is therefore a news item which does *not* go into the 'religion' slot; it is emphatically 'world affairs'" (80pfnd:3-4; 86bep:58). This "good news," the "announcement of a new fact," is what calls for conversion, "a turning to face the new fact" (86bep:58). That call is the fruit of evangelism, which "is properly the announcing of a fact — the presence of the reign of God in Jesus, and its presence in *foretaste* in the fellowship of those who have accepted the call to conversion" (67).

This emphasis on "secular event" and "news-bulletin" gives to "religion" a different place than many are accustomed to grant it: the gospel is not about "religion" but is emphatically "world affairs." The relationship between this understanding of the gospel and the critical modern discussions of religious plurality forms the focus of this chapter. The connection may be illustrated in a preliminary way by comparing the setting of Newbigin's treatment of religious pluralism in *The Finality of Christ* with that of his later discussion of it in *The Open Secret*. The impact of viewing the gospel as "secular announcement" has eventually meant the refinement of chapter titles and arrangements. The chapter prior to the one on "secular announcement" in the earlier work was entitled "Christianity Among the Religions," the form of the discussion of "the finality of Christ" which Newbigin had found to be most characteristic at the time due to the common "assumption that this is a discussion among the religions" (69fc:22). That chapter corresponds to the one in the later work on "The Gospel Among the Religions," which follows all the chapters — including the central and determinative one ("The Gospel and World History"). The notion of "secular announcement" came in the first instance following the discussion of interreligious relationship and served to suggest a weaning from the accepted notion of the fully and solely "religious" terms of the discussion and of Christianity as a partner in it. In the latter case, that ground has already been laid by the time the "religions" and their "religious" character are introduced. The gospel itself, fully introduced as a secular announcement, is the frame of reference from which the religions will be considered in both their "religiousness" and their relationship to the secular events about which the gospel speaks.[2] As the importance of this secularity of the announcement deepens, so also are the terms of the general debate moving from an earlier concentration on "continuity and discontinuity" to the need for a strategy for side-by-side living among peoples of various faith, the quest for a style of dialogue by which the purposes of God might be sought. The earlier article on "the religions" stayed to the center of the course and discussed Christianity vis-à-vis the other religions (cf. 69fc:45). The later one sets the religions more fully in their cultural contexts as confronted with this secular announcement which is the gospel. In both, that is the tendency of Newbigin's thought and the most notable contribution he makes to the discussion.

Lying forcefully at the center of Newbigin's suggestion for "dialogue" we discover his notion of "witness." The basis for the meeting with the person of another religion matches the purpose of the meeting: "I have been laid hold of by Jesus Christ to be his witness" (77bpmi:260).[3] It is especially crucial for an understanding of Newbigin's view of religions and their relationship to the "secular announcement" of the kingdom that his particular notion of "witness" be appreciated. In earlier chapters we have noted his emphasis on "bearing the witness of the Spirit" and have recognized that for Newbigin, witness is first of all the Spirit's work. It is important here to recognize that the gift of witness — which is a promise, not a command (cf. Acts 1:8, 78caw and 87mcw) — corresponds to the "news-bulletin" character of the gospel and establishes the nature of the Christian's manner of relationship with people of other faith. The church's evangelism does not have to do with "something in the 'private sector'" of life, with "our ideas of religion," or simply with "the meaning of my personal life." Nor is the church supporting a "good cause" about which one "might be optimistic or pessimistic." That question does not arise since the "rule of God" is a "fact" and not a cause. The church must simply be faithful to witness to it (80pfnd:4-5).

The connections here are especially worked out in Newbigin's commentary on the Fourth Gospel. "The gospel is — by definition — news," he begins. As something "new" it "has to be integrated into the general experience, particularly the religious experience, of mankind. We have to show that it has a place in the whole seamless fabric of human experience" (82lhc:12). The only way open by which to seek that integration, that introduction of what is "new" and therefore "news," is found in the attitude of John the Baptist.

> "Witness" is the proper word because the function of a witness is not to develop conclusions out of already known data, but simply to point to, report, affirm that which cannot come into the argument at all except simply as a new datum, a reality which is attested by a witness. (82lhc:14)

The witness is one who "gives his testimony in a trial where it is contested. The verdict as to what stands and what falls will only be given at the end" (86fg:64). The introduction of the courtroom analogy is an important component of Newbigin's thinking because it sets the evangelistic expression of the church in the context of the widely varying cultural "fabrics" which hear its announcement as "news" and warns the church not to become "judge" instead of "witness" in that setting (82ccee:151).

This set of ideas forms the framework for Newbigin's discussion of issues concerning the variety of the world's religious expressions. We shall note especially how he responds to (a) the ongoing debate about what continuity exists between the Christian faith and other faiths; (b) the kind of proposals currently being offered for attaining unity among the religions and their adherents; and (c) the persistent question of "universal salvation." Before investigating the way Newbigin relates to those issues, however, it will be necessary to look first at an issue that is determinative for them all and grows immediately out of the foregoing observations. That is the matter of the definition of "religion," especially its relationship to culture and what Newbigin calls "secular history."

In the survey which follows in these areas, the goal will be to display the range and character of Newbigin's view of the religions to discover implications in it for a theology of cultural plurality. This will be done not by attempting to create a paradigm for grasping the vast field of opinion on these matters and to identify his position in it. Such a pursuit lies beyond the scope of the present study. Nor will an attempt be made to compare and contrast his view thoroughly with all those with whom he interacts, which again would lead us into too extensive a project. Rather, Newbigin's view will be shown as it emerges in his responses to, comments upon, and criticisms of the views to which he refers. We shall seek to observe the kind of critique he tends to make and consider the view of cultural plurality which that exposes in his theology. This will mean that throughout the survey of the areas mentioned, these particular bodies of material will be in view: (a) his relation to the modern continuation of the Hendrik Kraemer–A. G. Hogg debate; (b) the distinctiveness of his view as compared with that of Karl Barth; (c) his engagement in debate with John Hick; (d) his references to William E. Hocking, Wilfred Cantwell Smith, Karl Rahner, Hans Küng, John Macquarrie, and Raimundo Panikkar; and (e) treatments of his views by Gabriel Fackre, Gavin D'Costa, and Stephen Travis.[4]

The Limitations of the Religion Concept

The most important and fundamental insight Newbigin brings to discussions of religious plurality is that religious plurality is a subset of a larger category, cultural plurality. If he is not asking by what authority it might be thought otherwise, he is reiterating the basic principle that the matters about which "religion" is concerned do not only touch areas of life known as "religious." Whether or not that is true at all in the general sense, it must of course be thoroughly true in regard to a gospel which is "secular announcement" and the "religion" which forms in terms of that announcement.

This already precipitates and anticipates several facets of Newbigin's view. Christianity is of course a "religion" like other religions (cf. 69fc:46-47). Salvation has to do with more than just "religion." To investigate the meaning of these statements will move us toward clarifying the definitions for "religion" which function in Newbigin's thought, the relationship of Christianity to salvation, and the relationship between religion and culture.

Newbigin finds in "the attack upon 'religion' in the name of the Gospel, launched with such power by Karl Barth and further developed by Dietrich Bonhoeffer," what he believes to be a "large element of truth" (66hrsm:9). He agrees that "in one sense the Gospel is indeed the end of religion." But "tantalizing" though they be, Bonhoeffer's "outlines for a 'religionless' Christianity" raise issues demanding "more careful thinking."

> Religion is much too great and permanent an element in human experience to be swept out of sight. The Gospel is the end of religion, as it is the end of the law. But law remains a reality in the life of the Christian, and so, I am persuaded, is religion. (9-10)

But the trend of the 1960s to look for the demise of religion was supplanted in the 1970s and 1980s by an almost exactly opposite trend. In proposal after proposal for the unity of religions, Newbigin finds the tendency to assume that in "religion" — in the devout practice of its prescriptions or the intuitions of its inner experience — is to be found the place where salvation occurs and the means of its mediation. Most relentlessly, Newbigin asks why this is so readily and unquestioningly assumed. He finds that Rahner "assumes, without proving, that it is religion among all the activities of the human spirit which is the sphere of God's saving action" (78os:195; cf. Travis 1983:33).[5] Similarly, Panikkar assumes without reason that "religion is the way by which men are saved and brought into union with God" (69fc:41; cf. 42-43). This is one of the more forceful questions Newbigin puts to Hogg in cross-examination. If Hogg is right that "God is always seeking to win his erring children to himself, why should it be assumed that religion is the human response to this endeavor? What ground is there for thinking that religion is the sphere of God's special working?"

(83cwr:22). Newbigin calls it "one of the unexamined assumptions of our [Western] culture" that what we call religion "is the only or the primary form of contact between the human race and its Creator" (86fg:88).

The gospel portrait of things leads to an altogether different picture. Even if we were to look for a single facet of human living to be the *locus* of salvation (which is more than Newbigin is willing to assume), the Bible would lead us away from the suggestion that it should be "religion." "Is a man nearer to Christ because he is religious?" The question can only find its answer by asking in the same breath, "Is the devout Pharisee nearer or farther than the semi-pagan prostitute?" (69fc:44).

> If the Bible is our guide, we cannot exclude the possibility that precisely religion may be the sphere of damnation — the place where man is farthest from the living God. Surely we must insist that the "light that lightens every man" shines not only, perhaps not even chiefly, in man's religion; rather we may see it shining in the ordinary fidelities of home, business and national life. (69fc:43)

The teaching of the New Testament draws a new line. "The parable of the Good Samaritan is a sharp and constantly needed reminder to the godly of all faiths that the boundary between religion and its absence is by no means to be construed as the boundary between light and darkness" (77cwps:10). The cross itself, happening as it did as the consequence of the reaction of the most religious, "stands throughout history over against all the claims of religion — including the claims of the Christian religion — to be the means of salvation" (77bpmi:261). Christianity, in its character as a religion, is no more privileged than any other to claim to be salvific.[6]

This perspective is confirmed by observation. Newbigin recognizes on the one hand that "religion — including the Christian religion — can be the sphere in which evil exhibits a power against which human reason and conscience are powerless" (77bpmi:257). "I have seen enough to know," he says, "how powerful a source of evil religion can be" (66hrsm:9). And even at their "points of highest ethical and spiritual achievement" the religions are threatened by, and "therefore ranged against, the Gospel" (77bpmi:257).

On the other hand, the fruit of the "light" is not confined to the religious dimension of life.

I expect to find and do find everywhere in the life of mankind signs of the kindness and justice of God which are manifested in Jesus. These signs are to be found throughout the life of mankind, not only — not even primarily — in his religion. (77bpmi:261)

Newbigin presses this point even farther by asking where, in most missionary experience, a "point of contact" is normally found. Does the gospel "come home" to an ordinary person "in the field of his religious experience"? No. It is more normally "in relation to some experience of his secular life which has no obvious reference to his religious beliefs and practices" that the gospel lodges and "becomes meaningful" (69fc:46-47).

"Religion," then, is relativized twice in Newbigin's thought. It is relativized once in that it stands under the radical judgment of the cross, and again in that it does not stand alone under that judgment. It is only a part of the whole fabric of human experience. The judgment does not overvalue the "religious" strand by isolating it for judgment. The judgment which comes from the word of the cross is part of a "secular announcement" which pronounces "radical judgment upon all human wisdom and upon the experience on which that wisdom is founded," whether that is "religious" wisdom or "secular" wisdom (69fc:57-58). The declaration of the Kingdom of God reveals religion to be merely a facet of the secular life and history of humankind, and not even its "saving" facet. The announcement of the cross means that religion shares the judgment of God on the whole of which it is a part, sometimes the part most deserving of judgment.

What then is "religion"? Newbigin's definitions are not so clear and crisp as are other elements of his thought. They contain on the surface a certain kind of oscillation from one position to another. On the one hand, he wants to refuse to "religion" the dominant, or even crucial, role in the full, culturally bounded life of humankind. Therefore he treats it as an "element" (66hrsm:9; 72bck:80; 77trsp:82), "aspect" (66hrsm:95; 69fc:48-49), or "dimension" (77trsp:82) of "the sum total of ways of living which shape the continuing life of a group," that is, culture (cf. 78os:159). It is a "sphere" — but only one of the spheres — of the full pattern of human life (77bpmi:257; cf. Oman 1925!).

Yet Newbigin wants to maintain that religion rightly has to do with all of life. "To speak of a separate department of life called 'religion' is to speak of an unreal abstraction" that divorces "the public life of man in history" from "his interior life of prayer and obedience and love towards

God" (77cwps:13). He challenges the "assumption (generally unexamined) that Christianity is one variety of the inclusive species 'religion'" (77mm:264). Religion is neither a "department" nor a "species." A particular religion is not "simply one of a class" (77trsp:82). In the case of Christianity, it is only by a radical reinterpretation of the Bible by the modern scientific worldview that it can be relegated to a privatized "sector of human affairs" (78os:97). Thus Newbigin's more formal definitions of "religion" convey a conception more comprehensive and all-pervading. As it was put in an earlier comment, "religion deals with the sacred, that is to say, with that which makes upon man a claim to which every other claim has, in principle, to be subordinated" (55qutr:23).[7]

The idea that in religion "a man surrenders himself to something greater than himself" (77bpmi:257) conveys that religion has to do with "beliefs and practices which are concerned with what we believe to be ultimate and decisive" (72bck:80).[8] Newbigin is willing to accept as appropriate the definition of the Birmingham "Agreed Syllabus of Religious Instruction," which speaks of "stances for living" (77trsp:82; cf. City of Birmingham 1975:5). Such a definition, including as it does ideologies, matches in that respect Newbigin's intent in his most comprehensive definition of religion, found in *The Open Secret*:

> The word "religion" is intended to denote all those commitments which, in the intention of their adherents, have an overriding authority over all other commitments and provide the framework within which all experience is grasped and all ideas are judged. . . . I am using ["religion"] to refer to that which has final authority for a believer or a society, both in the sense that it determines his scale of values and in the sense that it provides the models, the basic patterns through which the believer grasps and organizes his experience. (78os:181-182)

On this basis Newbigin shows how a "claimed" religion may not be the "real" religion — the "ultimately authoritative factor in [one's] thinking and acting" — as is the case for the Western person who lives not by the authority of the privatized field of religion but according to "his traditional tribal 'myth,'" that is, the "modern scientific world view" (78os:182). In the course of this line of thought, his definition comes remarkably close to one which would equally embrace "culture" (cf. 78os:159).

Thus the question arises, How are these two movements in Newbigin's thought related? On the one hand, he wants to ensure that we understand that religion is not the whole, and certainly not the salvific part of the whole, of human life. On the other hand, he refuses to resign religion to one "department" and claims that it has a pervasive character, touching all aspects of life. It is defined as a facet of culture and yet also as an essence of culture. The discussions in which he engages (as we shall see) reflect this oscillation. He speaks sometimes of religion in the totalistic sense and at other times in the limited sense.

This apparent inconsistency can only be understood in terms of Newbigin's effort to define "Christianity as a religion." His generalizations about religion grow out of that soil.[9] "Religion," as a facet of life, is a part of what Christianity is. "If the word 'religion' covers such things as the practice of individual and corporate worship, prayer, the reading and treasuring of sacred scriptures, then it requires no argument to prove that Christianity is a religion." It is "certainly one of the religions" (69fc:46-47). For the Christian community, the acts by which it remembers the words and life of Jesus and renews its life in the reenactment of Jesus' death and resurrection through baptism and the Lord's Supper, repeated and "formalized so that they may become the common possession of all races and all generations, constitute the visible substance of religion." It is by these visible forms that "the knowledge of God is expressed and renewed" (66hrsm:94-95).

And yet Christianity is more than merely a religious "facet" of life, more than one of the class of what are termed "religions" (69fc:47). By virtue of its formation in consequence of a "secular announcement" of the reign of God it is crucial for all facets of human experience. This must in the end mean that "Christianity as a religion" can never properly be privatized into an isolated "sector" of life but is always a matter of "world affairs," fully public in its concern and relevance. It is the gospel, of course, which is final and ultimate, and not the empirical movement called "Christianity." But that is never entirely separable. It is the nature of the gospel's message that there is an actual community which carries that message in history and always gives it an embodied form, that is, a culturally "religious" character.

> The claim that the fact of Christ is decisive for all human life is a meaningless claim except as it is interpreted in the life of a community which lives by the tradition of the apostolic testimony. There cannot, therefore, be a total disjunction between the Gospel and "Christianity." (69fc:77)

So then Christianity contains the characteristics of the religious dimension of life. But it also embraces as an ultimate claim — becoming for converts to it their ultimate commitment — all the dimensions of life. Therefore, it is not religion — not even "Christianity as a religion" — that is the ultimate, salvific element in culture. It is the secular events reported in the gospel which are salvific. But it must also be said that religion in general, and particularly Christianity (i.e., the community responding to the claims of the gospel), is not, and cannot be, separate from culture as a "whole way of living." By this conception of the interrelation of religion and culture Newbigin seeks to refuse both the idolization of religion which comes from reifying it and the reductionism which treats it as merely inner and private. He restricts to certain limits the use to which we put our abstraction of "religious" elements of human life and maintains the essential importance of ultimate perspectives and commitments for the way all of life is lived by everyone.

The Debate about Continuity

It is against the backdrop of the debate during and after the 1938 IMC meeting at Tambaram between A. G. Hogg and Hendrik Kraemer that Newbigin clarifies most fully his response to the question about any "continuity" which might exist "between faith in Jesus Christ and other forms of religious commitment" (69fc:59, 23-40; 83cwr). Kraemer characterized the issue in that debate as the choice between "two fundamental positions." "The first maintains the continuity between the essential tendencies and aspirations to be found in the ethnic religions and the essential gift of the Christian religion" (Kraemer 1939:13). Such a notion, whether cast in terms of "fulfillment" or a "natural theology" growing out of general revelation, he did not choose. His starting point was rather the second position, which "stresses the discontinuity" (14). Hogg, in response, pointed to the difference between talking about continuity with other "faiths" as "complexes of spiritual, ethical, intellectual and social elements" (called "religions") and asking about "non-Christian faith," the possibility of a "religious life which is not faith in Christ and yet is 'hid in God'" (Hogg 1939:84, 101). His conviction that the latter is truly possible suggests that such "faith" should be more determinative for our missionary approach than our attitude toward the "faiths" or religions

(101). In regard to such "non-Christian faith" we are right to see genuine continuity, according to Hogg, in that there is a genuine self-disclosure of God apprehended by it (110).

Newbigin declares himself for both continuity and discontinuity, not totaling siding, therefore, with either Kraemer or Hogg.

> The Gospel demands and effects a radical break with, and conversion from, the wisdom that is based upon other experience; yet mature reflection by those who have experienced this break suggests that it is the same God who has been dealing with them all along. (69fc:60)

There is "a radical discontinuity" which is at the same time "not a total discontinuity" (59). Or, put more positively, "there certainly is continuity"; but "the relation between non-Christian and Christian experience of God . . . cannot be described in terms of continuity alone" (36-39).

For Newbigin, it is the preaching of the cross which is the most vivid display of these twin facts. He terms it "the crux of any discussion about the continuity of Christian faith with the wider religious experience of mankind" that

> there was indeed a knowledge of God among the people whose life was rooted and nurtured in the faith of Israel; but in the name of that faith Israel solemnly and deliberately rejected Jesus as the enemy of God, as one under the curse of God. (79cjh:208)

This so-called question of the Pharisees, which Kraemer put to Hogg (Kraemer 1956), gains even more force from the example and testimony of Paul, who had to count as useless "the treasures which were his as a devout Pharisee" while acknowledging that "it was the living God who had been dealing with him when he was a Pharisee" (69fc:36-37, 58-59).

It is the "continuity" side of the argument that Newbigin must make compellingly in order to maintain the balanced joining of these affirmations which he seeks. The affinity of his view with that of Kraemer appears more obvious on the face of things, given his emphasis on the unique revelation of God in the incarnation, life, death, and resurrection of Jesus.[10] His position on the significance of the "total fact of Christ" and the necessity of conversion would suggest immediately a discontinuity. Is there room in that way of thinking for continuity? It is in his attempt to answer the charge against Kraemer that he left no such room for it that Newbigin establishes a sense of real continuity (cf. 83cwr:28).

It is important to note, in this connection, Newbigin's concurrence with Hogg at the point of his most insistent question (a question which Newbigin believes Kraemer "does not squarely face" 69fc:38). "Can there be no real two-sided communion with God *at all* until this grace has been acquired?" (Hogg 1939:102; cf. 109). Hogg's distinction of non-Christian "faith" from non-Christian "faiths" is based on the notion that "non-Christian faith is the result of a real divine self-disclosure," really known (69fc:35). The crucial clue which leads Newbigin to add his affirmative lies in the observation that the near-universal intuition of Bible translators (generally in situations of missionary encounter) has been to render the New Testament word *theos* "by the name given by the non-Christian peoples to the one whom they worshipped as the supreme being," such names obviously deriving their content "from non-Christian religious experience" (77bpmi:256; 69fc:36). In conversation with the "dean" of missionary linguist-translators, Eugene Nida, Newbigin confirmed that in those few instances where this pattern was not followed and a transliteration of the Hebrew or Greek word was used instead of the local one, "the converts have simply explained the foreign word in the text of their bibles by using the indigenous name for God" (77bpmi:256).

This insight fits with Newbigin's approach to "personal knowing" and his sense of the "paradigm shift" involved in conversion. In those terms, "total discontinuity is inconceivable. If something [were] totally discontinuous with my present experience I could not be aware of its existence." There is a continuity perceivable from within the "new perspective" by which "one can speak meaningfully" about "a real self-communication of God in the wider experience of mankind." Newbigin qualifies that by underscoring that it cannot be so perceived from outside the Christian faith and by adding the reminder that this self-communication does not merely occur in the "religious experience" of humankind but in the other facets of experience as well (79cjh:208-209). But the conviction that real revelation is present beyond "Christian faith" remains, a revelation which "happens when God actually communicates himself to men, and that communication happens only if there is human response" (69fc:75). In this, Newbigin stands over against Kraemer's argument for a virtual "total disjunction" between "revelation" and "faith."

The most important biblical foundation for Newbigin's agreement with Hogg on this point lies in the "overture" to the Fourth Gospel. Jesus is introduced there as "the true light that enlightens every man" (John 1:9). "To say this is to affirm that the presence and work of Jesus are not confined within the area where he is acknowledged" (77cwps:10). That fact ought to give Christians "an eager expectation of, a looking for, and a rejoicing in the evidence of that work" (78os:198). But the character of that work should not be too hastily assumed to be in the nature of "inner illumination of conscience and reason" (83cwr:28). The text, properly exegeted, is saying rather that Jesus is the one true light which "shines on every human being." The text does not proclaim that there is an inner light within each person, or still less that such inner illumination is to be equated with "various religions of mankind" (82lhc:6). Jesus, the light, shines on every person with a shining that reveals and judges. For together with the light comes the acknowledgment that it is in darkness that the light shines (John 1:5). So "this is not some sort of Christ-monism" (78os:197). The light can be pointed to and distinguished from darkness. All are called to face it and move towards it: "Go towards it and your path will be clear; turn your back on it and you will go into deeper darkness" (77cwps:10). Further, it should be added, this does not lead to an absolute dualism either, for "the darkness has not overcome" the light (John 1:5).[11]

The guidance of these and other texts leads Newbigin to show what "God at work in the non-Christian religions" is like in terms of the discussion of "faith" in the letter to the Hebrews. Faith is visible in those who look for "that which is not yet seen," not those "who are satisfied with what they have." Newbigin calls "faith" that hungering and thirsting — "whether religious or secular — which is open and eager for a reality beyond what now is" and which grows in answer to the light from the one who is the life. Newbigin affirms such hungering and thirsting to be "the sign of the active presence of him who is the source of the world's life" (83cwr:28-29).

In a sense, by redefining "faith" in this way Newbigin concurs with Hogg's insistence that the word be used in regard to non-Christian people. But the terms of its use are changed. Newbigin believes the change to be required by several fundamental difficulties in Hogg's position. In the first place, "faith and faiths cannot be so clearly distinguished" as Hogg would suggest (83cwr:21). The nature of both elements in the distinction prompts from Newbigin the question with which he faces others: "Why should it be assumed that religion" — whether the system of beliefs or the religious experience — "is the human response to this endeavor?" (22). Even more critically, the dilemma Hogg poses between the "occurrence" of revelation and its "content" is "a false one because occurrence is part of the content" (69fc:50; cf. Hogg 1939:115-116). Hogg comes near to missing the importance of the fact that "Jesus is not just the first Christian believer, but is the object of Christian believing." It is the notion of election which must provide the clue in this regard. On the one hand, as the Bible clearly declares, God self-discloses through concrete historical events (the "happenedness" which Kraemer emphasizes) and not directly to each individual as separate from the rest, contrary to Hogg's "unexamined assumption" that "God's efforts at self-disclosure must be directed to each person individually." On the other hand what we know of God through Jesus tells us that God's purpose of salvation embraces the whole world (the "content" which Hogg emphasizes). Then there can only be compatibility between the "occurrence" and the "content" if it is "also true that these particular events are, in some sense, for the sake of all" (83cwr:22-26). Election makes clear that this is so.

For these reasons, Newbigin does not see as parallel the "faith versus faiths" distinction of Hogg and the "Gospel versus Christianity" or "revelation versus religion" distinctions of Kraemer. In one sense Newbigin is right. But it is not the sense in which he makes the point, which he does by refusing Eric Sharpe's suggestion that Kraemer was separating between "the ideal and the actual" in religion. He grants that Hogg was probably not doing that either (83cwr:21-22). Rather, the difference between the two is better shown in terms of the earlier discussion of Newbigin's view and definition of "religion." Kraemer, like Barth, was declaring the finality of the revelation in Jesus in that it judges all religious expressions of humankind, even those spawned by yieldedness to that revelation. Hogg was making an analogous distinction between religions of humankind and the encounter with the revelation of God. But he was changing the effect of the dichotomy by replacing God's initiative of revelation with the human response to God's revelation as the first term in the equation. By doing this, he wished to broaden the field in which revelation is seen to be taking place and argue for a form of response to it which can take place within the framework of other "religions."

The effect of Newbigin's basic principle of the gospel as "secular announcement" can be applied similarly to both perspectives. To Kraemer it says that the cross does not solely judge the "religions" of humankind but all of life. But it also claims the inseparability of the gospel and the actual life experience of humanity. So Newbigin will say, "If God's revelatory act has not been in some measure understood and accepted, there has been no revelation; but if it has been understood and accepted, there has been a religious experience" (69fc:34).

It applies itself to Hogg, as well. The cross, as the heart of the "secular announcement" which judges not only religion, does not on the other hand omit religion from its judgment. That is true not only of the "religions" as systems of belief and practice but of "faith" as the human response to God's self-communication. Religious experience may prove itself to be the sphere of darkness just as may any other facet of human experience.

So then, both assume too readily that religion is the form of any salvific response to revelation, Kraemer viewing religion too uniquely as the object of judgment and Hogg viewing religious experience too hopefully as the subject of faith. Because of that, Kraemer holds the tension "between faith in Jesus Christ and other forms of religious commitment" too taut and Hogg relaxes it too completely.

Before leaving our consideration of this debate, it is important for our assessment of Newbigin's theology of cultural plurality to compare his thought with that of Karl Barth. While great similarity exists concerning the finality of God's revelation in Jesus Christ, Barth is not Newbigin's guide on matters concerning "religion" and "culture." Newbigin draws assistance from Barth at some crucial points. But his understanding of the possibilities of "natural revelation" and the gospel's affirmation of culture in general and many specifics of culture in particular forms itself independently from Barth's view and at many points in contrast to it.[12]

The large familiarity with Barth's work which Newbigin shows in his writings indicates a marked appreciation for Barth's contribution. His first association with him, through his commentary on Romans, did not immediately establish that. During his early struggle (while at Cambridge) to understand the atonement in terms which were compelling and challenging in the modern world, it was James Denney who was the "decisive agent" for him, not Karl Barth. Barth he found "incomprehensible" (85ua:30-31). Newbigin's formative years left him "more of an evangelical than a liberal," but it was not a distinctively neo-orthodox approach which influenced that shift.

During the early years of his missionary experience, Newbigin was already forming the basic sense of the "limits" of "religion" which we have surveyed. At a time when he had not yet "read Karl Barth and did not know that 'religion is unbelief'" (cf. Barth 1957a:297-325), other influences were leading him to "see that religion can be a way of protecting oneself from reality" (85ua:58). Those influences included the magisterial Barth-like volume of Kraemer (1938), which included an assessment of the Hindu school of Vishishtadvaita, known as "India's Religion of Grace" (168-173), and long, instructive contact with Hindu friends and scholars of that same school. Out of that came an increasing certainty "that the 'point of contact' for the Gospel is rather in the ordinary secular experiences of human life than in the sphere of religion" (85ua:57-58). Thus were forming the seeds of both his companionship with Kraemer's ideas and his difference from them. The conclusions he was drawing stood in contrast with those Kraemer was articulating when he said:

> This fundamental discontinuity of the world of spiritual reality, embodied in the revelation in Christ, to the whole range of human religion, *excludes* the possibility and legitimacy of a *theologia naturalis* in the sense of a science of God and man, conceived as an imperfect form of revelation, introductory to the world of divine grace in Christ. (1939:4; cf. 1938:101-141)

It was not until the Amsterdam 1948 WCC Assembly that Newbigin met Barth personally. Of the meeting he says, "I had not yet learned to appreciate either Barth or his theology as I was to do later" (85ua:115). What Newbigin found to be the "prophetic" force in Barth's Amsterdam address began that process. "Barth demolishes all one's plans with his terrific prophetic words, and one is left wondering what to do next; and his answer is, Just get on with the next plain duty" (117). That encounter was to gain added depth during the years which followed as the two served as part of the "Committee of Twenty-Five" assigned to draft the theme paper on "Hope" for the Evanston 1954 Assembly. Himself eventually the committee chairman, Newbigin found Barth sometimes "polemical," sometimes "in good form" and free of "his earlier tantrums" (131, 139). On one occasion he found Barth coming to his rescue when his own paper was being attacked on all sides (132). The appreciation growing from this depth of personal contact would lead at a later stage to a more deliberate study. That occurred upon Newbigin's retirement from Madras to England in 1974.

> I decided to do what I had not previously attempted: to read the whole of Barth's *Dogmatics*. It was an immensely rewarding experience. Barth

condensed and Barth quoted I had found totally unimpressive. But the real Barth, and especially the famous small-print notes, was enthralling. It was a needed preparation for the much more difficult missionary experience which (as I did not then realize) lay ahead. (241-242)[13]

We noted in the previous chapter that at an early stage Newbigin critiqued Barth's view of the church as giving insufficient place to the historicality of the church and the essential connection of that to the historical and redeeming work of Christ (cf. 53hg:48-49, which lectures were given in November 1952 between the second and third meetings of the Committee of Twenty-Five!). It is along the same lines that Newbigin stands apart from Barth on another occasion. In the unpublished response to Löffler in the "Thomas debate," Newbigin challenges the view expressed by Duraisingh and Krass (and, he thinks, agreed to by Thomas) that the baptism of the Spirit and water baptism should be looked upon as separate issues. He replies that "to speak again of two baptisms is to go back on the incarnation. Karl Barth notwithstanding" (73ck:10). This issue raises again the fundamental historical rootedness of Christian experience and hence the corporate experience of the church. This sort of division between Spirit- and water-baptism implies a "separation between the body of Christ and the Spirit of Christ" (72hsc:30).

That it is regarding an issue of historicality that we find Newbigin most emphatically opposing Barth is noteworthy because it is also regarding an issue of historicality that we find him most unambiguously agreeing with Barth and defending him, although, significantly, it has to do with a different application of it. Newbigin observes that while the trend of the "secular 60s" was to loosen the tie "to traditional theism," the 70s saw a swing in the opposite direction, and " 'transcendence' is back in fashion" (78cc:5). This new trend, exemplified by the authors of *The Myth of God Incarnate* (Hick 1977b), sharpens an important issue which Newbigin says English theology has been reluctant to face.

Either one can take the general religious experience of mankind as the clue for our understanding of the human situation, and then seek categories with which to fit Jesus into this understanding; or one can take Jesus as the absolutely crucial and determinative clue for all understanding and then try to understand the rest of human experience from this centre. This, of course, is the issue which Karl Barth pressed relentlessly in all his writing. (78cc:5)

On another occasion, as well, Newbigin speaks "in defence of Barth" on this very point. Maurice Wiles's suggestion that Barth begs the question when he says that "to separate Christian faith from historic events makes the faith false" draws a response from Newbigin (79cjh:201). The historicality of revelation, he says, is required by the character of personal knowledge if in fact the object of our knowing is personal. Further, the legitimacy of Barth's response to being challenged on this point, that he "must answer directly and without qualification, without being ashamed of his naivety, that Jesus Christ is the one and entire truth through which he is shown how to think and speak," is to be affirmed.

> On what grounds can it be shown that the understanding of how things are that is obtained from this child-like attention to Jesus as the clue to it all is inferior to that which can be obtained by the attempt to develop one's clues for grasping the vast complexity of experience? Indeed is not the former stance more appropriate for a creature before its creator, and for a forgiven sinner before its saviour? (79cjh:201-202; cf. Busch 1976:435)

On the side of the revelatory events, Newbigin finds Barth emphasizing their essential historicality. But on the side of the human experience of the effect of those events, he finds him unacceptably unhistorical.[14] This shows up especially when the question of continuity, of the possibility of God's self-communication beyond explicit Christian faith, of natural theology or general revelation vis-à-vis the non-Christian religions arises. As we have noted, Newbigin sets the stage for his *Honest Religion for Secular Man* by noting Barth's "attack upon 'religion' in the name of the Gospel" (66hrsm:9). But to speak of "the end of religion" must mean the end of its salvific claim, not its abolition in the life of one who believes the gospel. Newbigin suggests that it is right — Barth notwithstanding — to write a book about "Honest Religion," as his Cambridge professor John Oman had done. Another book by Oman, Newbigin says, received scant notice because of its theme: *The Natural and the Supernatural*. It unfortunately "appeared just at a time when the rise of Barthian theology was sweeping that question under the carpet." But, he says, "now . . . we are facing again the questions to which John Oman devoted his tremendous intellectual powers" (10). In a sense, Newbigin's book forms a supplement and corrective to the perspective of Barth.

Barth, Carl Braaten summarizes, believes that "from the human side there is sheer discontinuity. The contact of the Word of God and human culture is an event that occurs by grace alone and is always a miracle" (1977:30). It is only through the grace by which "there are justified sinners" that we may speak even of Christianity as a "true religion." That goal is only reached at the end of a "humble road" which begins by accepting the revealed judgment of God that "religion is unbelief" (Barth 1957a:325-328). Because "religion is the contradiction of revelation" there can be no point of contact between the two (302-303). Even for the Christian religion, it is only when the church "lives by grace" that it may be the "*locus* of true religion" (298).

With the "grace" and the "miracle" parts, Newbigin would not disagree. Nor would he disagree with Barth's conviction that "no culture can be normative. The only acceptable normative form of the word of God in history is the written word of God — the Bible" (Braaten 1977:30). But Newbigin's allowance that there is a kind of continuity between the religious life of the world's peoples and the revelation in Jesus Christ moves in a direction which Barth could not. The strong *"Nein!"* Barth pronounced against Emil Brunner's proposals for pursuing "natural theology" and positing that humankind has a "capacity for revelation" by which there is a natural "possibility of being addressed" rules out his companionship with Newbigin's approach (cf. Brunner and Barth 1946). For Newbigin, to affirm only discontinuity and to see it as absolute is to deny that Jesus is the "light that lightens every man" and that the normative word of God must always take form in a human, responding community which grows in terms of its cultural heritage. Grace captures and redeems, as well as it judges and sets aside, the riches of the world's cultures, including their religious dimensions. Conversion implies "radical discontinuity" but never an "absolute discontinuity."

The divergence between Newbigin and Barth can be further illustrated by the way in which Barth and Newbigin are compared in two treatments which look at both of their views. Gavin D'Costa, in a work attempting to construct a "theology of religious pluralism," develops a "pluralist, exclusivist, inclusivist" paradigm.[15] He compares the views of John Hick (pluralist), Hendrik Kraemer (exclusivist) and Karl Rahner (inclusivist). He opts for Karl Rahner's "inclusivism" which he says holds out the "possibility of grace in the dialogue partner's life and religion." This "avoids the *a priori* Barthian exclusivism which characterizes the partner's life and religion as erroneous" (1986:90). At one critical stage in his discussion, he asks regarding "Kraemer's very Barthian outlook" on "the difference between empirical Christianity and the revelation of Christ" whether "the two can be entirely separated" (74). His argument against such an "exclusivist" approach rests on the point he sees in Newbigin's critique of Kraemer, that is, that "the truth of the Gospel cannot be spoken of in abstraction from the communities' traditions which communicate it" (74). While he classes Newbigin as an "exclusivist" with Barth and Kraemer, D'Costa clearly notices that at a fundamental level Newbigin parts company on the issue of strict discontinuity.[16]

Gabriel Fackre also helps us to identify the nature of the divergence of Barth and Newbigin (1983). He himself comes close to Barth but feels compelled to move beyond him. In his construction, he claims to

> pursue the trajectory of Barth's thought (one aborted by Barth because of historically conditioned reasons — the "blood and soil" form in which extra-ecclesial truth claims were made in the formative period of his theology). Grace is power as well as favor. Therefore, there are consequences in fact as well as in principle from the particular reconciling deed of God in Christ. (45)

Two observations are important here. First, Fackre's suggestion "beyond Barth" is very close to the way Newbigin shows that it is the "one light," Christ, who shines on "every man," thus joining the uniqueness of the revelation in Christ to the universality it possesses by virtue of the fact that it is the revelation of the one who "made everything that is" and for whom all things are intended. Newbigin also goes beyond Barth at this point, although it is his sense that Barth has not altogether failed to do so himself. So he leans on him to make the point that "in Karl Barth's words, we must have ears to hear the voice of the Good Shepherd in the world at large" (77bpmi:266). And, as Barth would, Newbigin clarifies his own assertions about real continuity and divine self-communication in the context of non-Christian religions:

> So also the Christian sees the Gospel as the end of religion. God has spoken his word in Jesus Christ and whatever echoes of that word are to be found in the religions and cultures of mankind can be heard as echoes, not as parallel and independent messages. (77trsp:82)

Yet a distinction remains regarding the value placed on the cultural life of humankind, both secular and religious, as the arena in which God is self-disclosing amidst the ambiguities of light and darkness.

Second, Fackre's hint about Barth's early concern over the matter of the "blood and soil" claims to ultimacy and superiority give an important clue for the strength of his position. It certainly fueled "Barth's long struggle against 'natural theology'" which "lies behind this insistence on the Word enfleshed as the sole disclosure point for ultimate truth" (Fackre 1983:41). Newbigin finds in Barth's reaction to Hitler's "blood and soil" an important corrective for the missionary who seeks to contextualize the gospel. It warns that "to ascribe absolute value to the forms of social organization at any one time and place is both historically naive and theologically intolerable." But he adds that culture — the "powers" of the New Testament — must always be assessed both positively and negatively. "Their claim to absolute authority has been disallowed." But they are crucial to the purpose of Christ in that "we depend upon them to enable us to develop the very powers by which we can begin to question them" (78os:158-160). Culture — and its religious element — must not be absolutely valued. But neither must it be absolutely negated.[17]

It is certainly Newbigin's missionary history that brings him to a different position than Barth here. Fackre appreciates his "profound wrestle" with these questions (in the chapter in *The Open Secret* on "The Gospel Among the Religions"). He rightly assesses that his uniqueness lies in holding "a perspective that brings together themes from Karl Barth with a ministry in Indian and ecumenical contexts" (1983:42, n. 11). That combination enables him to see continuity and discontinuity together. Given his understanding that the clue to "the meaning of the public life of mankind" lies in Jesus, "the decisive turning point of human history," Newbigin can affirm:

> With this as my clue I expect to find and do find everywhere in the life of mankind signs of the kindness and justice of God which are manifested in Jesus. . . . The same clue enables me to recognize the fact that precisely these signs of God's goodness can be and are used as means by which men think to establish their own standing before God. (77bpmi:261)

The Dialogue of the Religions

In Newbigin's revision of his article on "The Basis, Purpose and Manner of Inter-Faith Dialogue" (77bpmi; cf. 78os: chapter 10), he does more than just add sections by which to interact with John Hick's response to it (cf. Hick 1977a). The terms of the discussion have changed. That change in many ways signals the culmination of a series of prior attempts to display by some reasonable typology either various proposals for a universal faith (61ftow:30-55), alternative standpoints by which to assess the claim of finality made for Christ (69fc:15-22), suggested models for interreligious dialogue (77bpmi:253-256), proposed structures for unity among the religions (77cwps:4-9), or possible meanings of the word "religion" in a religiously plural society (77trsp:82-84). Now in the concluding chapter of *The Open Secret* the question has shifted yet again. "It is now necessary to face the difficult questions which arise when this commitment ['to Jesus Christ as the one to whom all authority inheres'] is brought into contact with other unconditional commitments of the same kind" (78os:181). The discussion with adherents to other commitments is going on every day. It is at the gate. It is now only a matter of deciding what must be the faithful response in the discussion from one who is committed to Jesus Christ and the "secular announcement" he initiated into the world.

The conclusion to which Newbigin comes is "obedient witness" (78os:205-206). The church must have a "readiness for frank and searching discussion . . . with those outside the church" who are "of different cultures and traditions" (77cwps:17; cf. 18). The fashion of calling this "dialogue" he permits, so long as it is understood to refer not merely to the formal dialogue of scholars but to "the more elementary matter of day-to-day conversation with our neighbors of other faiths" (77cwps:18). In the revisions in *The Open Secret* to his earlier article on dialogue (77bpmi), a phrase enters the picture which subtly captures his new perspective: "the dialogue *of* the religions" (78os:210, emphasis mine). He treats that not as a project or program, not as something which must be attempted, not as something we must have *with* the *other* religions, but as a real and already present fact of life. People of different ultimate commitments *are* in discussion with one another. His attempt, therefore, is not to show why a Christian must engage in dialogue. But he seeks to show the purpose to be pursued in it and the manner appropriate to such an encounter with neighbors. The existing dialogue is assumed to be one which "the Christian will share" and which will "put his 'Christianity' at risk" (210).

By the time Newbigin was addressing the issue in this way, this new "fact of life" had only recently become a living fact for residents of the United Kingdom. What the church in India had always been accustomed to facing daily (and Newbigin with it), the church in England was experiencing as a fresh challenge. Newbigin describes it in a goading way: "Now the heathen are among us in their hundreds of thousands. They are much like ourselves except that — on the whole — they are more godly, more disciplined, more pious than we are" (76cc:25; cf. 85ua:243-244). During his first years back in England, Newbigin's primary response was to address the need of the church to have its "timidity in commending the Gospel" overcome. In his teaching at Selly Oak Colleges his goal was to "help these people to understand why the Church has to be missionary" (85ua:242-243). In the end, his theology of "dialogue" is simply his description of the "style of witness" which needs to characterize the "missionary" church in a religiously plural setting.

Understanding Newbigin's approach to "dialogue" requires a sense of the difficulties he sees in virtually all alternative approaches. Those are evident in the several places in which he offers a typology of responses to the issues stemming from religious plurality. The variations in those typologies from one to the next means that in no one of them do we find a standardized grid and that limits their helpfulness. What is important to note in them are the trends touching on certain kinds of responses and the typical questions he poses to them. By teasing out those general trends from a survey of his several typologies we shall be able to gain a sense of the place Newbigin himself chooses to stand and the reasons for it.

1. Generally Newbigin's typologies have included (usually as the first mentioned viewpoint) the "comparative study of religions," as representative of a perspective "from outside any of the religions." This is the perspective of the Enlightenment, which brings religions to the "bar of reason," admitting as true what falls "within the limits of pure reason," using the "scientific method as the clue" (77bpmi:253; 77trsp:83; 78os:183). In earlier typologies this was illustrated with the nineteenth-century tendency toward theories of "religion as illusion," following the schema of his mentor John Oman:

> theories of a Hegelian type which see religion as a primitive, anthropomorphic science; theories of the Schleiermacher type which see religion as a product of human psychology; and theories of a Kantian type which see religion as the result of the moral pressure of the community upon the individual. (77bpmi:254; 69fc:16; cf. Oman 1925:274ff.)

On one occasion Newbigin includes in this category ("from outside religion") what he makes a more discrete category elsewhere, that is, "programmes for political and social order" (77cwps:4-5). Here he has in mind dialogue prompted by the "practical need for political and social unity," typified by the approach of Indian colleagues like Paul Devanandan and M. M. Thomas. He mentions as a further example of this approach the sixteenth-century emperor, Akbar, as he does elsewhere to illustrate yet another separate category, "the point of view of [the] social function" of religions (77trsp:83). There Newbigin wishes to underscore a point of debate in which he had become engaged in connection with the Birmingham Syllabus for the nationally mandated religious education in the area's schools. He believes it to be a dominant British sentiment that religion "helps to keep the social fabric from splitting. The furor over the inclusion of Marxism in the Birmingham Syllabus arises largely (one suspects) from this way of looking at 'religion'" (77trsp:83). This "social function" approach is also, in reality, a subset of standpoints "from outside religions" by which they are to be judged.

In the end, these "from outside" approaches are explicitly dropped from Newbigin's typology (or perhaps included only in order to set them aside from consideration). He sets "comparative religion" apart from the discussion because "it does not envisage the possibility . . . of the meeting of different ultimate commitments," and that possibility is now the sharpened focus of his concern (78os:182).[18] But his critique of this type of approach is important to note because it is the same as that by which he measures other approaches. Whether unity is sought "on the basis of a view of reality drawn from science or philosophy" or on the basis of "a programme for political and social order," these programs "will necessarily be divisive, because not all men will accept either the proposed scientific understanding of reality or the proposed political and social order" (77cwps:5). They all have some particular perspective over against other possible and real ones, and any supposed "objectivity" fails to account for that.

2. A second "type" permeates Newbigin's attempts to set out the "types" in order, though it does not always show up in the same form. These are the perspectives which in one way or another suggest a unity based on what is "common" to all the religions. It presupposes a "common core of reality within all the varieties of religious experience" (77bpmi:254). On that basis it proposes a unity to be found by searching "within all the

religions for that which is the essence of them all" (77cwps:5). This approach therefore interprets religions as "varied manifestations of one common experience" (77trsp:83). In *The Open Secret* Newbigin treats these approaches as driven by a commendable reaction to "the clashing diversity of religious commitments." They have in common that they "seek some basis for unity among [the religious commitments], or at least some agreed common framework" (78os:184).

This was the embracing vision for all three of the views dealt with in Newbigin's earlier book, *A Faith for This One World?* (61ftow). Each provides an example of this search for a "universal faith" by which the world can be united. They differ only in the specifics of their proposals: Dr. S. Radhakrishnan speaks of the "inner essence of the actual religions" (30-41); Arnold Toynbee calls for an "alliance of the so-called higher religions" (41-46); William E. Hocking envisions a coming "confluence of the great religions" as a result of the discovery of the "universal mystical experience in the human race" (46-55). The inclusion of Radhakrishnan here is extremely important because the Hindu example runs as a thread throughout Newbigin's discussions of this general type, usually including reference to the famous "elephant and blind interpreters" story (69fc:16-17). And it bears an intimate companionship with views expressed by some Western theologians. Newbigin finds Paul Tillich, for example, expressing "with precision the Vedantic view of particular religions" (18; cf. Tillich 1963:97). Wilfred Cantwell Smith shares the Hindu model, Newbigin says, when he talks of "the religiousness which is the human response to the one transcendent reality" (77bpmi:254; cf. Smith 1962:173). John Hick, likewise, accepts "as axiomatic that there is one reality behind or within all the forms of religion" (77bpmi:254; cf. Hick 1973).

In a much earlier address at the University of Chicago in 1954 (55qutr), Newbigin presented more extensively than he has anywhere else in his published work a survey of the attitude of Hinduism toward non-Hindu faiths and its prospectus for achieving human unity. In the course of that survey, the lines of his continuing critique of similar Western suggestions emerge. He begins by reference to the visit of Swami Vivekananda to Chicago for the Parliament of World Religions toward the end of the nineteenth century. His speech there was noteworthy in that

> it was the first announcement of the claim of Hinduism to be not merely
> a religion, and not merely a world religion, but *the* world religion — the

religion within which the truths of all other religions had already been included and transcended. It is to the Hindu that the revelation of the unity of all religions has been given. (17)

This posture has pervaded India itself, where "the belief that all religions are in essence one has become not merely an article of faith but almost an axiom of thought" (17).

But Newbigin, who by then had spent almost two decades in India encountering the fruit of the perspective, found several points at which a critique must be made. For one thing, the unity envisioned can only be a negative one in that what "it offers is the cessation of strife, not the creation of a new community." In fact, it "would be quite contrary to its own nature to produce a historic community" because it "bids men seek beyond all the visible forms which are the mark of any human community." Hinduism, Newbigin says, "has no doctrine of the church" (55qutr:22-23).

More important for the present subject, however, is the way Newbigin responds to the implied spirit of "tolerance" in the attitude that stems from Vivekananda's conviction that "the contradictions between the religions are only apparent." The popular illustration of the elephant and the blind beggars raises the important question: what are "the credentials of the man who tells it and who implicitly claims that in the country of the blind he alone can see"? Newbigin finds

> a fundamental intolerance implied in the Hindu position, no less than in the Christian. His attitude of equal tolerance to all forms of religion rests upon a definite conviction in the light of which he believes all the forms of religion to be but varied refractions of the truth which he sees. (55qutr:19)[19]

This makes Hinduism's "universal perspective" but one more particular notion. With this fact Newbigin later challenged the religiously mixed community of the Vellore Christian Medical College:

> If you examine the doctrine that all religions are really the same, whether you find it for instance in the writings of Vivekananda or in those of Dr. Radhakrishnan, you will find that it rests upon a particular view of religion, a view of religion which Christians believe to be wrong. (68coec:84)

Not only Hinduism, but "every mature and universal religion will have its own interpretation of the multiplicity of religions" (55qutr:23). Hinduism is no more capable than any other religion of escaping the general truism that "there is no standpoint available to man which is not some particular standpoint, and every claim to reconcile men must share the precariousness which arises from that fact" (29).

Here we come to the heart of the issue for Newbigin. In the spate of articles which in the mid-seventies flowed in response to the issues of the religious plurality which had engulfed England, his constant refrain becomes the reiteration of this "given" fact: there is no standpoint above every other standpoint. Whether one stands outside of the religions to offer a unifying perspective or understanding, or whether one offers a proposal for unity from within a religious commitment, the result can never provide escape from the "precariousness" of particularity, which is our "fundamental human predicament." We are reminded that all of the historical efforts for "the putting together of truths from different religions" point toward the simple conclusion, that "the result is still only one proposal which has to be defended against others. A variety of relative truths do not become absolute by being combined" (77cwps:5).

In most of Newbigin's discussions in the mid- to late-1970s, these issues are pressed the most forcefully in response to the view of John Hick, who at the time lived in the same city (Birmingham). According to Newbigin, Hick's suggested "Copernican Revolution" requires a critique similar to that given to Hinduism. Hick has failed to come to terms with the inevitable particularity of any suggested understanding of the interrelationship of the religions, even one which accepts and embraces them all. Hence, there is a "logical fallacy" into which Newbigin says Hick falls. He calls for "a shift from the dogma that Christianity is at the centre to the realisation that it is God who is at the centre" (Hick 1973:131; cf. Newbigin 78os:184, 188-189). But Hick's analogy of "the sun and the planets" is not commensurate with "God and the religions." The physical universe consists of elements which are observable by the same methods. God and the religions are not.

> The two realities which are accessible and comparable are God as I conceive him and God as the world religions conceive him. What claims to be a model for the unity of religions turns out in fact to be the claim that one theologian's conception of God is the reality which is the central essence of all religions. (78os:184-185)

Hick, by the very use of the words "dogma" and "realisation" in his call for the shift masks what cannot be avoided (78os:188-189). His new "realisation" is as much a dogma as the old.

What Hick has failed to see, according to Newbigin, is that "the appearance of neutrality and objectivity is an illusion" (76cc:26). Such an "illusion" Newbigin found present also in the perspective of the Birmingham Syllabus (in the fashioning of which Hick had been involved). While it directed the curriculum "away from attempting to foster the claims of particular religious standpoints" (City of Birmingham 1975:4), it seemed to ignore that by adopting a "stance" regarding religious education in a plural society — which therefore involved a "stance" interpreting the nature, character, and purpose of "religions" — it would inevitably "rest upon one particular view in which religions should be regarded" (77trsp:83). On the one hand, to make of a "religion" simply "one of a class" is to reduce it so that it is "no longer an ultimate commitment, a stance for living." On the other hand, the view which thus classifies it must become itself a "stance for living," that is, by the definitions of the syllabus itself, religious in character. Newbigin's chief complaint about the syllabus was that it was only its own stance which was left out of the picture (82-84).[20]

Newbigin believes that it must be acknowledged in the end that "we have *no* neutral standpoint from which we can survey all the religions . . . and pronounce that they are all variants of one theme. There is no standpoint which is above all standpoints" (76cc:26). We cannot be free of "the taint of locality" (61ftow:53), and it is pretentious and illusory to think otherwise.

3. Newbigin completely agrees, therefore, with Hick's beginning observation about how things are. Disunity ("religious and other than religious," Newbigin would add) persists because of the "plurality of centres" in which each confessional stance "has the impression of standing at the centre of the world of meanings, with all other faiths dispersed around its periphery" (Hick 1977a:4-5). But every mature religion has some particular viewpoint about how itself and all the others fit together. And every claim to unity — whether from within or without the "religions" — "rests on some ultimate commitment" and thereby possesses particular religious character. Newbigin is convinced of

> the truth of Andre Dumas' thesis, that when a proposal for unity is made,
> if the proposer does not explicitly indicate the centre around which the

proposed unity is to be structured, then he is in fact proposing his own religion. (77cwps:7; cf. 3-4; Dumas 1974)

Every program for the unity of religions "is — as every programme must be — a programme which is built round a definite centre" (77cwps:5). This must be recognized and accepted. It is Newbigin's criticism of Hick that he has failed to do so and therefore has not solved the problem: he has only added one more chair to the ever-widening circle of suggested perspectives among which discussion must take place and from which credentials should be requested for the claims being made. The only possible response we can make to the fact of religious plurality, according to Newbigin, is the acceptance of the mutuality of possessing diverse and even contradictory ultimate commitments and the readiness to discuss those frankly and openly. This is the third model which permeates his typologies and it is the one he embraces as proper to the Christian perspective. This is an extension, really, of what he sometimes lists as a separate category from his "Christian" alternative, proposals which arise "from within the religious commitment itself" (77cwps:5). The Hindu suggestion is one such proposal from "within one of the religions" (69fc:17-18). The Christian's conviction is that in fact Jesus "is the centre around which the unity of mankind here in history is to be built" (61ftow:38). Both are particular standpoints. Neither is above all others.[21]

This perspective culminates most fully in *The Open Secret*. There his final model affirms "that the Christian goes to meet his neighbor of another religion on the basis of his commitment to Jesus Christ. . . . His confession is the starting point of his truth-seeking" (78os:190). Even the claim that the center is to be found in Jesus must give way to the recognition that "we are on the way to the knowledge of the true centre." "Jesus as I know him" must always give way to "Jesus as he really is" (77cwps:8-9). In this, the Christian sits in "the same position as his partners in dialogue" (78os:191).

So then, Newbigin's call to the Christian community is for a style of dialogue in which it does two things. First, it must be definite about its own center and the reasons it has for claiming that it is the center of the meaning of the history of the world. And if it is clear that Jesus is the center, the church must be willing to sit in the circle without assuming that it has a privileged place to sit at the center of the circle of ultimate commitments, nor at some point outside the circle, nor in any way above it. It is into a

pluralistic setting that God places the church and it is responsible only to
be a faithful witness there in the humble position of servant, subject to the
requirements of full humanity. Its witness is that of one in a trial, not
offering proofs or arguments, but introducing by the only means open to
it a new datum, the presence of the kingdom of God. Its "testimony" can
be contested. Therefore, there is risk and vulnerability. But it learns by the
encounter and it trusts the Spirit to provide that others will as well.[22]

The test for Newbigin will be whether he can and will live by the same
strictures that he lays down for everyone else. Will he claim "a standpoint
above every other" as a Christian? To be sure, there is a tension here. In his
book on *The Finality of Christ* it would appear that he is suggesting so. On
the one hand he says,

> if religion deals with men's ultimate commitments, then it is surely wise
> to recognize that a religious man does not have a point of view which
> transcends that commitment and which enables him to judge other
> religious commitments impartially. (69fc:20)

But on the other hand he goes on to suggest that if it can be shown that
the standpoint of the gospel is not one that is merely "within one of the
religions" (i.e., that it is a "secular announcement"), it would be "possible
to claim that Christ is the end of all religion, and that therefore this standpoint is one outside of the religions" (and in that sense "final"?) (69fc:22).
The position he develops does hinge on the continuing affirmation that
"God as he truly is" must be the recognized "centre of all things" and that
(not Christianity but) Jesus Christ is "God as he truly is" incarnate. "Therefore Jesus Christ is the centre, and all phenomena of religion (including
Christianity) and all the phenomena of irreligion and anti-religion are to
be judged and valued by their relation to him" (77cwps:7).

This claim forms Newbigin's ultimate commitment, and the interpretation of all the religions lies inherent within it. It is a claim which he
knows cannot be construed as "objective" or "above all other standpoints."
It must be given over to scrutiny. The key lies in the fact that Newbigin
knows that truth cannot be proven by rational argument, nor can it be
confirmed by cultural force. The only proof available to the Christian claim
lies at "the end," when everything will be made clear and the story will show
its point and meaning. As one laid hold of by Another, Newbigin gives his
simple witness that the "end" has been revealed ahead of time in the person

of Jesus. That is the claim which lives in daily, as yet unresolved, encounter with other claims and commitments.

In summary, Newbigin argues against all supposed ultimate perspectives regarding the religions. He accepts the position of one particular stance among many, each of which holds an ultimate vision. In regard to the dialogue itself, there are basically two types of opinion, the first of which he rejects and the second he embraces: (1) conversation proceeds based on some notion which ties all the religions together; (2) conversation proceeds based on the variety of commitments they represent. This latter he adopts in a way that seeks to preserve a full appreciation for cultural (and religious) plurality while maintaining the integrity of Christian witness.

The Problem of Universalism

Among the inevitable questions that arise in contemporary discussions of the relationship of Christianity to other faiths is the destiny of people who have no explicit faith in Jesus Christ. "Will the pious Hindu (or Muslim, or Buddhist) be saved?" (69fc:60). It is a question that certainly must come close on the heels of the case that Newbigin makes in all his writings for the "finality" and universal validity of the revelation of God in "the total fact of Christ." While he will want to exegete and critique the question itself, it is one in which he recognizes what he refers to as the "plausible logic" by which conclusions about the fate of large numbers of people could be drawn. His article on "Christ and the World of Religions" (83cwr) targets the question that grows out of the pressing fact that "death does reign in the world" alongside the claim that Jesus is uniquely "the life of the world" and his death is the crucial victory: "If it is indeed the decisive event for the deliverance of the world from death, does it not follow that all who have not explicitly accepted the gift of life in the name of Jesus are condemned to eternal death?" What are we to think about the millions before Christ or before the gospel who are condemned? Newbigin is aware that "questions such as these cannot be silenced" (16-17). What can or cannot, must or must not be said about them?

Newbigin's position on this issue has been identified (rightly) as "an intentional silence" on the destiny question, maintaining "an eschatological agnosticism about the non-knowers of Jesus Christ" (Fackre 1983:42). Not that he has been silent in the defense of that agnosticism! He prefers to refer to his position as one that refuses to cut the "enduring tension" between the idea of "Jesus as the unique Lord and Saviour of the world by reference to whom all men are finally judged" and the ideas, equally biblical, that he is "the universal saviour" and that "the object of [God's] saving love is not a few but the whole world" (77cwps:24). He defends the roots of both "the universalist perspective" and "the clear teaching about judgment" in the Bible.

> There can be no doubt that just as the perspective of the Bible is the whole history of humanity and of the cosmos, so also it is full of what one may call universalist overtones. . . . On the other hand there are equally clear and much more numerous passages, especially in the New Testament, which speak of a coming judgment and of the possibility of being rejected. . . . We would part company with the New Testament altogether if we ignored it. (78os:87-88)[23]

Because of this tension, Newbigin will not agree to either of the generally circulated notions. He directly challenges "universalism,"[24] which he defines as "the dogmatic belief that the possibility of eternal loss is excluded" (77cwps:24). His critique of Rahner is a most emphatic example at this point. The scheme by which he postulates that adherents of non-Christian religions might be considered to be "anonymous Christians" has the problem that "it assumes that our position as Christians entitles us to know and declare what is God's final judgment upon other people" (78os:195; cf. Rahner 1966, 1969). This is the constant reminder Newbigin gives as the rationale for his "intentional agnosticism." Content with what is given,

> [w]e must not presume to prejudge the last judgment. We know a few things, but they are enough: that the call of God is to all men; that those whom He chooses to convert are few; and that those few are chosen not for themselves but for the sake of all. If they forget that, they will be rejected. (66c:323)

"We cannot and must not try to know in advance what the final judgment is going to be" (77cwps:25).

It is just as presumptuous, in other words, to declare that "all are saved" as it is to declare that certain ones are not. It does not undo the presumption of it to be motivated by concern for the masses of people who otherwise might be thought condemned. Newbigin says,

> I cannot find anything in the New Testament to support what seems to be a widespread view today, namely that whereas it is tolerable to think of a few people being lost, it is intolerable to think of a majority of mankind being lost. (66c:323)

God does not govern by "referendum" (69fc:61). And in regard to proposals which suggest alternative ways God works and saves, the principle Newbigin states in a slightly different area of discussion applies here as well.

> The Bible gives us no ground for believing that God has other plans for the unity of mankind than that which he has set forth in Jesus Christ and of which he has made the Church to be first fruit, sign and instrument. . . . This is not popular doctrine at the moment, but it is scriptural. (69wwfo:131)

When faced most pointedly with the complaint which O. V. Jathanna laid at Kraemer's door — how can the decisive and saving deed of Christ "be effective for those who lived and died before Christ was born or before the gospel was brought to them?" — Newbigin attempts an answer based on an extensive survey of the Scriptures. At the end, his conclusion is that "none of this teaching can be construed to mean what is usually called 'universalism,' for it lies always in close relation with teaching about judgement and the dread possibility of final perdition" (83cwr:26-28).[25]

But it is not the universalist position alone that Newbigin finds guilty of presumption. He sees also some "who seem anxious to keep the doors of hell wide open so that there may not be any lack of funds or recruits for missionary work" (69fc:61). Whether for this or better motives, the adoption of some "opinion about who are to be finally saved and who finally lost" cuts the tension as well as does the universalist view. To rule some out, whether by the traditional guidelines of baptism or "belief," or by the more recent "moralistic" tendency to include those who "sincerely follow the light of their own conscience" or who are "sincere adherents" of other religions, falls prey to the same charge as to rule all in. "Neither of these positions has any real ground. We have no data to answer the question" (69fc:62).

Here Newbigin's argument turns. He recognizes the biblical foundation in the doctrine of judgment from which the "plausibility" of an ex-
cluding opinion might arise, but he guards the conclusions to be drawn
from that.

> It is certainly made clear that it is possible to refuse this opportunity and
> thereby to lose the possibility of salvation — to be lost. But it is not, I
> believe, implied that the vast multitudes who have never been presented
> with this Gospel call for conversion and commitment are thereby nec-
> essarily excluded from participation in God's on-going and completed
> work. (69fc:61)

Rather, he argues, the teaching of Scripture steers us away from "knowing"
the fate of anyone. When asked whether only "few" would be saved, "Jesus
declined to answer." He simply replied that his questioners should "do their
best to get in through the narrow door" (69fc:61-62). This poses the real
issue for Newbigin, which is the difference "between the quest for a kind
of assurance which has the future securely programmed in advance, and
the summons to a kind of faith which trusts everything to the living Lord."
Within that sort of faith one can humbly receive "the central emphasis of
the New Testament teaching about final judgment, which is that judgment
will always be surprising and that it will be those who are sure they belong
inside who find themselves outside" (77cwps:25; cf. Travis 1983:38).

It is Newbigin's persistent observation that judgment, as "surprise,"
is particularly addressed to those "who have received the gracious promises
of God." He notes that "the grave and terrible warnings that the New
Testament contains about the possibility of eternal loss are directed to those
who are confident that they are among the saved" (82ccee:151). For Paul,
the possibility of eternal loss was a threat "for him as a believer," according
to 1 Corinthians 9:27. And according to Romans 11:25f., "he is willing to
be convinced that all will be saved." This Newbigin calls the "true logic of
grace" which stands over against the "plausible logic" which would extend
from the redemption of Christ through the cross to the conclusion that we
may, or even must, "say openly that those who do not know that mercy are
lost." Newbigin feels the force of that argument but demurs. "I can only
answer that, while it seems plausible, it is not permitted for the simple
reason that my place in the whole transaction is that of a witness and not
that of a judge" (82ccee:151).

Before looking at several important criticisms of Newbigin's view, one more dimension of it should be mentioned. We have observed the nature and strength of his rejection of any presumption via a claim to know either that all are ruled in or that some are ruled out. That very way of looking at it hints at an objection he makes to the form of the question. He resists the idea of giving it an answer because it is asked in such restricted terms. It is too mathematical. "The universalism of the Bible will not be understood if we are thinking in terms of a multitude of spiritual monads and asking about the destiny of each one conceived as a separate individual" (78os:89). To ask about the personal destiny of individual souls strips away the meaning of salvation, which for Newbigin is both corporate, present, and oriented away from self-interest toward service. This becomes his primary criticism of the very debate about "universalism" and the various approaches to it. It is framed in terms too focused on individual destiny. Such is his response to the book by Gavin D'Costa in which Newbigin's views figure prominently, sometimes as a companion "exclusivist" to Kraemer, sometimes as the critic of Kraemer and support of Rahner, whom D'Costa essentially defends (D'Costa 1986). The whole layout of the issues, he says, is built on a false, because truncated, view of salvation. To talk about eternal destiny apart from relationships here and now is to do serious damage to the gospel (personal conversation, October 1986). The impression one easily gets from Newbigin is that he would prefer not to have to deal with a question such as "the eternal destiny of the individual soul." Yet the issue keeps returning and must be engaged, and so he does.[26]

Several criticisms can be made regarding Newbigin's insistence on maintaining an intentionally agnostic position. From the "inclusivist" D'Costa comes one line of critique. He observes of both Kraemer and Newbigin that they avoid giving an answer regarding what he sees to be the "awkward tension" in their position, that is, that a loving God denies salvation to millions. He agrees with Newbigin that we cannot know the mysterious workings of God. However, he says,

> this answer seems painfully inadequate in the light of the pressing questions before us and it is not clear, if we use our test case of Israel, why there are supposedly inadequate grounds for attempting to probe the issue further. Kraemer, Newbigin and others seem to want to relieve this exclusivist internal tension without paying the price in terms of the theological implications of their answer. (D'Costa 1986:68)

D'Costa's challenge is too forcefully pressed. The critique must be qualified by the broader context of his discussion. D'Costa builds a case for Rahner's view as an inclusivist model which stands between the pluralist and exclusivist models. The latter each emphasize one of "two traditionally held Christian axioms." The pluralists (represented in D'Costa's treatment by John Hick) stress "the universal salvific will of God" and the exclusivists (represented by Hendrik Kraemer) stress "salvation through Jesus Christ alone." The inclusivist model is that of Karl Rahner and it, D'Costa argues, is the only one which holds together the two axioms. Two major flaws in the case he makes are important here. First, as it turns out, the two axioms by which the various models are to be tested were originally drawn from Rahner (D'Costa 1986:83). This seriously prejudices the case by setting up the debate on Rahner's own terms. But second, the parties brought forward into the debate are an imbalanced match. Kraemer is an anachronism. He can hardly be expected to have anticipated and spoken in terms of our more modern pluralistic setting and the newer sensitivities which go with it. This difficulty forces D'Costa to lean on Newbigin as a second to Kraemer. But curiously, most of D'Costa's references to Newbigin make use of his critiques of Kraemer or gather from him what is taken to be implicit support for Rahner or D'Costa's own Rahnerian approach (74, 94-95, 105, 106, 121, 124, 136). His classification of Newbigin as an exclusivist is strained by this fact. His debate would have dealt more fairly with modern exclusivism had he chosen Newbigin from the beginning instead of Kraemer. That would have protected him from using the older Kraemer as a "straw man."

When we come to D'Costa's severe criticism of Newbigin's "agnostic" approach, then, we must understand where D'Costa is headed. It is also important to note that his source for the articulation of Newbigin's position is the very place in Newbigin's writings at which he critiques Rahner both for making "religion" the salvific realm and for presuming to pronounce on the salvation of the whole world (77bpmi:259-260; D'Costa drew the reference from the re-publication of the article in Rousseau 1981:20). No-where in his treatment of Rahner does D'Costa take up either criticism.

These factors complicate D'Costa's criticism of Newbigin's "agnostic" approach. He gives little evidence that he has fully heard the basis for that approach. And yet, it is a critique that cannot be taken lightly. Is Newbigin guilty of failing to do his "theological duty" as Hans Küng has said of such an approach? (78os:196; cf. Küng 1976:99). At the point in *The Open Secret* where Newbigin speaks to this issue, there is an expansion of the text from the earlier article from which it is drawn, and this suggests that the force of the charge has not escaped Newbigin's attention (cf. 77bpmi:260). He adds Küng's emotive word, "supercilious," to set the stage for his response. In it he expands the biblical case for the note of "surprise" he finds emphasized in the New Testament. He underscores judgment as threatening the secure. He ends on the note of Jesus' refusal to answer "are there few?" He personalizes by adding,

> It is almost impossible for me to enter into simple, honest, open, and friendly communication with another person as long as I have at the back of my mind the feeling that I am one of the saved and he is one of the lost. Such a gulf is too vast to be bridged by any ordinary human communication. (78os:196-197)

But is his argument finally convincing? That it culminates in so un-characteristic an appeal to a sense of personal "impossibility" to overcome a gulf "too vast to be bridged by any ordinary human communication" suggests how close and tenuous is the case for his agnostic approach over against the more distinctly "exclusivist" approach which he acknowledges follows a kind of "plausible logic." After all, if there is ever a case in which the clear indication of the Scriptures leads toward what can only be conceived as humanly impossible, does that not simply make more emphatic the need for grace and the power of the Spirit? He would surely argue this way in other cases.

Perhaps the most direct challenge to Newbigin's "agnostic" stance from the more "exclusivist" side comes from Paul Schrotenboer in response to Newbigin's article on evangelical-ecumenical differences (1982; cf. 82ccee). Schrotenboer is sensitive to the tension of which Newbigin speaks and with which he wrestles. But he confesses that he is

> not impressed by Bishop Newbigin's comments that we are not judges, for the person who is spiritual judges all things (1 Cor. 2:15). On the basis that we are only witnesses and not judges, it does not follow that to affirm that people who don't know Christ are lost is an act of judging. To my way of thinking, that kind of statement is simply a witness to the exclusive saving power in Jesus Christ. (1982:153)

Schrotenboer's point is important. Newbigin's courtroom analogy of "witness" and "judge" is helpful for clarifying the style of witness for which the Bible calls. But it does breed the tendency to equivocate on the meaning of "judging." Newbigin assumes that to express an "opinion about who are to be finally saved" (77cwps:25) must necessarily "judge" them in the sense against which we are warned in the New Testament. But that ignores the distinction between acting as judge by consigning people to a particular fate and identifying (giving witness to!) the basis on which a judge has indicated such a decision will be made.

Newbigin's dichotomy has the potential to narrow the very notion of "witness." This can be observed in two respects. First, if the church bears the witness of the Spirit, then it would follow that it witnesses to those things about which the Spirit is concerned to witness. John 16:8-11 identifies some of the things that are involved. The Spirit, among other things, "will prove the world wrong about . . . judgment," or as the RSV has it, "will convince the world . . . of judgment." Newbigin's treatment of this item in his commentary draws back from its most direct meaning. He limits the idea by dwelling on a part of it, that the Spirit "exposes as false the world's idea of judgment" (82lhc:213). The plain meaning of the text cannot be only that the Spirit exposes the world's idea. It must be also that the Spirit exposes judgment itself, rightly understood. It is difficult to see how judgment can be convincingly exposed without some criteria of discrimination or differentiation. To join the Spirit in giving witness to what Jesus has told us about those criteria cannot be construed as an unwarranted judging of individuals. It is witness to what is revealed about the basis for and fact of judgment. This moves beyond affirming the mere "possibility of eternal perdition" to the report of the indication that there will be such for some.

The idea of witness may also be narrowed if its meaning is wrested away from its relationship with other biblical models of the church's calling. If "witness" can be sharply contrasted with "judge" in terms of courtroom imagery, it is more difficult to distance the companion images of "ambassador" or "herald" from the function of God's judgment (cf. 2 Corinthians 5:20 et al.). Neither the ambassador nor the herald are themselves judges, but they clearly are commissioned to represent the judgment of one who is. The appeal to biblical language will have to account for the implications of all these models.

Additional questions may be raised about the biblical case Newbigin makes for his view. These represent areas in which further exegetical work would be necessary if his position is to be sustained.

First of all, "surprise" is certainly a feature of the New Testament teaching about judgment, but a more nuanced assessment of its implications is needed. What are the biblical indications that the surprise element is intended to settle us into an agnostic stance? Do we really know nothing about the judgment that comes? Does not the revelation of the element of "surprise" already tell us a great deal? As Newbigin himself has emphasized, the "religious" are generally the least likely to respond to the light. That tells us something about the lines that will be drawn by judgment. A better reading might be that Jesus came revealing judgment to those who had ears to hear and whom his Father chose, and the very thing he came revealing was the new surprising basis on which judgment would take place. Isn't this after all part of the "secret" made "open" by the Spirit's life in the church?

Second, the argument from Luke 13:23-30 (where Jesus responds to the question, "will only a few be saved?") is not convincing. Newbigin's often repeated claim that Jesus refused to answer the question about the "few" is open to serious challenge. In the first place, we are not told that the question was from a "disciple" as Newbigin says (780s:88). It was "someone." It is Luke's habit to be painstakingly clear about such identifications. The context as well seems to imply someone not a disciple. More to the point, it is hard to construe Jesus' response to the question as a refusal to answer regarding the "few" in that he plainly says "many, I tell you, will try to enter and will not be able" (Luke 13:24). In addition, the text cannot be totally isolated from its parallel in Matthew 7:13-14. In that collection of sayings Jesus adds: "For the gate is narrow and the road is hard that leads to life, and there are few who find it." Newbigin raises important exegetical issues regarding our interpretation of these passages, and his hearing of the passages must be seriously engaged. But his exegetical argument as it stands does not yet bear the weight he places on it.

One final comment may be added. If there should be some possibility — as Newbigin seems to hold some hope for — that God will bring about the salvation (holistically understood) of some, or many, by a route altogether "other" than by the way of election, each one bearing the message to the neighbor, then it would appear that the whole fabric of the socio-historical and missionary character of the church as the sign and instrument of the kingdom is threatened. What such a possibility might mean apart from the method of election, which Newbigin asserts is alone congruent with human nature and destiny as well as divine personhood and purpose,

Newbigin does not suggest. Lacking some such "fitting" description, the relationship between his intentionally "agnostic" stance and his sense of the "inner logic of election" is not evident.

To dwell on these challenges to the argument Newbigin advances in support of his view should not be taken to suggest that its value is eliminated, or even diminished. Newbigin has provided important elements to the whole debate on universalism by qualifying and recasting the questions themselves, and the field as a whole will be richer if it pays attention to them. (The implications of this will be revisited in chapter seven.) Beyond that, his view is important to consider precisely because it lives so close to a distinctly "exclusivist" view while differentiating itself from it. The two views share important territory. They both find deficient the more bold affirmations of the pluralist view, and to a certain extent the inclusivist view. They both find it crucial to be rooted in biblical affirmations that take seriously both the "uniqueness" of Christ and the universality of God's love for the world. It is important that the dialogue of these theological "cousins" — the dialogue between Newbigin's view rooted in his "election logic" and the exclusivist view he acknowledges is also following a certain "plausible logic" — should continue.

CHAPTER 7

A Theology of Cultural Plurality:
Charting the Agenda

This exposition of the structure of Lesslie Newbigin's missionary theology (which is more than a theology of mission though more pointed than a complete "dogmatics") has intended to show that he offers in it an implicit "theology of cultural plurality." It rests on the "missionary character" of the biblical doctrine of election. One is chosen by God to bear the blessing to another. The particularity of the choice reflects both the personal character of God (which implies the freedom to act and to choose the time and place of such action) and the social character of human life. It is congruent with the nature of salvation (it reconciles as it is received at the hand of an "other") and the scope of it (it is intended for all). Far from creating or intensifying the "problem" of particularity, election for witness is the pattern which makes the inevitable particularity of a personal God's historical actions universal. The particular choice is designed to bear the blessing to all.

Election is the principle by which one event is seen to be significant for providing meaning for the whole. Some are chosen to be the witnesses of the disclosure of the meaning of the history of the world which comes in the only way possible, by revelation. The point of history can be known only at the end of the story. That cannot be known in advance unless it is shown by the one whose purpose the end fulfills. Central to the series of God's acts of self-communication is the life, teaching, death, and resurrection of Jesus, which disclosed the end by announcing the commencement of the "reign of God." The resurrection affirmation that in Jesus' death there was victory over death speaks at once of the judgment and hope of the world, giving meaning both to the history of the world as a whole and to the lives of the individual persons whose histories are a part of it.

We come to grasp that this is so not by the coercion of another, nor even by our own rational choice, but by the action of the Spirit of God, who chooses to make us witnesses by conversion. Conversion is always a radical "U-turn" but never totally discontinuous with culturally formed models and patterns in terms of which the Spirit's witness has approached and challenged us. Within the culture of every newly converted person and community, the Spirit forms a new response to the lordship of Christ over all of life. But the Spirit-directed independence of the new convert to judge what form that obedience should take is not total. Its form is certainly not determined by the culture of the one chosen to bear the Spirit's witness to the new convert, but neither can it remain independent of the preceding forms of discipleship. The new convert is necessarily part of the community of chosen witnesses, bonded by the reconciliation of one receiving the blessing at the hand of another. Mutual recognition that each one's culture stands under the judgment of the cross while also containing riches to be brought into captivity to Christ forces both to listen to the Scriptures and to learn from each other.

The relationship with every neighbor who does not share this commitment is established by this election for witness. Election has in view the universal scope and meaning of the "secular announcement" intended for all and addressed to the whole of life. That announcement is "world affairs" in that it does not merely address the "religious department" of life but the total spectrum of its concerns. "Religion," then, is not made the salvific element of culture. Nor is it excluded from view, since in every configuration of culture there is a religious dimension in the sense of an "ultimate commitment." The Christian relates continuously to people of ultimate commitments that differ from that which is indicated by the gospel. Therefore, living as one committed to a particular standpoint and not claiming a standpoint above every other, the Christian's relationship must be on the basis that one has been laid hold of by Another to give a witness to a fact which can be contested. In that relationship it is recognized that others will speak from their standpoints, and, because of that, one's own form of Christianity will be at risk. The Christian's hope is that both partners in the dialogue of cultures (including religions) will be converted to Christ in the process.

This summary of Newbigin's theological foundations for approaching the world's culturally plural circumstances in mission makes apparent that his theological reflection casts a field of thought which may rightly be called a "theology of cultural plurality." Entwined within his election "logic" are responses to questions anticipated earlier as those which any such theology must engage and to which Newbigin is constantly attentive: What is the meaning of the plurality of cultures, and how is that fact to be valued? What is the meaning of the fortunes of history by which these cultures are placed in relationship with one another? How is the Christian message to be understood in light of this plurality? What forms of Christian mission correspond to these understandings?

Newbigin most directly answers questions like these when he describes what is involved in "the missionary encounter" between the gospel and a given culture. That encounter he construes as part of a larger "triangular relationship" between the local culture, the Christianity of the missionary church (understood as a culturally ecumenical fellowship), and the witness of the Bible (78os:165-172; cf. 86fg:7-9).[1] This "triangle of forces" sets in juxtaposition three axes of special concern for a theology of cultural plurality: on the one side, the gospel-culture (or, Christ-culture, Bible-culture) encounter itself; on the other side, the "reciprocal relationship" between the Bible and the community whose life is determined by it; and along the base, the "missionary dialogue" between that community and the cultures as they are both addressed by the Bible (Figure 1, p. 238). Most approaches tend to focus on either the first or the third of these axes. One type of approach envisions primarily the first axis. H. Richard Niebuhr's classic treatment deals with *Christ and Culture* (1951). Bruce Nicholls similarly focuses on the development of a "Theology of Gospel and Culture" (1979). Representative of approaches which emphasize the base of the triangle (the third axis) are Louis Luzbetak's *The Church and Cultures* (1970) and Charles Kraft's *Christianity in Culture* (1979).[2] The Willowbank Consultation, sponsored in 1978 by the Lausanne Committee for World Evangelization (LCWE), shows the ambiguity that persists between these two dominant ways of construing the issues. Its theme was identified as "gospel and culture," but the abridged American edition of its published compendium bears the subtitle, "Studies in Christianity and Culture." Likewise, when Aylward Shorter defines "inculturation" as "the on-going dialogue between faith and culture or cultures" or more fully as "the creative and dynamic relationship between the Christian message and a culture or cul-

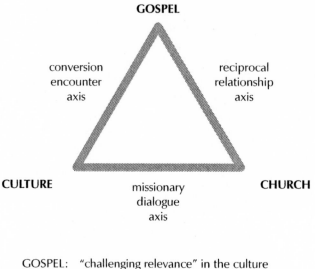

GOSPEL: "challenging relevance" in the culture
          "hermeneutical circle" with the church

CULTURE: radical discontinuity regarding the gospel
         radical independence regarding the church

CHURCH: adherence to the given tradition
        dialogue with the varied cultures

FIGURE 1. A Triangular Model of Gospel-Culture Relationships

tures," he seems to equate the gospel message with the church's grasp of it
(1988:11). Gospel and church, in Newbigin's triangle, are thus collapsed.
Over against tendencies such as these, Newbigin's model maintains a wider
and fresher dynamism by stressing this third side of the triangle, that is,
the "reciprocal relation" between the church and the Bible by which the
church represents the Bible in the encounter with cultures and the Bible
critiques and reforms the church while it is doing so.

    In this concluding chapter, these three axes will be used as a frame-
work for marking out some of the contours of what a theology of cultural
plurality entails and for assessing the value of Newbigin's contributions to
the agenda of such a field. Several interrelated questions will be kept in
view regarding his theological proposals: (a) what are Newbigin's valuable
insights that hold promise for further development? (b) what are the limits

and weaknesses that need to be identified and addressed? (c) how do his perspectives challenge the way issues are generally posed and what agenda does he thus forge for the field? and (d) in what ways might his views profitably be built upon? A survey along these lines will provide the basis for showing finally how Newbigin's theology of cultural plurality undergirds the "gospel and Western culture" venture and the recovery of the missionary character of the churches of the West.

The Gospel-Culture Encounter

For Newbigin, the missionary encounter is at the most essential level a Christ-culture, Bible-culture, gospel-culture conversion encounter. This is the form of the question he puts in regard to the "missionary problem" of post-Enlightenment culture. What would be involved, he asks, in a "genuinely missionary encounter between the gospel and this modern Western culture?" For an answer he draws from his basic understanding of "the issues raised by the cross-cultural communication of the gospel" (86fg:4ff.). His most fundamental premise is that

> there can never be a culture-free gospel. Yet the gospel, which is from the beginning to the end embodied in culturally conditioned forms, calls into question all cultures, including the one in which it was originally embodied. (86fg:4)[3]

Paul's conversion provides Newbigin with an illustration of the dynamics of the encounter. The voice that interrupted his trip to Damascus spoke to him not in Greek but in Hebrew, "the language of the home and the heart, the mother tongue" (cf. Acts 26). But it called him into question: "Why do you persecute me?" Such a confrontation as that — the challenge to a radical U-turn of ultimate commitment — can only be brought into the picture with any "right" or "power" by God. This then is Newbigin's model for the encounter of gospel and culture. The gospel is communicated "in the language of the receptor culture," provisionally accepting the understandings embodied in that language. It will always "involve contradiction, and call for conversion." That conversion can only be the supernatural work of the sovereign Spirit, never the "calculable" achievement of a human communicator or persuader (86fg:5-6).

In several of Newbigin's articulations of his triangular model his discussion begins at the most visible axis, the relationship between the missionary's culture and the receptor culture (78ctc, 78os:164-180). But in those cases as well it is clear that the most essential and elementary facet of the dynamic is reached only when the third corner of the picture comes into view and it is clear that the Bible acts as a force that critiques both cultures. The missionary's efforts at communication are most properly to be understood as pointers to the most basic encounter, which is an action of God. The missionary communication must aim in the direction toward which that encounter is known to be headed. The goal is best summarized for Newbigin by the expression of A. G. Hogg — "challenging relevance" (78ctc:11-12).[4] Newbigin highly values the model provided by Hogg's "experiment" of theology done in "faithful dialogue" with the Hindu culture (as shared in his book, *Karma and Redemption*, 1909). In the process of the dialogue, "the Hindu reader hears himself addressed wholly in terms with which he has learned to understand his world" (the "relevance"), while at the same time being "introduced to Jesus as one who, standing within that familiar model, bursts it open with the power of a wholly new fact" (the "challenge"; 78ctc:11-12). Communication which seeks to embody the gospel within the language and forms of the receptor culture but fails to challenge it leads to "syncretism." When it seeks to challenge apart from such embodiment it becomes "irrelevant" and fails to communicate (86fg:7).[5]

The concern to maintain both these dimensions in full force in the encounter leads Newbigin to stress the notion of "contextualization" over the older emphases on "indigenization" and "adaptation." For him, "the value of the word *contextualization* is that it suggests the placing of the gospel in the total context of a culture at a particular moment, a moment that is shaped by the past and looks to the future." It does not suggest identifying with the more traditional and "conservative" elements in the culture, as does "indigenization," nor does it imply, as does "adaptation," that the missionary comes with a pure, unembodied gospel which only has to be "adapted" to the new culture (86fg:2). The "challenging relevance" is maintained by recognizing that the gospel refuses to be either too "fitted" or too "foreign" to the culture taken as a present whole.[6]

It should be obvious that this model for the gospel-culture encounter depends on the theological foundations we observed in chapter five. It is the sovereign Spirit who converts. The fruitfulness of that element of Newbigin's theology of cultural plurality becomes most apparent here. The Spirit produces by conversion a "radical discontinuity" with the convert's culture by virtue of the "paradigm shift" to embrace a new ultimate commitment at the center, yet not a total one, as can be observed from the vantage point of this new center. At the same time, the Spirit unites the new convert to the whole historical strand represented by the missionary, yet preserving a "radical discontinuity" of the new convert from the cultural embodiments of the prior church and a certain "independence" for new converts to give conversion its form within the terms of their own culture. This is one of Newbigin's major contributions to discussions of cultural plurality, the dividing of the continuity question into two and setting each in creative tension with the other. Especially in regard to the issue as it is seen in discussions of "religious pluralism," this has potential to personalize the question, to show separate axes along which the question must be asked (both the gospel-culture axis and the receptor-missionary axis), and to suggest a way in which both radical conversion and continuity with one's culture may be maintained simultaneously.

For the practice of mission it has implications as well. While it is the work of the Spirit to convert in this gospel-culture encounter, the "missionary" character of the church is not ruled out. But it is clearly in a secondary role that must be played out in concert with the manner in which the Spirit proceeds. The Spirit always converts by an embodied form of the gospel, never by some "distilled, pure, unadulterated" gospel, which can only be an illusion (86fg:4). The crucial insight here is that the embodied form which is involved in the encounter is that formed primarily in terms of the receptor culture, not the missionary's culture. The embodiment in the culture of the missionary of necessity becomes accessible and is part of the communication, but its importance is qualified in relation to the more important embodiment in the culture of the person called into conversion. This is the foundation for the "independence" of the form of the new conversion vis-à-vis the missionary's culture. Mission becomes servanthood to a gospel which belongs to the "other," not the extension of one's own church.

It may be added at this point that it is in this connection that we should regard Newbigin's constant — almost "belaboring" — insistence on a "trinitarian" structure of mission theology (cf. especially 63rtdt; 78os). His treatments themselves never quite provide the consistent precision that would make its importance obvious. In *The Open Secret* the dynamic of the whole theology is really supplied by the "inner logic" of election, and the trinitarian chapters seem almost to be forced into the picture. His recourse to the cumbersome term "prevenience" ("the previousness of the kingdom," 78os:63) in the chapter on the Spirit betrays a difficulty in making the "trinitarian basis" work. However, an appreciation for the issues pressing upon Newbigin at the time that this trinitarian emphasis emerged in his thought helps us understand what is at stake. And reading his trin-itarianism in terms of his implicit theology of cultural plurality provides the basis for a simpler and more useful explication of it.

The notion became important to Newbigin at the time in the 1950s and 1960s when "God at work in the world" was the radical new insight. For many who used the language of "trinitarian mission" at the time, this was its major, if not only, reference point. The recognition that the "mission of God" includes the work of God beyond the boundaries of the church and beyond the explicit acknowledgment of Jesus as Lord provided the fundamental impetus to move beyond seeing the "Son" and his "great commission" as the primary or sole focus of mission. The mission of the "Father" must enlarge our frame of reference.

But particularly in the early 1960s, the attention given to "God's work in the world" chipped away at the importance attached to "conversion." Our survey has indicated that it is in this connection that Newbigin places emphasis on the role of the Spirit in mission. Granted that God (the Father) is at work "out there," conversion is still relevant because the Spirit is the one who sovereignly and freely converts "out there" also. Thus the "trini-tarian basis" is completed. It is only whole if the conversioning of the Spirit is affirmed in this way. The presence and announcement of the kingdom of God in Jesus' life and in the call to be his disciples is a secular announce-ment linked to the universal purpose and action of the Father to reconcile all things to himself, and it is linked also to the Spirit's sovereign planting of chosen witnesses through conversion. The trinitarian basis, seen in this light, is brought into the service of a theology of cultural plurality — which is in reality the way it has functioned for Newbigin all along.

In all that has been said thus far, it should be obvious that the "cultural conditioning" in terms of which Newbigin sees the Spirit bringing about conversion is not accepted by the Spirit as a mere necessity to which there must be a grudging capitulation. Newbigin construes as the mind of the Spirit a positive valuation of the full range of cultures. The "radical inde-pendence" of the new convert from the prior church's forms underscores the positive expectation that in the new culture the conversion will yield fruit for the ecumenical fellowship and bring into captivity to Christ the "riches" of that culture. On this point his view has correspondence with that of Lamin Sanneh. Sanneh makes the case for "mission as *translation*" and the inherent quality of "translatability" in the Christian faith based on the instinctive response of missionaries in the New Testament period and ever since, the instinct to translate the gospel's message into the vernacular. And mission by translation, he argues, asserts that the recipient culture is "the true and final locus of the proclamation," "the authentic destination of God's salvific promise" (1989:29, 31). Not even the "attendant safeguards against cultural absolutism" can strip from human cultures this essential dignity and value.

Even a culture's need for critique and transformation maintains this genuinely "high view" of cultures. The element of "challenge" does not negate but rather heightens the value placed on cultures. Those who claim to hold a "high view" of cultures because they see them as in need of little or no change in order to embrace Christianity (e.g., McGavran 1974, Inch 1982) do not in fact hold a "high" view. Newbigin's view takes cultures more seriously by recognizing that they include at the center a "standpoint" of ultimate commitments by which those of that culture organize their patterns of life. As a dynamic force, they are never neutral. Newbigin affirms that not even language is neutral, because "it embodies beliefs to which its users are committed" (78os:164). To treat cultures as Newbigin does makes a truer claim to a "high view" of cultures, believing them to possess greater power and importance in matters of truth and ethics than those who count them to be "neutral in essence" (as does Kraft, e.g., 1979:113). Newbigin affirms that even though our attempts to give form to the gospel in the idioms of our cultures are less than ultimate and absolute and in fact distort the truth (78os:164), yet by mutual correction in the ecumenical fellowship they fulfill their potential to enrich the genuine display of the truth.

This sense of the positive valuing of human cultures indicated by Newbigin's theology of the Spirit and conversion shows up in his interpretation of Genesis 10–11, probably the most pivotal of texts in the Bible for a theology of cultural plurality. It is, of course, especially critical for Newbigin's own theology because it forms the prelude to the announcement of God's choice of Abraham which in regard to the biblical doctrine of election is so paradigmatic, not only for all the chosen "people of God" who follow but for the very principle that one particular event has signif-

icance for the whole of the world and its history (Genesis 12). The clue
which Newbigin sees in election touches on this important nerve center in
the Old Testament, the shift from the so-called universal history of the
world's variegated cultures to the "salvation history" of God's particular
dealings with Abraham and his descendants. Newbigin reminds us, as we
have noted in chapter four, that the dichotomy of two "separate" histories
which that often represents to people is false to the method of election and
the mode of the New Testament gospel as a "secular announcement." More
importantly, these chapters of Genesis show that God's workings by the
method of election are portrayed against the backdrop of the "Table of
Nations" and the "Tower of Babel," which must have bearing on the way
in which the universal multiplicity of cultures is appreciated.

The interpretation of Genesis 10–11 is the spawning ground for any
biblically oriented theology of cultural plurality. The conclusions reached
here give shape and hue to all that follows. (And conversely, they betray
what presuppositions are brought to the text in the first place!) One's
interpretation of these chapters displays what attitude and posture God is
assumed to have toward the endless variations of cultural configuration.
Given how crucial this is, it is remarkable that missiological literature
touching on biblical foundations has offered so little careful examination
of it. This is evidenced by the wide-ranging divergence of opinion whenever
the subject *is* addressed, however lightly or briefly. In order to highlight the
need for development in this regard, a survey of some representative positions is offered here in order to set out a typology to help chart the course
ahead. In this context, Newbigin's valuation of the cultures — as indicated
by his interpretive comments on Genesis 10–12 and the New Testament
parallel in Acts 2 — will be set over against other suggestions in order to
show the biblical foundations for his theology of cultural plurality and
indicate the value of his position for further biblical theological study.

The Table and the Tower

The Genesis accounts of the dispersion and differentiation of the progeny
of Noah in chapter 10 (the "table of nations") and the incident at Babel in
chapter 11 are inseparably tied together and form the critical and immediate
backdrop for the particularizing covenant with Abraham in chapter 12.
These accounts are crucial for a theology of cultural plurality, for "the basis

for the universalism of Scripture is to be found in this chapter (10)" (Claus Westermann 1967:27; cf. Kenneth Cracknell 1982:6-7). This makes it all the more noteworthy that Arthur Glasser, after indicating the great need for a theology of culture in an otherwise intensive biblical survey, skips chapter 10, although in connection with the tower of Babel an implicit reference to the earlier chapter appears (Glasser 1981). Richard De Ridder, as well, in a treatment of "The Old Testament Roots of Mission" moves from Genesis 1–3 directly to Genesis 12 (1983:175). Thom Hopler, in a helpful look at progressive cultural change among the people of God throughout Genesis, omits reference to chapter 10 altogether, mentioning Babel in only the slightest way (1981:32). Stuhlmueller (who did the Old Testament portion of the work he and Senior co-authored), otherwise sensitive to sociocultural dynamics and developments, appears unconcerned to draw out the implications of either chapter except to make the point, very important in another connection, that Israel's progenitors lived amongst peoples like (and unlike!) themselves before their special calling (Senior and Stuhlmueller 1983:10-11).

This trend toward omission notwithstanding, the answers to the basic questions with which these two chapters confront us are crucial for missiology. How should we understand the multiplication of diverse "clans, nations, languages" in chapter 10? The answer to that will depend on exactly what is identified as the nature of the sin of the people of Shinar in chapter 11 and the relationship of the confusion of languages by God in chapter 11 to the proliferation of languages in chapter 10. Does the Babel incident, told later, give the origin and interpretation of the earlier stated development? Or does it reflect a subsequent event growing out of the context of the proliferation? Or are both giving parallel accounts and complementary interpretations of the same development seen from different angles? Missiological discussions surveyed here, where they touch at all on these chapters, give evidence that these issues have neither been well focused nor fully thought through. These cases taken together show a very wide divergence of opinion.

The tendencies worthy of special note may be represented along five lines. Their most important divergence regards the stated or implied assessment of the tribal-national-linguistic ("cultural," to use our modern term) plurality displayed in chapter 10. Before proceeding to delineate these assessments we may note two viewpoints regarding the protohistorical material in Genesis 1–11 for which this typology does not apply. Both Meredith Kline and Modupe Oduyoye trace cultural differentiation from the time of Adam's sons onward. For each, the patterns are fully established before the flood, and the post-flood history merely plays out the drama. They each take definite stands with a particular strata of the cultural development. Kline identifies two tendencies regarding city-building: metapolis (the city of God) and megalopolis (the city of man) (1983:39, 23). The prediluvian pattern found in Genesis 3–8 repeats itself in the history of Genesis 9–12 (86). Oduyoye, on the other hand, draws the distinction between settled, agrarian, urbanizing life and the biblically commended nomadic, pilgrim life of Abel, Abraham, and the Christian (1984:71ff.). Both have so clearly taken cultural sides before coming to Genesis 10 and 11 that the issue as we are addressing it does not exist for them.

1. *Negative Assessments.* Bengt Sundkler's foundational understanding of mission as "translation" appeals to Babel for part of its grounding. The confusion of Babel is "an event which is painted as nothing less than catastrophe. . . . The vast variety of languages of man is not only beauty and richness: it is also a curse." Mission, therefore, has as its purpose "to break the curse and replace it by understanding and unity." It was because of the catastrophe of Babel that "the blessing had to be concentrated upon one people" (1965:11-14).

A similar negative cast emerges in Harvie Conn's theological reformulation of church growth thought.

> Our quest is directed to the recovery of the universal shalom of paradise lost. Our solidarity in Adam, not our particularity, is our holy grail. As fallen creatures this side of the history of Babel, we cannot, in that quest, shed our unique ethnicities. They remain the guardians of God's common grace against the unchecked presumption of an undivided and sinful development of humanity (Gen 11:1-9). (1983:86)[7]

Understanding the Babel incident to predate the developments recorded in the Table of Nations, Conn sees the nations as "simultaneously signs of God's will to peace and of his judgment." They are bound up with the "curse" of Babel.

> Genesis 11 and the confusion of tongues provide the reason for God's division of the nations. God initiates differentiation in judgment on

humankind's arrogant attempt to remedy the divisive impact of sin by establishing unity in their own honor. . . . The dispersion movement of Genesis 10 appears as a curse, a centrifugal force separating people and retarding the subjugation of the earth. (90)

Conn appears to see this "curse" of Babel, the proliferation of the nations and languages, as an extension of the Fall and curse of the Garden of Eden. Its function as "guardian of common grace" forms a close correspondence to the exclusion of Adam and Eve from the Garden lest they should eat of the tree of life.

The main difficulty with these and other negative assessments of the plurality of Genesis 10 is that they tend to take the events of chapter 11 as the prior explanatory situation without adequately facing the question that must remain: Why then does the finished literary work place chapter 10 first? While the historical reconstruction they adopt is a possible one and is hinted by the opening words of chapter 11 indicating a unity of language, it is not the only possibility. A local reference, identified by the placing of the event on the "plains of Shinar" might as well indicate a local unity of language. An isolated reading of the Babel incident apart from a sense of the flow of thought from the graciousness of chapter 9 and the expansive scattering of chapter 10 too easily assigns "curse" to what emerges on the face of the text as "blessing."

2. *Dialectical Assessments.* When it is recognized that the writer who placed the Table before the Tower, having thus displayed the "blessing" which issues in diversity, quickly calls us up short with a statement about God's judgmental "curse" of confusion and alienation through language diversification, we are confronted with an inevitable tension. Unity and diversity do not yield here an easy resolution. This sense of the text leads Karl Barth, in an in-depth exegetical treatment of Genesis 10–11, to a dialectical approach to the ethical problem of "near and distant neighbors" (1961). It is most forcefully stated in his general conclusion:

The separation and division of the peoples, although right as concerns the divine will and actions, is altogether wrong as concerns the human. . . . It would certainly be wrong to maintain that there is an order of creation separating the nations, which is obviously excluded by Genesis 1–11. (317)

For Barth there are two understandings of the existence of the "nations" given in the two chapters before us which must be understood as being "placed alongside" each other, chapter 10 giving the long development and chapter 11 a single particular incident (313). In the first place, the nations are "divinely ordered for the humanity reconstituted by the deliverance of Noah." Until then it had not been so:

> As the main theme was previously the one people from Adam to Noah, it is now Noah's descendant Abraham and his one people and its hope. But there now emerge necessarily as a subsidiary theme the many nations who together constitute the race, and history in the form of the universal history within which this one history is to be enacted. (311-312)

But from chapter 11 we learn another factor inherent in the development of nations. It comes from the judgment of God on the sinful "intention" of the people of Shinar. Their sin is at the heart "a departure from grace." Their act itself was not inherently sinful. Rather it was wrong "to try to assure and assert by human resolve and enterprise the unity already given and not really threatened from any quarter." Therefore, for this one humanity, "its possibility of unity must be taken from it." So our human lot is changed: Our "being as humanity must now be one in the antithesis of near and distant neighbors, who can neither of them constitute the whole of humanity, but only relative totalities with geographic frontiers and divergent histories" (314-315).

The dialectic involved looks forward to the reconciliation of God. "The sentence pronounced is not an ultimate but only a penultimate word. . . . The curves of the separated ways are so ordered in advance that they will finally come together again" (317). It is here that the problem emerges. While the dialectical approach seeks to maintain the tension of grace and judgment, unity and diversity, blessing and curse, in the end it bears a negative assessment of the diversity. Barth's strong assertion that the race constituted one humanity until the post-flood events of Genesis 10 and 11 and that that original unity, "forfeited and lost by its sin and guilt," is "ultimate" and due to be finally restored presents diversity as only provisional and as an interruption of the ideal. Cultural plurality can only then be seen in an ultimately negative light.[8]

It is true that elsewhere (in his 1926 essay on "Church and Culture") Barth suggests a positive stance toward "culture" as a "serious," although not "ultimately" serious, "game" in which the church ought to be engaged with genuine earnestness (1926:349). Such an evaluation does not contradict what is being said here because the concept of "culture" with which Barth was working was wholly different from what we today envision when we speak of cultural plurality. Given the youthfulness of the field of cultural anthropology at the time, it is reasonable that this difference should exist. "Culture" indicated to Barth something like "the sum of the aims proceeding from human activity and in turn stimulating human activity" or, in the German sense of *Kultur,* "the idea of the final goal and the totality of norms by which human activity should be guided" (1926:337). Culture, then, is a "task" to which humanity puts its effort (343-344). It is something to be "done" (345). Barth's concern is with "cultural achievement," "cultural activity," "striving" for a cultural "goal" (349). In his essay he does not envision the multiple "ways of living" which make up the given worldviews, values, and behavior patterns of the world's variegated peoples.

Hendrik Kraemer's view shows some similarity to that of Barth's, although his treatment of the Genesis passages is much slimmer. He sees in the two chapters "the paradoxical oneness of divine blessing and divine condemnation, both of which in their unity are the sustaining powers in the pilgrimage of mankind." He sees more of the created order manifesting itself in the plurality than does Barth: "In this story the predicament of man in his cultural and religious achievements is admirably expressed. The cultural and religious creative urge is . . . implanted by God in man." But "man's accomplishments . . . appear always infected by corruption and pride, which has its root . . . in the forgetfulness of God." In the face of "the riddle of the unity and diversity of the nations" the sin of Shinar was the people's "impatience to solve it." It was their "urge for one organized life," to be achieved by their "own means and to [their] own glory" which brought the scattering response of God. In the new age of Pentecost "God's Holy Spirit restores the God-willed, but destroyed, unity of mankind" (1956:254).

While not as open to the charge of an ultimately negative appraisal of pluralism as Barth might be, Kraemer does not entirely remove himself from the problem inherent in a dialectical approach. The condemnation too easily dominates over the blessing unless more is said to prevent that conclusion. This he has not done. His overriding emphasis placed on "unity," destroyed and to be restored, suggests a similar undercurrent to that of Barth's. Something about the diversity is depreciated. Diversity thwarts the intended unity. The unity is the more ultimate.[9]

3. *Neutral Assessments.* Several authors hint toward a positive affirmation of plurality but in their lack of full engagement with the text fall short of a definitive positive statement. Kenneth Cracknell, in his survey bearing directly on our subject, makes only the most general comments regarding the Table of Nations. The expansion is "within the purposes of God," and the nations are to "flourish with his blessing." The peoples share a common ancestry and a "common destiny to live in harmony in spite of racial and linguistic differences" (1982:6). He passes over the "deeply significant" account of Babel with the simple observation that "it is part of the human situation with which God has to deal in his redemptive activity in history" (7). A blandly neutral position is what emerges: plurality is the arena in which we share a common destiny to live in harmony and the arena with which God must deal to bring redemption. It is simply a "given."

In not dissimilar fashion, D. T. Niles says, "The world of mankind in its differences is what the Gospel is meant to redeem and reconcile." In Genesis 10 we find "those particularities of mankind . . . which are the stuff of history. With this history God is concerned, and over it God will triumph." He goes on to indicate that it is the differentiations which are the cause of strife, yet in the end they will become part of the glory of God. It was because of them that the builders of Shinar "gave up building" (1962:248). The impression that they ceased a "good" project because of their strife seems to strip away from the text any suggestion of judgment from God. Neither he nor Cracknell attempts to describe the nature of the sin of the people at Babel. For both, these glaring omissions leave vulnerable their common desire to accentuate the positive. That in part accounts for the fact that in the end they really only argue for plurality as a historical reality which must be taken into account. Plurality is not highly significant in their assessment of these texts.

4. *Positive Assessments.* Much more forceful in their affirmation of plurality are a number who see the expansion of nations in chapter 10 as the fulfillment of the creation mandate renewed now under Noah. The view of C. Peter Wagner is offered in defense of the "homogenous unit principle" of the church growth school. According to Wagner, the Table of Nations confirms "that social pluralism was part of God's creational plan." The sin of the people of Shinar was that they were attempting to "counteract what they correctly understood to be God's purpose in diversifying the human race. . . . Apparently, then, God punished this early resistance to pluralism"

(1979:111-112).[10] Presumably, then, their punishment was gentle — to send them back to the task of diversifying.

Others speak similarly about the nature of the people's sin in Genesis 11. Art Glasser likewise envisions a broken mandate:

> Fallen man reveals his insecurity, vanity and self-centeredness by disobeying the command to scatter and populate the earth. Had they scattered they would have gradually and peaceably divided into diverse linguistic and cultural groupings. The judgment was an acceleration of the process of linguistic change that provoked such discord and tension that they fled from one another. Ethnic pluralism should not automatically be regarded as God's judgment upon human sinfulness. (1981, 2:5)

In the latter comment he is surely right. But it must be asked whether in his very intriguing suggestion about "acceleration" there is not a substantial weakening of the judgment of God.

More importantly, for Wagner and Glasser, as well as for Herbert Kane who joins them in the suggestion that "the postdiluvians disobeyed God's command to 'replenish' the earth and instead built the Tower of Babel" (1976:21), the problem lies in the assumption that the word of God telling them to "be fruitful and multiply" was first a command. To make of it a responsibility which when resisted was punished controverts the whole tone of freshness and newness flowing from chapter 9. It places the setting again in a new Garden of Eden where the spreading across the earth is not "before the Lord" (Genesis 10:9) in the enjoyment of his blessing but in testing. To make of plurality a hardened command contains dangerous potential for ethnocentrism and national pride of the worst sort.

In this connection it is worth mentioning that Barth identifies this particular view as that of the Neo-German "pseudo-theology" accompanying the rise of Nazism. One of their exegetes held that the building of Babel was "in reaction against the dispersal of humanity." The point of the text is then that God "reinstituted His order of national life" against the "concentrated force of the vaunted human attempt at unity" (Barth 1961:313). That ought to give us due pause to guard against paralleling that argument.

5. *Progressive Assessments.* The final type of assessment we identify here was anticipated by Johannes Blauw, though not fully developed by him. Following the "unelaborated" hint he found in Karl Hartenstein, Blauw

gave full place to the "special importance for a theology of mission" which the first chapters of Genesis hold. Particularly in Genesis 10–11 we find what he called "the fundamental kerygma regarding the nations" (1962:18, 20).

Blauw's approach to chapter 10 finds its clue in the covenant with Noah from which its events flow.

> In the Table of Nations in Gen. 10 we have a consequence of the announcement in Gen. 9 regarding the new covenant with the earth. This covenant shows its effectiveness in the filling of the earth with a multitude of the nations. The joy of the creator has won over his sadness and wrath (cf. Acts 17:26). The world of nations is the result of the peace made with man after the Flood. (1962:19-20)

The plurality is "consequence, effect, result," not responsibility and mandate. Seeing in it the blossoming of God's joy, Blauw refuses to break the back of his positive assessment of plurality with the judgment of the next chapter. Without weakening the force of that judgment, he refers it rather forward, where it is counterbalanced by the call of Abraham in chapter 12. The Tower "does not carry the same weight" as the Table. Both salvation and judgment emerge, but "salvation prevails" (20). Thus he refuses to adopt a stringent dialectic.[11]

The insight begins to fade, however, as Blauw looks on to chapter 12 in light of 10 and 11. He sees the call of Abraham as "the beginning of the restoration of the lost unity of mankind and of the broken fellowship with God" set against the backdrop of the "unresolved problem of the relation of God to the nations" (1962:19). Thus he appears to be setting aside the "beginning" of new covenant results in chapter 10. A sense of the continuity between the covenants of God with Noah and Abraham is wanting. The earlier "beginning" needs a dimension of progressive ripening.

Bishop Newbigin's analysis of these two chapters provides that farther-reaching dimension. It is Newbigin's assumption that "God's plan for the salvation of the world is a consistent whole, the means congruent with the end" (61ftow:79). He sees, as did Blauw, the necessary connection between Genesis 9 and Genesis 10. "The Bible," he says, "does not see the world as a monochrome mass; rather it speaks of the 'nations' whose distinct existence is itself the first fruit of God's primal covenant of blessing" (77wilc:21). It is for the sake of the fulfillment and redemption of that "first fruit" that God will choose Abraham and with him Israel. Of course, he acknowledges, the confusion of languages at Babel was "not a sign of God's blessing but of God's rejection of man's effort to construct his own 'heavenly city,'" that is, to bring to finality the first fruits already given. The resulting judgment of God needs to be clearly distinguished from the diversity which is a blessing in chapter 10. "Diversity is part of God's gracious purpose for the human family, but separation and mutual rejection is not." When that curse of Babel is reversed at Pentecost, there remains a variety of languages. The Holy Spirit there provides "the baptism of the languages, not their extinction" (21-22).

Newbigin envisions the ever-increasing blossoming of the "first fruits" given in the "primal covenant" as the redemption of God unfolds.

> An essential part of the history of salvation is the history of the bringing into obedience to Christ of the rich multiplicity of ethical, cultural, spiritual treasures which God has lavished upon mankind. . . . All these gifts will be truly received and understood when the Holy Spirit takes them and declares their true meaning and use to the Church. (77bpmi:262-263)

Newbigin, then, does not see the "constitution of the one humanity in a world of nations" as a movement by God away from the desired goal, as did Barth. Rather it moves squarely toward the goal. The interference of Babel highlights the way in which God must yet move toward that goal, bringing reconciliation through redemption. But Newbigin's highly positive evaluation of cultural plurality is not swamped by the judgment at Babel. Nor does it ignore it. Rather it presses forward toward the salvation from all the rightful curses of God which thwart the beauty and richness of the treasures God desires and deserves.

For Newbigin, diversity is not a departure from the ideal ("unity"), from which departure we need salvation ("restored unity"). Nor is it merely the created order of things from which we have strayed ("seeking false, disobedient unities") and to which we need to be restored. Rather it is a beginning harbinger and first fruit of redemption which in its captivity to Christ and use by the Holy Spirit manifests God's glory. It is not a diversity in the way of unity but a diversity on the way to unified diversity.

Newbigin is not alone in suggesting such a progressive assessment of the cultural plurality in the Table of Nations. C. S. Song does, as well, although in a very different vein. Whereas Newbigin sees plurality in terms of the progression of redemption, Song sees it in relation to the progression of creation. Basic to Song's interpretation of Babel is his notion that "culture as a whole is none other than the manifestation of God's creative power translated into actual forms and events. Thus, creation may be regarded as God's culture in its totality" (1975:25). So, the cultural task of the Christian mission is to

> search for and appreciate different shapes which the cultural dynamic of God's creation takes in different cultural and historical contexts. . . . Diversity in shapes of culture is not witness against the unity and sovereignty of God's creation. Rather it is an affirmation of the richness of God's nature and His relation to the world. (28)

In light of his view that culture is positive in all its forms, it is not surprising that Song sets the action of God at Shinar in the most positive light possible.

> Very few exegetes have understood dispersion to the world not as God's punishment for human pride but as fulfillment of God's command. . . . Disruption of the tower construction is to implement God's purpose for "the development and progress of humanity." (1982:23)

He goes on to suggest that God's action was a gracious move to assist greater human unity: " 'Uprootedness' seems one of the ways in which God brings peoples and nations into close proximity with one another. We cannot fail to recognize a remarkable correspondence here between the tower of Babel and the call of Abraham" (30).

Song's progressive assessment of plurality sees diverse cultures as expressions of the maturation and continual unfolding of creation. He brings to his interpretation his bias that we must understand redemption in terms of creation and its continuing character. In the process he appears to have rather absorbed redemption into creation. He shows no strong sense of sin or judgment which requires restoration through redemption. This is in sharp contrast to Newbigin's "progressive" approach. Newbigin preserves a positive sense of creation while taking with full seriousness human sin and divine judgment. His progressive assessment of cultural plurality embraces both creation and redemption.

Summary. The wide diffusion of opinion regarding these two critical chapters calls for serious and studied rethinking. Theological bias regarding "unity" as the fruit of the gospel often tends to prejudice the case too quickly toward negative views of diversity in culture. Ethnic imperialisms leading the "way to unity" cannot be far behind. On the other hand, a positive stance toward contemporary plurality runs the danger of imposing itself too uncritically on the text and failing to see the tragedy in Babel which brings to fuller light the radicality and renovating reconciliation of the gospel. Human unity and cultural diversity need to find a firmer weldpoint in missiological reflection upon these texts in Genesis, which need to be kept prominent on our continuing biblical agenda. Newbigin's approach, bringing to bear a wide-ranging appreciation for the diversity within a fuller vision of the directions in which God's redemption moves, makes an important contribution.

The Bible-Church Relationship

The gospel-culture encounter we have been considering does not take place in a vacuum. Although the conversion it seeks occurs only as a supernatural act of the Holy Spirit, the Spirit never brings that about outside the culturally bounded events of real history. The original form of the gospel was an incarnation and every successive communication of it is necessarily the same. Newbigin counts it as a firm fact that in the missionary encounter between the gospel and a culture, "the first party will be represented by a community for which the Bible is the determinative clue to the character and activity of the one whose purpose is the final meaning of history" (86fg:62). Therefore, the mission of the church is to know that the Spirit is *the* witness and to bear in its own life that witness as those chosen for that purpose.

The clue to the nature of this community which represents the gospel in the encounter lies in the fact that it lives on the other side of the boundary marked by conversion. Former ultimate commitments have been exchanged for "the Bible as the determinative clue." The people of a receptor culture meet the gospel first in a community of "people called missionaries who already organize their corporate life around a story that is told in a book and is continually re-enacted by word and sacramental action in their liturgy." The gospel's encounter with any culture "takes place in a whole complex of contacts between the community organized in this way and the people to whom they come" (86fg:42). In the missionary dialogue which takes place between those communities we find the base of the "triangle" of forces — gospel, culture, church.

But before that can adequately be explored, the relationship implied between the gospel and the community which represents it in the encounter must be appreciated. At the very heart of Newbigin's important description of the authority of the Bible in the encounter of the gospel with Western culture he makes his case hinge on the relationship between the Bible and this community determined by it. Just as the community is the "people of the book," so also "the Bible comes into our hands as the book of a community, and neither the book nor the community are properly understood except in their reciprocal relationship with each other" (86fg:55). The "pre-understanding" of the community which is shaped by its tradition fashions the way the Bible is understood and heard. But the community and its tradition have taken shape as they have been "constantly modified as each new generation of believers endeavors to be faithful in understanding and living out Scripture." This hermeneutical circle "operating *within the believing community*" means that there is between the tradition and the Scriptures a "constantly developing reciprocal relationship" (56, 58).

This "reciprocal relationship" places the church in a very important location for the gospel-culture encounter. Newbigin finds the notion of a "hermeneutical circle" to be true of the Bible-church relationship but inadequate "to describe what is involved in the encounter between Scripture and our culture" (86fg:51). Unless there is a commitment to the Bible's authority, there is no way for it to have authority, because something else will hold the place of authority and by that standard the Scriptures will be judged. This is the problem, Newbigin says, with post-Enlightenment efforts to establish the Bible's authority, whether by the view that it "is a body of factually inerrant statements about nature and history," or that it "bears witness to authentic personal experience . . . continuous with the total religious experience of the human race," whether one believes that the Bible "embodies concepts and principles that can be distilled from its material and can stand in their own right," or that it records "divine revelation in the history behind the story" (86fg:59; cf. 45-50). All such efforts are made on the basis of the more basic commitments implicit in the Enlightenment. A hermeneutical circle cannot genuinely operate apart from the paradigm shift called conversion, a conversion such as that into which the Christian community has been chosen (53). Election thus becomes the clue for understanding the Bible's authority:

> The Bible functions as authority only within a community that is committed to faith and obedience and is embodying that commitment in an active discipleship that embraces the whole of life, public and private. This is the plausibility structure within which the faith is nourished. (58)

This reciprocal relationship, then, means that the church may rightly be identified as "the pillar and bulwark of the truth" along with the Bible (86fg:58; cf. 1 Timothy 3:15-16). Even the Scripture "as we have it" must be recognized to be "the result of the operation of this same hermeneutical circle from the very beginning" (56). Yet Newbigin clearly affirms that "within the reciprocity of this relation, it is Scripture that always has the primacy" because it "renders accessible to us the character and actions and purposes of God" (58, 59). In that way he preserves in this discussion of authority what he says elsewhere about the role of the Bible as the third factor in the missionary encounter. "The missionary dialogue with other cultures is not simply a dialogue between cultures; the Bible functions decisively . . . as a third and independent party in the developing relationship" (78ctc:15).

That his theology of cultural plurality has brought Newbigin to focus on this sense of the relationship between the Bible and the church touches on two areas in which his thought casts — or, re-casts — the agenda for the field and offers important proposals. First, the role election plays in his theology places the church center-stage in the gospel-culture encounter. The church catholic, then, as those gathered into conversion out of the diversity of cultures, is what makes the gospel accessible to the cultures in the encounter. Newbigin, by his way of engaging *ecumenism and pluriformity*, helps shape an essential "inter-cultural ecclesiology." Second, election to be witnesses to what has been revealed about the end of the story, and therefore its meaning, places the understanding of "revelation" at the heart of the cultural plurality agenda. The "personal" character of God and what it means for God to be "known" in terms of the culturally conditioned nature of human life form the most basic of assumptions for Newbigin. Discussions touching on cultural plurality cannot avoid dealing with issues of *revelation and relativity*.

Ecumenism and Pluriformity

In chapter five we observed Newbigin's insistence about the necessity of incorporation into the living, visible, historically rooted church as a consequence of conversion. The principle of the "radical independence" of the new convert forces the issue of the cultural conditioning which must be assumed in regard to all the actual forms that church takes. The total church, therefore, is viewed by Newbigin as essentially "pluriform" (69wwfo:126-127).[12] Far from militating against the argument for the church's obligatory "movement" toward unity, this pluriformity of the church draws more vividly the lines along which the unity must manifest itself. Each local church "must embody a catholicity which calls in question the life-style of that place" and true catholicity "will confirm a proper particularity in the life-style of each local church" (77wilc:21). So as Newbigin proceeds step by step to spell out what is involved in the "continually developing" triangular relationship, the corner of it which originally is identified as the "Christianity of the missionary" (78os:165, 168) is acknowledged to be much more profound and complex. Ultimately he envisions that corner to be "the church as a global fellowship," "the ecumenical fellowship representing the witness of Christians from other cultures" (169, 172).

This perspective offers to the ecumenical discussions two suggestive reformulations which have prospects for stimulating the development of an "inter-cultural ecclesiology" as part of a larger theology of cultural plurality.

1. Newbigin shifts the focus of ecumenical discussion from a "cross-confessional" or even "cross-national" one to a "cross-cultural" one. He calls for a "movement" into a unity that embraces the diversity while healing the alienation and the breaches which manifest themselves at the points of our cultural difference. For every Christian community there is a "discontinuity," which is at the same time "continuous," in regard to its own culture, taking the form of a double relationship of "identification" and "separation." Sustaining this relationship requires the fellowship of "mutual learning and of mutual correction among all of every culture who now confess [Jesus] as Lord and who seek to make their confession challengingly relevant in their several situations." The ecumenical dialogue is not for the purpose of producing by stages an approach to a final uniformity. But its goal is "faithful adherence to the tradition" by incarnational forms which embody the challenge and relevance of the gospel in all the world's myriad of cultural

configurations. The commitment to such a path in openness to "real mutual understanding, learning, and criticism" lies at "the very heart of the ecumenical task" (78ctc:13-15). This is the character of the worldwide ecumenical movement "when it is true to itself." Each local church, "perceiving Christ through the spectacle of one culture, can help the other to see how much the vision has been blurred or distorted" (86fg:9).

But this mutual correction takes place in the context of "extremely complex and constantly changing patterns of relationship between Church and culture" (78ctc:14). The recognition of that complexity and the refusal to yield to an oversimplification of it constitutes one of the major contributions Newbigin makes for an assessment of cultural plurality. His major essay on this matter (78ctc; cf. 78os:164-180) gives the reader the impression that its author is almost breathlessly overwhelmed by the potential variations that defy simplistic constructs. It is not only cultures themselves which possess an unlimited range of possible variation and which in fact undergo constant patterns of change. But it is also the church-culture relationship which has such a variable and dynamic character. The possibilities both for cultures and for church-culture relationships are brilliantly kaleidoscopic!

It is in this regard that Newbigin offers an advance on Niebuhr's standard typology of "Christ and culture" postures. To the flat description of five basic types of relationship, Newbigin adds the dimensions of cultural difference and historical change. First of all, he says, it must be recognized that "all the elements of culture, even in the most stable communities, are changing" (78os:161). So a Christian's relationship to the culture can never remain static. Within the culture there are "conservative" elements and "reforming" elements. To attempt to "transform" some facet of the culture means to "accommodate" to another element. Some elements which today reform, tomorrow conserve the fruit of the change. The picture is further complicated when it is realized that the internal patterns of change just identified are in constant association with similar sets of patterns in other societies (161-162). We live in a world where there is an "infinitely complex pattern of intercultural influence on a global scale" helping to produce "an almost infinite variety of different situations, and none of them static" (168, 167).

Other factors enter in, as well, to produce a "complicated and unpredictable evolution" (78ctc:5). "The battles to be fought in different cultural groups will be different: what is radical in one group will be reactionary in another" (73snhc:10). And the way in which a first generation convert reacts to the traditional or emerging culture will not be the same as the reaction of a second or third generation believer. In each community, the impulses toward rapid change or identity preservation will be paralleled by changing needs in the Christian part of the population. Its status as minority or as majority, as influential or oppressed, as respected or denounced, and the changes which occur in that status, will all play a role in fashioning the evolving posture toward the culture. "The church within a given culture does not retain a fixed relation to that culture" (78ctc:13).[13]

In his most direct and pointed expansion (correction?) of Niebuhr's model, Newbigin shows what happens when there is a meeting of churches from different cultures with "different relations to their cultures" due to their particular histories and circumstances.

> A North American Christian, for example, highly critical of his own culture and very sympathetic to the relatively strange culture of India, is repelled when he meets a city congregation in India which is relatively unsympathetic to traditional Indian culture and very open to the West. (78ctc:14)

They appear to be poles apart in their attitudes when in reality they have an almost identical posture vis-à-vis their own culture and that of others. Likewise those from different cultures who share similar outlooks may do so because one is a cultural conservative while the other is a cultural radical.

These questions regarding Niebuhr's approach signal the need for an even larger reappraisal of his typology. A more nuanced sense of cultural difference, cultural change, and cultural history, viewed against an appreciation for the multiplicity of the world's cultures and the gospel's incarnations within them, alters the terms of the debate. Niebuhr's insights formed against the backdrop of the church's attitudes within the course of Western civilization may continue to make a contribution, but the missionary experience of cross-cultural encounter which Newbigin brings to bear on his typology sets the agenda for a new type of discussion and for the development of models for patient intercultural contact in the ecumenical fellowship.

2. Second, Newbigin calls those involved in the theological task to pursue it in ecumenical terms set by the conditions of cultural plurality. This vision is no doubt what he underscores by his recounting of the incident in which Karl Barth was found on the lawn at Bossey during the

meetings of the Committee of Twenty-Five, surrounded by papers and attempting to draft the final section of the report as he had been assigned. Newbigin found him "looking much dishevelled" and commented that he looked as if he were in trouble. Barth replied, "I am. This is a task for some great ecumenical theologian" (85ua:140). In a way, Newbigin himself is a model of what such an "ecumenical" theologian might be. In any event, it is his conviction that theology belongs to a universal church which is culturally ecumenical in its fellowship.

In this respect we notice that the triangular model we have been viewing is not applied simplistically by Newbigin. In a sense, he keeps shifting the way he says the three-cornered relationship is experienced. The complex evolution of relationships between the local culture, the ecumenical Christian community, and the Scriptures is something experienced, on the one hand, "within the receptor community" (78os:168). But the same pattern of relationships is always developing in "the church as a global fellowship" (169) and more generally in "the interaction between gospel and culture" (172). But it is ultimately in the interest of the way theology is to be done that he develops the model, and he has in mind most particularly "Christology." In all of the church's theological work, its theology must be "*in via*, and the way is a missionary way, the way which the Church must take from the culture of first-century Palestine to all the nations and their cultures, to the ends of the earth and to the end of time" (78ctc:10). It must do its theology, therefore, in terms of the model of cross-cultural missionary encounter and under three "mutually interlocked" conditions:

> it must be done in the openness of dialogue with the varied cultures of mankind; it must be done in the openness of learning within the ecumenical fellowship of all Christians; it must be done in faithful adherence to the given tradition. (10)

This immediately suggests the importance and value of so-called third-world theologies in the service of genuinely universal theology. Newbigin finds it unfortunate that

> we are still far from such a truly ecumenical theology because we have created a situation in which the only languages in which the ecumenical conversation can be conducted are the languages of western Europe, and consequently the only theologians of the Third World who can play a

real part in the conversation are those who have been co-opted into the dominant European culture with its accepted myths and models. (79tewp:73)

African Independent Churches and the rise of Pentecostalism are to New-bigin the signs of protest against this fact. They represent a kind of theolo-gizing which already is part of the life of the church throughout the world, but a part to which the ecumenical movement has given itself insufficient access. While what we call third-world theology is too much an "echo" of western theologies (78os:171-172), there is another kind, "namely, that which is being continuously produced in the languages of the churches of the Third World — in the form of preaching, catechesis, song, story, and drama." While he acknowledges that "it will always be extremely difficult to bring the insights of this 'vernacular' Third World theology into the mainstream of the ecumenical debate," Newbigin asserts that "without it that debate will be beating the air" (80m80:154).

Without genuinely ecumenical theology, there is the danger that the gospel will be judged by each part of the church "in the light of" the local "myth." It is in response to that possibility that Newbigin suggests the theological agenda: "the real task of ecumenical theology will be to learn how to use the different myths of different cultures to communicate a Gospel which transcends them all" (79tewp:73). This conveys his sense of theology in general.

> I believe that the task of a Christian theologian is not to seek to place the story of Jesus within the general religious experience of mankind, but to place the myths of our contemporary culture in the light which streams from him when he is acknowledged as Lord. (79cjh:210)

A relevant and challenging statement of the gospel lies at the heart of theology. Newbigin holds a fascination for the Fourth Gospel as a prime example of it. He calls it "the boldest and most brilliant essay in the com-munication of the gospel to a particular culture in all Christian history." In it

> the language and the thought-forms of that Hellenistic world are so employed that Gnostics in all ages have thought that the book was written especially for them. And yet nowhere in Scripture is the absolute contra-

diction between the word of God and human culture stated with more terrible clarity. (86fg:53)

Of course, the need for this kind of theology is most keenly felt by Newbigin in the West. Upon his return to Britain after his retirement from Madras in 1974 he was confronted with a form of Christianity which he found to be "profoundly syncretistic" (86bep:60). It is his assessment that "there has seldom been any awareness among Western theologians of the extent to which their own theologies have been the result of a failure to challenge the assumptions of their own culture" (78os:172). The failure is precisely because the ecumenical movement has remained dominated by Western forms as the framework for its theologizing. The real value in this charge of Western syncretism is that it levels the ground. It challenges the too-easy assumption in the West that "syncretism" is something that happens when one of the cultures "out there" is encountered by the gospel and twists and distorts what we have delivered more or less purely. Newbigin would probably not go so far as to use the word "syncretism" to describe all theology. But his insistence that all theology is culturally conditioned, and therefore less than ultimate, implies the suggestion of M. M. Thomas that we speak in terms of a "Christ-centered syncretism" (Thomas 1979). A cultural ecumenism implies a universal syncretism which must constantly be open to mutual correction.

This emphasis of Newbigin's suggests another important agenda for the theology of cultural plurality. There is a need for "culture encounter" exposition of the sort that Newbigin provides in his commentary on the Fourth Gospel. It grows out of the breadth of his experience of the type of ecumenical fellowship he calls for. Bearing the marks of his theology of cultural plurality and his triangular model of gospel-culture encounter, his purpose in the commentary is directly stated: "My task is to make clear to myself and (if possible) to others the word which is spoken in the Gospel in such a way that it may be heard in the language of this culture of which I am a part with all its power to question that culture" (82lhc:ix). The commentary has as its obvious backdrop what he has learned from India's fascination and consternation with the message of the Fourth Gospel. That window on the text lets in fresh light for Newbigin's own encounter with his native British culture.

By "culture encounter" exposition we should not only mean the exposition of biblical texts which interprets them for particular cultures based

on a vision of a culturally plural world in which the gospel ranges intend-
ingly among the varied cultures in order to call their peoples to a radical
conversion. We should mean also the kind of statements which give exposition to the cultures themselves, laying bare the issues which the gospel
brings. In the 1960s Newbigin provided an example in *Honest Religion for
Secular Man,* as he did also in the 1980s with *Foolishness to the Greeks.*
Newbigin has indicated the personal vulnerability to misreading the situation which is always involved. In the earlier case, he was too easily swept
along with the mood of the "secular decade." His current interpretation of
the contemporary scene in Western culture, undoubtedly made with greater
caution, must run the same risk. The greatest contribution it makes, however, lies beyond the correctness of its analysis and in the kind of effort he
makes for showing the "challenging relevance" of the gospel. His model
suggests the agenda.

Revelation and Relativity

There are important clues in Newbigin's theology of plurality for developing
a theology of "revelation."[14] Newbigin emphasizes the "personal" character
of God, which means that God can act in historical terms and choose the
time and place of those actions. By such historical action God relates to
other — human — "persons" and the encounter is the basis on which
"knowing" takes place.

　　A complementary assumption which from the beginning has under-
girded Newbigin's thought has to do with what it means to be human in a
way that corresponds to God's personal knowable-ness. Human life and
meaning are social and corporate. Salvation intends the restoration of
wholeness in the social fabric of humankind on the way to a final destiny
which is corporate as well as individual. Salvation, therefore, works by way
of election, which brings divine and human persons together into mutual
"knowing" and reconciliation.

　　Newbigin's view of revelation embraces both of these assumptions
(cf. 36r:1-2). The pervasive effect of those assumptions is that his view of
"revelation" reflects itself at a great many points in his theology of cultural
plurality, as we have seen. It is not my intention here to give full and
systematic definition to his view. Rather, it is my concern to bring it into
relation to particular issues that arise when divine revelation is affirmed in

tandem with an acknowledgment of cultural relativity. The intersection of divine action that is historical and self-disclosing with the patterns of human social intercourse that are culturally circumscribed and conditioned is a crucial nexus for reflection in the interest of a theology of cultural plurality.

It is immediately obvious that this will be of greatest concern to those who share in any sense both a "revelational positivism" in which real "revealing" of God's person is believed to be possible and an actual part of what has, in fact, historically "occurred," and a "cultural relativism" which appreciates the variety of cultures and knows the inevitability that all human life and thought is culturally conditioned. In evangelical missiological circles focused on the cross-cultural communication of the gospel these are shared, and issues growing up around a "theology of revelation and plurality" have been debated within that orbit of conversation. Tracing some of the elements of that conversation, particularly as it has engaged two participants in the Lausanne Committee's Willowbank Consultation, provides a helpful framework in terms of which Newbigin's view may be explained and allowed to suggest ways in which such discussions may be moved ahead.

It has not been in these explicit terms that Newbigin has framed his view of revelation, nor has he specifically engaged the debate to which we are about to make reference. But because his theology of cultural plurality has foundational assumptions in common and reflects at its heart a perspective (i.e., election et al.) which ultimately raises similar issues, the potential of his view for providing an advance in the debate will be displayed in order to mark out the lines along which a key agenda for the theology of cultural plurality is set.

Charles Kraft and Bruce Nicholls represent among evangelical missio-anthropologists two diametrically opposed views of "God and culture." Starting from a common conception supplied by William Smalley (1955), they ultimately diverge into contrary positions that remain at loggerheads and have thus arrived at a *cul-de-sac* of evangelical thinking which begs for a third way. Their respective treatments of "God as supracultural" are not isolated views but are representative of two trends within evangelical discussion (Kraft 1979:120-128; Nicholls 1979:13-15; cf. Nicholls 1980:53-55).

Careful to avoid the possible implications of the noun form of the word Smalley used ("superculture") which might suggest "an absolute set of cultural forms," Kraft uses the adjective "supracultural" to indicate "the transcendence of God with respect to culture." By that he means that God is "above and outside culture" and is "not bound by any specific culture" (1979:120). In this he joins Smalley in beginning to answer the question:

> Granted that there is a God above and beyond all human culture, that He has revealed Himself to man in several cultural forms . . . and that He has taken an active interest in parts of man's cultural behavior through time, proscribing and prescribing at various times and places . . . , what in human experience is God's absolute, unchanging, permanent will, and what is His will for particular times and places, and what is neutral? (Smalley 1955:58-59; cf. Kraft 1979:121)

Kraft also turns to Eugene Nida for help in answering such a question, although not without an important qualification. Nida had stated emphatically:

> The only absolute in Christianity is the triune God. Anything which involves man, who is finite and limited, must of necessity be limited, and hence relative. Biblical cultural relativism is an obligatory feature of our incarnational religion, for without it we would either absolutize human institutions or relativize God. (Nida 1954:282, n. 22)

Kraft adopts Nida's "biblical cultural relativism" as a means to avoid an impossible and God-excluding "absolute relativism" by embracing a kind of "relative relativism" (Nida 1954:50; cf. Kraft 1979:124-125). Only Kraft wishes to modify Nida's core affirmation about God as the "only absolute" in a way suggested by Smalley. He broadens what must be meant by the "supracultural and absolute" by employing the terms exclusively for

> God Himself, His nature, attributes and character, for the moral principles which stem from what He is (but not for particular acts of behavior which may attempt to fulfill those principles), for His plan and total will. (Smalley 1955:60; cf. pp. 59, 62; Kraft 1979:122)

The deliberate exclusion of God's acts from the definition and the constant emphasis made by both Smalley and Kraft on God's "principles" and "will" lead toward what becomes Kraft's principal interest, the question of the communication, via revelation, of "supracultural truth" (1979:122, 129ff.).

In his view, "God as above culture" uses culture as "the vehicle for interaction with human beings." The "forms" and "functions" of culture are "neutral in essence" and supracultural truth supplies "meanings" and directs "usage" within that milieu (113).[15]

Nicholls, on the other hand, moves in an opposite direction. Whereas Kraft abstracts God's principles and will from the revealing actions of God within cultures, Nicholls reifies God's revealing actions as embodying God's principles and will. He starts, as Kraft does, by adopting the term "supra-cultural." But he focuses on an aspect of it which Kraft notes only briefly in passing, the fact that "supracultural" would seem to have to refer also to the "realm" of angels, demons, and Satan (cf. Kraft 1979:120-121).[16] Nicholls treats the "supra-cultural" as a "realm of reality" which is in interaction with "human cultural factors." For him, the term "supra-cultural" refers to "the phenomena of cultural belief and behavior that have their source outside of human culture." He accepts that there are two such realms, the "spiritual realm of God and his kingdom" and the realm of "Satan and his kingdom," the former the more ultimate because of the victory of the cross (1979:13; cf. p. 14). When the "supra-cultural realm" of God's kingdom interacts with human cultures, it transforms them to conform to that supracultural pattern. In other words, the kingdom of God is an ideal culture which God is seeking to achieve "in and through" human societies. To reveal that pattern, God "overshadowed the cultural forms" of the Hebrew culture and "transformed it over the centuries" so that divine revelation within the forms of that culture would have this "supra-cultural character" (1980:53).

> The culture of the Hebrews was not just the product of their environment but was the interaction of the supra-cultural and the Hebrews in their environment and history. The Word of God changes the direction of culture and transforms it. (1979:13)

The same dynamic is present now in the church. Nicholls envisions "a progressive movement toward a 'Christian culture'" that will come to its consummation at the return of Christ to "establish his reign on earth." "A truly Christian culture will then be manifest" (13-15).

> The hope of the resurrection includes total transformation of culture when the supra-cultural kingdom of God is established on earth and

Christ is Lord of all of creation. In this present age the church as the new community of the people of God is the visible manifestation of this new society to the extent that Christ is Lord. Thus the resurrection stands as the ultimate model of both the universality and the humanity of the final Christian culture. (18)

God has one particular culture in mind, according to this view, toward which God is moving history.[17]

The two models are poles apart. Kraft's "above and beyond" model takes cultures to be simply vehicles for the communication of God's principles in the process of revelation. The Bible, then, is like a casebook in which the biblical cultures in terms of which it comes are neutral vehicles containing revelations of the disembodied message. Nicholls's "in and through" model treats cultures as perversions of a divinely intended ideal and recipients of the restored ideal by God's revealing action. The Bible, in that case, is more like a textbook in which the biblical cultures of the recipients and conveyors of revelation have become part and parcel of the content of what is being revealed.

Kraft has preserved cultural relativity and avoided the danger into which Nicholls falls, that of absolutizing a particular culture. In the process, however, he has so abstracted God from culture and so neutralized culture that the ethical dimension of revelation is lost and revelation itself is relativized. There is ample space for missionary "relevance" (e.g., Kraft's proposals regarding "dynamic equivalence") but little for missionary "challenge." On the other hand, Nicholls has avoided the danger of relativizing revelation in such a way that the ethical potential and "challenge" of God's meeting with cultures would be lost. But he runs aground on the danger of absolutizing one particular culture and risks a potential legalism or cultural imperialism. In the process, it is God who is in danger of being relativized by being made captive to God's own "realm."

The problem with both these views is that they each extract from God what they term the "supracultural" element that gives to revelation its normative character and authoritative content. Kraft envisions an unenculturated message containing "eternal truths" which are above and outside culture. Nicholls looks to a cultural realm beyond any cultures we construct which embodies "eternal truths" that God reveals "in and through" human cultures. The impasse is in need of a third way.

Here the perspective of Newbigin holds promise. A theology of revelation must begin with "God as personal." The principles and will of God must not be abstracted out from God's person and actions in order that they may somehow "be communicated." What God wishes to disclose is always God's *self*, and such a disclosure is made by the free actions through which God interacts with human persons in real history. "The eternal emphatically *has a history*, however shocking it may be to the philosopher" (61ftow:48). "Time is real to God" because it is "the form of His creation" (53hg:135-136; cf. 41kgip 3:8-10). Transcendence over it is not nullified by God's participation in it.

Likewise, because personal, God's desires, judgments, and challenges are brought to bear in relatedness, not by the mere transposition of forms to match an ideal. Nor are divine judgments encased within a prescribed culture. This principle allows to God the full range of personal response to each person and culture and yields to God's desire that all the cultures be guided by means of reconciliation and the presence of the Spirit into a pluriformity of expressions of trust and obedience.

If it is a personal God whose self-disclosure we meet in the Bible, then we know that God cannot be encased in any of the forms by which or in which the self-disclosure is made, nor is there any aloofness from history in such a way that only the divine will and eternal principles may become known. This is why the Bible comes as primarily narrative. It is neither a casebook nor a textbook but a "storybook," which by the stories it recounts renders accessible to us "the character, actions and purposes of God." By beginning with a personal God who acts personally in history, an understanding of revelation is formed which neither abstracts God from divine characteristics ("principles and will") nor reduces God to an enculturation of specific divine goals.

Linked with this principle is another. Revelation is communal. By it God meets not cultures but the people who are living dynamically in terms of them. The meeting has to do with their meetings with one another as much as with God. The meeting engages their response. That is why "if God's revelatory act has not been in some measure understood and accepted, there has been no revelation" (69fc:34). The full dignity and personhood of people is thus protected. They are not merely the receptors of an encoded message (as they tend to become for Kraft) or the consignees of a conscripted culture (as they may become under Nicholls's view), but they are image-bearers of God with whom God seeks to be reconciled. Their cultures will neither be neutralized nor absolutized. The believing community which bears the witness to the revelational acts of God will be neither nullified as insignificant to any other culture nor deified as the bearers of a divine culture.[18]

The Church-Culture Dialogue

In what has been said already in connection with the gospel-culture encounter and the Bible-church reciprocal relationship, we have anticipated much of what has a bearing on the church-culture missionary dialogue. That dialogue takes place in light of the primary witness of the sovereign Spirit who brings about in conversion within the new culture a new addition to the pluriformity of the church. The form of that conversion cannot be forced into a continuity, with the missionary church "extending" itself into the new culture, but neither can it remain disconnected from the church as an ecumenical fellowship. By conversion, persons of the new culture join the same reciprocal relation to the Bible that other Christians have held. They bring new pre-understandings to the interpretation and "hearing" of the Bible, while they also join the whole community as those under the Bible's authority and determined by it.

The church's missionary dialogue recognizes and expects this supernatural work of conversion by the free Spirit. Therefore the missionary church lives out its relationship of "hermeneutical circle" with the Bible in open dialogue with the public plurality of cultures,

> in dialogue with those who inhabit cultural worlds outside of the Church (whether these are religious or secular) in order to learn through this dialogue more of the fulness of what Lordship means, a fulness which will finally be made manifest only when every tongue confesses that Jesus Christ is Lord to the glory of God the Father. (78ctc:21-22)

This leads to the conclusion that the church's missionary witness can never rightly be a one-way conversation. It is always dialogic, including both the church's inner dialogue with its own culture and its outward dialogue with all others and their respective cultures.

Because this third axis gives rise to the issues we have already surveyed under the headings of the other two and relies on the insights to be gained there, it will only be necessary here to add a brief assessment of several additional aspects of Bishop Newbigin's theology of plurality. In this section we shall note the agenda implications growing out of Newbigin's sense of the "secularity" of the announcement of the gospel (especially impacting the nature of "religious pluralism" discussions), and of his way of seeing in election the solution to the problem of particularity and universality which is at issue in the Christian-culture witness encounter.

Culture and Religious Pluralism

Newbigin's approach to "dialogue" makes it clear that for him it is not just a matter of relating to "the religions" or even "those of other religious faith." It involves the broader range of what is involved in "culture." Therefore it has to do with the Christian's relationship to every other person who does not share the same "ultimate commitment." It is linked without apology to "obedient witness" for which the Christian has been "laid hold of" and which is a gift from the Spirit to be lived out in companionship with the Spirit's own "witness." By "dialogue" Newbigin means the basic missionary character of the church. He calls for that to be done in a humble and faithful manner.

This broader sense of "dialogue with cultures" makes the assertion that "cultural plurality" is the larger field in terms of which we must raise whatever questions are necessary in regard to "religious plurality."[19] This calls for a significant recasting of the field of discussion. In several important areas, specific notions Newbigin uses sketch out for us the particular ways he believes the discussions should be revised. We shall note four of them.

1. The classic "continuity of Christianity with the other religions" question is recast by Newbigin's division of the question into two. What has divided the question is the fact that Newbigin asks it from the point of view of the newly converted person. It is no longer a philosophical matter of seeing or not seeing logical and conceptual continuities between religious systems. Now it becomes a matter of pastoral assistance for the new convert who must wrestle in two directions. There is the question about continuity with the culture in terms of which all of life until now has been lived. But there is also the question of continuity with the new community into which participation has been secured by the gospel. This dividing of the question, asked as it is from this new point of view, suggests an expansion if not an alteration in the terms of the continuity debates.

2. Newbigin claims an approach to "dialogue" which might be said to be more genuinely "pluralistic" than those approaches which usually go by that name. That is true because he offers no overarching understanding of "all" the religions which claims for itself a "standpoint above every other standpoint." He owns the assessment of all religions which he believes the Christian faith requires but does that only to carry out his own commitment to that faith, as those of any faith must. Every standpoint has or implies some view of "all the religions," and he expects in the encounter with other standpoints for those other views to be represented. This is more pluralistic than a procedure by which a view is fashioned which suggests how all the standpoints fit together in a larger unitary structure of thought. That, to Newbigin, is mere illusion.[20] Newbigin's frequent urging that this be acknowledged by those such as the framers of the Birmingham Syllabus is an important principle for the way ahead in interreligious conversations. It leads also to a more forthright confidence in the gospel and encouragement to give a witness to that for which we are "laid hold of," without that reverting into a witness born of presumption and bigotry.

The value of this observation of Newbigin's is linked to the value of his overall apologetic, which stresses that every position begins from the standpoint of some fundamental axioms which are not proved and cannot be proved by any other set of axioms which are more ultimate. All thinking starts from some presupposed "faith-decision." These are generally the culturally defined perspective about "the ways things are" and just as generally are unexamined. His constant pressing of this issue has value for putting into the discussions of pluralism a better and truer mutual understanding based on a more clear self-understanding.[21]

It is important, however, to question whether Newbigin presses this issue too hard and long (undoubtedly due to his sense that others miss it too frequently). He acknowledges at points that the necessity for an assumed beginning point for all thought means accepting such a presupposition "provisionally" and working from there to test and revise the beginning assumption. That must mean that for all of us, unless we have lived in an absolutely static way, we have engaged in a constant reciprocal process of thought by which the current "provisional" assumption is tested and revised, recast in the form of a new "provisional clue" and tested again. His emphasis on the "fundamental axiom" blurs the process of thought and argument which then becomes the proper agenda. Recourse to the "fundamental axiom" cannot forever exclude the debate about the relative merits of one axiom or another, given experience and reflection regarding the ability of each to give coherence and meaning.

3. Newbigin challenges what he sees as the all-too-frequent assumption in discussions of religious plurality that "religion" is the facet of human existence in which the "salvific" element is necessarily to be found. He finds in both experience and Scripture evidence that if anything the reverse is closer to the truth, for the "religious" dimension of life is often the realm of greatest darkness. But he goes beyond solely theological grounds for this challenge. Religion is relativized not only by the biblical revelation and the implications of the cross, but on the more mundane basis of the relationship between religion and culture. Religion has to do with those facets of culture which do bear upon concerns for salvation, but areas of life other than the religious do as well. The phenomenon of desacralization has left much of modern life stripped of "religious" features, but desacralized life is no less founded on ultimate commitments and values taken to be absolute by those who hold them and live by them. The religious dimension is not all there is to the religious character of culture.

Several corollaries must be added to this. While Newbigin asserts that religion is not necessarily the salvific dimension of life and that the gospel as a "secular announcement" speaks to the whole of the cultural life of humankind, not just the religious part of it, he does not do so in such a way as to admit that religion can properly be seen as a separate realm of life in the first place. He resists the danger of isolating religion into a separate and private "department" of life that would remove any "religious" concern from the public realm and restrict it to the private sphere. As a dimension of culture, religion is intimately related to all of life and cannot rightly be cut off from it in a genuinely plural society, unless by the dominance of another ultimate commitment that consigns it to the realm of private opinion or values (as the case of the West has illustrated).

This line of thought has much to commend it, and it promises a fruitful depth in discussions of religious plurality. Newbigin's suggestions do not yet provide a sufficiently full or clear definition concerning the distinction between "culture" and "religion" and the relationship between the two. But beginning with his clue about the frequent "salvific assumption" and his concern over the "privatization of religion," a more thorough framework of "culture and religion" can and must be developed. This constitutes an important part of the agenda ahead for the theology of cultural plurality as a field which includes within it a theology of religious plurality.

4. In chapter six, some assessment was made of Newbigin's "intentional agnosticism" about the question of the destiny of those who have not explicitly acknowledged Jesus as Lord. At this point it should be added that apart from what might be said about his view as a "conscientious position," it certainly has value as an intentional "silent protest" (not so silently made!). In the first place, he is concerned to level the ground regarding the presumption involved in both the so-called inclusivist and exclusivist approaches. No less than those who hold that there is no hope for those outside of explicit faith in Christ, those who hold that all will ultimately be saved are presuming to know in advance the outcome of the final judgment. Even Karl Rahner's gracious inclusion of those he calls "anonymous Christians" (1969) must be tested against the standard of presumption. Newbigin's personal avoidance of either stance should not dull the important effect of this leveling. It presents a new basis for conversations between groups that tend to stay out of contact about the issue of "universal salvation" to acknowledge that those usually construed to be on the side of "refusing to decide for someone else of another culture" may in fact be doing so in reverse.

Newbigin protests also that the religious plurality discussions focus on such a narrow aspect of salvation, the "eternal destiny of the individual human soul," that they are reductionistic in the extreme. The present and social dimensions of salvation are not brought into the picture. Were this to be taken seriously, as it must, it would first of all have impact on the labels so commonly used in typologies in the field, labels which focus almost exclusively on how various views approach the "soul destiny" question ("exclusivism, inclusivism, pluralism"; cf. Race 1982, D'Costa 1986). An agenda for the "theology of religious pluralism" is to make of it something more than a "theology of soul destiny."

Newbigin's protest in this regard may be too loud and long. The deliberateness with which he protects in other areas the inclusion of the sense of the individual along with the sense of corporate salvation (e.g., the concern for individual historical meaning along with the meaning of world history as a whole, over against Marxism), must have a bearing on this area as well. As much as Newbigin is right to press the charge of reductionism, he cannot with consistency omit the issue of the ultimate destiny of the individual person as either partaker in the corporate salvation or nonpartaker. His own theology requires that this remain part of the "religious pluralism" — or better, "cultural pluralism" — discussion.

Election and Biblical Theology

An essential part of the point that has been made in this study is that the missionary character of election, as Newbigin describes it, lies at the heart of his theology of cultural plurality and gives it its value and strength. This theological center constitutes the most important contribution he makes toward the development of the field we have been attempting to circumscribe. What stands out is his way of turning the question of particularity around to ask it from the point of view of the one encountered by the "witness" who has come from another culture. The question, therefore, focuses his attention on the mission of God which is justified from the charge of caprice by the universalizing movement envisioned in the pattern of election, each one chosen to bear the blessing to the "other." A "personal" God and a meaningful history are thus established by the only means congruent. Election forms the clue toward the "solution" of the problem of particularity; it does not comprise the problem, which must be overcome another way. Election is a corollary to the nature of God and the character of the mission on which God is embarked in this divinely originated world. The universal mission of the church in a culturally (and thus religiously) plural world of diverse particularities is defended on this ground.

This "inner logic" of God's mission designed to work by way of election will not, of course, convince everyone or finally lay to rest the issue of "the particular and the universal." Arnold Toynbee, who otherwise spoke appreciatively of Newbigin's fair treatment of his view in *A Faith for This One World?* and described his own acknowledgment of the necessity of an assumed beginning "standpoint" in ways very similar to Newbigin's, remained unconvinced by the election argument in the book.

> In all the religions of the Judaic family, I find an inner contradiction between their picture of what God is like and their account of God's acts. As I see it, love and exclusiveness are incompatible. . . . I do not think this inner contradiction is permanently tenable. (Toynbee 1961:3)

In Newbigin's own terms, we may say that what he provides is a rationality visible from within Christian faith. While he reframes the question to be that of the "other" who is met by the Christian witness, the inner logic he explicates is directed in the end to the Christian witness who is genuinely bothered by the implications of the question from the "other" and is designed to provide a place to stand and a confidence to bear the Spirit's witness even in the face of the severest challenge of "particularity." It is not hinted that Newbigin believes his presentation of election as "solution" will convincingly resolve the issue for people who judge it from another standpoint. He does not seem to expect that this will answer and turn aside the question coming from the lips of a Hindu, for example. In Hindu terms, the question will remain a damning one. But for the Indian Christian who meets the Hindu neighbor, election gives a foundation for faithful witness.

The value that is here affirmed for Newbigin's articulation of "the missionary significance of the biblical doctrine of election" does not deny that there are two areas in which important limitations are evident and in which further work may productively be done.

1. Newbigin's view of "election for responsibility" must bear the weight of the criticism leveled against the "election for service" view of H. H. Rowley. Robert Cushman asks whether "Rowley's attractive generalization is not largely a reading of the Old Testament in the light of the New" (1981:203). Newbigin's identification of "witness" as that for which the people of God are chosen intensifies the question in regard to his own view of election responsibility. The close connection he always maintains between the revelation of the end, the promise of the Spirit, and the calling to be witnesses would seem to create a structure of thought implying of the Old Testament "chosen-for-witness" people that the beginning of the eschatological end and the presence of the Spirit are already true for them. The hard line between Old and New Testaments which he draws on other issues (e.g., law and grace), is not drawn here, and the result is somewhat a flattening of the picture. There is not a sense of the unfolding or progression of the basic conception which would make it a convincingly "biblical theological" idea.

This does not disqualify his contribution, of course. He does not intend to provide such a biblical theological treatment of the Old Testament and mission. But the fact that he places his notion in this arena, emphasizing that he is referring to the "biblical doctrine of election," means that a need remains for a more complete biblical theological assessment of its value as a fresh hermeneutic both for approaching the cultural pluralisms present in the Old Testament history and literature and for searching out the Old Testament conception of "mission" in the minds of both the Israelite community and God. He contributes to the search that its promise is not to be sought by finding an explicit "commission" but rather by looking for the "inner logic" of the way God proceeds in mission by the manner of election.

2. There is another area in which Newbigin's election thesis cannot avoid further essential questions. His concentration on the responsibility and corporate dimensions of election places the discussion in a different arena from that of the classical Protestant predestination debates. But Newbigin does not see only responsibility or only the corporate dimension. He affirms that there is still a rightful, humble sense in which the elect do possess real blessing, real salvation. And he affirms on this issue and others that the corporate dimension of salvation and election does not erase the individual aspect. Because of this, his view cannot ultimately avoid tackling at least in some respects the classical questions, albeit while revising the questions themselves. His view of election does not get us entirely out of the woods on the matter of the problem of the "antithesis" of the chosen and the unchosen, God's choosing and not choosing, the reception of the news and the nonreception, the gaining and the losing of eternal life. The clues he does give provide fresh possibilities for a bridge by which the classical questions and the modern missiological perspective may be joined and engaged together.

Final Conclusions

At the outset, it was proposed that Newbigin's theological foundations for dealing with issues of cultural plurality held promise because his has been a crucial voice in at least three major arenas of missiological discussion: the validity and character of cross-cultural mission, the necessity and forms of the church's unity, and the basis and mode of interreligious dialogue. Each has to do with a heightened experience of "cultural plurality," and in each case the participants in the discussion respond in terms of some fundamental, theological attitude toward that plurality. In light of the small amount of attention given to clarity about the theological convictions implicitly undergirding the discussions, Newbigin's instinctive and extensive effort to provide that is one of his most important contributions. Because he makes that contribution on a number of fronts, his theological structure is all the more important. It possesses a certain integrative force, bringing into intimate relationship discussions which have tended to remain too much in isolation from each other. It calls upon the participants in all those arenas to do two things: to bridge out from the isolation of one conversation into other related ones and to explore more consciously their own root theological assumptions and test their adequacy in the face of the expanded experience of cultural plurality. In this way Newbigin has provided an enrichment to the field called "missiology."

A more explicit contribution is made by his casting a field of theological inquiry. This he has done not by deliberate intention but simply in the process of responding to challenge after challenge placed before him. What this book has attempted to show is that as a result of his work we can see the lines along which such a field is marked out. Rooted in his understanding of election, he has shown that a theology of cultural plurality must take up questions of history and eschatology and provide foundations for public, political action on the part of the church. He has shown further that it will involve critical attention to conversion and its communal implications, issues foundational for an adequate ecclesiology. And he has shown that the field must deal with how we understand "religion" in its relation to "culture" and to a gospel which comes as a "secular announcement," with a view toward finding appropriate patterns of relationship with people to whom witness to Christ is being given. In the end, Newbigin invites us to proceed in terms of a triangular understanding of the relationships between gospel, culture, and church. When these features are taken together they represent the contours of a field in need of more conscious and explicit theological attention. His particular proposals are a significant contribution to such a field.

But what is perhaps the most important contribution of Newbigin's "theology of cultural plurality" lies in a more practical area. In service to pastors and church leaders who are drawn to take up his challenge regarding the encounter of the gospel with their own culture, he provides a theoretical and theological undergirding for their missional engagement. Here is a vision and perspective with the power to sustain a transforming way of life for churches of all sorts.

In the first place, it has the power to enable churches to engage their "own" culture in a missionary way. It supplies the theological ground on which the conversion encounter takes place and envisions what sort of conversion the Spirit desires and intends, no less among people of the West than among people elsewhere. It shows the encounter to be one in which the gospel calls for a fundamental U-turn in mind and behavior, but always roots that new planting of Christian discipleship and community in terms provided by the culture of the "converted." Thus the gospel approaches every culture with affirmation and reception (so that there is no place given to culture-rejection or culture-bashing), yet with the element of critique and discontinuity (calling the people of every culture into new community). For the churches of the West, this means maintaining the readiness to recognize unwarranted accommodations to their culture in order to disentangle themselves, while discovering the Spirit's creative work to make the church a faithfully Western incarnation of the gospel. The church in the West, as much as any other church, is called to be part of the variegated flowering of Christian faith across the earth.

In the second place, Newbigin's perspective gives churches powerful resources for the "inner dialogue" in which they must be engaged. The missionary engagement with one's own culture is always first an inward dialogue before it can be an outward one. That is to say, the church must never deceive itself to think that the culture is somehow "out there" in people outside the church. It is always as much the culture shared by the people in the church as by those outside, and it cannot be otherwise. The difference is that the church is a community called into a living, reciprocal relationship with the Scriptures by which the gospel is as much "reading" them as they are reading it. As those addressed by the gospel, the church learns to live as the place where their own culture — the one that has shaped their instincts and inclinations and preferences and judgments — is first and foremost greeted by God and confronted with its need to be transformed by the knowledge of God. The church is always a community being converted, day by day. It lives rightly when it stays open to the encounter of the gospel with the culture by which it thinks and lives, ready for the fresh witness of the Spirit.

Third, Newbigin's vision nourishes congregations toward their calling to be "the hermeneutic of the gospel," the interpretive lens through which people will see and read what this gospel has to do with them and the world in which they live. It has the power to open up dynamic ways for churches to be living, speaking, acting signs of the reign of God. It has the power to sustain the church as a community that gives living demonstration that God is known and God's purposes are achieved in the life, death, and resurrection of Jesus Christ, and that it is both thinkable and feasible to live as though that is true!

This agenda for the church's life lies at the heart of Newbigin's passion, and it was for this cause that he sought to understand the missional mind of the Spirit of God. He offered the fruit of his effort as his legacy to the churches so that they may live out their vocation in the joy of the resurrection and the hope of the coming reign of God.

The Literature of the
Thomas-Newbigin Debate

Published Portions of the Debate

1. The article by Kaj Baago (1966) in *IRM* (July), upon which both Newbigin (66c and 69fc) and Thomas (1971) later comment.
2. Newbigin's article containing the substance of his address at the
   Nasrapur Consultation on "mission" (March 1966), in which he discusses conversion and responds to the view of Baago (66c, published
   in August 1966). His response to Baago was made even more explicit
   in the revised version of the article (chapter 5 of 69fc).
3. The published dialogue between M. M. Thomas and Hendrikus Berkhof (Löffler 1968), which carried on a discussion begun at Mexico City
   in 1963.
4. Newbigin's article (69cmcu) containing an assessment of the dialogue
   between Thomas and Berkhof (Löffler 1968).
5. Thomas's book on *Salvation and Humanisation* (1971), in which he
   comments on the views of both Baago (1966) and Newbigin (69fc,
   69cmcu, 57tfd, 69wwfo).
6. Newbigin's extensive review (71rsh) of *Salvation and Humanisation*,
   published in *Religion and Society*.
7. The publication in *Religion and Society* (March 1972) of an exchange
   of letters between Thomas and Newbigin with comments by Alfred C.
   Krass (72bck). The exchange was included in an issue containing some

of the material presented at the November 1971 Bienniel Consultation of the CISRS on the theme "Conversion and Baptism" (cf. Christopher Duraisingh 1972, Richard W. Taylor 1972). More particularly, the exchange included:

a. A letter dated "21st October 1971" from Thomas to Newbigin (Thomas 1972:69-74), including a response to a manuscript of Newbigin's address in 1971 at a seminar of the Jesuit Educational Association of India (72sad).
b. A letter dated "17th November 1971" (but compare the date of "18-11-71" at the conclusion of the letter, which is the correct one) from Newbigin to Thomas (72bck:75-84).
c. A comment by Alfred C. Krass (1972a) on Thomas's book (1971), Newbigin's original review article (71rsh), and Thomas's letter of October 21, 1971 (1972:69-74).
d. A letter dated "20th December 1971" from Thomas to Newbigin (1972:87-90).

Unpublished Materials of the Debate

Several unpublished items, including those listed below, were originally intended to be incorporated with some of the published materials and published in a separate volume, a project which was ultimately abandoned.

8. An undated response by Alfred Krass to Newbigin's November 18, 1971, reply to Thomas's letter of October 21, 1971 (Krass 1971, 2 pages).
9. A letter dated "January 3, 1972," from Alfred Krass to Thomas in response to Thomas's letter to Newbigin dated December 20, 1971 (Krass 1972b, 2 pages).
10. A letter dated "30 January 1973," from Paul Löffler to both Thomas and Newbigin, complaining that they had come too quickly to "a near agreement on all essential points" and raising questions to foster further debate (Löffler 1973, 3 pages).
11. A mimeographed manuscript by Newbigin entitled "The Church and the Kingdom" containing extensive comments by Newbigin in response to Löffler's letter (73ck, 12 pages; cf. Löffler 1973). In it Newbigin interacts further with Thomas (1972:87-90) and Krass (1971, 1972b) but especially engages the articles of Duraisingh (1972) and Taylor

(1972) which had appeared in the March 1972 issue of *Religion and Society*. The last page of the draft bears the date "July 1972," but that must surely indicate July 1973 since the letter of Löffler to which it responds was dated "30 January 1973." Löffler's letter could not have been misdated for an actual "30 January 1972" because it makes explicit reference to the March 1972 issue of *Religion and Society* in which the original exchange of letters between Thomas and Newbigin appeared.

Writings of Lesslie Newbigin:
An Annotated Bibliography

This bibliography of Bishop Newbigin's works contains both the published and the unpublished materials that form the basis for the present study and relate to its theme. Hence although it is extensive it does not claim to be complete. Most of the items noted here, but not all, are referenced at some point in the text. The bibliography is briefly annotated in order to provide information regarding the setting in which an address or essay was first given and in order to trace the various forms and places in which materials have been republished from time to time. In most cases, essays are included in the listing only once at the point of initial or primary publication. Revised editions of books have been listed a second time in those cases in which the revisions are especially important to note.

Each of the materials is identified by a reference code that consists of the last two digits of the year of publication followed by up to four lowercase letters representing the first letters of the key words in the title. This procedure is followed so that the reader may more easily identify and recall each particular item as it is referenced in the text. The materials are listed in order by year. Within each year, they are listed alphabetically by code. This does not preserve the exact alphabetical order of the titles in all cases, but it will facilitate referencing the sometimes large number of items included in a given year.

33svmu   "The Student Volunteer Missionary Union." In *The Christian Faith Today,* pp. 95-104. London: SCM Press.

36r   "Revelation." Unpublished theology paper presented at Westminster College, Cambridge.

37cfmw   *Christian Freedom in the Modern World.* London: SCM Press.

38cibc   "Can I Be Christian? — VIII." *The Spectator* May 6, 1938:800.

38tns   *Things Not Shaken: Glimpses of the Foreign Missions of the Church of Scotland in 1937.* Unsigned. Edinburgh: Church of Scotland Foreign Mission Committee.

39le   *Living Epistles: Impressions of the Foreign Mission Work of the Church of Scotland in 1938.* Unsigned. Edinburgh: Church of Scotland Foreign Mission Committee.

41kgip   "The Kingdom of God and the Idea of Progress." Unpublished notes of four lectures given at United Theological College. Bangalore.

42wig   *What Is the Gospel?* SCM Study Series No. 6. Madras: CLSI.

44cg   "The Church and the Gospel." In *The Church and Union,* by the Committee on Church Union, SIUC, pp. 46-59. Madras: CLSI.

44f   Foreword to *The Church and Union,* by the Committee on Church Union, SIUC. Madras: CLSI.

45ofmi   "Ordained Foreign Missionary in the Indian Church." *International Review of Missions* 34:86-94.

46ib   "I Believe." In *I Believe,* edited by M. A. Thomas, pp. 73-88. Madras: SCM Press. Address given at the Regional Leaders' Conference, Madras, December 1945.

46ibc   "I Believe in Christ." In *I Believe,* edited by M. A. Thomas, pp. 101-114. Madras: SCM Press. Address given at the Regional Leaders' Conference, Madras, December 1945.

46ibg   "I Believe in God." In *I Believe,* edited by M. A. Thomas, pp. 89-100. Madras: SCM Press. Address given at the Regional Leaders' Conference, Madras, December 1945.

48csu   "The Ceylon Scheme of Union: A South Indian View." *South India Churchman* June 1948:162-163. Acknowledgment to the *Morning Star,* Jaffna.

48dacp   "The Duty and Authority of the Church to Preach the Gospel." In *The Church's Witness to God's Design,* Amsterdam Assembly Series, vol. 2, pp. 19-35. New York: Harper and Brothers.

48hcsi   "The Heritage of the Church of South India: Our Presbyterian Heritage." *South India Churchman* January 1948:52-54.

48rc   *The Reunion of the Church: A Defence of the South India Scheme.* London: SCM Press. Republished in a revised second edition in 1960 (60rc).

50eea   "The Evangelization of Eastern Asia." In *The Christian Prospect in Eastern Asia: Papers and Minutes of the Eastern Asia Christian Conference, Bangkok, December 3-11, 1949,* pp. 77-87. New York: Friendship Press. Republished in the *International Review of Missions* 39 (1950):137-145.

51cccw   "Comments on 'The Church, the Churches and the World Council of Churches.'" *Ecumenical Review* 3:252-254.

51ott   "Our Task Today: A Charge to Be Given to the Fourth Meeting of the Diocesan Council, Tirumangalam, 18-20 December, 1951." Unpublished paper.

51sid   *A South India Diary.* London: SCM Press. Republished in 1952 in an American edition entitled *That All May Be One,* New York: Association Press. Introduction by E. H. Johnson. A revised edition was published in 1960 by SCM Press, London (60sid).

52clwc   "The Christian Layman in the World and in the Church." *National Christian Council Review* 72:185-189.

52nch   "The Nature of the Christian Hope." *Ecumenical Review* 4:282-284.

52ot   "Odd Theologians." *South India Churchman* January 1952:2-4.

52rcg   Review of *The Communication of the Gospel,* by David H. C. Read. *International Review of Missions* 41:526-528.

53afc   "Ambassadors for Christ." *South India Churchman* August 1953:3-4.

53ccgc   "Can the Churches Give a Common Message to the World?" *Theology Today* 9:512-518.

53ch   "The Christian Hope." In *Missions Under the Cross,* edited by Norman Goodall, pp. 107-116. London: Edinburgh House Press. Address given in 1952 at the Enlarged Meeting of the IMC at Willingen.

53hg   *The Household of God: Lectures on the Nature of the Church.* London: SCM Press. The Kerr Lectures given at Trinity College, Glasgow, in November 1952. An American edition was published in 1954 by Friendship Press, New York, with more complete sectioning (the present study uses the pagination of this edition). Republished in a slightly revised edition in 1964 by SCM Press.

53mc   "The Ministry of the Church." *National Christian Council Review* 73:351-355. Published form of a draft entitled "Statement for the consideration of the dioceses on the ministry of the church — ordained and unordained, paid and unpaid; Madura, 1953."

54c   "Conversion." *The Guardian (Madras)* December 23, 1954:409.

54lwlc   "The Life and Witness of the Local Church." In *The Church in a Changing World: Addresses and Reports of the National Christian Council of India, Gumtur, November 5-10, 1953*. Mysore: Wesley Press.

54pccc   "The Present Christ and the Coming Christ." *Ecumenical Review* 6:118-123.

54wsot   "Why Study the Old Testament?" *National Christian Council Review* 74:71-76.

55qutr   "The Quest for Unity Through Religion." *Journal of Religion* 35:17-33. The Thomas Memorial Lecture at the University of Chicago in 1954. Republished in the *Indian Journal of Theology* 4, 2 (1955):1-17.

56nms   "National Missionary Society." *South India Churchman* January 1956:6-7. Address at a meeting of the Golden Jubilee Celebration of the National Missionary Society, Madras, November 1955.

56ss   *Sin and Salvation*. London: SCM Press.

56wgc   "The Wretchedness and Greatness of the Church." *National Christian Council Review* 76:472-477. Sermon preached at the united service during the triennial meeting of the NCCI, Allahabad.

57iwia   "I When I Am Lifted Up. . . ." Unpublished sermon given at the Uniting Synod of the Congregational and Evangelical and Reformed Churches, Cleveland, 1957.

57tfd   "A Time for Decision." In *Revolution in Missions*, edited by Blaise Levai, appendices. Vellore: The Popular Press.

58acr   "Anglicans and Christian Reunion." *Theology* 61:223-227.

58obog   *One Body, One Gospel, One World: The Christian Mission Today.*
           London and New York: International Missionary Council. Par-
           tially republished in the *Ecumenical Review* 11 (1958):143-156.

59guhc   "The Gathering Up of History into Christ." In *The Missionary
           Church in East and West,* edited by Charles C. West and
           David M. Paton, pp. 81-90. London: SCM Press. Address given
           in 1957 at the Ecumenical Institute in Bossey.

59nuws   "The Nature of the Unity We Seek." Unpublished paper, ap-
           proximate date.

59scmt   "The Summons to Christian Mission Today." *International
           Review of Missions* 48:177-189. Address given at the Annual
           Dinner of the North American Advisory Committee of the
           International Missionary Council, New York, November 1958.

59wgdu   "Will God Dwell Upon Earth?" *National Christian Council
           Review* 79:99-102. Text of a sermon preached at the dedication
           of a chapel in a Christian College.

60bicu   "Basic Issues in Church Union." In *We Were Brought Together,*
           edited by David M. Taylor, pp. 155-169. Sydney: Australian
           Council for the WCC. Address given at the National Confer-
           ence of Australian Churches, Melbourne, February 1960.

60bnfw   "Bishop Newbigin's Final Word." In *We Were Brought Together,*
           edited by David M. Taylor, pp. 128-130. Sydney: Australian
           Council for the WCC. Address given at the National Confer-
           ence of Australian Churches, Melbourne, February 1960.

60bsft   "Bible Studies: Four Talks on 1 Peter by Bishop Newbigin." In
           We Were Brought Together, edited by David M. Taylor, pp. 93-
           123. Sydney: Australian Council for the WCC. Addresses given
           at the National Conference of Australian Churches, Mel-
           bourne, February 1960.

60cbww   "The Cup of Blessing Which We Bless." Unpublished sermon
           preached at Grace Cathedral, San Francisco, December 9,
           1960.

60csi   Letter to the Editor: "Church of South India." *Faith and Unity*
           5, 8:24.

60fwlb   "Forgetting What Lies Behind. . . ." Unpublished sermon
           preached at the Riverside Church, New York City, at the 50th
           anniversary observance of the Edinburgh 1910 World Mis-
           sionary Conference, May 25, 1960.

60lmc   "The Life and Mission of the Church." In *We Were Brought Together,* edited by David M. Taylor, pp. 59-69. Sydney: Australian Council for the WCC. Keynote address at the National Conference of Australian Churches, Melbourne, February 1960.

60mcsi   "The Ministry of the Church of South India: A Letter from Bishop Lesslie Newbigin to Fr. Dalby, S.S.J.E." *Faith and Unity* 5, 7:12-14.

60mm   "Mission and Missions." *Christianity Today* 4, no. 22 (August 1, 1960):911.

60muc   *The Mission and Unity of the Church.* Grahamstown: Rhodes University. The Eleventh Peter Ainslee Memorial Lecture, October 17, 1960. Republished under the title "Is There Still a Missionary Job Today?" in *563 St. Columba: Fourteenth Centenary 1963.* Glasgow: The Iona Cummunity Publications Department, for the Church of Scotland.

60pp   "The Pattern of Partnership." In *A Decisive Hour for the Christian World Mission,* by Norman Goodall, J. E. Lesslie Newbigin, W. A. Wisser 't Hooft, and D. T. Niles, pp. 34-45. London: SCM Press. One of the John R. Mott Memorial Lectures at the Founding Assembly of the East Asia Christian Conference, Kuala Lumpur, May 1959.

60rc   *The Reunion of the Church: A Defence of the South India Scheme.* Revised edition of 48rc. London: SCM Press.

60sid   *A South India Diary.* Revised edition of 51sid, including a new foreword and epilogue. London: SCM Press.

60taii   "The Truth As It Is in Jesus." Pamphlet. U.S.A.: North American Ecumenical Youth Assembly. Address given at a Faith and Order luncheon in San Francisco, December 1960.

60um   "The Unification of the Ministry." *Faith and Unity* 6:4-10. Republication of 60rc:xx-xxvii, a portion of the introduction added in the revised edition of 48rc.

60whsl   "The Work of the Holy Spirit in the Life of the Asian Churches." In *A Decisive Hour for the Christian World Mission,* by Norman Goodall, J. E. Lesslie Newbigin, W. A. Wisser 't Hooft, and D. T. Niles, pp. 18-33. London: SCM Press. One of the John R. Mott Memorial Lectures at the Founding Assembly of the East Asia Christian Conference, Kuala Lumpur, May 1959.

61abln   "Address by Bishop Lesslie Newbigin to Africa Committee, January 27th, 1961." Unpublished address, refined and published as 61sic.

61ec   "Ecumenical Comments." *Lutheran World* 8:74-77. An invited response to an article by Peter Brunner entitled "The LWF as an Ecclesiological Problem," *Lutheran World* 7:237ff.

61f   Foreword to *The Theology of the Christian Mission*, edited by Gerald H. Anderson, pp. xi-xiii. New York: McGraw-Hill, and London: SCM Press.

61ftow   *A Faith for This One World?* London: SCM Press. The William Belden Noble Lectures given at Harvard, November 1958.

61icd   *Is Christ Divided? A Plea for Christian Unity in a Revolutionary Age.* Grand Rapids: William B. Eerdmans Publishing Company.

61sic   "Sugar in the Coffee." *Frontier* 4:93-97. A refined and published form of 61abln.

62bomm   "Bringing Our Missionary Methods Under the Word of God." *Occasional Bulletin from the Missionary Research Library* 13:1-9. Address at a mission consultation of the Presbyterian Church, US.

62clu   "The Church — Local and Universal." In *The Church — Local and Universal; Things We Face Together, No. 2,* by Leslie T. Lyall and Lesslie Newbigin, pp. 20-28. London: World Dominion Press.

62f/mm   Foreword to *Missionary Methods: St. Paul's or Ours?*, by Roland Allen, American edition, pp. i-iii. Grand Rapids: William B. Eerdmans Publishing Company.

62f/ue   Foreword to *Upon the Earth*, by D. T. Niles, pp. 7-8. London: Lutterworth Press.

62mdem   "The Missionary Dimension of the Ecumenical Movement." *Ecumenical Review* 14:207-215. Republished in the *International Review of Mission* 70 (1981):240-246.

62ommt   *The Ordained Ministry and the Missionary Task.* Pamphlet. Geneva: WCC.

62p   "Preface." In *Survey of the Training of the Ministry in the Middle East,* by Douglas Webster and K. L. Nasir. Geneva, London, New York: Commission on World Mission and Evangelism, WCC.

62rdwm   "Report of the Division of World Mission and Evangelism to the Central Committee." *Ecumenical Review* 15:88-94.

62rsce   "Rapid Social Change and Evangelism." Unpublished paper. Approximate date.

63dd62   "Developments During 1962: An Editorial Survey." *International Review of Missions* 52:3-14. Unsigned.

63en   "Editor's Notes." *International Review of Missions* 52:242-246, 369-373, 508-512. Unsigned.

63gdpt   "Gesta Dei per Tamulos." *Frontier* 5:553-555. Review of *The Dispersion of the Tamil Church* by N. C. Sargant.

63jam   "Joint Action for Mission." *National Christian Council Review* 83:17-23.

63jsmc   "Jesus the Servant and Man's Community." Unpublished address given at a congress of the SCM.

63mm   "The Message and the Messengers. Notes of Bible Studies Given at the Singapore Situation Conference. (1 Cor. 1–4)." *South East Asia Journal of Theology* 5:85-98. Republished in *One People — One Mission,* edited by J. R. Fleming. East Asia Christian Conference, 1963.

63rtdt   *The Relevance of Trinitarian Doctrine for Today's Mission.* London: Edinburgh House Press. Republished in 1964 in an American edition entitled *Trinitarian Faith and Today's Mission.* Richmond, Va.: John Knox Press.

63wc   "World Christianity: Result of the Missionary Expansion." Unpublished address given at Biblical Seminary, New York City. Approximate date.

64ccre   "The Church: Catholic, Reformed, and Evangelical." *Episcopalian* 129:12-15, 48.

64en   "Editor's Notes." *International Review of Missions* 53:248-252, 376-379, 512-517. Unsigned.

64f   Foreword to *God for All Men,* by Robert C. Latham, p. 4. London: Edinburgh House, New York: Friendship Press, and Geneva: WCC.

64sy63   "Survey of the Year 1962-3: By the Editor." *International Review of Missions* 53:3-82. Unsigned.

65fe   "From the Editor." *International Review of Missions* 54:145-150 (unsigned), 273-280 (unsigned), 417-427 (initialed).

65hmmc   "The Healing Ministry in the Mission of the Church." In *The*

	Healing Church, pp. 8-15. Geneva: Division of World Mission and Evangelism, WCC.
65i	Introduction to *The Programme Fund of the Division of World Mission and Evangelism.* Geneva: WCC.
65ibln	"Introduction by Lesslie Newbigin." In *All Africa Conference of Churches.* Geneva: WCC.
65im	"Integration et Mission." *Rythmes du Monde* (Brugge-Paris) 13:139-147.
65ml	"Ministry and Laity." *National Christian Council Review* 85:479-483. Summary of a talk given to the United Mission of Nepal at Kathmandu, March 1965.
65p	Preface to *The Healing Church,* pp. 5-6. Geneva: Division of World Mission and Evangelism, WCC.
65sy64	"Survey of the Year 1963-4: By the Editor." *International Review of Missions* 54:3-75. Unsigned.
66c	"Conversion." *National Christian Council Review* 86:309-323. Notes of an address given at the Nasrapur Consultation, March 1966. Republished in *Religion and Society* 13, no. 4 (1966):30-42 and in *Renewal for Mission,* edited by David Lyon and Albert Manuel, pp. 33-46. Madras: CLS, 1967.
66hrsm	*Honest Religion for Secular Man.* Philadelphia: Westminster Press and London: SCM Press. The Firth Lectures, University of Nottingham, November 1964.
66sy65	"A Survey of the Year 1964-65." *International Review of Missions* 55:3-80. Unsigned.
67ggg	"Glory, Glory, Glory." *The Lutheran Standard (USA)* May 30, 1967:13, 16. Bible study on John 17 given at the 1966 meeting of the National Council of Churches of Christ of the USA, Miami Beach.
67hh	"The Hinge of History." *The Lutheran Standard (USA)* April 4, 1967:10-11. Bible study on John 17 given at the 1966 meeting of the National Council of Churches of Christ of the USA, Miami Beach.
67jwie	"Just Who Is the Enemy?" *The Lutheran Standard (USA)* May 2, 1967:12-13. Bible study on John 17 given at the 1966 meeting of the National Council of Churches of Christ of the USA, Miami Beach.
67pwmw	"A Point from Which to Move the World." *The Lutheran Stan-*

dard (USA) May 16, 1967:9, 30. Bible study on John 17 given at the 1966 meeting of the National Council of Churches of Christ of the USA, Miami Beach.

67sfow   "The Spiritual Foundations of Our Work." In *The Christian College and National Development,* pp. 1-8. Madras: CLS.

67srd   "Strong Roots of Driftwood." *The Lutheran Standard (USA)* April 18, 1967:9-10. Bible study on John 17 given at the 1966 meeting of the National Council of Churches of Christ of the USA, Miami Beach.

68amim   "Anglicans, Methodists and Intercommunion: A Moment for Decision." *The Churchman* 82:281-285.

68bima   *Behold I Make All Things New.* Madras: CLS. Talks given at youth conferences in Kerala, May 1968.

68bsgn   "Bible Studies Given at the National Christian Council Triennial Assembly, Shillong." *National Christian Council Review* 88:9-14, 73-78, 125-131, 177-185. Four studies given in October 1967. Republished in 1968 in *Renewal for Mission,* edited by David Lyon and Albert Manuel, pp. 192-213. Second revised and enlarged edition. Madras: CLS.

68coec   *Christ Our Eternal Contemporary.* Madras: CLS. Meditations given at the Christian Medical College, Vellore, July 1966.

68rtr   Review of *Theology in Reconstruction* by T. F. Torrance. *Indian Journal of Theology* 17:43-45.

68wmc   "The World Mission of the Church." *South India Churchman* September 1968:2-4.

69cmcu   "The Call to Mission — A Call to Unity." In *The Church Crossing Frontiers,* edited by Peter Beyerhaus and Carl F. Hallencreutz, pp. 254-265. Lund: Gleerup. Contribution to a collection of essays on the nature of mission in honour of Bengt Sundkler.

69cuww   "Church Union: Which Way Forward?" *National Christian Council Review* 89:356-363.

69fc   *The Finality of Christ.* London: SCM Press and Richmond, Va.: John Knox Press. The Lyman Beecher Lectures, Yale University Divinity School, April 1966. Also given as the James Reid Lectures at Cambridge University.

69sfbs   *Set Free to Be a Servant: Studies in Paul's Letter to the Galatians.* Madras: CLS.

69wwfo   "Which Way for 'Faith and Order'?" In *What Unity Implies: Six Essays After Uppsala*, World Council Studies No. 7, edited by Reinhard Groscurth, pp. 115-132. Geneva: WCC.

70bsl   "The Bible Study Lectures." In *Digest of the Proceedings of the Ninth Meeting (COCU)*, pp. 193-231. Princeton, N.J.: Consultation on Church Union. Lectures given in March 1970.

70cu   "Cooperation and Unity." *International Review of Mission* 59:67-74.

70msc   "Mission to Six Continents." In *The Ecumenical Advance: A History of the Ecumenical Movement, Vol. 2, 1948-1968*, edited by Harold E. Fey, pp. 171-197. London: SPCK.

70smd   "Stewardship, Mission and Development." Unpublished address given at the Annual Stewardship Conference of the British Council of Churches, Stanwick, June 1970.

71c   "Conversion." In *Concise Dictionary of the Christian World Mission*, edited by Stephen Neill, Gerald H. Anderson, and John Goodwin, pp. 147-148. Nashville and New York: Abingdon Press.

71csc   "The Church as a Servant Community." *National Christian Council Review* 91:256-264. Lecture given at the Consultation on Love and Justice in the World of Tomorrow, October 1970.

71jc   "Jesus Christ." In *Concise Dictionary of the Christian World Mission*, edited by Stephen Neill, Gerald H. Anderson, and John Goodwin, pp. 307-309. Nashville and New York: Abingdon Press.

71rsh   Review of *Salvation and Humanisation* by M. M. Thomas. *Religion and Society* 18, 1:71-80.

71s   "Salvation." In *Concise Dictionary of the Christian World Mission*, edited by Stephen Neill, Gerald H. Anderson, and John Goodwin, pp. 537-538. Nashville and New York: Abingdon Press.

71t   "Trinitarianism." In *Concise Dictionary of the Christian World Mission*, edited by Stephen Neill, Gerald H. Anderson, and John Goodwin, pp. 607. Nashville and New York: Abingdon Press.

72amtj   "Address on the Main Theme, 'Jesus, Saviour of the World,' at the Synod Assembly of January 1972." *South India Churchman* February 1972:5-8.

72bck   "Baptism, the Church and Koinonia: Three Letters and a Comment." *Religion and Society* 19, 1:69-90. An exchange of letters between Lesslie Newbigin and M. M. Thomas with a comment by Alfred C. Krass. Letter of 17 November 1971 ("18-11-71") by Lesslie Newbigin, pp. 75-84. Republished in 1977 in *Some Theological Dialogues,* by M. M. Thomas, pp. 110-144. Madras: CLS.

72csit   "The Church of South India — Twenty-Five Years After." *Christian Advocate* December 21, 1972:13-14.

72foii   "Faith and Order in India Now." *National Christian Council Review* 92:433-436. Guest editorial.

72hsc   *The Holy Spirit and the Church.* Madras: CLS. Addresses originally given at a convention in Madras, April 1972.

72jij   *Journey into Joy.* Madras: CLS and Delhi: ISPCK. Transcription of taped addresses given at the Christian Medical College, Vellore, October 1971. Republished in 1973 in an American edition, Grand Rapids: William B. Eerdmans Publishing Company.

72sad   "The Secular-Apostolic Dilemma." In *Not Without a Compass: JEA Seminar on Christian Education in the India of Today,* edited by T. Mathias et al., pp. 61-71. New Delhi: Jesuit Educational Association of India. With reactions by Pierre Fallon, G. Casimir, and G. Soares, pp. 72-78.

72ssl   "Servants of the Servant Lord." *Vivekananda Kendra Patrika* February 1972:153-155.

72tfyc   "Twenty-Five Years of C.S.I." *National Christian Council Review* 92:141-145.

72tfyo   "Twenty-Five Years Old: How Fares the Church of South India?" *Presbyterian Life (Philadelphia)* 25, 9:38-40.

73ccas   "The Churches and CASA." *National Christian Council Review* 93:543-549. A paper written for the consultation between CASA and heads of churches at Delhi, September 1973.

73ck   "The Church and the Kingdom." An unpublished paper written in response to a letter by Paul Löffler (dated "30 January 1973") encouraging further debate between Lesslie Newbigin and M. M. Thomas. (The paper bears the date "July 1972" but it must have been written in July 1973, responding as it does to Löffler's letter. A January 1972 date is impossible to conjecture for Löffler's letter since it refers to the March 1972 issue of *Religion and Society.*)

73fsvu   "The Form and Structure of the Visible Unity of the Church." In *So sende Ich Euch: Festschrift für D. Dr. Martin Porksen zum 70. Geburtstag,* edited by Otto Wack et al., pp. 124-141. Korntal bei Stuttgart: Evang. Missionsverlag. Originally published in two parts as "The Form and Structure of the Visible Unity of the Church, (1st Part)," *National Christian Council Review* 92 (1972):444-451, and "The Form and Structure of the Visible Unity of the Church, (2nd Part)," *National Christian Council Review* 93 (1973):4-18. Republished in *One in Christ* 13 (1977):107-126.

73rcyc   Review of *Christ and the Younger Churches* by Georg F. Vicedom. *Indian Journal of Theology* 22:183-185.

73snhc   "Salvation, the New Humanity and Cultural-Communal Solidarity." *Bangalore Theological Forum* 5, 2:1-11.

73tsb   "The Taste of Salvation at Bangkok." *Indian Journal of Theology* 22:49-53.

74cfm   "Christian Faith and Marxism." *Madras Christian College Magazine* 1974:21-26. The substance of an address given to students at the Fellowship Breakfast organized by the SCM of Madras Christian College, February 11, 1973.

74gs   *The Good Shepherd: Meditations on Christian Ministry in Today's World.* Madras: CLS. Talks originally given to meetings of the clergy working in the CSI in the city of Madras. Republished in a revised edition in 1977, Leighton Buzzard, Beds., U.K.: The Faith Press (77gs).

74lwc   "Living with Change." *Religion and Society* 21, 4:14-28. An address given to a Conference at Coventry Cathedral.

75bwku   ". . . But What Kind of Unity?" *National Christian Council Review* 95:487-491.

75rcdt   Review of *Crisis of Dependency in Third World Ministries* by James A. Berquist and P. Kambar Manickam. *Religion and Society* 22:81-82.

75rcp   Review of *Canterbury Pilgrim* by A. Michael Ramsey. *Ecumenical Review* 27:171.

75rgcc   Review of *Great Christian Centuries to Come. Ecumenical Review* 27:171-172.

75rilc   Review of *India and the Latin Captivity of the Church* by Robin
            Boyd. *Scottish Journal of Theology* 28, 1:90-92.
75rim   "Reflections on an Indian Ministry." *Frontier* 18:25-27.
76aopa   "All in One Place or All of One Sort: On Unity and Diversity
            in the Church." In *Creation, Christ and Culture: A Festschrift
            in Honour of Professor Thomas F. Torrance,* edited by Richard
            W. A. McKinney, pp. 288-306. Edinburgh: T. & T. Clark. A
            response to *Christian Unity and Christian Diversity* by John
            Macquarrie, London: SCM Press. Republished in *Mid-Stream*
            15 (1976):323-341.
76cc   "The Centrality of Christ." *Fraternal* 177:20-28. An address
            given at the Ministers' Session of the 1976 Assembly of the
            Baptist Ministers' Fellowship.
76cuan   "Christian Unity at Nairobi: Some Personal Reflections." *Mid-
            Stream* 15:152-162. Excerpts republished under the title
            "Nairobi 1975: A Personal Report." *National Christian Council
            Review* 96:345-356.
76rnwc   Review of *New Ways for Christ* by Michael Wright. *Inter-
            national Review of Mission* 65:228-229.
77bmm   "The Bishop and the Ministry of Mission." In *Today's Church
            and Today's World,* edited by J. Howe, pp. 242-247. London:
            CIO Publishing. A contribution to the preparatory volume for
            the Lambeth Conference, 1978.
77bpmi   "The Basis, Purpose and Manner of Inter-Faith Dialogue." *Scot-
            tish Journal of Theology* 30:253-270. Originally prepared for the
            Lutheran Church in America, Division for World Mission and
            Ecumenism. It was written in November 1975 and distributed by
            the LCA in pamphlet form under the title *Interfaith Dialogue*
            (1976). Republished in 1977 in two German translations:
            "Christen im Dialog mit Nichtchristen," *Theologie der Gegenwart*
            3:159-166; and "Dialog zwischen verschiedenen Glauben," *Zeit-
            schrift für Mission* 3, 2:83-98. Republished in Rousseau 1981:13-
            31. Modified as chapter ten of *The Open Secret* (78os), "The
            Gospel Among the Religions," republished in *Mission Trends No.
            5: Faith Meets Faith,* edited by Gerald H. Anderson and
            Thomas F. Stransky, C.S.P., pp. 3-19, New York: Paulist Press.
77cu   "Conciliar Unity: A Letter to the Editor." *South India Church-
            man* March 1977:10.

77cwps   *Christian Witness in a Plural Society.* London: British Council of Churches. A paper presented to the Assembly of the British Council of Churches, April 1977.

77fmm   "The Future of Missions and Missionaries." *Review and Expositor* 74, 2:209-218.

77gs   *The Good Shepherd: Meditations on Christian Ministry in Today's World.* Revised edition of 74gs. Leighton Buzzard, Beds., U.K.: The Faith Press. Foreword by the archbishop of Canterbury.

77mm   "Recent Thinking on Christian Beliefs: VIII. Mission and Missions." *The Expository Times* 88, 9:260-264. A review of mission theology from 1950 to 1976.

77trsp   "Teaching Religion in a Secular Plural Society." *Learning for Living* 17, 2:82-88. Address given at the annual general meeting of the Christian Education Movement. Republished in 1978 in *Christianity in the Classroom,* pp. 1-11. London: Christian Education Movement. Republished in 1982 in *New Directions in Religious Education,* edited by John Hull, pp. 97-108. London: The Falmer Press.

77wilc   "What Is a 'Local Church Truly United'?" In *In Each Place,* by J. E. L. Newbigin et al., pp. 14-29. Geneva: WCC. Republished in the *Ecumenical Review* 29:115-128.

78caw   "The Church as Witness: A Meditation." *Reformed World* 35 (March):5-9.

78cc   *Context and Conversion.* London: Church Missionary Society. The 1978 CMS Annual Sermon, delivered at St. Andrew's Church, London, December 4, 1978. Republished in the *International Review of Mission* 68:301-312.

78ctc   "Christ and the Cultures." *Scottish Journal of Theology* 31:1-22. A paper read to the 1977 Conference of the Society for the Study of Theology. Adapted as part of chapter nine of *The Open Secret* (78os).

78eqfu   "Episcopacy and the Quest for Unity." Unpublished notes of a contribution to a discussion at the Annual Conference of CCLEPE and Ecumenical Officers at Stanwick, September 1978.

78os   *The Open Secret: Sketches for a Missionary Theology.* Grand Rapids: William B. Eerdmans Publishing Company. Republished in a revised edition in 1995, Grand Rapids: William B. Eerdmans Publishing Company (95os).

78rfl   "The Right to Fullness of Life." In *A Vision for Man: Essays on Faith, Theology and Society,* edited by Samuel Amirtham, pp. 339-347. Madras: CLS. A contribution to a collection of essays in honor of Joshua Russell Chandran on the occasion of his sixtieth birthday.

78tiol   *This Is Our Life.* Leeds: John Paul the Preacher's Press. Moderator's address to the General Assembly of the United Reformed Church, Southport, 1978.

79cjh   "The Centrality of Jesus for History." In *Incarnation and Myth: The Debate Continued,* edited by Michael Goulder, pp. 197-210. Grand Rapids: William B. Eerdmans Publishing Company. Followed by a "Comment on Lesslie Newbigin's Essay," by Maurice Wiles, pp. 211-213.

79nwwh   "Not Whole Without the Handicapped." In *Partners in Life: The Handicapped and the Church,* Faith and Order Paper No. 89, edited by Geiko Müller-Fahrenholz, pp. 17-25. Geneva: WCC.

79pals   "Presiding at the Lord's Supper." Unpublished paper written as a contribution to the discussion in the United Reformed Church regarding "the presidency at the Lord's Supper of members other than those ordained."

79pct   *Preaching Christ Today.* Birmingham, U.K.: Overdale College. The eighteenth Joseph Smith Memorial Lecture, published as a pamphlet.

79tewp   "Theological Education in a World Perspective." In *Ministers for the 1980s,* edited by Jock Stein, pp. 63-75. Edinburgh: The Handsel Press. Republished from *The Churchman* 94, 2:105-115 with an introduction added. The substance of a paper given to the Conference of the Staffs of the Church of England Theological Colleges, January 3, 1978. Also published in 1978 in *Ministerial Formation* 4:3-10 and in 1984 in *Missions and Theological Education in World Perspective,* edited by Harvie M. Conn and Samuel F. Rowan, pp. 3-18, Farmington, Mich.: Associates of Urbanus.

79ttgv   "Toespraak tot de Gezamenlijke Vergadering van de Synoden van de Nederlandse Hervormde Kerk en de Gereformeerde

Kerken in Nederland op 22 November 1978 in De Blije Werelt te Lunteren." *Wereld en Zending* 8, 1:96-109.

80cwu "Common Witness and Unity." *International Review of Mission* 69:158-160. Written for the Joint Working Group Study on Common Witness of the Roman Catholic Church and the World Council of Churches, Venice, May 29–June 2, 1979.

80m80 "Mission in the 1980s." *Occasional Bulletin of Missionary Research* 4, 4:154-155.

80pfnd *Priorities for a New Decade.* Reprinted from *Reform* (URC). Birmingham, U.K.: National Student Christian Congress and Resource Centre.

80sk *Sign of the Kingdom.* Grand Rapids: William B. Eerdmans Publishing Company. First published in Great Britain under the title, *Your Kingdom Come,* Leeds: John Paul the Preacher's Press. Originally written in preparation for the Melbourne 1980 conference of the Commission on World Mission and Evangelism, WCC, and presented as the Waldstrom Lectures at the Theological Seminary of the Swedish Covenant Church, Lidingo, September 1979.

81ispr "Integration — Some Personal Reflections 1981." *International Review of Mission* 70:247-255.

81pc "Politics and the Covenant." *Theology* 84:356-363.

82buc "Bishops in a United Church." In *Bishops, But What Kind?* edited by Peter Moore, pp. 149-161. London: SPCK.

82ccee "Cross-Currents in Ecumenical and Evangelical Understandings of Mission." *International Bulletin of Missionary Research* 6, 4:146-151. Responses by Paul G. Schrotenboer and C. Peter Wagner, pp. 152-154, and a reply by Lesslie Newbigin, pp. 154-155.

82eis "L'Eglise de l'Inde du Sud." *Unity Chretienne* 65:9-15.

82lhc *The Light Has Come: An Exposition of the Fourth Gospel.* Grand Rapids: William B. Eerdmans Publishing Company.

82lt "Living Together." *Now* (The Methodist Church Overseas Division, London) June 1982:18-19.

82m "Ministry." Unpublished address given at a conference in Croydon, U.K. Approximate date.

82tc "Text and Context: The Bible in the Church." *Theological Review (Near East)* 5, 1:5-13. Originally written for the *Festschrift* in honor of Bishop Kulandran published in India in 1981 under the title *God's Word in God's World*, edited by D. J. Ambalavanar.

83ckc   "Christ, Kingdom and Church: A Reflection on the Papers of George Yule and Andrew Kirk." Unpublished paper. Approximate date.

83cwr   "Christ and the World of Religions." *The Churchman* 97:16-30. Written for a collection of reflections on the theme of the Vancouver 1983 WCC Assembly, "Jesus Christ, the Life of the World." Republished in *Reformed Review* 37, 3:202-213.

83hswu   "How Should We Understand Sacraments and Ministry?" Unpublished paper. Written for a consultation jointly mandated by the Anglican Consultative Council and the World Alliance of Reformed Churches, London, January 1983.

83os84   *The Other Side of 1984: Questions for the Churches.* Geneva: WCC. With a postscript by S. Wesley Ariarajah.

83rim   "Renewal in Mind." *GEAR* (Group for Evangelism and Renewal in the URC) No. 29:4-7. Text of an address given at the Birmingham (U.K.) GEAR Day, February 26, 1983.

83rmu   Rejoinder to "Mission and Unity in the Missionary Ecclesiology of Max A. C. Warren" by Ossi Haaramaki. *International Review of Mission* 72:271-272.

84bfu   "The Basis and the Forms of Unity." *Mid-Stream* 23:1-12. The Second Peter Ainslee Lecture, given at the Council on Christian Unity luncheon, San Antonio, Texas, September 24, 1983.

84bocm   "The Bible and Our Contemporary Mission." *The Clergy Review* 69, 1:9-17. The fourth Thomas Worden Memorial Lecture, given at the Upholland Northern Institute, May 4, 1983.

84ffem   "Faith and Faithfulness in the Ecumenical Movement." In *Faith and Faithfulness: Essays on Contemporary Ecumenical Themes,* edited by Pauline Webb. Geneva: WCC. Essays in tribute to Philip A. Potter.

84sctb   "The Sending of the Church — Three Bible Studies." *New Perspectives on World Mission and Unity,* Occasional Paper No. 1:1-14. Church of Scotland Board of World Mission and Unity. Addresses given at a Conference on World Mission and Unity, Edinburgh, November 1984.

85bfao   "By Faith Abraham Obeyed. . . ." Unpublished address given at a celebration of the seventy-fifth anniversary of the Edinburgh 1910 World Missionary Conference. Abridged version published under the title, "Ecumenical Pilgrims," in the *Catholic Gazette* (The Catholic Missionary Society) 77, 2 (1986): 6-8.

85cwbc   "Can the West Be Converted?" *Princeton Seminary Bulletin* 6, 1:25-37. Originally published by the Friends of St. Colm's, the Education Center and College of the Church of Scotland. Republished in 1987 in the *International Bulletin of Missionary Research* 11, 1:2-7.

85dssn   "Does Society Still Need the Parish Church?" Transcript of a taped address given at the Centre for Explorations in Social Concern on November 5, 1985, and distributed "for private circulation only."

85fc   "A Fellowship of Churches." *Ecumenical Review* 37, 2:175-181.

85gpow   "'Going Public' Operates with. . . ." Unpublished notes following correspondence with Peter Wright about *Going Public: A Report on Ministry of Full-Time Chaplains in Polytechnics,* London: National Standing Committee of Polytechnic Chaplains. (Cf. 85rgp.)

85hiao   "How I Arrived at the Other Side of 1984." *Selly Oak Journal* No. 2:6-8. An introduction to a series of six responses to *The Other Side of 1984* (83os84; cf. 85rtr).

85rboc   "The Role of the Bible in Our Church." Unpublished remarks given at a meeting of the URC Forward Policy Group, April 17-18, 1985.

85rgp   "Re 'Going Public.'" Unpublished letter to Peter Wright regarding *Going Public: A Report on Ministry of Full-Time Chaplains in Polytechnics,* London: National Standing Committee of Polytechnic Chaplains. (Cf. 85gpow.)

85rnwc   Review of *A New World Coming* by Andrew Kirk. Prepublication draft.

85rtr   "A Response to the Responses." *Selly Oak Journal* no. 2:33-36. Newbigin's comments on the series of six responses to *The Other Side of 1984* (83os84; cf. 85hiao).

85ua   *Unfinished Agenda: An Autobiography.* Grand Rapids: William B. Eerdmans Publishing Company. First published in London: SPCK (1985). Republished in a revised edition in 1993, Edinburgh: St. Andrew Press (93ua).

85wscp   *The Welfare State: A Christian Perspective.* Oxford: Oxford In-
          stitute for Church and Society. Republished in *Theology*
          88:173-182.

86bep   "A British and European Perspective." In *Entering the Kingdom:
          A Fresh Look at Conversion,* edited by Monica Hill, pp. 57-68.
          Middlesex, U.K.: British Church Growth Association and
          MARC Europe.

86bvdw   "The Biblical Vision: Deed and Word Inseparable." *Concern*
          28, 8:1-3, 36.

86eafm   "England as a Foreign Mission Field." Reproduced text of an
          address given at the Assembly of the Birmingham Council of
          Christian Churches, March 10, 1986.

86f   Foreword to *Redeeming Time: Atonement Through Education,*
          by Timothy Gorringe, pp. ix-x. London: Darton, Longman and
          Todd.

86fg   *Foolishness to the Greeks: The Gospel and Western Culture.*
          Grand Rapids: William B. Eerdmans Publishing Company.
          The Benjamin B. Warfield Lectures given at Princeton Theo-
          logical Seminary, March 1984.

86olp   "One of the Loveliest of the Psalms. . . ." Unpublished address
          given on the BBC.

86wbp   "Witness in a Biblical Perspective." *Mission Studies* 3, 2:80-84.

87mcw   *Mission in Christ's Way.* Geneva: WCC Publications.

88cfwr   "The Christian Faith and the World Religions." In *Keeping the
          Faith: Essays to Mark the Centenary of Lux Mundi,* edited by
          Geoffrey Wainwright, pp. 310-340. Philadelphia: Fortress Press.

88evcc   "The Enduring Validity of Cross-Cultural Mission." *Inter-
          national Bulletin of Missionary Research* 12, 2:50-53.

88obc   "On Being the Church for the World." In *The Parish Church?*
          edited by Giles Ecclestone, pp. 25-42. London: Mowbray.

88spts   "A Sermon Preached at the Thanksgiving Service for the Fif-
          tieth Anniversary of the Tambaram Conference of the Inter-
          national Missionary Council." *International Review of Mission*
          77:325-331.

88st   "The Significance of Tambaram — Fifty Years Later." *Mission-
          alia* 16:79-85.

89gcbw   "Gospel and Culture — But Which Culture?" *Missionalia*
          17:213-215.

89gps   *The Gospel in a Pluralist Society.* Grand Rapids: William B. Eerdmans Publishing Company and Geneva: WCC Publications.

89mcwc   *Mission and the Crisis of Western Culture.* Edinburgh: The Handsel Press.

89rmcu   Review of *The Myth of Christian Uniqueness,* edited by John Hick and Paul Knitter. *Ecumenical Review* 41, 3:468-471.

89rpuj   "Religious Pluralism and the Uniqueness of Jesus Christ." *International Bulletin of Missionary Research* 13, 2:50-54.

90chs   *Come Holy Spirit, Renew the Whole Creation.* Occasional Paper No. 6. Birmingham, U.K.: Selly Oak Colleges. An address on the theme chosen for the 1991 Assembly of the World Council of Churches in Canberra, Australia.

90rfm   "Religion for the Marketplace." In *Christian Uniqueness Reconsidered: The Myth of a Pluralistic Theology of Religions,* edited by Gavin D'Costa, pp. 135-148. Maryknoll, N.Y.: Orbis Books.

91tt   *Truth to Tell: The Gospel as Public Truth.* Grand Rapids: William B. Eerdmans Publishing Company and Geneva: WCC Publications.

92gpt   "The Gospel as Public Truth." Editorial in *Touchstone: A Journal of Ecumenical Orthodoxy* 5 (Summer):1-2.

92wow   "Way Out West: The Gospel in a Post-Enlightenment World." *Touchstone: A Journal of Ecumenical Orthodoxy* 5 (Summer):22-24.

93cf   "Certain Faith: What Kind of Certainty?" *Tyndale Bulletin* 44:339-350.

93ct   "Culture and Theology." *The Blackwell Encyclopedia of Modern Christian Thought,* edited by Alister E. McGrath, pp. 98-100. Cambridge, Mass.: Blackwell Publishers.

93kgoh   "The Kingdom of God and Our Hopes for the Future." In *The Kingdom of God and Human Society,* edited by R. S. Barbour, pp. 1-12. Edinburgh: T. & T. Clark.

93rp   Religious Pluralism: A Missiological Approach." *Studia Missionalia* 42:227-244.

93ua   *Unfinished Agenda: An Updated Autobiography.* Revised edition of 85ua. Edinburgh: St. Andrew Press.

94ccmr   "Confessing Christ in a Multi-Religion Society." *Scottish Bulletin of Evangelical Theology* 12 (Autumn):125-136.

94wis   *A Word in Season: Perspectives on Christian World Missions.*
           Grand Rapids: William B. Eerdmans Publishing Company and
           Edinburgh: St. Andrew Press. A collection of mostly unpub-
           lished addresses and essays, a few from the early 1960s but
           most from the late 1980s and early 1990s.

95f   Foreword to *Roland Allen*, by Hubert J. B. Allen, pp. xiii-xv.
           Cincinnati: Forward Movement Publications.

95os   *The Open Secret: An Introduction to the Theology of Mission.*
           Revised edition of 78os. Grand Rapids: William B. Eerdmans
           Publishing Company.

95pc   *Proper Confidence: Faith, Doubt, and Certainty in Christian
           Discipleship.* Grand Rapids: William B. Eerdmans Publishing
           Company.

Other References Cited

Abbott, Walter M., S.J., ed. 1966. *The Documents of Vatican II.* New York: Guild Press, America Press, Association Press.

Allen, Roland. 1962. *Missionary Methods: St. Paul's or Ours?* Grand Rapids: William B. Eerdmans Publishing Company.

Amalorpavadass, Duraisamy. 1979. "Evangelization and Culture." In *Evangelism and the World Today,* edited by Norbert Greinacher and Alois Müller, pp. 61-71. New York: The Seabury Press.

Ariarajah, S. Wesley. 1985. *The Bible and People of Other Faiths.* Geneva: World Council of Churches.

Baago, Kaj. 1966. "The Post-Colonial Crisis of Missions." *International Review of Missions* 55:322-332.

Balasuriya, Tissa. 1984. *Planetary Theology.* Maryknoll, N.Y.: Orbis Books.

Barth, Karl. 1926. "Church and Culture." Published in English translation in 1962 in *Theology and Church: Shorter Writings 1920-1928,* translated by Louise Pettibone Smith, pp. 334-354. London: SCM Press.

————. 1948. "The Church — The Living Congregation of the Living Lord Jesus Christ." In *The Universal Church in God's Design,* Amsterdam Assembly Series, vol. 1, pp. 67-76. New York: Harper & Brothers.

————. 1957a. *Church Dogmatics,* vol. 1, part 2: *The Doctrine of the Word of God,* ET. Edinburgh: T. & T. Clark.

————. 1957b. *Church Dogmatics,* vol. 2, part 2: *The Doctrine of God,* ET. Edinburgh: T. & T. Clark.

————. 1957c. "The Perfections of the Divine Freedom." In *Church Dog-*

matics, vol. 2, part 1: *The Doctrine of God,* ET, par. 31, pp. 440-677. Edinburgh: T. & T. Clark.

————. 1961. Excursus on "Near and Distant Neighbors." In *Church Dogmatics,* vol. 3, part 4: *The Doctrine of Creation,* ET, pp. 307-323. Edinburgh: T. & T. Clark.

————. 1962. *Church Dogmatics,* vol. 4, part 3, second half: *The Doctrine of Reconciliation,* ET. Edinburgh: T. & T. Clark.

Berkhof, Hendrikus. 1962. *Christ and the Powers,* ET. Translated by John Howard Yoder. Scottdale, Pa.: Herald Press.

————. 1979. *Christian Faith: An Introduction to the Study of the Faith,* ET. Grand Rapids: William B. Eerdmans Publishing Company.

Berkouwer, G. C. 1960. *Divine Election.* Grand Rapids: William B. Eerdmans Publishing Company.

Bevans, Stephen, S.V.D. 1992. *John Oman and His Doctrine of God.* Cambridge: Cambridge University Press.

Blauw, Johannes. 1950. *Goden en Mensen.* Groningen: J. C. Niemeyer.

————. 1962. *The Missionary Nature of the Church: A Survey of the Biblical Theology of Mission.* London: Lutterworth Press.

Boer, Harry R. 1961. *Pentecost and Missions.* London: Lutterworth Press.

Bosch, David J. 1977. *Theology of Religions.* Pretoria: University of South Africa.

————. 1978. "The Why and How of a True Biblical Foundation for Mission." In *Zending op Weg naar de Toekomst,* Festschrift for Dr. J. Verkuyl, pp. 33-45. Kampen: J. H. Kok.

————. 1980. *Witness to the World: The Christian Mission in Theological Perspective.* Atlanta: John Knox Press.

————. 1983. "The Structure of Mission: An Exposition of Matthew 28:16-20." In *Exploring Church Growth,* edited by Wilbert R. Shenk, pp. 218-248. Grand Rapids: William B. Eerdmans Publishing Company.

Braaten, Carl E. 1977. *The Flaming Center: A Theology of Christian Mission.* Philadelphia: Fortress Press.

————. 1980. "Who Do We Say That He Is? On the Uniqueness and Universality of Jesus Christ." *Missiology* 8:13-30.

————. 1985. *The Apostolic Imperative: Nature and Aim of the Church's Mission and Ministry.* Minneapolis: Augsburg Publishing House.

British Council of Churches. 1987. "The Gospel and Our Culture: A British Council of Churches Programme for This Side of 1984." Pamphlet. London: British Council of Churches.

Bruggeman, Antonio, S.J. 1965. *The Ecclesiology of Lesslie Newbigin.* Excerpta ex Dissertatione ad Lauream in Facultate Theologica Pontificiae Universitatis Gregorianae. Ranchi, India: Pontificia Universitas Gregoriana.

Brunner, Heinrich Emil, and Karl Barth. 1946. *Natural Theology: Comprising Nature and Grace by Prof. Dr. Emil Brunner and the Reply "No!" by Dr. Karl Barth.* Translated by Peter Fraenkel. London: Geoffrey Bles.

Bultmann, Rudolph. 1962. *Kerygma and Myth.* London: SPCK.

Busch, Eberhart. 1976. *Karl Barth: His Life from Letters and Autobiographical Texts.* London: SCM Press and Philadelphia: Fortress Press.

Castro, Emilio. 1966. "Conversion and Social Transformation." In *Christian Social Ethics in a Changing World: An Ecumenical Theological Inquiry,* edited by John C. Bennett, pp. 348-366. London: SCM Press and New York: Association Press.

Childs, Brevard S. 1970. *Biblical Theology in Crisis.* Philadelphia: Westminster Press.

City of Birmingham Education Committee. 1975. *Agreed Syllabus of Religious Instruction.* Birmingham, U.K.: City of Birmingham Education Committee.

Coe, Shoki. 1976. "Contextualizing Theology." In *Mission Trends No. 3: Third World Theologies,* edited by Gerald H. Anderson and Thomas F. Stransky, C.S.P., pp. 19-24. Grand Rapids: William B. Eerdmans Publishing Company.

Conn, Harvie M. 1983. "Looking for a Method: Backgrounds and Suggestions." In *Exploring Church Growth,* edited by Wilbert R. Shenk, pp. 79-94. Grand Rapids: William B. Eerdmans Publishing Company.

———. 1984. *Eternal Word and Changing Worlds: Theology, Anthropology and Mission in Trialogue.* Grand Rapids: Zondervan Press.

Cox, James L. 1979. "Faith and Faiths: The Significance of A. G. Hogg's Missionary Thought for a Theology of Dialogue." *Scottish Journal of Theology* 32:241-256.

Cracknell, Kenneth. 1982. "God and the Nations: Biblical Protology and Eschatology as Clues to Understanding the Divine Purposes Among Humankind." In *Dialogue in Community,* edited by C. D. Jathanna. Balmatta, Mangalore: Karnataka Theological Research Institute.

Cullmann, Oscar. 1964. *Christ and Time: The Primitive Christian Conception of Time and History.* Revised edition. Translated by Floyd V. Filson. Philadelphia: The Westminster Press.

Cushman, Robert E. 1981. *Faith Seeking Understanding: Essays Theological and Critical.* Durham, N.C.: Duke University Press.

Daane, James. 1973. *The Freedom of God: A Study of Election and Pulpit.* Grand Rapids: William B. Eerdmans Publishing Company.

Dawson, Christopher. 1956. *The Dynamics of World History.* Edited by John J. Mulloy. New York: Sheed and Ward Inc.

D'Costa, Gavin. 1986. *Theology and Religious Pluralism: The Challenge of Other Religions.* Oxford and New York: Basil Blackwell Ltd.

De Groot, A. 1964. *De Bijbel over het Heil der Volken.* Roermond: Romens.

De Ridder, Richard R. 1971. *Discipling the Nations.* Grand Rapids: Baker Book House.

————. 1983. "The Old Testament Roots of Mission." In *Exploring Church Growth,* edited by Wilbert R. Shenk, pp. 171-180. Grand Rapids: William B. Eerdmans Publishing Company.

Devanandan, Paul D. 1962. Review of *A Faith for This One World?* by J. E. Lesslie Newbigin. *National Christian Council Review* 82:127-128.

————. 1983. *Selections from the Books of P. D. Devanandan.* Bangalore: CISRS.

Dumas, Andre. 1974. "The Unity of the Church and the Unity of Mankind." *Study Encounter* 10, 2 (SE/61):1-16.

Duraisingh, Christopher. 1972. "Some Dominant Motifs in the New Testament Doctrine of Baptism." *Religion and Society* 19, 1:5-17.

Fackre, Gabriel. 1983. "The Scandals of Particularity and Universality." *Mid-Stream* 22, 1:32-52.

Freytag, Walter. 1957. *The Gospel and the Religions,* IMC Research Pamphlet No. 5. London: SCM Press.

Geertz, Clifford. 1973. *The Interpretation of Cultures.* New York: Basic Books, Inc.

Glasser, Arthur F. 1981. "Old Testament: Contribution to a Theology of Mission." Class notes at Reformed Theological Seminary, Jackson, Mississippi. Spring 1981.

Godsey, John D. 1967. "History of Salvation and World History." In *Christian Mission in Theological Perspective: An Inquiry by Methodists,* edited by Gerald H. Anderson, pp. 56-76. Nashville: Abingdon Press.

Gottwald, Norman K. 1967. *The Church Unbound: A Human Church in a Human World.* Philadelphia and New York: J. B. Lippincott.

Guder, Darrell L. 1985. *Be My Witnesses: The Church's Mission, Message, and Messengers.* Grand Rapids: William B. Eerdmans Publishing Company.

———, ed. 1998. *Missional Church: A Vision for the Sending of the Church in North America.* Grand Rapids: William B. Eerdmans Publishing Company.

Hahn, Ferdinand. 1965. *Mission in the New Testament*, ET. London: SCM Press.

Handspicker, Meredith B. 1970. "Faith and Order 1948-1968." In *The Ecumenical Advance: A History of the Ecumenical Movement, Volume 2, 1948-1968*, edited by Harold E. Fey, pp. 143-170. Philadelphia: Westminster Press.

Hasel, Gerhard F. 1975. *Old Testament Theology: Basic Issues in the Current Debate.* Revised edition. Grand Rapids: William B. Eerdmans Publishing Company.

Hick, John. 1973. *God and the Universe of Faiths.* New York: St. Martin's Press.

———. 1977a. "Christian Theology and Inter-Religious Dialogue." *World Faiths: Journal of the World Congress of Faiths* No. 103 (August): 2-19, 30.

———, ed. 1977b. *The Myth of God Incarnate.* Philadelphia: Westminster Press.

Hiebert, Paul G. 1983. *Cultural Anthropology.* Second edition. Grand Rapids: Baker Book House.

———. 1985. *Anthropological Insights for Missionaries.* Grand Rapids: Baker Book House.

Hogg, A. G. 1909. *Karma and Redemption: An Essay Toward the Interpretation of Hinduism and the Re-statement of Christianity.* London, Madras, Colombo: Christian Literature Society.

———. 1939. "The Christian Attitude to Non-Christian Faith." In *The Authority of the Faith*, "The Madras Series" vol. 1, pp. 94-116. New York: International Missionary Council.

Hopler, Thom. 1981. *A World of Difference.* Downers Grove, Ill.: InterVarsity Press.

Hunsberger, George R. 1987. Review of *The Bible and People of Other Faiths* by S. Wesley Ariarajah. *Missiology* 15:122-123.

———, and Craig Van Gelder, eds. 1996. *The Church Between Gospel and*

Culture: The Emerging Mission in North America. Grand Rapids: William B. Eerdmans Publishing Company.

Inch, Morris. 1982. *Doing Theology Across Cultures.* Grand Rapids: Baker Book House.

Jacobs, Donald R. 1980. "Conversion and Culture: An Anthropological Perspective with Reference to East Africa." In *Down to Earth: Studies in Christianity and Culture,* edited by John R. W. Stott and Robert Coote, pp. 131-145. Grand Rapids: William B. Eerdmans Publishing Company.

Jathanna, O. V. 1981. *The Decisiveness of the Christ-event and the Universality of Christianity in a World of Religious Plurality.* Berne: Peter Lang.

Jewett, Paul K. 1985. *Election and Predestination.* Grand Rapids: William B. Eerdmans Publishing Company.

Jocz, Jakob. 1958. *A Theology of Election: Israel and the Church.* London: SPCK.

Kane, J. Herbert. 1976. *Christian Mission in Biblical Perspective.* Grand Rapids: Baker Book House.

Kline, Meredith. 1983. *Kingdom Prologue,* vol. 2. Unpublished monograph.

Knitter, Paul F. 1985. *No Other Name? A Critical Survey of Christian Attitudes Toward the World Religions.* Maryknoll, N.Y.: Orbis Books.

Kraemer, Hendrik. 1938. *The Christian Message in a Non-Christian World.* London: Edinburgh House Press.

————. 1939. "Continuity or Discontinuity." In *The Authority of the Faith,* "The Madras Series" vol. 1, pp. 1-21. New York: International Missionary Council.

————. 1956. *Religion and the Christian Faith.* Philadelphia: Westminster Press.

Kraft, Charles H. 1979. *Christianity in Culture: A Study in Dynamic Biblical Theologizing in Cross-cultural Perspective.* Maryknoll, N.Y.: Orbis Books.

Krass, Alfred C. 1971. Letter to Lesslie Newbigin. Unpublished.

————. 1972a. "A Comment by the Rev. Alfred C. Krass." *Religion and Society* 19, 1:84-87.

————. 1972b. Letter to M. M. Thomas. Unpublished. January 3, 1972.

Kuhn, Thomas S. 1962. *The Structure of Scientific Revolutions.* Chicago: The University of Chicago Press.

Kumar, S. Ananda. 1980. "Culture and the Old Testament." In *Down to Earth: Studies in Christianity and Culture,* edited by John R. W. Stott and Robert Coote, pp. 33-48. Grand Rapids: William B. Eerdmans Publishing Company.

Küng, Hans. 1976. *On Being a Christian*. Translated by Edward Quinn. Garden City, N.Y.: Doubleday.

Löffler, Paul. 1965. "The Biblical Concept of Conversion." *Study Encounter* 1:93-101.

————. 1967a. "Conversion in an Ecumenical Context." *The Ecumenical Review* 19:252-260.

————. 1967b. "Conversion: Introduction." *The Ecumenical Review* 19:249-251.

————, ed. 1968. *Secular Man and Christian Mission*. Geneva: World Council of Churches.

————. 1973. Letter to M. M. Thomas and Lesslie Newbigin. Unpublished. January 30, 1973.

Luzbetak, Louis J., S.V.D. 1970. *The Church and Cultures*. Techny, Ill.: Divine Word Publications.

Macquarrie, John. 1975. *Christian Unity and Christian Diversity*. London: SCM Press.

Marshall, I. Howard. 1980. "Culture and the New Testament." In *Down to Earth: Studies in Christianity and Culture*, edited by John R. W. Stott and Robert Coote, pp. 17-32. Grand Rapids: William B. Eerdmans Publishing Company.

Martin-Achard, Robert. 1959. *Israel et les nations*. Neuchatel and Paris: Delachaux et Niestle.

————. 1962. *A Light to the Nations*. London: Oliver and Boyd.

McGavran, Donald A. 1974. *The Clash Between Christianity and Cultures*. Washington, D.C.: Canon Press.

————. 1981. *The Bridges of God: A Study in the Strategy of Missions*. Revised edition. United Kingdom: World Dominion Press.

Mesters, Carlos. 1989. *Defenseless Flower: A New Reading of the Bible*. Maryknoll, N.Y.: Orbis Books.

Michalson, Carl. 1967. "The Issue: Ultimate Meaning in History." In *Christian Mission in Theological Perspective: An Inquiry by Methodists*, edited by Gerald H. Anderson, pp. 77-88. Nashville: Abingdon Press.

Nicholls, Bruce J. 1979. *Contextualization: A Theology of Gospel and Culture*. Downers Grove, Ill.: InterVarsity Press.

————. 1980. "Towards a Theology of Gospel and Culture." In *Down to Earth: Studies in Christianity and Culture*, edited by John R. W. Stott and Robert Coote, pp. 49-62. Grand Rapids: William B. Eerdmans Publishing Company.

Nida, Eugene A. 1954. *Customs and Cultures: Anthropology for Christian Missions*. New York: Harper & Row.

Niebuhr, H. Richard. 1951. *Christ and Culture*. New York: Harper & Row.

Niles, D. T. 1962. *Upon the Earth*. London: Lutterworth Press.

———. 1969. "Karl Barth — A Personal Memory." *The South East Asian Journal of Theology* 11:10-13.

Oduyoye, Modupe. 1984. *The Sons of the Gods and the Daughters of Men*. Maryknoll, N.Y.: Orbis Books.

Oman, John. 1917. *Grace and Personality*. London: Hodder and Stoughton.

———. 1925. "The Sphere of Religion." In *Science, Religion and Reality*, edited by Joseph Needham, pp. 261-299. New York: The Macmillan Company.

———. 1931. *The Natural and the Supernatural*. Cambridge: Cambridge University Press.

Panikkar, Raimundo. 1984. "Religious Pluralism: The Metaphysical Challenge." In *Religious Pluralism*, edited by Leroy S. Rouner, pp. 97-115. Notre Dame: University of Notre Dame Press.

Pannenberg, Wolfhart. 1977. *Human Nature, Election and History*. Philadelphia: Westminster Press.

Peters, George W. 1972. *A Biblical Theology of Missions*. Chicago: Moody Press.

Piet, John H. 1970. *The Road Ahead: A Theology for the Church in Mission*. Grand Rapids: William B. Eerdmans Publishing Company.

Polanyi, Michael. 1958. *Personal Knowledge: Towards a Post-critical Philosophy*. Chicago: University of Chicago Press.

Race, Alan. 1982. *Christians and Religious Pluralism: Patterns in the Christian Theology of Religions*. Maryknoll, N.Y.: Orbis Books.

Rahner, Karl. 1966. "Christianity and the Non-Christian Religions." In *Theological Investigations*, vol. 5, translated by Karl-H. Kruger, pp. 115-134. Baltimore: Helicon Press and London: Darton, Longman & Todd.

———. 1969. "Anonymous Christians." In *Theological Investigations*, vol. 6, translated by Karl-H. and Boniface Kruger, pp. 390-398. London: Darton, Longman & Todd and New York: Seabury Press.

Ramseyer, Robert L. 1983. "Christian Mission and Cultural Anthropology."

In *Exploring Church Growth*, edited by Wilbert R. Shenk, pp. 108-116. Grand Rapids: William B. Eerdmans Publishing Company.

Reilly, John, S.J. 1978. *Evangelism and Ecumenism in the Writings of Lesslie Newbigin and Their Basis in His Christology*. Dissertation presented to the Faculty of Theology, Pontifical Gregorian University, Rome.

————. 1979. *Evangelism and Ecumenism in the Writings of Lesslie Newbigin and Their Basis in His Christology*. Excerpta ex Dissertatione ad Doctoratum in Facultate Theologiae Pontificiae Universitatis Gregorianae. Roma: Pontificia Universitas Gregoriana.

Richardson, Alan. 1949. "Instrument of God: The Unity of the Biblical Doctrine of Salvation." *Interpretation* 3, 3:273-285.

Richardson, Don. 1981. *Eternity in Their Hearts*. Ventura, Calif.: Regal Books.

Robinson, John A. T. 1963. *Honest to God*. London: SCM Press.

Rousseau, Richard W., S.J., ed. 1981. *Interreligious Dialogue: Facing the Next Frontier*. Scranton, Pa.: Ridge Row Press.

Rowley, H. H. 1945. *The Missionary Message of the Old Testament*. London: Carey Kingsgate Press.

————. 1950. *The Biblical Doctrine of Election*. London: Lutterworth Press.

Sanneh, Lamin. 1989. *Translating the Message: The Missionary Impact on Culture*. Maryknoll, N.Y.: Orbis Books.

Satari, Paul Russ. 1996. "'Translatability' in the Missional Approach of Lamin Sanneh." In *The Church Between Gospel and Culture*, edited by George R. Hunsberger and Craig Van Gelder, pp. 270-283. Grand Rapids: William B. Eerdmans Publishing Company.

Schineller, Peter, S.J. 1990. *A Handbook of Inculturation*. Mahwah, N.J.: Paulist Press.

Schreiter, Robert J., C.PP.S. 1985. *Constructing Local Theologies*. Maryknoll, N.Y.: Orbis Books.

Schrotenboer, Paul G. 1982. "Responses to the Article by Lesslie Newbigin." *International Bulletin of Missionary Research* 6:152-153.

Seebass, Horst. 1977. "Bachar, II-III." In *Theological Dictionary of the Old Testament*, vol. 2, edited by G. Johannes Botterweck and Helmer Ringgren, pp. 74-87. Revised edition. Grand Rapids: William B. Eerdmans Publishing Company.

Segundo, Juan Luis, S.J. 1973. *The Community Called Church*. Maryknoll, N.Y.: Orbis Books.

———. 1978. *The Hidden Motives of Pastoral Action: Latin American Reflections,* ET. Maryknoll, N.Y.: Orbis Books.

Senior, Donald, C.P., and Carroll Stuhlmueller, C.P. 1983. *The Biblical Foundations for Mission.* Maryknoll, N.Y.: Orbis Books.

Shorter, Aylward, W.F. 1988. *Toward a Theology of Inculturation.* Maryknoll, N.Y.: Orbis Books.

Smalley, William A. 1955. "Culture and Superculture." *Practical Anthropology* 2:58-91.

Smith, Wilfred Cantwell. 1962. *The Meaning and End of Religion: A New Approach to the Religious Traditions of Mankind.* New York: Mentor Books.

Song, C. S. 1975. *Christian Mission in Reconstruction: An Asian Analysis.* Maryknoll, N.Y.: Orbis Books.

———. 1982. *The Compassionate God.* Maryknoll, N.Y.: Orbis Books.

Stott, John R. W., and Robert Coote, eds. 1980. *Down to Earth: Studies in Christianity and Culture.* Grand Rapids: William B. Eerdmans Publishing Company.

Sundkler, Bengt. 1965. *The World of Mission,* ET. Grand Rapids: William B. Eerdmans Publishing Company.

Taylor, John V. 1958. *The Growth of the Church in Buganda.* London: SCM Press.

Taylor, Mark Kline. 1986. *Beyond Explanation: Religious Dimensions in Cultural Anthropology.* Macon, Ga.: Mercer University Press.

Taylor, Richard W. 1972. "On Acknowledging the Lordship of Jesus Christ Without Shifting Tents." *Religion and Society* 19, 1:59-68.

Thangasamy, D. A. 1966. *The Theology of Chenchiah with Selections from his Writings,* Confessing the Faith in India Series No. 1. Bangalore: CISRS.

Thomas, Joe Matthew. 1996. *The Centrality of Christ and Inter-Religious Dialogue in the Theology of Lesslie Newbigin.* Dissertation presented to the Faculty of Theology, University of St. Matthew's College, Toronto, Canada.

Thomas, M. M. 1969. "What Bishop Newbigin Has Meant to Me." In *Bishop Newbigin's Sixtieth Birthday Celebration Brochure.* Madras.

———. 1971. *Salvation and Humanisation: Some Crucial Issues of the Theology of Mission in Contemporary India.* Madras: CLS.

———. 1972. "Baptism, the Church, and Koinonia: Three Letters and a Comment." By M. M. Thomas, Lesslie Newbigin, and Alfred C. Krass.

Letters dated 21st October 1971 (pp. 69-74) and 20th December 1971 (pp. 87-90). *Religion and Society* 19:69-90.

————. 1979. "Christ-Centred Syncretism." *Religion and Society* 26:26-35.

————. 1984. "Mission and Modern Culture." *Ecumenical Review* 36, 3:316-322.

————. 1986. "Christology and Pluralistic Consciousness." *International Bulletin of Missionary Research* 10, 3:106-108.

Tillich, Paul. 1959. *A Theology of Culture.* Edited by Robert C. Kimball. Oxford: Oxford University Press.

————. 1963. *Christianity and the Encounter of the World Religions.* New York: Columbia University Press.

Toynbee, Arnold J. 1961. "Arnold J. Toynbee Writes." *SCM Press Book Club Bulletin* 145 (November): 2-4. Naperville, Ill.: SCM Press.

Travis, Stephen H. 1983. "The Life of the World and Future Judgement." *The Churchman* 97:31-40.

van Buren, Paul. 1963. *The Secular Meaning of the Gospel.* New York: Macmillan and London: SCM Press.

van Dijk, I. 1917. "De Leer der Verkiezing in het N.T." *Gezam. Geschr.* I.

Van Engen, Charles Edward. 1981. *The Growth of the True Church.* Amsterdam: Rodopi.

van Leeuwen, Arend Th. 1964. *Christianity in World History: The Meeting of the Faiths of East and West.* New York: Charles Scribner's Sons.

Verkuyl, Johannes. 1978. *Contemporary Missiology: An Introduction.* Translated and edited by Dale Cooper. Grand Rapids: William B. Eerdmans Publishing Company.

Vicedom, Georg F. 1965. *The Mission of God: An Introduction to a Theology of Mission,* ET. Saint Louis, Mo.: Concordia Publishing House.

Vischer, Lukas, ed. 1963. *A Documentary History of the Faith and Order Movement 1927-1963.* Saint Louis, Mo.: Bethany Press.

von Rad, Gerhard. 1961. *Genesis: A Commentary,* ET. Translated by John H. Marks. Philadelphia: Westminster Press.

Vriezen, Th. C. 1953. *Die Erwählung Israels nach dem Alten Testament.* Zurich: Zwingli Verlag.

Wagner, C. Peter. 1979. *Our Kind of People: The Ethical Dimensions of Church Growth in America.* Atlanta: John Knox Press.

Watson, David Lowes. 1984. "Salt to the World: An Ecclesiology of Liberation." *Missiology* 12:453-476.

Weber, Hans-Reudi. 1963. "God's Arithmetic." *Frontier* 6 (Winter): 298ff.

Republished in 1975 in *Mission Trends No. 2: Evangelization,* edited by Gerald H. Anderson and Thomas F. Stransky, C.S.P., pp. 64-69. New York: Paulist Press and Grand Rapids: William B. Eerdmans Publishing Company.

West, Charles C. 1959. "This Ministry: A Biblical Introduction." In *The Missionary Church in East and West,* edited by Charles C. West and David M. Paton. London: SCM Press.

Westermann, Claus. 1967. *Handbook to the Old Testament.* Translated and edited by Robert H. Boyd. Minneapolis: Augsburg Publishing House.

Wickeri, Philip L. 1985. "Selfhood as Gift and Task: The Example of Self-Propagation in Chinese Christianity." *Missiology* 13:261-273.

Wiles, Maurice. 1979. "Comment on Lesslie Newbigin's Essay." In *Incarnation and Myth: The Debate Continued,* edited by Michael Goulder, pp. 211-213. Grand Rapids: William B. Eerdmans Publishing Company.

Willowbank Consultation. 1978. "The Willowbank Report." In *Down to Earth: Studies in Christianity and Culture,* edited by John R. W. Stott and Robert Coote, pp. 308-339. Grand Rapids: William B. Eerdmans Publishing Company, 1980.

Winter, Ralph D. 1974. "The Two Structures of God's Redemptive Mission." *Missiology* 2:121-129.

Endnotes

Notes to Chapter 1

1. Note, e.g., the use Charles H. Kraft makes of the paradigm — albeit with the significant shift from addressing "Christ" and culture (in reality addressing Christian postures vis-à-vis culture) to models of "God" and culture, thus moving the focus of the conversation from a theology of human responsibility to a theology of divine revelation (1979:103-115). Kraft's perspectives have been very influential in evangelical missiology.

2. References to Bishop Newbigin's writings will be made by means of the coded designations used in the bibliography for each item. In each case, the code begins with the last two digits of the year of publication (or of writing, in the case of unpublished materials), followed immediately by the initial letters of the key words in the title (up to four). For authors other than Newbigin, the standard author-date system of reference within the text will be used.

3. His definition is similar to but less static than the collective definition attempted by the participants at the Willowbank Consultation on "Gospel and Culture," sponsored by the Lausanne Committee for World Evangelization (LCWE) in 1978. The report of the consultation defined "culture" as "an integrated system of beliefs, of values, of customs, and of institutions which express these beliefs, values and customs, which binds a society together and gives it a sense of identity, dignity, security, and continuity" (Willowbank Consultation 1978: section 2).

4. Newbigin indicated in personal conversation (July 1986) that this has been his source (cf. 86fg:3). He added that he has done no significant or extensive reading in the field of cultural anthropology.

5. The recent study process on "Gospel and Cultures" in the World Council of Churches and the WCC's 1996 Conference on World Mission and Evangelism in Salvador, Brazil, on the theme "Called to One Hope: The Gospel in Diverse

Cultures" holds promise for a new wave of insights to emerge in a broader ecumenical arena.

6. The operative concept of culture Marshall uses is largely uninformed by the best of modern cultural anthropological understanding, indicating the serious problem of a lack of cross-pollination between evangelical missionary theology and biblical scholarship. The technical definition used by Marshall has some validity but is put in terms which are at best vague and confusing: "Thus, in summary, the word 'culture' can refer variously to the particular ways in which people learn to control their environment, to develop intellectual and aesthetic values and expressions of them, and to produce an ideology which upholds these values. Culture is a social phenomenon, and can have various, separable parts. Culture means a way of thinking, an approach to life in the world" (1980:19-20). His fuller treatment, however, emphasizes the "aesthetic values" dimension of that definition, which becomes extremely problematic. "High culture" is not something he finds addressed in the New Testament, understandably. But that misses the point.

7. A reversal in the titles of the essays requested of Kumar and Marshall and a pluralizing of the referent "culture" — "The Old (New) Testament and Cultures" — might have helped the focus.

8. That there is an undefended leap from saying that "God desires the salvation of all humankind" to speaking of the "universal salvific will of God" might be mentioned as well. Such a conclusion at least overlooks the immediate context of the biblical text which asserts the idea. God not only desires the salvation of all but desires for all "to come to a knowledge of the truth" (1 Timothy 2:4).

9. Cf. the similar theological development in Balasuriya 1984. There he affirms the fatherhood of God and brotherhood and sisterhood of humankind to be the essential theological foundation for a "planetary theology."

10. Wherever reference is made in the present study to Newbigin's book, *The Household of God*, the pagination of the reference will be that of the 1954 American edition which contains full section divisions, even though the 1953 date of the original publication will be preserved in the reference. The importance of the book requires that its original date be kept clearly in mind.

11. Minor exceptions to this are found in his "catechetical" work, *Sin and Salvation* (56ss), another work containing pastoral instruction, *The Holy Spirit and the Church* (72hsc), and, to a lesser degree, his major ecclesiological contribution, *The Household of God* (53hg).

12. In this respect, his pursuit is unlike that of Johannes Blauw, who sought to provide "a conception of missionary work that is as closely as possible related to what the Bible tells us" (1962:12). In his watershed volume, Blauw develops his "biblical theology of missionary work" in a more thematic and descriptive fashion, attempting to show the development of a "missionary faith and theology" in the biblical record.

13. In this he is like Johannes Verkuyl, who speaks of considering the "very structure of the whole biblical message" (1978:90), and David Bosch, whose method

it is "to establish the central thrust of the message of Scripture" as he searches for "the essentially missionary dimension of God's revelation in [Jesus]" (1980:48).

Notes to Chapter 2

1. In the descriptions that follow, the publication dates of materials that were based on addresses or lectures play a role secondary to the dates of the lectures themselves.

2. For an excellent summary of Oman's theology on this and other themes, see Stephen Bevans, S.V.D., *John Oman and His Doctrine of God* (1992).

3. At the time, Newbigin appears not to have taken note of the critique of Paul D. Devanandan, who said that "to the Indian reader the claim that the world is becoming one civilization is not sufficiently convincing" (1962:128).

4. The term "apologetics" as used here envisions a different dimension of Newbigin's work than that mentioned by Devanandan, when he said about *A Faith for This One World?*, "It is, however, in the third and fourth lectures that our author is at his best, for Newbigin's *forte* seems, at least to this reviewer, to be Biblical exegesis, not Christian apologetics" (Devanandan 1962:128). By "apologetics" Devanandan means Newbigin's analysis of the contemporary historical scene, not the effort (which would surface in these later writings) to build an epistemological framework for personal faith in the God who revealed himself in Jesus Christ.

Notes to Chapter 3

1. In several distinctively missiological works that might appear to contradict this assertion, the emphasis on election is dependent on Newbigin. Darrell Guder's book in the field, *Be My Witnesses*, carries as a pervasive theme the breaking of the benefits/mission dichotomy and calls for a sense of election which sees in it responsibility (e.g., 1985:9ff., 37-40, 91-96). Even though the book is mostly undocumented, it is not hard to trace the strong influence of Newbigin (cf. xiii). In another mission theology, David Bosch includes at the most basic level of his formulation the argument from election which establishes the meaning and purpose of history (1980:58-59, cf. 50-52). That he is dependent upon Newbigin is clear from the inclusion of the illustration Newbigin frequently uses to show the radical difference between biblical and Hindu approaches to historicality and universal truth (59). In the more comprehensive theological work of Karl Barth, election is, of course, foundational for the whole, including the implications he draws regarding the mission of the church (cf. 1962:681-901). Comparisons to be made along the way will show, however, that Newbigin's sense of the "missionary character" of election is distinct from Barth's and more closely tied to the development of a rationale for mission across cultural frontiers.

2. Those who, like Newbigin, struggle with the "problem of the antithesis" are to be differentiated from those for whom the antithesis is an intentional dualism. Such is the approach of Meredith Kline (1983) and, in an opposite way, Modupe Oduyoye (1984). Don Richardson employs a similar structure but with a more yielding set of possibilities on the "unchosen" side (1981).

3. By the phrase "correction of Calvin," Newbigin means to indicate the confirmation he finds in Barth's argument for a "purpose" approach to election (personal conversation, October 1986).

4. Similar views are expressed by Alan Richardson (1949:276), David J. Bosch (1978:38), Johannes Verkuyl (1978:94), and Juan Luis Segundo, S.J. (1973:40-42, 82-84; 1978:136-139). Hendrikus Berkhof, in his survey of the Christian faith, intentionally places his discussion of election at the conclusion of his section on human responsibility, following the order he sees in Calvin (1979:480-482). This affirms a similar perspective as well.

5. Note also his similar emphasis in 61ftow:78-79, cf. 81f.; 66hrsm:100-101; 69fc:112-113; and 72jij:73-74.

6. Some seem incapable of feeling the potency of this question from "the other." Rowley is puzzled as to why God's particular actions and choices should be "repugnant" to anyone (1950:41). Blauw believes the problem to have been swept away by the "election for service" view of Rowley and others, leaving "no ground for the reproach still often heard within the younger Churches of Asia" (1962:23). Both too quickly dismiss the importance of the challenge.

7. Compare Robert E. Cushman's critique of too easy an identification of election as "for service" (1981:199-200).

8. It is worth noting that, in a passing reference, Hendrik Kraemer refers to the election of Israel and God's particular dealings with her as a "special revelational experiment." The fleeting suggestion only occurs in order to underscore what he considers more "deeply significant," that before God begins the experiment "the 'everlasting Covenant between God and every living creature' is stated as an established and irremovable fact." This he holds to be of "the greatest significance for a Biblically-based theology of religion" (1956:253-254). This slight and backhanded reference to election confirms the judgment Newbigin makes that Kraemer failed to turn his attention to the "missionary significance" of election (83cwr:24).

9. Newbigin does, in his ecclesiology, stop short of saying that the church is a "sacrament" of salvation for the world. In his judgment, such an affirmation — which places the church as a "symbol" of "universal salvation," establishing a "soteriological universalism" — goes beyond the warrant of the Scriptures. It breaks the necessary eschatological tension and realizes prematurely the "final" judgment. Cf. 78os:87ff.

10. Pannenberg is certainly right to point out the serious danger of "abstraction" when theology addresses only the issue of individual election. He uses the designation appropriately when he says, "Since in the classical doctrine the object

of election, the individual person, is presented in abstraction from any social and temporal context, it shall be called the 'abstract' concept of election" (1977:47). But the danger exists on the other side as well. To make the purpose of election "primarily symbolic," as he does (36), is equally "abstracting," in this case abstracted from the personal and particular context. The relevance of the personal and individual aspect of election (which Pannenberg acknowledges) must be maintained for a proper understanding of the purpose of the corporate election. To deal with the individuality of the chosen in the context of the corporate choice in fact removes the onus of "abstraction." To dismiss individual election altogether would ultimately set aside particularity.

11. Note especially Harry Boer (1961:68), Johannes Verkuyl (1978:92), Bengt Sundkler (1965:13-14), and Richard De Ridder (1971:31). Cf. Hendrik Kraemer (1956:253-254).

12. Newbigin's point here about the "freedom" of God is part of his larger argument about the "necessity" that God should give self-disclosure by means of election. These two are not contradictory. He supports the kind of contention that Daane makes regarding the need to move beyond emphasis on the decree of God and see with full force the freedom of God operating in election (1973; cf. Barth 1957c). Newbigin builds on that by looking at the personal character of God. Necessity only comes by the requirements of God's own personal nature and the way the world has been made to be lived in relationship to God.

13. These include Karl Barth (1962:573-576), David J. Bosch (1978:39), Charles Van Engen (1981:134), Johannes Verkuyl (1978:94), and Herbert Kane (1976:23).

14. Guder continuously argues against dichotomizing the benefits and mission implied in election (1985). Cf. Berkouwer 1960:320-322, where he notes that A. Kuyper had already posed the purpose question in the past century, but without separating service from salvation (cf. H. Berkhof 1979:245). Daane indicates that "there is a consensus among Reformed theologians that election is not merely a summons to service," while showing that most of them "do not include the idea of salvation in their concept of Israel's election" as part of that "more than service" dimension (1973:111-112). Though for other reasons than those of Rowley, the representatives of the so-called decretal theology share a similar divorce of salvation from election for Old Testament Israel.

15. Cf. Bengt Sundkler (1965:14ff.), Charles Van Engen (1981:121), and Carroll Stuhlmueller, C.P. (Senior and Stuhlmueller, 1983:83ff.).

16. Duraisamy Amalorpavadass hints at this relation of particularism and universality in regard to the incarnation but does not extend it to include the nature of election as God's missional way of bearing witness to it (1979:63; cf. Carl Michalson 1967:82).

17. The tendency to look at the issue almost exclusively from the point of view of Israel's consciousness should be apparent in many of the perspectives identified above. Note as illustrations Rowley 1950, Blauw 1962, Senior and Stuhl-

mueller 1983, and Ariarajah 1985 (who treats election simply as the "self-understanding" of a religious group, 1985:11).

18. It is difficult to determine what Blauw means by his critique of the assumption that "mission is a postulate of universalism" (1962:30). It would appear that he means to critique the idea that the notion of mission — understood in direct terms — must emerge from a sense of universalism. If that is so, he begins a line of critique that Newbigin's thought completes. It is the mission of God, which ultimately works by way of election, that casts itself upon the whole world with universal scope.

Notes to Chapter 4

1. Cf. 59scmt:185; 61icd:31; 68bima:12, 27; 71t:607.

2. See 41kgip; 61ftow; 63rtdt; 66hrsm; 68coec; 69fc.

3. Cf. 69fc:65-67, 69, following Nicol Macnicol.

4. The word "clue" — one that is pervasive in Newbigin's writings — is especially important to define in this context. Newbigin views a "clue" as a potential "model" by which the mind may be able to grasp and understand a particular field of inquiry. To "accept" a clue as the key to understanding such a field (as, for example, the meaning of history) is to accept it provisionally. All of us think and evaluate by the adoption of "provisional clues" which are presupposed until and unless there comes a point at which they are no longer adequate to bear the burden of explanation required of them. A "paradigm shift" to an interpretation based on another "clue" may be made when one perceives the possibility that it provides the potential for larger understanding. The word "clue," therefore, does not mean "evidence" or "proof" in Newbigin's usage.

5. These two core assumptions were stated together in Newbigin's senior theology paper at Westminster College, Cambridge, on the topic of "Revelation." He identifies them as the two beliefs upon which "the central importance ascribed to revelation in Christianity depends" (36r:1-2).

6. On this score he critiques the view of Maurice Wiles that resting a knowledge of God on "certain historical events" is no more secure than resting it on "a more general historical experience" for which the historicity of particular events is not essential. Newbigin levels the ground by pointing out that preferring the fruit of "general historical experience" is no less dependent upon "models and concepts which we take as provisional clues" (79cjh:202).

7. This line of thought shows why it became so important to Newbigin to identify "the abandonment of teleology as the key to the understanding of nature" as the most important feature of Enlightenment culture, as seen over against the gospel. In that respect, Newbigin claims, Western culture has come to agree with the Eastern religions (86fg:34, 39).

8. Cf. 61ftow:96ff.; 68coec:39ff.; 78os:115ff.; 86fg:134-136.

9. This argument is repeated in 61ftow:98; 68coec:42; 78os:117ff.; and 86fg:136.

10. See especially 41kgip 4:1-10; 53ch:114-116; 78os:115-119; and 86fg:135-137.

11. Thomas's quotation of this statement omits the opening definite article, which creates the potential for a radically different understanding of the meaning.

12. H. Berkhof, in the original phase of the dialogue, drew attention to Thomas's approach, which outlined the gospel as "the affirmation and fulfillment" of the "quest of modern man" that his sociology had helped him formulate (Loffler 1968:16).

13. Note allusions of this sort in 41kgip 4:9; 61ftow:101; 68coec:47; and 86fg:137.

14. This Newbigin says in defense of M. M. Thomas's effort to see the work of God in the religious renaissance and the political and human revolutions of Asia.

15. See also 59scmt; 60whsl; 63jsmc; and 63rtdt.

16. Note, for example, Newbigin's care to speak "with great diffidence" (72sad:68 and 74lwc:23) and his concern to note the "provisional" character of all such interpretations (78os:100 and 69fc:82).

17. Also relevant in this connection is his admission that he had been vulnerable to being impressed by the German "Student Movement" in the early 1930s and that he had had to learn important lessons from that (85ua:24-25).

18. Paul Devanandan's comment that Newbigin's *forte* seems to him "to be Biblical exegesis, not Christian apologetics" does not contradict what is being said — as it might appear — but rather confirms it. By "apologetics" he refers to Newbigin's "claim that the world is becoming one civilization," that is, Newbigin's attempt to interpret the current scene (1962:128). Interestingly, Devanandan critiques that interpretation as "not sufficiently convincing" to an Indian reader. Today, Newbigin would likely agree. But in an intriguing reverse movement, Devanandan's protégé, M. M. Thomas, credits his mentor for helping shape his current assertions regarding pluralism, which are founded on an "awareness of our common responsibility to a common historical human destiny," which in turn presents "the moral challenge of the single history" (1986:106)!

19. Cf. van Leeuwen 1964:331ff., 402ff. See also 74lwc:15; 65fe:420.

20. Cf. Newbigin's treatment of liberation theology and Marxism as vulnerable to the development of a moralistic legalism, 78os:106ff., 125.

21. See Newbigin's extended discussions on this theme in 59guhc:84-85, 87-88; 63rtdt:38-41; and 59scmt:185. Briefer allusions occur also in 69fc:86-87 and 61ftow:28.

22. Note Newbigin's dependence on the work of Paul Devanandan and M. M. Thomas in regard to the interpretation of the resurgence of Hindu religion (cf. 63rtdt:45).

23. Cf. 61ftow:17; 63rtdt:45; and 66hrsm:45.

24. Newbigin makes reference to the quip about William Miller's students

who, it is said, "had received such an effective prophylactic dose of Christianity that they were quite immune from catching the real thing!" (72sad:64).

25. Cf. 66hrsm:56; 74lwc:22; and 79cjh:210.

26. Newbigin does not, in the several places where these ideas are mentioned, give a specific reference. In fact, what he indicates in his 1966 publication had been said by Dawson "more than thirty-five years ago" (66hrsm:50), he eight years later identifies with the expression "more than twenty-five years ago" (74lwc:22), adding to the complication. At any rate, Dawson does say something of this sort in 1956:105-106 (an article which first appeared in 1934).

27. Behind all this lies Newbigin's resistance to definitions of "time" or "eternity" in regard to God which remove him from time as we experience it. His conviction is that time is the "form" of God's creation; that time is real; and that since God is personal and relates to his creation in personal terms as a real creation, "time is real to God," while it remains subject to him (53hg:135-136; cf. 41kgip 3:8-10).

28. This emphasis on the gospel as a secular announcement will be picked up again in chapter six in its important connection with the question of the limits of the idea of "religion."

Notes to Chapter 5

1. Cf. 66c:312; 68coec:85; 78os:135-136; and Löffler 1965:97-98.

2. The comment about a "later diaconical decision" Newbigin draws from a paper delivered at the meeting of the Central Committee of the WCC in 1965. The author is not named in either of Newbigin's references to it. In the earlier reference (66c:311) he adds that in the Central Committee's discussion the idea "was immediately challenged."

3. In the earlier publication (66c) of the material revised and used as chapter 5 in *The Finality of Christ* (69fc), Newbigin critiqued Castro's paper without naming its author (66c:311). His critique at that time was more incautious. In the later revision, he adds, along with Castro's name, both the acknowledgment that Castro gave "a very clear refutation" of the "two conversions" idea and a softening of his critique: "there seems to be a remnant of the wrong idea" (69fc:94).

4. In this connection Newbigin mentions the Sermon on the Mount, which he says is not a "legal code" but "an outline, a series of hints" (68coec:90). His concern to avoid legalism has led squarely into a very complex and thorny issue. How does the ethical teaching of Jesus bear the authority of the revelation of the will of God and yet remain a series of hints? (Cf. Matthew 7:21, 24, 29; James 2:8, 11.) As it is here stated, his approach appears to be too casual, although it breaks open one of the most important issues facing a theology of cultural plurality. This issue will receive further attention in the concluding chapter.

5. It is this which Paul Löffler quotes from Newbigin to make most vividly his case for a similar point. That he does in the article which Newbigin credits and

quotes as a substantial source for *his* thinking about conversion as it appears in the revised form of chapter 5 of *The Finality of Christ* (Löffler 1965:100; cf. 69fc:7, 113).

6. It is less certain from Löffler's essays on the subject that he does not in some sense concur in this sort of universalism, his own comment notwithstanding. Cf. his comment that "conversion is no end in itself, but a representative response by some on behalf of all men leading to the exemplary realization of the Kingdom" (1967a:260).

7. The earlier version of this chapter of *The Finality of Christ*, which was delivered at the Nasrapur Consultation on mission in 1966 and first published in the *National Christian Council Review* (vol. 86, August 1966), contains a glaring omission of the word "not" which inverts the meaning on this point. It reads, "On the other hand, the other meaning of the *pro* is wholly excluded" (66c:313). In Newbigin's personal copy of the original article he has inserted a marginal note adding the word "not." The reprint of the article in *Religion and Society* (13, 4:30-42) preserves the error.

8. Cf. similar arguments in 78os:16-18; 79cjh:200-205; and 86fg:99-100.

9. Cf. the frequent places where this idea appears in Newbigin's thinking: 53hg:168ff.; 65fe:149; 66c:322; 69wwfo:130-132; 78os:163, 169; 78cc:6-13. It would appear that when Newbigin in 63rtdt:43 argues that the Christian's actions are "signs rather than instruments," he counters the idea that the instrumentality is involved at all. It is no contradiction. He is only guarding against the notion that our "acts" are themselves the very building of the Kingdom of God. The acts, which are a sign of that Kingdom, are not the means to establish it but "the witnesses to its present reality." By that witness the Church's action is "instrumental" in the sense that it "bears the witness of the Spirit" to the world, which is the means for the inclusion of others in the blessings of salvation.

10. See, for example, 58obog:19; 66c:322; 69wwfo:130; and 71rsh:73.

11. See 86fg:117; 69wwfo:119; 76aopa:298; 71rsh:73; and 66c:322.

12. This is affirmed as well by Newbigin's strict avoidance of the term "sacrament" to describe the church's relationship to the world as inappropriate to the biblical indications. Cf. the language of Vatican II in *Lumen Gentium* (Abbott 1966:15, 79) and also that of Pannenberg 1977:36ff. and Braaten 1977:56.

13. The discussion of continuity in this context must be distinguished from the manner in which we are more accustomed to encounter it. The more common "continuity-discontinuity" debate, as sparked by Hendrik Kraemer and A. G. Hogg in the late 1930s, continues to ask what possible lines of "continuity" Christian faith might have with other religions or faiths (cf. Kraemer 1939, Hogg 1939). Here, however, Newbigin asks a different question: What lines of continuity ought a newly converted person to establish and/or maintain with the Christian "faith" or religion (i.e., "Christianity") into which she or he has entered? Newbigin's perspective on this question provides the context in which he discusses the one more commonly raised (as will be more fully discussed in the next chapter).

14. It is not accidental that McGavran's book was first published (in 1955)

by the press that published many of Allen's works, World Dominion Press (see the comment in the foreword by Kenneth G. Grubb, 1981:v).

15. For a full survey of the literature involved in the debate and the pattern of their responses back and forth, see pp. 280-282 in this volume.

16. Chenchiah's view of the church places almost no stock in its historical character. His thesis that "the Children of God are the next step in evolution and the Kingdom of God the next step in cosmos" is matched with the assessment that "all through history, the Church has never been the cradle of new life" (Thangasamy 1966:16, 28).

17. It is interesting, in light of this aspect of the debate, that in a more recent treatment of these issues Thomas expands and clarifies his suggestion. The impact of the debate with Newbigin is clearly visible when he speaks of "three levels of koinonia in Christ: first, the koinonia of the eucharistic community of the church, itself a unity of diverse peoples acknowledging the *Person* of Jesus as the Messiah; second, a larger koinonia of dialogue among people of different faiths inwardly being renewed by their acknowledgment of the ultimacy of the *pattern* of suffering servanthood as exemplified by the crucified Jesus; third, a still larger koinonia of those involved in the power-political struggle for new societies and world community based on secular anthropologies *informed by* the agape of the cross" (1986:108).

18. The exegetical treatment of Matthew 28:16-20 by David J. Bosch stands as one of the most comprehensive to date (Bosch 1983). He there supplies, as Newbigin does not, an exegetical critique of McGavran's interpretation of the "Great Commission" text which forms the basis for his distinction between discipling and perfecting (pp. 230-233).

19. Cf. on this issue the critique by Robert Ramseyer of the anthropological perspective of another representative of the church growth movement, Charles Kraft (Ramseyer 1983:114; cf. Kraft 1979:113).

20. Cf. 59scmt:186; 76aopa:305.

Notes to Chapter 6

1. Newbigin would not have called the historically rooted gospel events the "convergence" of "salvation history" and "secular history" as Löffler did (Löffler 1965:97; cf. p. 101). Rather he would say that the events are secular ones, as God's dealings have been from the beginning. The secular history of the world is itself salvation history in that it contains the events which are saving, secular events on behalf of all.

2. The title used in *The Open Secret* undoubtedly builds upon the title of the booklet by Walter Freytag entitled *The Gospel and the Religions* (1957), a source from which Newbigin draws an important illustration in the course of the chapter. The change from "and" to "among" less ambiguously declares the distinction he seeks to make.

3. The last chapter of *The Open Secret* is a revision of an article published a year earlier with the more descriptive but cumbersome title "The Basis, Purpose and Manner of Inter-Faith Dialogue" (77bpmi). Most of the revisions were made in order to interact with the view of John Hick. In many places the chapter and the article are identical.

4. The limitations outlined here may save us from some of the difficulty hinted at in Newbigin's comment about "the jungle of argumentative literature which has grown up . . . in the last fifty years" around some of these issues (83cwr:17)! However the need for a more extensive survey of Newbigin's views remains. The most complete analysis of Newbigin's theology of religions and response to religious pluralism is the very helpful doctoral dissertation of Joe Matthew Thomas entitled *The Centrality of Christ and Inter-Religious Dialogue in the Theology of Lesslie Newbigin* (University of Toronto and Toronto School of Theology, 1996). Thomas's dissertation treats the themes of the current chapter of this book in an expanded and comprehensive way that sheds important light on the full structure of Newbigin's perspective.

5. D'Costa's comparison of Hick, Kraemer, and Rahner is also done wholly from within this assumption. Cf., e.g., 1986:75.

6. Newbigin's examples from the Scriptures to illustrate this point are drawn primarily from the New Testament, particularly from Jesus' interaction with the Pharisees. The point can be strengthened by reference to the Old Testament prophets, who speak against a religiosity devoid of spirit and practical righteousness. (This Newbigin begins to approach in 66hrsm:95. Cf. Isaiah 1, Jeremiah 7, Psalm 51).

7. The influence of John Oman is particularly evident here. Cf. Oman's concept of the "sacred" as the "valuation as of absolute worth" (1925:289). Thus defined, the sacred is distinctively the "one mark of the sphere of religion" (296).

8. Note here the influence of Paul Tillich's now classic definition of religion as "the state of being grasped by an ultimate concern, a concern which qualifies all other concerns as preliminary and which itself contains the answer to the question of the meaning of our life" (1963:4).

9. It is right, in Newbigin's terms, that this should be the case, since every religion contains within itself its own "philosophy of religions" (78os:191). See also his display of this fact in his address on "The Quest for Unity Through Religion," in which he shows Hinduism's distinctive approach and interpretation of all other religions in terms of its own essential intuition (55qutr).

10. Not surprisingly, D'Costa classes Newbigin with Kraemer as an "exclusivist" (1986:15, 74, et al.). He acknowledges it is not an uncritical companionship. In fact, his critique of Kraemer and the defense of many of his own positions over against Kraemer ironically depend very heavily on Newbigin, which suggests the flaw in D'Costa's paradigm (cf. 1986:74-75, 105, 106, 121, 124, 136). James L. Cox maintains a healthy appraisal of the relationship when he says that "it would be wrong in this context to dismiss Newbigin as a latter-day exponent of Kraemer's position" (Cox 1979:254).

11. Gabriel Fackre seizes on this image of light, together with "life," in his attempt to build a similar case for a theory of revelation and redemption in which each holds together and integrates both particularity and universality. His assertion that "a Christic grace does its illuminating work in the whole created order" is very like Newbigin's view (1983:45; cf. 77bpmi:255). Fackre, however, misses Newbigin's full perspective. He builds his suggestion as one which contrasts with views that do not preserve the necessary union of particularity and universality. That includes Newbigin's view, which he identifies as "developed out of" the view expressed by Karl Barth, labeled "centrifugal singularity" in Fackre's paradigm (42). Newbigin anticipated much that Fackre suggests, except for the latter's recourse in the end to a post-death provision for those who "have not had the opportunity for a decision of faith in this world" (51). In this, Fackre moves at the last moment in a direction similar to that of O. V. Jathanna, who invokes the idea of "reincarnation for a 'second chance'" (Newbigin 83cwr:28; cf. Jathanna 1981:470-481).

12. Especially in view here is the position articulated in the so-called early Barth of *Church Dogmatics* vol. 1, part 2; cf. paragraph 17, "The Revelation of God as the Abolition of Religion" (1957a).

13. Newbigin often noted that he read the *Church Dogmatics* backwards! Wanting to know the end, which would show the meaning of the whole, he began with the last section and worked his way back toward the beginning. This is consistent with Newbigin's eschatology!

14. Cf. D'Costa's description of Barth's approach as "unhistorical and *a priori*" (1986:64). This he gleans from a comment by D. T. Niles: "When asked how he [Barth] knew that Hinduism was unbelief when he had never met a Hindu, his immediate reply was '*a priori*'!" (Niles 1969:10-11; cf. D'Costa 1986:59).

15. Cf. Alan Race for another example of the same threefold paradigm (1982).

16. Cf. also Paul Knitter's similar assessment of the distinction of Newbigin's view from Barth's (1985:108-110). More consistently than D'Costa, Knitter places Newbigin in a part of his paradigm ("mainline Protestant") which stands over against Barth.

17. Further implications of this point of contrast between Barth and Newbigin will be dealt with in the concluding chapter where their interpretations of Genesis 10–11 will be considered.

18. Note, however, that the "from outside" approach present in the Western scientific worldview reenters as highly important in his later discussions of the encounter of the gospel with the West. This scientific worldview, which is happy to "keep a place" for religion, albeit a private realm, encourages religion as "a deeply inner" experience in which the variety of religions "can find a kinship" (86fg:40-41). Here we find this first dominant model joined to the second one, which we shall observe shortly.

19. Newbigin says it also elsewhere: "within such a view of reality, there is room for almost infinite tolerance. . . . The one thing which on this view cannot be tolerated is the assertion which Christianity is bound to make, namely, that the

Supreme Being has, once and for all, revealed himself in a historic person" (61ftow:38). Cf. also the way in which C. Badrinath picks up Kraemer's phrase, "pseudo-tolerance," for his description of the Hindu impact on some Indian Christian theologians (Badrinath, quoted from an unpublished paper in 83cwr:25-26; cf. Kraemer 1938:207).

20. It may be noted here that it is in regard to this debate over religious education in Britain that Newbigin comes the closest to giving the sort of specific portrait of a "pluralistic society" that M. M. Thomas challenges him to give. He asks what Newbigin "expects by way of positive response from the institutions of public life in pluralistic societies" (1984:319). Newbigin suggests that the combined phrase "secular plural society" points the way. "There can be a society which is secular in the sense that it holds together a plurality of different groups each of which has a set of shared values which is — to some extent — distinctive" and which "can co-exist and fruitfully interact" (77trsp:85). The questions of ethics in government, standard norms of behavior, and the limits of pluralism (is "racism" an acceptable member of the club?) lead Newbigin to speak of the "limits to the possibilities of a secular society even in the pluralist sense" (77trsp:86). These sketches, of course, do not satisfy the depth of Thomas's concerns. How does one, on this basis, avoid creating a new "pluralistic Christendom" pattern?

21. In a fascinating comment in the SCM Press Book Club Bulletin of November 1961, Arnold Toynbee responded to a question Newbigin asked of him in the book which dealt with his views (61ftow:43). Toynbee confirmed that he did not claim "a standpoint above all religions" and identified his own perspective in terms similar to Newbigin's: "I am making judgments because doing this (at one's peril) is, I should say, one of the inescapable consequences of being human. Things seem to us right or wrong, true or false, and each of us has to choose what seems to him right and true, though he knows that his judgment is fallible. In other words, I think I have arrived at my views in the same way that Bishop Newbigin has arrived at his acceptance of what is, for him and for all orthodox Christians, 'the total fact of Christ' " (1961:2-3).

22. Newbigin adds to this sort of portrait of the church in dialogue a diagram drawn from Walter Freytag (77bpmi:264; 78os:204; cf. Freytag 1957:21). It enters as somewhat an enigma in that it does not immediately suggest what Newbigin has been driving at. He uses it to make the additional point that the Christian's meeting with someone of another faith involves a "self-emptying" (78os:205). That, of course, is a uniquely Christian perspective of the "unity" in the encounter. Newbigin also has altered the intent of Freytag from the original use of the diagram. Freytag had drawn it from Javanese tradition to affirm that "the higher mysticism ascends, the more it departs from the cross" (1957:21). It illustrated his major point, which was to contradict the notion that the religions "form a whole as the ascending religious development of humanity" (2). Newbigin too quickly and uncritically transposed that into a model for "all the religions, including Christianity." To use the model in this way, which contradicts the notions of other religions about themselves, is to fall again into the trap Newbigin has warned others to avoid.

23. Newbigin holds these two together in his exegesis on either side. This is more helpful than the approaches of Ariarajah, who polemically offers a countering of "exclusivist" texts with a survey of his own "universalist" texts (1985; cf. Hunsberger 1987), or Braaten, whose barrage of passages "piled verse upon verse" seems designed for the same purpose (1980:23). He is also more careful than D'Costa, who following Rahner transmutes the biblical phrase "God desires the salvation of all humankind" to the affirmation of "the universal salvific will of God" without making a case for it (1986:4, 25; Rahner 1969:391; cf. Travis 1983:34 and his distinction between "God's saving *purpose*" and "what *will* happen").

24. This "universalism" he sometimes calls "general universalism" (66c:323) or subdivides into "rationalistic universalism" and "romanticism" (82ccee:150-151). He does not equate this form of universalism with "biblical universalism" (78os:87, 89). Nor is it to be understood as the equivalent of "universalism" as a reference to the "universality" of Christ, i.e. the claim for his finality and uniqueness.

25. He therefore contends that Jathanna's solution of invoking "the idea of reincarnation as a 'second chance'" is unnecessary given the Bible's steady portrait of a history which is "in some sense a unity," centered upon the incarnation of Jesus. The individual in relatedness to the whole is the direction in which the question "has to be answered" (83cwr:28).

26. This personal destiny dimension of the discussions is the reason why they are so dominated by terms such as those used in D'Costa's threefold typology (1986; cf. Race 1982 for an identical typology but a different preference). The terms "pluralist," "exclusivist," and "inclusivist" are alike in that they each make primary reference to the paths and destinies of people relative to their deaths. To allow that dimension to so dominate a "theology of religions" raises important questions for the whole debate.

Notes to Chapter 7

1. Increasingly, work in this field is being done using a similar threefold framework. The Roman Catholic scholar Robert J. Schreiter, C.PP.S., who shares Newbigin's dominantly linguistic orientation to the definition of cultures, has offered a schema for *Constructing Local Theologies* (1985; cf. pp. 49ff.). He sees as the interacting roots of local theology "gospel, church, and culture" (20-21). While similar in outline, his treatment differs from Newbigin's in that the "church" component is conceived in a more monolithic fashion (suggesting more the sum of its prior incarnations than the result of mutual correction and re-formation in ecumenical fellowship) and the "gospel" appears to be a more "established" entity by virtue of the church's tradition. Compare also in this regard the similar approach of Peter Schineller, S.J., although his model envisions as one of the three "poles" the pastoral agent, in the place the church holds in other models (1990:61-73). The triadic approach is also reflected in Carlos Mesters's *Defenseless Flower* (1989:106ff.),

where he describes the three forces at work when the Bible is interpreted in and for a community: the *pre-text* (the situation we are living in today), the *text* (its literal meaning), and the *context* (the faith of the community which receives and reads the Bible as its book).

2. Kraft includes a small but important chapter on "God's attitude toward culture" in which he builds upon Niebuhr's "Christ and culture" paradigm, focusing at that point on the first axis (103-115). While he and Niebuhr deal with "God" or "Christ" and culture, they are really dealing more directly with a variety of Christian understandings of that and the resulting Christian postures vis-à-vis culture, hence their treatments are not much different from those which deal with "church and culture."

3. Newbigin's most distilled definition of what the gospel "is" has to do with that concrete, historical original embodiment. "In speaking of 'the gospel,' I am, of course, referring to the announcement that in the series of events that have their center in the life, ministry, death, and resurrection of Jesus Christ something has happened that alters the total human situation and must therefore call into question every human culture" (86fg:3-4).

4. Cf. 80m80:155; 82tc:5; 86fg:7.

5. Philip Wickeri's study of the growth of "self-propagation" in the Three-Self Patriotic Movement in China demonstrates this dynamic in similar terms. The focus he gives to that pursuit is the question whether and how such a minority Christian community can "challenge and affirm the Chinese experiment without becoming either irrelevant or syncretistic" (1985:271).

6. Shoki Coe, who is credited with coining the word "contextualization," joined it to the idea of "contextuality," which is "the missiological discernment of the signs of the times, seeing where God is at work and calling us to participate in it" (1976:21). He sees contextualization as achieving the gospel's "fit" with the culture in a dynamic, future-oriented way, while "contextuality" refers to the "challenge" to sociopolitical action perceived in the situation. Such an application of a "relevance-challenge" schema to the social struggles in which Christians must become engaged bears a compatibility, if not identity, with Newbigin's application of it to the encounter leading to conversion. Further exploration of the correspondence of these two discussions and the relationships between them would benefit an emerging theology of cultural plurality. This would increase the bridging between sociological and anthropological analysis.

7. Cf. Hopler's statement that the judgment on Babel had as its purpose "to protect man from himself" (1981:32).

8. One is tempted to wonder as well whether for Barth Genesis 10–11 is more the "Fall" of humanity than is Genesis 3! (Cf. 1961:310).

9. Could this ultimately negative appraisal of cultural plurality in the dialectic of Kraemer and, especially, of Barth, partially unspoken yet forcefully felt, explain the strength of the reaction against them by the Indian theologians before and after Tambaram 1938?

10. Cf. Harvie Conn's critique of Wagner's position, 1983:90.

11. This is in contrast to Gerhard von Rad's sense that the "primeval history" breaks off in "shrill dissonance" (1961:149). Von Rad's view is more suggestive of the dialectical assessment mentioned above.

12. Cf. 73snhc:10; 77wilc:21-22; 73fsvu.

13. Cf. the observation of Donald R. Jacobs in the African context that a new community of Christians tends to move successively through several stages of relationship to the traditional culture: the rejection phase, the accommodation phase, and the reestablishment of identity (1980:140-145).

14. It is interesting in this connection to observe that Oscar Cullmann, in a footnote, entertained using the term *Offenbarungsgeschichte* as more comprehensive than the term *Heilsgeschichte* (1964:26, n. 10). One wonders what might have been the effect of such a choice and a corresponding English rendering of his theological project as "revelation history" instead of "salvation history." At the least, it would have sharpened our attention on a needed field.

15. A major criticism of Kraft's view is made by Robert Ramseyer regarding the faulty anthropology this represents. He faults Kraft for "neutralizing" culture by his bifurcation between "principles and behavior, meaning and form" (1983:114). This, we may add, occurs not only in regard to human culture but in regard to the person and action of God, as well.

16. Kraft dwells on the subject only long enough to suggest the extremely cumbersome notion of the angelic and demonic realm as that of "supracultural nonabsolute beings"!

17. Thom Hopler shares a similar view of a "progression" toward a divine model of culture. God works to "establish his ideal" and reveals a "biblical way of life" for the people of God to follow (1981:32, 45-46).

18. As Lamin Sanneh puts it, all human cultures are both "destigmatized" (revitalized) and "de-absolutized" (relativized) by the gospel (1989:1ff.) For a helpful synopsis of Sanneh's view, see Paul Russ Satari, " 'Translatability' in the Missional Approach of Lamin Sanneh" (1996).

19. Raimundo Panikkar makes important suggestions in this same direction. He calls for religious pluralism to be discussed in a parallel fashion with "linguistic, cultural, and philosophical pluralism." He says that "only after the acceptance of these three pluralisms will we be prepared to discuss and eventually accept the legitimacy of religious pluralism" (1984:100-101).

20. In John Oman's *The Natural and the Supernatural*, there is an almost identical approach to "standpoint" mentioned as prolegomenon to the "classification of religions" (1931:358-359; cf. the earlier chapter on "Standpoint," 74-98).

21. Some of the fullest expressions of Newbigin's fundamental apologetic approach are to be found in *The Gospel in a Pluralist Society* (89gps, especially the first 65 pages), *Truth to Tell* (91tt), and *Proper Confidence* (95pc). An older work which is less accessible in the West, *Christ Our Eternal Contemporary* (68coec) is an important precursor.

Index of Persons

Allen, Roland, 23, 168, 172-73, 174-76, 179, 190, 326n.14
Amalorpavadass, Duraisamy, 321n.16
Ariarajah, S. Wesley, 20-21, 90, 322n.17, 330n.23

Baago, Kaj, 157, 177-79, 189
Badrinath, C., 329n.19
Balasuriya, Tissa, 10, 21, 318n.9
Barth, Karl, 32, 41, 68, 85-87, 88, 94, 184, 198, 199, 208, 209-15, 247-49, 251, 253, 260-61, 319n.1(ch.3), 320n.3, 321n.13, 328n.11, 328n.12, 328n.14, 328n.16, 328n.17, 331n.8, 332n.9
Berkhof, Hendrikus, 99-100, 176-77, 320n.4, 321n.14, 323n.12
Berkouwer, G. C., 84, 92, 321n.14
Bevans, Stephen, S.V.D., 319n.2
Beyerhaus, Peter, 134-35
Blauw, Johannes, 66-67, 88, 90-91, 102, 108, 109, 111, 251-52, 318n.12, 320n.6, 321n.17, 322n.18
Boer, Harry R., 97-98, 108-9, 321n.11
Bonhoeffer, Dietrich, 199
Bosch, David J., 111, 318n.13, 319n.1(ch.3), 320n.4, 321n.13, 326n.18

Braaten, Carl E., 15, 111, 212-13, 325n.12, 330n.23
Brunner, Heinrich Emil, 213
Bultmann, Rudolph, 117, 147

Calvin, John, 320n.3, 320n.4
Castro, Emilio, 157, 162, 324n.3
Chenchiah, Pandipeddi, 53, 135, 153, 180, 326n.16
Childs, Brevard S., 40
Coe, Shoki, 331n.6
Conn, Harvie M., 18, 246-47, 332n.10
Cox, James L., 327n.10
Cracknell, Kenneth, 245, 250
Cullmann, Oscar, 98, 109, 110, 153, 332n.14
Cushman, Robert E., 105, 108, 276, 320n.7

D'Costa, Gavin, 19-20, 31, 198, 213-14, 229-30, 274, 327n.5, 327n.10, 328n.14, 328n.16, 330n.23, 330n.26
Daane, James, 83, 87-88, 321n.12, 321n.14
Dawson, Christopher, 150-51, 324n.26
Denney, James, 32, 209
De Ridder, Richard R., 102, 245, 321n.11

333

Index of Subjects

Printed in the United States
19163LVS00003B/169-171